BUDDHISM IN TIBET

BUDDHISM IN TIBET

illustrated by

LITERARY DOCUMENTS AND OBJECTS OF RELIGIOUS WORSHIP

with an

ACCOUNT OF THE BUDDHIST SYSTEMS PRECEDING IT IN INDIA

By

Emil Schlagintweit

BOOK FAITH INDIA

Delhi

BUDDHISM IN TIBET

Published by
BOOK FAITH INDIA
414-416 Express Tower
Azadpur Commercial Complex
Delhi, India 110033
Tel. [91-11] 713-2459. Fax [91-11] 724-9674
E-mail: pilgriın@del2.vsnl.net.in

Distributed by
PILGRIMS BOOK HOUSE
P.O.Box 3872
Kathmandu, Nepal
Tel. [977-1] 424942. Fax [977-1] 424943.
E-mail: pilgrims@wlink.com.np
WebSite: pilgrimsbooks.com

Varanasi Branch
PILGRIMS BOOK HOUSE
B 27/98-A-8, Durga Kund
Varanasi, India 221001
Tel. [91-542] 314060. Fax [91-542] 314059, 312788
E-mail: pilgrim@lw1.vsnl.net.in

First Book Faith India Edition 1999

ISBN 81-7303-201-7

Printed in India by Jay Kay Offset Printers.

Preface to the New Edition

The early religion of Tibet, the Bon-po faith was more a kind of animistic or shamanistic belief than a religion but with the introduction of buddhism from India the old religion assimilated much of the new. This is why we see a lot of very strange, almost hideous looking demonic gods displayed in Tibetan monasteries.

The famous King Srongtsam Gyampo, who was reputed to have been greatly influenced by his two wives, encouraged the development of Tibetan Buddhism. These two wives are depicted on thangkas as the two Taras, one being the Nepalese Princess Bhrikuti, the other being from China.

The other great exponent of the religion was Tsongkhapa. He helped to eradicate some of the earlier practices and published manuscripts about his strict doctrines relating to Buddhist development in Tibet.

The different sects which evolved, the Gelukpa, Nyingmapa, Karmarpa and Sakyapa and others are explained, as well as such terms as *chortens* and *mani* walls, which can be seen all over Nepal and Tibet.

Some of the more important Boddhisattvas, such as Guru Rimpoche, Manjushri, Lokeswar and Chenresig who are often displayed in Tibetan and Nepalese Monasteries, are considered. Lamaism and the general principles of Tibetan beliefs are well documented.

The development of the great monastic institutions in Tibet is well documented, as are the ceremonies and the daily life of the monks. The rituals and facts surrounding the origins, art and methods of displaying deities and Buddhas are discussed in detail.

Illustrations, drawings and diagrams, together with references and other detailed information are included at the end of the narrative to fully inform the student of this most complex subject.

Bob Gibbons
Kathmandu 1998.

PREFACE

THE religious systems of all ages—paganism in its rudest form perhaps excepted—have undergone changes and modifications which, if not materially affecting their principles, have at least exercised a certain influence upon their development. Buddhism may be considered a remarkable illustration of this; for not only have the rites suffered notable changes, but even the dogmas themselves have, in the course of time, become much altered. Although plain and simple in the earlier stages of its existence, it was in time greatly modified by the successive introduction of new doctrines, laws, and rites; so-called reformers arose, who assembled around them a greater or less number of followers; and these by degrees formed schools, which by-and-by developed into sects. The shifting of its original seat also exercised a considerable influence: the difference between a tropical and a cold and desert region, and between the physical character of tribes separated by the distinctive marks of the Arian and Turanian races, had to be smoothed over, partly at least, and obliterated by the influence of time.

The present work has for its object the description of Buddhism as we now find it in Tíbet, after an existence in this country of upwards of twelve centuries.

The information obtained by my brothers Hermann, Adolphe, and Robert de Schlagintweit, when on the scientific mission undertaken between the years 1854-58, which gave them the opportunity of visiting various parts of Tíbet and of the Buddhist countries in the Himálaya, has been the chief source on which I have drawn for my remarks and descriptions. The reports of former travellers have also been consulted and compared with the contributions received from my brothers. Not less important for my subject, as enabling one to judge of the fundamental laws of Buddhism, and their subsequent modifications, were the researches of the oriental philologists and intelligent writers on Buddhist doctrines, amongst whom Hodgson and Burnouf have so successfully led the way to the analysis of the original native works.

For the greater part of the objects here treated of and for most of the native explanatory remarks, I am indebted to my brother Hermann. He had engaged in Síkkim the services of Chibu Lama, a very intelligent Lepcha, then a political agent of the Rāja of Síkkim at Darjíling. Through this personage he was enabled to obtain numerous objects which had come from Lhássa, the centre of the Buddhist faith in Tíbet. Mr. Hodgson and Dr. Campbell, besides giving him much valuable information, were also so kind as to present him with various articles of interest for this subject. In Western Tíbet, it was particularly at the monastery of Hímis and in Leh, the capital of Ladák, that Hermann's wishes were the most readily accomplished. In Gnári Khórsum Adolphe, who was at that time accompanied by Robert, succeeded in persuading the Lamas of Gyúngul and Mángnang to sell him even objects which he had seen treated with the greatest respect and awe.

The folio atlas of twenty plates, two feet high and one and a half broad, contains facsimiles of representations of deities and of objects used for keeping off evil spirits. The originals were reproduced by means of transfer-paper, a method which has the great advantage that the alterations are entirely avoided which the artists are but too willing to make. The drawings being mechanically copied, retain entirely the stamp of foreign art. The details in reference to the method employed for the reproduction are given in the introduction to the atlas. The plates have been printed in the lithographic establishment of Dr. C. Wolf and Son at Munich.

For the illustrations accompanying the text I selected those of a more scientific nature in preference to those of a descriptive character. They consist of copies taken from original woodcuts, and of prints in Tibetan characters of the texts translated. These tables have been executed in the imperial printing office at Vienna. Their correct execution was kindly undertaken by Mr. de Auer, the director of this institution, so well known for its excellence in typographical and artistical reproductions.

In my studies of Tibetan I have been greatly assisted by Mr. A. Schiefner at St. Petersburg, to whose publications I shall often have occasion to allude. This gentleman also afforded me the welcome opportunity of laying the verbal explanatory details of the priests *in loco* a second time before a Lama, the Buriat Galsang Gombojew, who is engaged at St. Petersburg as teacher of Mongolian; he made for me, besides, various abstracts from books contained in the imperial oriental libraries having a bearing upon these objects.

I may be allowed to mention that I had the honour of presenting to the Royal Academy of Munich the Address to the Buddhas of Confession (contained in Chapter XI.), a sacred imploration, of which a translation in German was inserted in the Proceedings of this Institution (February, 1863).

ALPHABET USED FOR TRANSCRIPTION

a (ā ă ã), ä; b; ch; chh; d; e (ē ĕ ẽ); f; g; h; i (ī ĭ) j; k; l; m; n; o (ō ŏ), ö; p; r; s; sh; t; ts (tsʿh) u (ū ũ), ü; v; y; z; zh.[1]

1. RULES FOR PRONOUNCIATION.

Vowels.

1. *a, e, i, o, u,* as in German and Italian.
2. *ä, ö, ü,* as in German.
3. Diphthongs give the sound of the two component vowels combined.

Consonants.

1. *b, d, f, g, h, k, l, m, n, p, r, s, t,* are pronounced as in German and English.

[1] This is the same that has been adopted by my brothers in their "Results of a scientific Mission to India and High Asia;" for details *see* Vol. I., pp. 66 to 70; Vol. III., pp. 148-160.

2. *h*, after a consonant is an audible aspiration except in *ch*, *sh*, *zh*. In *ts̓h* it is separated from *ts* by the Greek *spiritus asper* ̔, in order to prevent this letter from being pronounced as *t* and *sh*.

3. *ch*, as in English (*church*).

4. *sh*, as in English (*shade*).

5. *j*, as in English (*just*).

6. *v*, as the *w* in German (*Wasser*), being different from *v* in *very*, and *w* in *water*.

7. *y*, as *y* in the English word *yes*, and *j* in the German *ja*.

8. *z*, soft as in English (*zeal*).

9. *ẓh*, sounds like the French *j* in *jour*.

Signs.

1. ¯ over a vowel indicates that it is long.

2. ˘ this, the sign of imperfect formation (= *u* in *but*, *e* in *herd*) placed over *a* and *e*, I had no occasion to use in Tibetan and Sanskrit terminology: it occurs, however, in modern geographical names, as *e. g.* Bĕrma.

3. ˜ indicates a nasal sound of the vowel.

4. ′ marks the syllable on which the accent falls. Accents have been, however, introduced in geographical names only; in the other native words I have limited myself to distinguishing the quantity of the syllables which are long.

5. ’, the Greek *spiritus lenis* I used for rendering the Tibetan soft aspirate; in this I followed the advice of Prof. Lepsius, in his recent supplement to his well-known "Standard Alphabet."[1]

2. DETAILED TRANSLITERATION OF THE TIBETAN ALPHABET.

The thirty *simple* letters of the Tibetan language are represented in Roman characters in the following manner:

ཀ k; ཁ kh; ག g; ང ng; ཅ ch; ཆ chh;

ཇ j; ཉ ny; ཏ t; ཐ th; ད d; ན n;

པ p; ཕ ph; བ b; མ m; ཙ ts; ཚ tsʻh;

ཛ dz; ཝ v; ཞ zh; ཟ z; འ ’; ཡ y;

ར r; ལ l; ཤ sh; ས s; ཧ h; ཨ a.

The point separating the syllables in Tibetan words and sentences, is rendered by a small horizontal line.

The *compound letters*, seventy-four in number, and formed by having another letter subjoined or surmounted, are transliterated thus: the subjoined letter is written behind the radical, as *e. g.* ཀྲ is rendered by *kr*,—the surmounting precedes the radical letter, as *e. g.* ལྷ *lh.*

[1] "Ueber Chinesische und Tibetanische Lautverhältnisse, und über die Umschrift jener Sprachen." Abhandlungen der Akademie der Wissenschaften von Berlin, 1861, p. 479.

The letters which according to grammatical rules ought to be silent, are printed with Italics, as *e. g.* rk is printed *r*k.

In order to facilitate the reading, I have spelt the Tibetan terms as they sound (with the omission of the mute letters); the reprinting in Tibetan letters is also left out in the text, but an alphabetical Glossary of Tibetan terms has been added at the end of the volume, in which the native spelling of every word and the detailed transliteration are given.

CONTENTS

PART I.

THE VARIOUS SYSTEMS OF BUDDHISM.

SECTION I.

INDIAN BUDDHISM.

SECTION II.

TIBETAN BUDDHISM.

(*For additions see p.* 393.)

PART II.

PRESENT LAMAIC INSTITUTIONS.

APPENDIX.

LIST OF ILLUSTRATIONS

PLATES OF THE ATLAS.

Group I.

Representations of Deities.

Group II.

Sentences and Figures for averting the dangers arising from evil spirits.

TABLES OF NATIVE PRINT IN THE TEXT.

ERRATA

Page						
Page	3	in the heading;	*for*	exislence	*read*	existence.
»	9	» »	»	» developement	»	development.
»	16,	line 26;	*for*	fourtth	»	fourth.
»	35,	» 10	»	kundzabchi	»	kundzobchi.
»	37,	» 23	»	well-towards-disposed	»	well-disposed towards.
»	42,	» 10	»	Togpa nyi	»	Togpa nyid.
»	78,	» 12	»	Palchen	»	Phalchen.
»	97,	» 11	»	Stavirās	»	Sthavirās.
»	129,	» 13	»	*r*Nams-par	»	*r*Nam-par.
»	133,	note 1	»	Nyon-thos	»	Nyan-thos.
»	258,	line 27	»	Lhonab	»	Lhonub.
»	276,	» 6	»	Chag	»	Phag.

Errors in Tables V. to VIII. of Native Print:

Page						
Page 2,	line 12;	*for*	gshegs-sa	*read*	gshegs-pa.
» 3	» 8	»	rnams-par	»	rnam-par.
» 4	» 3	»	mi-dkor	»	me-dkor.
	» 11	»	rnam-la-phyag	»	rnams-la-phyag.
» 5	» 2	»	nyon-thos	»	nyan-thos.
» 6	» 5	»	bshas-pa-rnam	»	bshas-pa-rnams.
	» 7	»	thar-par	»	thar-bar.
	» 11	»	bskal-ba	»	bskal-pa.
» 7	» 1	»	mts'hun	»	mts'hon.
	» 2	»	rnam-sa	»	rnam-pa.
	» 2	»	glu-ru-len	»	glu-rum-len.

PART I

THE VARIOUS SYSTEMS OF BUDDHISM

SECTION I

INDIAN BUDDHISM

CHAPTER I

SKETCH OF THE LIFE OF SĀKYAMUNI, THE FOUNDER OF BUDDHISM

ORIGIN.—THE PRINCIPAL EVENTS IN HIS LIFE.—HIS ATTAINMENT OF THE PERFECTION OF A BUDDHA.—PERIOD OF HIS EXISLENCE.

ALTHOUGH the numerous legends respecting the life and works of Sākyamuni, the reputed founder of the Buddhist faith, contain much that is fabulous, yet most of the incidents mentioned therein, when deprived of the marvellous garb with which early historians invariably used to embellish their tales, seem to be based on matters of fact. At present scientific researches have put Sākyamuni's real existence beyond a doubt;[1] but the period in which he lived will ever remain somewhat vaguely defined.

[1] See for details the biographies published by Csoma de Körös, "Notices of the life of Shakya," in the Asiatic Researches, Vol. XX., pp. 285-318; Hardy, "Manual of Buddhism," pp. 138-359; Schiefner, "Eine tibetanische Lebensbeschreibung Sākyamuni's," in the "Mémoires des Savants étrangers," Vol. VI., pp. 231-332. For Tibetan and Singhalese traditions about the Sākya race, see Foe koue ki, English translation, Calcutta, 1848, p. 203.

Sākyamuni was born at Kapilavastu in Gorakhpúr. The legends tell us that his father, the king Suddhodana (in Tibetan Zastang), requested one hundred and eight learned Brahmans to inform him of his son's destiny; the Brahmans, the legends say, after a careful examination of the prince's body, expressed their conviction that, "if he remained a layman during his lifetime, he would become a powerful monarch of vast territories; but in the event of his turning recluse, he would enter the state of a supreme Buddha or wise man: and in solemn assembly they declared that this prince would hereafter prove a blessing to the world, and that he himself would also enjoy great prosperity." It was in consequence of this answer, that the prince received the name of Siddhārtha, "the establisher."[1]

Siddhārtha proved to be endowed with extraordinary faculties, and the legends even go so far as to assert that, when he was about to be taught his letters, he could already distinguish them, and his eminent qualities were manifest, not only in his mental, but also in bodily perfection. It is added as particularly characteristic that already in his youth he was inclined to retirement and

[1] In the sacred legends he is generally characterised by other names. Those of Sākyamuni—in Tibetan Shakya Thub-pa, "Sākya, the mighty"—Gautama, or Sramana Gautama, "the ascetic of the Gautamas," refer alike to his family and career. The names of Bhagavat, "the fortunate," Sugata, "the welcome," Buddha, "the wise," designate his supreme perfection. A name which is very frequently given to the Buddhas in sacred books is Tathāgata, in Tibetan Dezhin, or Dezhin shegpa, "he who has gone in the manner of his predecessors." See Abel Rémusat, "Note sur quelques épithètes descriptives de Bouddha." Journ. des Savans, 1817, p. 702. Burnouf "Introduction," p. 70 *et seq.* Barthélemy St. Hilaire, "Le Bouddha et sa Religion", p. 75.

solitude: he abandoned his gay, playful comrades and buried himself in the dark recesses of dense forests, where he gave himself up to profound meditation. Suddhodana, the father, however, wished his son to become rather a powerful monarch, than a lonely ascetic. When, therefore, after a renewed consultation with the Brahmans, he learned that Siddhārtha would certainly leave his magnificent palace and become an ascetic, in the event of his seeing four things, viz. decrepitude, sickness, a dead body, and a recluse, he placed guards on all sides of the palace, in order that these dreaded objects might not come near his beloved son. Moreover, in order to weaken his love of solitude and meditation, he married him to Gopā (in Tibetan Sa Tsoma), the daughter of Dandapāni, of the race of the Sākyas, and gave orders that he should be provided with every kind of pleasure. But all these precautions proved futile. Siddhārtha, though living in the midst of festivities and in the enjoyment of all wordly pleasures, never ceased to reflect upon the pains which arise from birth, sickness, decay, and death; upon their causes, and upon the remedies to be used against them. He found that *existence* is the real cause of these pains, that desire produces existence, and that the extinction of desire causes cessation of existence. He then determined—as he had already done a hundred times before—to lead human beings to salvation by teaching them the practice of virtues and by detaching them from the service of the world. Although he had hitherto often hesitated, his resolution to renounce the world and to become an ascetic was finally put into execution, when he happened, on his walk to a garden in the vicinity of the palace, to meet at four different periods an old man, a leper, a dead body, and a man in a religious garb. He had attained the age of twenty-nine years, when he left his palace, his wife, and the infant son to whom she is said to have given birth at the very moment of her husband's meeting with the recluse.[1]

Siddhārtha began his ascetic life by assiduously studying the doctrines of the Brahmans and by becoming the disciple of the most learned of them. Being, however, dissatisfied with their theories and practices, which, he declared, did not offer the true means of salvation, he left them altogether, and gave himself up during the next six years to earnest meditation and the exercise of great austerities; the latter, however, he soon renounced, perceiving from his own experience, that the mortifications practised by the Brahmans were not of a nature to lead to the attainment of perfection. The six years past, he proceeded to the holy spot Bōdhimanda, where the Bōdhisattvas become Buddhas; and it was here, that, having seated himself upon a couch of grass of the *kusa* species, he arrived at supreme perfection, which became manifest by his remembering the exact circumstances of all human beings that had ever existed; by his obtain-

[1] It is more probable, says Wassiljew, in his "Buddhismus," p. 12, that Sākyamuni was led to view existence as the cause of pain and sorrow in consequence of a war in which the Sākya tribe was defeated, and which obliged him to wander about, rather than by his seeing the four dreaded objects mentioned; for there is a legend which says that the Sākya race was almost entirely exterminated during the life of the Buddha.

ing the divine eye, by the aid of which he could see all things within the space of the infinite worlds, and by his receiving the knowledge that unfolds the causes of the ever-recurring circle of existence.

Sākyamuni being now endowed with all these wonderful and marvellous faculties, became the wisest man, the most perfect *Buddha*. But having arrived at this state of perfection, he still hesitated whether he should make known his doctrines and propound them to men, his principles being, in his opinion, opposed to all those then adhered to. He was, at first, afraid of being exposed to the insults of animated beings, who are unwise and filled with evil designs. But, moved by compassion, and reflecting, that there would remain nevertheless many beings who would understand him and be delivered by him from existence—the cause of pains and sorrows—he at once resolved to teach the law that had been revealed to him.[1]

Sākyamuni died, the books say, after having attained an age of eighty years. The data contained in the sacred books as the year of this event, differ considerably, the most distant periods mentioned being the years 2422 and 544 B.C. Lassen, in his examination of these materials, gives preference to the literature of the southern Buddhists, which places his death in 544 or 543 B.C. Westergaard, however, in a recent essay on this subject, believes even this epoch to be by far too early, and calculates his death to have taken

[1] Barthélemy St. Hilaire, "Le Buddha et sa Religion," p. 32.

place in the period from 370 to 368 B.C., or about one generation before Alexander the Great took the throne.[1]

[1] Lassen "Indische Alterthumskunde," Vol. II., p. 51. Westergaard, "Ueber Buddha's Todesjahr;" German translation, p. 94.

CHAPTER II

GRADUAL RISE AND PRESENT AREA OF THE BUDDHIST RELIGION

DEVELOPEMENT AND DECLINE IN INDIA.—EXTENSION OVER VARIOUS PARTS OF ASIA.—COMPARISON OF THE NUMBER OF BUDDHISTS WITH THAT OF CHRISTIANS.

SCARCELY had Sākyamuni begun to teach his new religion in India, when he obtained a great many followers. His system had an extraordinary success both on account of its simplicity and of the abolition of castes; the Buddha admits to the blessings of which he is the dispenser the highest classes of man (Brahmans) as well as the lowest. Already at his death the number of Buddhists seems to have been very considerable; and about the middle of the third century B.C., during the reign of Asoka, Buddhism began to spread all over India. It then continued to flourish for eight hundred years (till the fifth century of our era), when a series of violent persecutions was commenced (instituted by Brahmanical sectaries, particularly by the adherents to the worship of Siva) which almost caused the extirpation of Buddhism. Hiuen Thsang, a Chinese pilgrim who had passed much of his life in India during extensive travels between the years 629 and 645 A.D., mentions numerous Buddhist temples, monasteries, and monuments, which in his time were already deserted, and even fallen into ruins—buildings which, two centuries before, Fa Hian, another Chinese traveller, had found in the most prosperous condition. Nevertheless, in many parts of India, Buddhists were still in existence, and in Benáres, now again a centre of Brahmanism, they are reported to have been the prevalent sect until the eleventh century, and in the northern parts of Gujrát even as late as the twelth. After that period, Buddhism ceased to exist in India, by reason of a combination of circumstances, amongst which the jealousy of the various schools and the invasion of the Mussalmáns are to be mentioned as perhaps the most important.[1]

As present the area of Buddhism includes vast territories, from Ceylon and the Indian Archipelago in the south to the Baikal Lake in Central Asia, and from the Caucasus eastward to Japan; and the number of its adherents may be considered as being at least equal to, if it does not exceed, that of the followers of the Christian religion, as will be seen from the following data.[2]

[1] Compare Mountstuart Elphinstone's "History of India," Vol. I., p. 212. Lassen, "Ind. Alterthumskunde," Vol. IV., p. 707.

[2] Prof. Neumann of Munich has computed the number of Buddhists in China, Tibet, the Indo-Chinese countries, and Tartary at 369 millions. Ungewitter, "Neueste Erdbeschreibung," Vol. I., p. 51, estimates the total of

The late Professor Dieterici, in his well-known compilation of the census of the globe,[1] estimates the population of *China* at four hundred millions, of *Japan* at thirty-five; and for the *Indo-Chinese Peninsula* he gives fifteen millions as the number of inhabitants in the independent territories. The data for the Indian dependencies in the peninsula are of great variety. Thornton's "Gazeteer" gives for Arrakán, Pégu, and Tenásserim a population of about one million; but in a note contained in Allens Indian Mail, 1861, the inhabitants of Pégu alone are calculated to amount to one million. An average of two millions for these three provinces is, perhaps, most in accordance with their area when compared with the remainder of the peninsula.[2] The inhabitants of the *Indo-Chinese Archipelago* are set down by Dieterici at eighty millions, of which twenty belong to the Dutch and Spanish possessions. The population of *Ceylon*, which is all Buddhist, exceeds, according to M^c^Carthey, two millions.[3] In *India Proper* there are scarcely any Buddhists at all.

For these regions of Asia we obtain, therefore, ac-

Buddhists at 325 millions. Colonel Sykes, whose accuracy in every branch of science, especially, however, in statistics, is so well known, also considers it certain that the Buddhists out-number the followers of any other creed: see his essay "On Indian Characters." London 1859.

[1] "Die Bevölkerung der Erde," in Petermann's "Geographische Mittheilungen," 1859, p. 1.

[2] Thornton's "Gazeteer." Allen's Indian Mail, 1861, p. 802.

[3] Report of the Proceedings of the fourth Session of the International Statistical Congress; London, 1861, p. 84. Compare Hardy, "Eastern Monachism," p. 310.

cording to these calculations an approximate total of 534 millions of inhabitants. At least two-thirds of this population may be considered to be Buddhists; the remainder includes the followers of Confucius and Lao-tse, the adherents of religions prevalent among the inhabitants of China Proper,[1] the Mussalmáns (numerous in Chinese Tartary), and the Pagan tribes of the Chinese peninsula and the Archipelago; the numbers of the latter are comparatively small, since in their districts the population is very thin. We may therefore estimate *the total of Buddhists* to amount to 340 millions.

The contribution to this number from other parts of the globe is comparatively small, but nevertheless it seems to amount to more than a million. The eastern provinces of the *Russian Empire* contain some 400,000 Buddhists, viz. 82,000 Kirghises and 119,162 Kalmuks inhabiting Europe,[2] and the Buriats (to the number of about 190,000 souls) living in Sibiria; these are almost all followers of Buddhism.[3] There are still to be added for the Himálaya and Western Tíbet, independant of China, the inhabitants of *Bhután*, to the number of 145,200, the whole of them, according to Pemberton,

[1] For China, Gützlaff states the Buddhists to be "the most popular and numerous sect," adding "that their religious establishments may be estimated at two-thirds of the whole of the religious edifices throughout China." R. As. Soc., Vol. XVI., p. 89. Schott, "Buddhaismus," p. 23, was of the opinion (in 1844) that the Buddhists were the minority.

[2] Notices taken from P. v. Köppen's memoir "Ueber die Anfertigung der ethnographischen Karte des europäischen Russlands." Bulletin hist.-phil. de l'Académie de St. Pétersbourg, Vol. IX., Table to face p. 335.

[3] Latham, "Descriptive Ethnology," Vol. I., p. 306. The same was told me by Gombojew, a Buriat of Selenginsk.

belonging to the Buddhist faith.[1] The population of *Síkkim*, together with the Buddhist inhabitants of *Nepál*, which chiefly include those of Tibetan origin, I estimate at 500,000 to 550,000.[2] The Buddhist province of *Spíti*, under English protection, was found, according to the census made by Major Hay in the year 1849, to have a population of 1,607.[3] Ladák, now a province of the kingdom of Kashmír, is reported by Cunningham to be inhabited by 178,000 souls; the native population is exclusively Buddhist, but since the annexation to Kashmír some Hindu members of the administration and some Mussalmán merchants have settled there.

The total of this group would amount even to one million and a quarter.[4]

For the sake of comparison I add that Prof. Dieterici found the total number of Christians spread over

[1] Report on Bhután, p. 151. A recent estimate by Hughes, quoted by the *Allgemeine Zeitung*, Jan. 1862, gives 1,500,000 inhabitants, a number which appears to be somewhat too large.

[2] Hughes estimates Nepál to contain 1,940,000 inhabitants, of which 500,000 Buddhists. This number will not appear too high, if we remember that the actual professed Buddhists in Nepál are divided into four sects, and that Buddhist doctrines have passed to a great extent into the primitive creed of the various tribes of Tibetan origin inhabiting this kingdom. See Hamilton, as quoted by Ritter. "Asien," Vol. III., pp. 120, 123, 125, 129; Hodgson, "Languages," &c.; As. Res., Vol. XVI., p. 435; the same on the Aborigines of the Sub-Himalayan in "Records of the Govt of Bengal," p. 129.

[3] Report on the valley of Spíti, in Journ. As. Soc. Beng., Vol. XIX., p. 437.

[4] Buddhism had also become known in Mexico by Chinese priests in the fifth century A.D., and had followers in that country until the thirteenth century; but the victorious Azteks, who took possession of Mexico in the beginning of that century, put an end to Buddhism. See Lassen, "Ind. Alterth.," Vol. IV., pp. 749 *et seq.*

the globe to be 335 millions, of which 170 millions are Roman Catholics, 89 millions Protestants, and 76 millions belong to the Greek church; their numerical strength appears therefore to be five millions less than the average estimate of Buddhists given above.

CHAPTER III

THE RELIGIOUS SYSTEM OF SĀKYAMUNI

THE FUNDAMENTAL LAW.—THE DOGMA OF THE FOUR TRUTHS, AND THE PATHS LEADING TO SALVATION.

SĀKYAMUNI, although the founder of Buddhism, is, at the present day, no longer considered to have been the first Buddha. Many most perfect Buddhas preceded him (so it is now believed), and many more shall appear hereafter; but they all teach the same law. [1]

The original religious system, as taught by Sākyamuni himself, is plain in its principles, but characterized by bold, philosophical speculation; its *fundamental dogma* is the following:— [2]

All existence is an evil; for birth originates sorrow,

[1] This theory seems to have been introduced into Buddhist mythology already by the Sautrāntika school. See Wassiljew, "Der Buddhismus," p. 314. To this dogma also the name of Tathāgata refers (see p. 4); for the philosophical explanation of this term with "thus gone," quoted by Hodgson from original works, see Burnouf, "Introduction," p. 75.

[2] See the valuable exposition of Köppen, "Die Religion des Buddha," pp. 213—26. Notices on the earliest dogma of Buddhism occur in numerous passages of Burnouf's "Introduction dans le Buddhisme Indien," and "Lotus de la Bonne Loi;" in Hardy's "Eastern Monachism," and "Manual of Buddhism."

pain, decay, and death. The present life is not the first one; innumerable births have preceded it in previous ages. The reproduction of a new existence is the consequence of the desire for existing objects, and of the works which have been aggregated in an unbroken succession from the commencement of existence. Proneness to the pleasures of life produces the new being; the works of the former existences fix the condition in which this new being is to be born. If these works have been good the being will come to existence in a state of happiness and distinction; if, on the contrary, they have been bad, the being will be born into a state of misery and degradation. The absolute annihilation of the conditions and pains of existence—Nirvāna—is attained by the most perfect dominion over passion, evil desire, and natural sensation.

Sākyamuni has explained this fundamental doctrine in the theory of the *four excellent truths*: THE PAIN, THE PRODUCTION, THE CESSATION, THE PATH; they are called in Sanskrit Āryāni Satyāni, and in Tibetan Phagpai denpa zhi. Their meaning may be defined as follows:

1. Pain cannot be separated from existence.
2. Existence is produced by passions and evil desires.
3. Existence is brought to an end by the cessation of evil desires.
4. Revelation of the path to this cessation.

In detailing the moral precepts of the fourtth truth he has indicated eight good paths:

1. The right opinion or orthodoxy.
2. The right judgment, which dissipates every doubt and incertitude.

THE FUNDAMENTAL DOGMA OF THE BUDDHIST FAITH.

1. In Sanskrit, written with Tibetan characters.

ཡེ་དྷརྨཱ་ཧེ་ཏུ་པྲ་བྷ་ཝཱ། ཧེ་ཏུནྟེཥཱནྟ་ཐཱ་ག་ཏོ་ཧྱ་བ་དཏ།

ཏེཥཱཉྩ་ཡོ་ནི་རོ་དྷ། ཨེ་ཝཾ་བཱ་དཱི་མ་ཧཱ་ཤྲ་མ་ཎཿ།

སརྦ་པཱ་པསྱཱ་ཀ་ར་ཎཾ། ཀུ་ཤ་ལ་སྱོ་པ་ས་མྤ་དཾ།

སྭ་ཙིཏྟ་པ་རི་ད་མ་ནཾ། ཨེ་ཏདྦུདྡྷཱ་ནུ་ཤཱ་ས་ནཾ།།

2. A Tibetan translation of the same.

ཆོས་རྣམས་ཐམས་ཅད་རྒྱུ་ལས་བྱུང་།

དེ་རྒྱུ་དེ་བཞིན་གཤེགས་པས་གསུངས།

རྒྱུ་ལ་འགོག་པ་གང་ཡིན་པ།

འདི་སྐད་གསུང་བ་དགེ་སྦྱོང་ཆེ།

སྡིག་པ་ཅི་ཡང་མི་བྱ་སྟེ།

དགེ་བ་ཕུན་སུམ་ཚོགས་པར་སྤྱད།

རང་གི་སེམས་ནི་ཡོངས་སུ་གདུལ།

སངས་རྒྱས་བསྟན་པ་འདི་ཡིན་ནོ།།

3. The right words, or perfect meditation.
4. The right mode of acting, or of keeping in view in every action a pure and honest aim.
5. The right way of supporting life, or of gaining a subsistence by an honest profession unstained by sins.
6. The rightly directed intelligence, which leads to final salvation ("to the other side of the river").
7. The right memory, which enables man to impress strongly in his mind what should not be forgotten.
8. The right meditation, or tranquil mind, by which alone steadiness in meditation can be attained, undisturbed by any event whatever.

It has been doubted with much reason, whether Sākyamuni taught the four truths in this form; but as he must have spoken about the means of arriving at final liberation, or salvation, I have added here these eight classes of the path, which are suggested to him already in very early Sūtras.[1]

The theory of the four truths has been formulated in a short sentence, which has been discovered on many ancient Buddhist images, and which is besides actually recited as a kind of confession of faith, and added to religious treatises. It runs thus: "Of all things proceeding from cause, the cause of their procession hath the Tathāgata explained. The great Sramana has likewise declared the cause of the extinction of all things."[2] Tathāgatha and

[1] Concerning the four truths see: Csoma "Notices," in As. Res., Vol. XX., pp. 294, 303; Burnouf's "Introduction," pp. 290, 629, and "Le Lotus de la Bonne Loi," App. V. Another series of eight classes, which is decidedly the produce of the later schools, will be noticed in the next chapter.

[2] This sentence is also the conclusion in the address to the Buddhas of

Sramana are two epithets of Sākyamuni, as explained before.

The ancient religious works apply to Sākyamuni's followers the title of Srāvakas "*hearers*," a name also having reference to their spiritual perfection. The Buddhists of this period seem to have called themselves Sramanas, "those who restrain their thoughts, the purely acting," in allusion to their moral virtues as well as their general conduct.[1]

confession, for which see Chapter XI.—In the translation of this sentence I have followed Hodgson; see his "Illustrations," p. 158. Other translations of various readings have been published by Prinsep, Csoma, Mill, and recently compared by Colonel Sykes. See his "Miniature Chaityas and inscriptions of the Buddhist religious dogma," in R. As. Soc., Vol. XVI., p. 37. The Sanskrit text written with Tibetan characters, and the Tibetan version is given in Plate I.

[1] Wassiljew, "Der Buddhismus," p. 69.

CHAPTER IV

THE HĪNAYĀNA SYSTEM

CONTROVERSIES ABOUT SĀKYAMUNI'S LAWS.—THE HĪNAYĀNA DOCTRINES. The twelve Nidānas; character of the precepts; incitation to abstract meditation: gradations of perfection.

AT the time of Sākyamuni's death the inhabitants of India were not yet so advanced in civilisation as to have a literature, and the claims of the Buddhist to scriptural documents of his law written down during his life (as the Nepalese believe), or immediately after his death (which is the opinion of the Chinese), are decidedly groundless. New researches have made it very probable that the alphabets in which the earliest historical records we know, the inscriptions of king Asoka (about 250 B.C.), are written, were imitated from the Phœnician alphabet, communicated to the Indians by merchants of that nation as early perhaps as the fifth century B.C., at which period already Greek letters became known in the ancient districts of Gandhāra and Sindhu, the countries at the foot of the

Himálaya drained by the Indus.[1] We are now able to assert that the words and doctrines attributed to Sākyamuni were transmitted orally down to the first century before the Christian era. The scriptural record was undertaken by the southern and the northern Buddhists independently of each other. In Ceylon the priests wrote them down during the reign of king Vartagāmani, 88—76 B.C.; their northern brethern brought them into a written form at an assembly of the priests, or synod, arranged by the Turuschka king Kanishka, 10—40 A.D. The Singhalese chose the vernacular language, from which the books were translated into the sacred Pāli dialect at the beginning of the fifth century A.D.; the northern branch used the Sanskrit.[2] Up to this periods, the religion had been preserved orally, and although, according to Buddhist history, Sākyamuni's words were brought into a well-defined and precise form already in the year of his death, yet it is very doubtful whether the natural changes to which oral tradition is subject allowed his original law to remain unaltered. Moreover, we have a positive proof that arbitrary alterations and additions have been purposely made, especially with reference to the historical details given in the earlier compilations.

[1] A. Weber, Zschr. d. d. Morgenl. Ges., Vol. X., p. 396. Westergaard, "Ueber den ältesten Zeitraum der Indischen Geschichte," pp. 35. *seq.* 80. Wassiljew, "Der Buddhismus," p. 30, is, however, of opinion that Buddhist missionaries had become acquainted with Greek letters in the third century B.C. in Bactria, and induced Asoka to model after them the alphabets used in his inscriptions.

[2] Turnour, "Mahāvanso," p. 207. Lassen, "Indische Alt.," Vol. II., pp. 435, 490. Westergaard, l. c., p. 41.

Such changes soon became numerous and assumed an importance not properly belonging to them, owing to the claim set forth by each new sect, that *its* peculiar dogmas had been revealed by Sākyamuni. The orthodoxy of each new and dogmatic school is maintained on the supposition, that the word of the Buddha is to be taken in a double sense, as he had often been compelled, in consideration of the mental capabilities of his hearers to give explanations about certain subjects quite at variance with his real opinion, and the new sects do not base their existence upon the rejection of previous works as spurious, but claim to have discovered the true meaning.[1]

During the first century after Sākyamuni's death there was no controversy about his laws, but after this period a numerous fraternity of monks (12,000 it is said) asserted the validity of ten indulgences. Their doctrine was rejected by the assembled priests at the synod of Vaisāli, a place north of Pátna (Pātaliputra), on the eastern bank of the Gándak river, and as they would not submit to the judgment, the first schism took place.[2] At this new

[1] Burnouf, "Introduction," p. 219; Wassiljew, "Der Buddhismus," pp. 7, 329.

[2] See Turnour, Pāli Buddhistical Annals. Journ. As. Soc. Beng. Vol. VI., p. 729. It was at this synod that the following dogma was propounded: "That can only pass as the true doctrine of the Buddha which is not in contradiction to sound reason". The formation of various schools was the immediate consequence of the acceptance of such a doctrine, and these schools, in their frequent attacks on each other, essayed to prove the correctness of their dogmas in solemn disputation before a great assembly of priests and laymen. In the earlier stage of Buddhism, only the leaders of the antagonistic schools were allowed to engage in disputation, and the vanquished controversialist was compelled either to put an end to his existence, to become the slave of his more successful opponent, to adopt the other's creed, or, if in possession of wealth,

stage of Buddhism, in which the fundamental dogmas of Sākyamuni began to be interpreted from various points of view, the ancient sects are called the Hīnayāna system.[1] The name means "little vehicle," and has originated with the later Buddhists. The epithet "little" was given because the adherents of this system restrict themselves to morality and to external observance only, without making use of such an abstruse, refined, and highly mystical theology, as did, at a later period, the Mahāyāna schools, or those of the "great vehicle." Yāna, vehicle, is a mystical expression, indicating, that man may escape the troubles attendant upon birth and death by practising the virtues inculcated by the Buddhas, and finally attain salvation.

The following details may be quoted as particularly characteristic of the Hīnayāna system.[2]

I. It distinguishes itself from the Srāvakas in the mode of explaining the principle of Buddhism: that the world must be abandoned because it entails upon man existence, pain and death. The source of existence is no longer demonstrated from the four truths only, but

to relinquish the same in favour of the victor. But in later periods entire monasteries took part in such disputations, and the establishments of the defeated party were destroyed—a circumstance which propably explains in many instances the radical disappearance of monasteries in India. Wassiljew, "Der Buddhismus," p. 72. Further particulars about the ancient schools may be found in the work of Vasumitra, a translation of which is added as an appendix to Wassiljew's work, pp. 244-84.—About the geographical position of Pātaliputra and Vaisāli, see Foe koue ki, English translation, p. 259, where an interesting note is added to the French original; compare also Burnouf, "Introduction," p. 86.

[1] See Foe koue ki, p. 9. Köppen, "Die Religion des Buddha." Vol. I., p. 417.

[2] Concerning its dogmas see Wassiljew, pp. 97-128, 149.

also from the twelve Nidānas (in Tibetan Tenbrel chugnyi), which are based upon the four truths.

The Nidānas, the theory of the causal connection, or concatenation of the causes of existence, are formulated as follows: "On account of ignorance, merit and demerit are produced; on account of merit and demerit, consciousness; on account of consciousness, body and mind; on account of body and mind, the six organs of sense; on account of the six organs of sense, touch (or contact); on account of contact, desire; on account of desire, sensation (of pleasure or pain); on account of sensation, cleaving (or clinging) to existing objects; on account of clinging to existing objects, renewed existence (or reproduction after death); on account of reproduction of existence, birth; on account of birth, decay, death, sorrow, pain, disgust, and passionate discontent. Thus is produced the complete body of sorrow. From the complete separation from and cessation of ignorance, is the *cessation* of merit and demerit; from the cessation of merit and demerit is the cessation of consciousness; from the cessation of consciousness is the cessation of (the existence of) body and mind; from the cessation of (the existence of) body and mind is the cessation of (the production of) the six organs; from the cessation of (the production of) the six organs is the cessation of touch; from the cessation of touch is the cessation of desire; from the cessation of desire is the cessation of (pleasurable or painful) sensation; from the cessation of sensation is the cessation of the cleaving to existing objects; from the cessation of cleaving to existing objects is the cessation of a reproduction of existence; from the cessation of a reproduction of existence is the cessation of birth; from the cessation of birth is the cessation of decay. Thus the whole body of sorrow ceases to exist."[1]

II. In the books of discipline attached to this system we also meet with a vast accumulation of precepts and rules intended to release its followers from the ties binding them to the present and future states of existence, and to strengthen them in moral virtues. One curious feature predominating throughout is worthy of mention. The whole of the precepts (which are comprised in 250 articles) display a negative character; thus, charity is inculcated, not by the command "to give," but by the prohibition "to take," save when the gift be offered as alms.

Already this school had put forth the doctrine, that perfection in abstract meditation is indispensable for final salvation; this perfection guarantees an energy not to be derived from the mere practice of simple virtues. Nevertheless the idea is not carried so far as to assign to mental speculation a higher value, than to virtues. Assiduity in undisturbed reflection was, however, found under any circumstances to be a most difficult task; certain preparatory exercises are, therefore, recommended, in order to finally lead the mind to abstraction from outward (worldly) objects; but here already we meet in Buddhism with decided extravagances in moral considerations. The counting of inhalations and exhalations is named as an

[1] Hardy's "Manual of Buddhism," p. 391. Burnouf, "Le Lotus de la Bonne Loi," Appendix No. VI., "Introduction," p. 623. Foe koue ki, p. 291.

excellent means for obtaining tranquillity of mind. Detestation of the world is said to result from meditating upon the attributes of the body: if, therefore, one begins with regarding his body as an abscess, he will be convinced that the body contains nothing but misery and decay, and he will then easily cast off all affection for it, and will even end by considering food also as a mass of putridity, with which he will become disgusted.[1]

III. As regards the degree of perfection which man has attained in virtues and science, this system acknowledges several gradations, which are based upon the following philosophical considerations. The comprehension of the doctrines as taught by Sākyamuni is different with different men. There are several degrees of comprehension. Those who have succeeded in arriving at the highest degree are superior to those of a lower one. There are four paths to comprehension, and in order to arrive at final emancipation from re-birth, at Nirvāna, it is indispensable to have entered one of them at least. Emancipation takes place either instantaneously, on account of the merit accumulated in previous existences, or by assiduous attention to the various exercises prescribed. To each of the four paths to comprehension are assigned particular faculties arising from its pursuit. Those who have not yet entered any of the paths, are designated in the sacred books by the name of "unwise

[1] Such moral fanaticism does not seem, however, to have had its exclusive origin in Buddhism, for the Buddhists themselves state, that these practices were known also to the Tīrthikas, the Brahmanical ascetics, or the "unbelievers." See Hardy, "Eastern Monachism," p. 250. Burnouf, "Introduction," p. 280.

men," or those who live in the meshes of the cleaving to existence, of evil desire, ignorance, and impurity. These unwise men have not availed themselves of the means revealed by the Buddha to obtain freedom from metempsychosis; "their minds are still obscure, slow, incapable of clear comprehension; such beings are not in the path securing final liberation, which is only accorded to one of the paths of wisdom."

The gradually increasing importance of the four paths is defined by the Buddhists as follows:—[1]

First path. This is attained by the Srōtāpatti, or "the man who have entered the stream" leading to Nirvāna, and have thus advanced one step towards salvation. Nirvāna is reached by rejecting the error which teaches "I am," or "this is mine," by not doubting the real existence of the Buddhas, and by perceiving that the practises and exercises ordained by them must be carefully attended to. From the time of entering this path up to the attainment of Nirvāna itself, there remain only seven more births, but none can take place in any of the four hells; such a saint constantly wanders about, and according to Chinese notions, his migrations last 80,000 kalpas, or periods of a mundane revolution.

Second path. The graduate is here called Sakridāgāmin, "he who will receive birth once more." Such a graduate's mind is enlightened upon the subject of the three doctrines understood by the Srōtāpatti, and is,

[1] See Foe koue ki, Engl. transl., p. 94. Burnouf, "Introduction," pp. 288-98. Hardy, "Eastern Monachism," Chapter XXII. Each path is subdivided into two classes, and thus we get the other system of eight paths, to which I have already alluded. See p. 17.

moreover, freed from the desire of cleaving to sensuous objects, and of wishing evil to others. He may either enter this path in the world of men and afterwards be born in a world appropriated to gods, or he may enter it in a world of gods, and afterwards be born in the world of men. He has still to wait 60,000 kalpas, before he arrives at Nirvāna.

Third path. Here the graduate, Anāgāmin, "he who will not be born again," is free from the five errors already cast off by the Sakridāgāmin, and also from evil desire, ignorance, doubt of the precepts of the sceptics, and hatred. He may enter, by the apparitional birth, a world of gods, and from that world attain Nirvāna, for which, however, he has still to wait 40,000 kalpas.

Fourth path. This, the highest path to perfection, is attained by the Arhats, Arhants, or Archats, a title meaning that they deserve to become members of the assembly of the faithfuls (samgha). In the earliest period of Buddhism the name Arhat was given to every one who had arrived at the comprehension of the four truths. But such a steadiness of the mind, the Hīnayāna followers say, can only be attained by those who have renounced the world, viz. by the priests; and these alone consequently enjoy the advantages of entering the fourth path, which consists in nothing less than the emancipation from re-birth, and the possession of five supernatural faculties, or the Abhijnās. To allege of any one that he has "seen Nirvāna," is the same as saying, that he has become Arhat. The restriction of Nirvāna to the clergy cannot be imputed to Sākyamuni, who, on the contrary, admits all his followers to the full blessings of his law.[1]

At the early period of the Hīnayāna system the list of the different gradations must have been closed with the Arhats, the Buddha even not being originally called by another name; but in the progressive developement of this system the Arhat was superseded by the Pratyēka Buddhas, the Bōdhisattvas, and the most perfect Buddhas.

Pratyēka Buddhas are those men who, though attaining by their own unaided exertions the Bōdhi of the supreme Buddhas, remain limited in their powers as well as their intellects. They are unable to release any one from the repetition of existence, as they only care for their own salvation, without contributing in the least towards that of other men. Pratyēka Buddhas are accordingly never said in the legends to have accomplished miraculous works similar to those of the supreme Buddhas, and are further considered never to appear when a real Buddha is living upon earth.[2]

Bōdhisattvas are the candidates for the Buddhaship, or those men who, by assiduity in the practice of virtues and meditation, have finally arrived at the intelligence, or Bōdhi, of the supreme Buddha. Whoever strives to attain this sublime rank, has to pass through countless phases of existence, during which he gradually accumu-

[1] I shall have occasion, in the chapter on Tibetan priesthood, to resume the admittance or non-admittance of this dogma by the various schools.—About the Abhijnās, see Burnouf, "Le Lotus de la Bonne Loi," p. 820.

[2] See Foe koue ki, English translation, pp. 10, 95, 158; Burnouf's "Introduction," p. 297; Hardy's "Monachism," and "Manual," Index, *voce* Pase Buddha.

lates a greater degree of merit; he gains thereby the favour of a Buddha of contemporaneous existence on earth, and by his assistance he rises to one of the celestial regions above the earth, where he awaits his next birth as Saviour. Such candidates are not enumerated in the sacred Hīnayāna books amongst the companions of the Buddha Sākyamuni, with whom indeed no Bōdhisattva could be contemporaneous; nor are they believed to take an active part in the general welfare of man. The title simply denotes the condition of those who shall attain the Buddhaship at their following birth.[1]

The most perfect Buddhas (whose plurality has been promulgated by the Santrāntika-Hīnayāna) are those Bōdhisattvas who, at their last birth, have arrived at the sublime wisdom which enables them to direct man to the path leading to the cessation of existence. From the moment of departure from earth they have left behind them every kind of personality and form, and all connection with the world; they interfere with nothing and leave it to man to seek salvation by his own energy. This dogma was still further enlarged by some of the Hīnayāna sects, the Mahāsāmghika school even going so far as to discuss the infinity, eternity, and omnipotence of the Buddha.

[1] Burnouf's "Introduction," p. 110; Hardy, l. c., Index, *voce* Bōdhisattva.

CHAPTER V

THE MAHĀYĀNA SYSTEMS

NĀGĀRJUNA.—THE FUNDAMENTAL MAHĀYĀNA PRINCIPLES.—THE CONTEMPLATIVE MAHĀYĀNA (YOGĀCHĀRYA) SYSTEM.—THE PRASANGA-MADHYAMIKA SCHOOL.

Nāgārjuna.

MOST of the sacred Tibetan writers consider Nāgārjuna (in Tibetan Lugrub) as the founder of this system, which means "great vehicle." Nāgārjuna is reported in their books to have lived in the southern parts of India, four hundred years after the death of the Buddha Sākyamuni or according to Westergaards calculation in the first century A.D.; the sacred books of the Southern Buddhists give the second century B.C.[1] The Tibetan historiograph Tārānātha, however, is of opinion, that the most important Mahāyāna books had already appeared

[1] *See* p. 7.—The Tibetans are decidedly wrong in considering Nāgārjuna as the author of the numerous Mahāyāna writings; for the treatises which they refer to him are ascribed in the Chinese translations to other authors. According to Wassiljew's opinion he is most probably a mythological personage, without any real existence; in which case we should have to regard Nāgārjuna as the generic name of the various authors who wrote upon the Mahāyāna doctrine before the time of Āryāsanga. See his "Buddhismus," pp. 140, 219.

in the Time of Srī Saraha, or Rāhulabhadra, who lived shortly before Nāgārjuna.

According to some Tibetan legends, Nāgārjuna received the book Paramārtha, according to others the book Avatamsaka, from the Nāgas, fabulous creatures of the nature of serpents, who occupy a place among the beings superior to man, and are regarded as protectors of the law of the Buddha.[1] To these spiritual beings Sākyamuni is said to have taught a more philosophical religious system than to men, who were not sufficiently advanced to understand it at the time of his appearance. In a Chinese biography Nāgārjuna is described as an exceedingly clever man, who considered his theory to be entirely different from that of Buddhism in its contemporaneous form, until, after conversation with the Nāgas, he discovered an exactly similar doctrine to have been taught by the Buddha Sākyamuni himself. Hence the biographer infers the system to contain the same principles as those of genuine Buddhism, though it is more sublime. This vindication of orthodoxy naturally leads to the conclusion, that Nāgārjuna's followers were well aware of their being in opposition to the Hīnayāna schools, which they would have reproached with heresy, had the latter not adopted some of the principles established in the new system, and by doing so, admitted the correctness of the innovations thus introduced. The Hīnayāna system existed still for many centuries; Hiuen Thsang, in his reports, frequently mentions that he has met during his travels adherents of the "little vehicle."

[1] Concerning the Nāgas see, Foe koue ki, English translation, p. 155.

In none of the sacred books treating on the Mahāyāna system do we find a record of the historical development of its theories prior to the appearance of Āryāsanga (in Tibetan Chagpa thogmed), a reformer who founded the Yogāchārya school (in Tibetan, Naljor chodpa).[1] It is impossible, therefore, to indicate, with any approximation to accuracy, either the origin, or the authors, of the divergent theories to be clearly traced in the Mahāyāna religious books, which were all of them written before Āryāsanga's time. In the works relating to this system two divisions essentially different are apparent: the first illustrating the principles of Nāgārjuna, which have been adopted by the Madhyamika schools (Tib. Bumapa); the second, which is the more developed one, being appropriated by the Yogāchārya school, or the contemplative Mahāyāna. I shall treat these divisions separately as also the peculiarities that developed in the Prasanga branch, the most important of the Madhyamika system.

The fundamental Mahāyāna principles.

The leading principles of this doctrine are to be found in the earliest works attributed to Nāgārjuna, among

[1] Aryāsanga is said to have been taught his doctrine by the future Buddha Maitreya, the president of the region Tushita, from whom he received back the five short treatises in verse known in Tibet as "the five books of Maitreya," or Champai chos nga. Csoma places him in the seventh century, but according to Wassiljew's researches (pp. 225, 230) he must have lived much sooner, as the biography of his younger brother, Vasubandhu, was translated by the celebrated Tshin thi into Chinese under the dynasty Tshin, who ruled between the years 557-588 A.D. Also the the remarks of Wilson in R. As. Soc., Vol. VI., p. 240, on the period when the principal works still extant in Sanskrit were written, may be quoted in prove of the period being an earlier one. He believes it now "established, that they have been written at the latest, from a century and a half before to as much after, the era of Christianity."

which may be specially mentioned: Samādhirāja, Buddhāvatamsaka, and Ratnakūta.

I. The fundamental dogma is that of the emptiness, or nothingness of things (in Tib. Tongpanyid, in Sanskrit Sūnyatā); it is also called Prajnā Pāramitā (in Tib. Pharchin, also Sherchin), "the supreme intelligence which arrives at the other side of the river."[1] This dogma, it is evident, is simply an enlargement and development of the principal law of Buddhism:—All is perishable, or partakes of impermanence, misery, and unreality. The idea of emptiness is referred both to single objects and also to absolute existence in general. When relating to single objects, the expression "void or ideal" signifies that which we consider in any object as original, existing by itself, and permanent; hence, even the Buddha is but the product of judicious reflection and meditation. When referred to absolute existence, emptiness is the abstract essence, existing in every thing without causal connexion, and comprising all though containing nothing.

Sākyamuni is said to have connected this dogma with the consideration, "that no existing object has a nature, Ngovonyid, whence it follows, that there is neither beginning nor end—that from time immemorial all has been perfect quietude, Zodmanas zhiba (viz. nothing has manifested itself in any form), and is entirely immersed in Nirvāna." The Mahāyāna schools demonstrate the doctrine of voidness by the dogma of the three characteristic

[1] There is an interesting treatise on nothingness, called the Vajramandā Dhāranī, which contains a *resumé* of the ideas connected with this dogma. It is translated by Burnouf, in his "Introduction," p. 548. Concerning the dogmas of the Mahāyāna system see Wassiljew, l. c., pp. 128-43, 319-24, 330.

marks, and of the two truths; the three characteristic marks enumerating the properties of any existing object, and the two truths showing how by the perfect understanding of these properties clear comprehension shall be attained.

The three characteristic marks are the following: Parikalpita (Tib. Kun tag), Paratantra (Tib. Zhan vang), and Parinishpanna (Tib. Yong grub).

Parikalpita is the supposition, or the error. Of this kind is the belief in absolute existence to which those beings adhere who are incapable of understanding that every thing is empty; of this kind is also whatever exists in idea only, without specific quality; or, in other words, whatever is attributed by our reflections and meditations to any object. The error can be two-fold; some believing a thing existing which does not, as *e. g.* the Non-ego; others assert the real existence of an object which only exists in the idea, as *e. g.* all outward things.

Paratantra is whatever exists by a dependent or causal connexion; it forms the basis of the error. Of this kind are: the soul, the sense, comprehension, and also imperfect philosophical meditation. Every object exists by concatenation, and has a specific nature; therefore, it is called dependent upon others, Paratantra.

Parinishpanna, "completely perfect," or simply "perfect," is the unchangeable and unassignable true existence, which is also the scope of the path, the *summum bonum,* the absolute. Of this kind can be only that which enters the mind clear and undarkened, as for instance, the emptiness, or the Non-ego. In order, therefore, that his mind may become free from all that would in any way attract his attention, it is necessary that man view every thing existing as ideal, because it is dependent upon something else; then only—as a natural consequence—he arrives at a right understanding of the Non-ego, and to a knowledge of how the voidness is alone self-existent and perfect.[1]

We now come to the two truths. They are: Samvritisatya (Tib. Kundzabchi denpa) and Paramārthasatya (Tib. Dondampai denpa), or the relative truth and the absolute one. Numerous are the definitions given of these technical terms in the sacred books, but the two principal stand as follows:—

1. Samvriti is that which is supposed as the efficiency of a name, or of a characteristic sign; Paramārtha is the opposite. A difference prevails between the Yogāchāryas and the Madhyamikas with reference to the interpretation of Paramārtha; the former say that Paramārtha is also what is dependent upon other things (Paratantra); the latter say that it is limited to Parinishpanna, or to that which has the character of absolute perfection. In consequence, for the Yogāchāryas Samvriti is Parikalpita *and* Paratantra, for the Madhyamikas Parikalpita only.

2. Samvriti is that which is the origin of illusion, but Paramārtha is the self-consciousness[2] of the saint in

[1] These technical terms were introduced by the Yogāchārya school.—For a comparison of Nirvāna with the wind, to illustrate the nature of Nirvāna, see Hardy's Eastern Monachism, p. 295.

[2] Sanskrit Svasamvedana, "the reflection which analyses itself."

his self-meditation, which is able to dissipate illusions, *i. e.*, which is above all (parama) and contains the true understanding (artha).

II. The world, or the Samsāra, must be renounced, not because it is a source of sorrow and pain, as Sākyamuni himself and the Hīnayāna followers say, but on account of its unreality, as it contains nothing which can satisfy the mind.

III. Besides the cleaving to existing objects, even thinking of any object or properties whatever, is sufficient to hinder final perfection, and the obtaining of the intelligence (Bōdhi) of a Buddha. Man must, therefore, not only curb his passions and abstain from the pleasures of life, but it is not even permissible for him to allow any notion to become the object of his meditation.

IV. Ordinary morality is not sufficient for deliverance from metempsychosis. Those who really strive after final emancipation, must assiduously practise the six transcendental, or cardinal virtues.

These cardinal virtues are:—[1]

1. Charity. 3. Patience. 5. Meditation.
2. Morality. 4. Industry, or earnest application. 6. Ingenuity.

V. The term "Bōdhisattva" has almost entirely lost its original meaning, and is now used in a double sense. In the one sense it is applied to all those who practise the six Pāramitās; in the other to the perfect beings who pass between the different worlds. We find

[1] In numerous religious books four more virtues are added: 1. Method, or manner; 2. Wish, or prayer; 3. Fortitude; 4. Fore-knowledge, or knowledge. See Csoma, in As Res., Vol. XX., p. 399; Burnouf, "Le Lotus de la Bonne Loi," p. 544.

them in the legends contemporaneous with the Buddhas, travelling with them, and listening to the words of the Buddhas, who occasionally send them to remote regions to deliver a message, or receive particular instructions. These Bōdhisattvas are subdivided into several classes, the most sublime among them being nearly equal to the Buddhas, from whom also it is possible they may have emanated; to some of them indeed a rank seems to have been assigned (though apparently without success) which is superior even to that of the Buddhas. They have fulfilled all the conditions for the attainment of the Buddhaship, and might immediately become most perfect Buddhas, did they not prefer, from unlimited charity towards animated beings, to remain still subject to the law of metempsychosis, and to re-incorporate themselves in human shape for the benefit of man. When once arrived at the estate of a most perfect Buddha it would be beyond their power to contribute to man's salvation, the Buddhas caring no longer for the world when they have once left it.[1] In cases of need, therefore, prayers for assistance are addressed not to the Buddhas, but to the Bōdhisattvas, who have shown themselves so friendly and well-towards disposed man. The addressing of prayers to the Buddhas residing in other regions, we must consider as only a further development of Mahāyāna Buddhism.[2]

[1] Concerning this important dogma see Hardy "Eastern Monachism," p. 228.

[2] The dogma of celestial Bōdhisattvas, the progeny of such Buddhas, has been developed only in mysticism, and not in the genuine Mahāyāna system.

VI. The Mahāyāna system does not exclude laymen from Nirvāna; it admits every one, layman as well as priest, to the condition of a supreme Buddha, and applies this name to all who have attained Nirvāna. With regard to the nature of the Buddhas, their definition is materially altered: they are no longer entirely deprived of every personality, and are believed to have a body with certain qualities, and to possess various faculties. By the Mahāyānas they have three different kinds of bodies ascribed to them, and, on leaving the world to return to the higher regions, are supposed to strip off only the last and least sublime of these earthly encumbrances, called the Nirmānakāya. These bodies are styled:—

1. *Nirmānakāya* (Tib. Prulpai ku), which is the Nirvāna with the remains, or body in which the Bōdhisattva appears upon earth in order to teach man, after entering by the six Pāramitās, the path, or career of the Buddhas.

2. *Sambhogakāya* (Tib. Longchod dzogpai ku), or the body of bliss and the reward of fulfilling the three conditions of perfection.

3. *Dharmakāya* (Tib. Chos ku), or the Nirvāna without any remains. This ideal body (the most sublime one) is obtained by the Buddha who abandons the world for ever, and leaves behind everything that has any connexion with it.[1]

[1] Schott, "Buddhaismus," p. 9; Csoma, "Notices" in Journ. As. Soc. Beng., Vol. VII., p. 142; Schmidt, "Grundlehren," in Mémoires de l'Académie de St. Petersbourg, Vol. I., pp. 224 *et seq.* For the Tibetan terms, see A. Schiefner, "Buddhistische Triglotte," leaf 4.

The Contemplative Mahāyāna (Yogāchārya) system.

The contemplative system is described in those works which, in viewing the doctrine of the Pāramitās, have started from the consideration that the three worlds exist only in imagination (Tib. Semtsamo). Such works are the Ghanavyūha (the Gandavyūha of Burnouf), the Mahāsamaya, and certain others. The saints Nanda (Tib. Gavo), Utarasena (Tib. Dampai de), and Samyaksatya (Tib. Yangdag den), are probably among the number teaching in this sense previous to Āryāsanga; the latter, however, must be considered as the real founder of the system.[1]

Like the preceding, the present system also requires abstinence from every kind of reflection, as interfering with clear comprehension; but the most important dogma established by this theory is decidedly the personification of the voidness, by supposing that a soul, Ālaya (Tib. Tsang, also Nyingpo), is the basis of every thing. This soul exists from time immemorial, and in every object; "it reflects itself in every thing, like the moon in clear and tranquil water." It was the loss of its original purity that caused it to wander about in the various spheres of existence. The restoration of the soul to its purity can be attained by the same means as in the preceding system; but now the motive and the success become evident; ignorance is annihilated and the illusion that anything can be real is dissipated; man understands at

[1] Wassiljew, l. c., pp. 143 *et seq.*; 164, 174, 334-47.

length clearly, that the three worlds are but ideal; he gets rid of impurity, and returns to his original nature, and it is thus that he becomes emancipated from metempsychosis. Of course, as with everything belonging to the world, this nature also is only ideal; but the dogma once established that an absolute pure nature exists, Buddhism soon proceeded in the mystical school further to endow it with the character of an all-embracing deity.[1] A material modification of its original character was thus established.

This idea of the soul, Ālaya, is the chief dogma of the Yogāchārya system, which is so called because "he who is strong in the Yoga (meditation) is able to introduce his soul by means of the Yoga into the true nature of existence." There occur, however, amongst the Tibetans, several explanations of this term, as well as other titles given to this school; but this name is the most common, and the line of arguments already instanced is ascribed to Āryāsanga. To the importance which, from the very first, this school has attributed to meditation, may be traced the germs which subsequently led to its losing itself in mysticism.

Āryāsanga and his successors managed to endow their doctrines with such splendour, that the Nāgārjuna school with the principles taught by it (which had been adopted by the Madhyamikas, Tib. Bumapa) had sunk almost entirely into oblivion for many centuries. It revived, however,

[1] Japanese Buddhism also speaks of a supreme Buddha, who sits throned in the diamond world and has created all the Buddhas. See Hoffmann, "Buddha Pantheon von Nippon," in v. Siebold's "Beschreibung von Japan," Vol. II., p. 57.

in the seventh century under the name of the Prasanga branch; and this still remains to be treated before concluding our notices of the Mahāyāna systems.

The Prasanga-Madhyamika school.

This school,[1] in Tibetan probably called Thal gyurva, was founded by Buddhapālita, and soon succeeded in superseding all other schools of the Mahāyāna system, notwithstanding the attacks made upon it by Bhavya, the originator of the Svatantra-Madhyamika school. The success attained by the Prasanga school is due, in a great measure, to the excellent commentaries and introductory works written in the eighth and ninth centuries by Chandrakirti (Tib. Dava Dagpa) and other learned men. These events coinciding with a numerous immigration of Indian priests into Tíbet, caused the Prasanga school to be at present considered by the Tibetan Lamas as that which alone taught and gave the true explanation of the faith revealed by the Buddha.

The Prasanga school obtained its name from the peculiar mode which it adopted of deducing the absurdity and erroneousness of every esoteric opinion. "The Prasangas say that the two truths, Samvriti and Paramārtha, cannot be maintained as either identical or different; if they were identical, we should strip off the Paramārtha together with Samvriti, and if they were different, we should not be able to become delivered from Samvriti.

[1] Wassiljew, "Der Buddhismus," pp. 327; 357-67. Compare Csomas' Notices, in Journ. As. Soc. Beng., Vol. VII., p. 144.

In understanding by the term Non-ego all objects which are compound, or exist in Samvriti, we attribute to it a character identical with being existent and uncompounded (Paramārtha); but if this is already the character of Samvriti, it denotes that the objects have already a perfect existence; hence they have already arrived at salvation (Tib. Dolzin). From such and similar hair-splitting considerations the Prasangas deduce that both truths have 'one and the same nature' (Tib. Ngovo chig), but two distinct meanings (Tib. Togpa nyi). These speculations are called Prasanga."

The Prasanga school maintains that the doctrines of the Buddha establish two paths—one leading to the highest regions of the universe, to the heaven, Sukhavatī,[1] where man enjoys perfect happiness but connected with personal existence; the other conducting to entire emancipation from the world, viz. to Nirvāna. The former path is attained by the practice of virtues, the latter by the highest perfection of intelligence. They reckon eight (according to some writers even eleven) peculiarities by which their system distinguishes itself from all the others; out of these eleven peculiarities, as given by the Tibetan Jam yang shadpa, I select the following as the most characteristic, the others being but a repetition of general Mahāyāna principles, or deductions contained in their own.

1. The principal dogma is the negation of existence as well as of non-existence; they admit neither self-existence (absolute existence), Paramārtha, nor existence

[1] See for particulars Chapter IX.

by causal connexion, Samvriti: in order not to fall into extremes. For, not to say of what has never existed, to be; and of the truly existing, not to be; this is to take a middle way, Madhyama.[1] This dogma is formulated as follows:—"By denying the extreme of existence is also denied, in consequence of conditional appearance, the extreme of non-existence, which is not in Paramārtha." The arguments in proof of this thesis are most circumstantial; the following most curious syllogisms occur in Jam yang shadpa's work:—

1. If the plant grew by its own specific nature, it would not be a composition, Tenbrel; it is demonstrated, however, that it is a composition.
2. If anything in nature were self-existent, we should certainly hear and see it; for the sensation of seeing and hearing would in this case be absolutely identical.
3. The quality of being general would not be peculiar to many things, because it would be an indivisible unity, as such a unity we should be obliged to take the *ego*, if there were an *ego*.
4. The plant would not be compelled to grew anew, because it would continue to exist.
5. If any Skandha,[2] as sensation, were self-existent,

[1] They are also called, on account of this theory, "those who deny existence (nature)," in Tibetan, Ngovonyid medpar mraba.

[2] The Buddhists enumerate five essential properties of sentient existence, which are styled Skandhas, or Sīlaskandhas, in Tibetan, Tsulkhrim kyi phungpo, "the aggregates of morals." They are: 1. The organized body; 2. Sensation; 3. Perception; 4. Discrimination; 5. Consciousness. See Burnouf, Index, *voce* Skandha; Hardy's Manual of Buddhism, pp. 388, 399-424.—For the Tibetan designations of the five Skandhas see "Buddhistische Triglotte," by A. Schiefner, leaf 9.

another Skandha, as *e.g.* the organized body, would be also self-existent; but it is impossible to produce by the self-existence of sensation that of the organized body, because the plastic power and the object to be formed are identical.

2. The Ālaya has an absolute eternal existence; those treatises do not teach the right doctrine which attribute to it only a relative existence.

3. Not only the Arhats, but also simple men, if they have entered the path, can arrive at the rude comprehension of the sixteen kinds of the four truths by "very evident (earnest) meditation" (Tib. Naljor ngonsum); but those systems are considered wrong which pretend, as the Hīnayāna, that the knowledge (Vishnāna) derived from such meditation (which is nothing but a manifestation of the Ālaya) be not liable to errors (Sansk. Vikalpa, Tib. Namtog). Even the Arhat goes to hell in case he doubt anything. This reproach is meant to be made to the schools by which the Arhats are admitted to Nirvāna under any condition.[1]

4. The three periods: the present, the past, and the future, are compounds, correlative to each other. The Buddha has declared: "A harsh word, uttered in past times, is not lost (literally *destroyed*), but returns again;" and, therefore, the past time is the present time, as is also the future, though as yet it has not come into existence.

5. The Buddha has two kinds of Nirvāna: Nirvāna with remains and Nirvāna without remains; the latter

[1] The means of avoiding the error have been more fully developed by mysticism in the exigencies of Vipasyana and Samatha. *See* p. 54.

kind only is entire extinction of personality, or the state where the notion of *ego* ceases, where the outward and inward man is destroyed. In this state, the Buddha has assumed the body Dharmakāya, in which there is neither beginning nor end; whilst in the Nirvāna with remains he has obtained only the Nirmānakāya body, in which, though rendered impervious to outward impressions, he has not yet thrown off habitual errors (the influence of passions), of which nothing remains in the other kind of Nirvāna.

The Prasangas admit as orthodox the greater part of the hymns in the Tanjur, and those of the Sūtras which are contained in the Kanjur; in these, they say, the true meaning of the word of the Buddha (viz. the Madhyamika doctrine) is explained. There exist a large number of such books, the most important of which are the seventeen books of the Prajnāpāramitā, then the Akshayamatinirdesa, the Samādhirāja, the Anavataptapariprichchhā, Dharmasamgīti, the Sagarapariprichchha, the Manjusrīvikrīdita, the first chapter of the Ratnakūta, and the chapter of Kāsyapa, which is quoted by Nāgārjuna and his disciples in support of their dogmas.[1]

It is remarkable to see at what extravagances Buddhist speculation has arrived by its tendency to follow abstract ideas without the consideration of the limits presented by bodily experience and the laws of nature. But the case is rather not an isolated one; we meet instances of analogous dreams in ancient and modern times.

[1] Wassiljew in his examination of the most important Mahāyāna Sūtras, pp. 157-202, presents an analysis of the Manjusrīvikrīdita and the Ratnakūta.

CHAPTER VI

THE SYSTEM OF MYSTICISM

General Character.—The Kāla Chakra System; its Origin and Dogmas.

The contact of the Buddhists with their various pagan neighbours gradually introduced into their creed ideas foreign to Buddhism, and the consequence of this was the rise of a new system full of mystic modifications. We see already in the later Mahāyāna schools, particularly in the Yogāchārya branch, a more general yielding to the current superstitious notions; but the principles of mystic theology such as we find them in the actual Buddhism of the present day have chiefly been developed in the most modern system, which originated independently of the earlier ones, in Central Asia. Its theories were afterwards even engrafted upon later productions by a subsequent incorporation, to such a degree, that without a knowledge of this system, we should often be almost at a loss how to understand the Mahāyāna sacred books.

European orientalists use to apply to this third system the name of Yogāchārya; and if we bear in mind, that Yoga means in Sanskrit "abstract devotion, by which supernatural faculties are acquired,"[1] it becomes evident that they were led to do so by the conformity of the name with the system to which they applied it. But Wassiljew has clearly proved in his work, that Yogāchārya is but a branch of the Mahāyāna system, and he therefore substituted the name of "Mysticism," which I have also adopted. This name was chosen because this system places meditation, the recital of certain prayers, and the practise of mystical rites above the observance of precepts and even above moral deportment.

Mysticism appears for the first time as a specific system in the tenth century of our era; it is called in the sacred books Dus kyi khorlo, in Sanskrit Kāla Chakra, "the circle of time."[2] It is reported to have originated in the fabulous country Sambhala (Tib. Dejung), "source or origin of happiness." Csoma, from careful investigations, places this country beyond the Sir Deriáu (Yaxartes) between 45° and 50° north latitude. It was first known in India in the year 965 A.D.; and it was in-

[1] Wilson, "Glossary of Judicial and Revenue Terms," *see* the article Yoga.

[2] See Csoma, "On the origin of the Kāla Chakra system," Journ. As. Soc. Beng., Vol. II., p. 57. "Grammar," 192. "Analysis," As. Res., Vol. XX., pp. 488, 564. Compare also Burnouf, "Introduction," Section V. Hodgson, "Notice on Buddhist Symbols," R. As. Soc., Vol. XVIII., p. 397. Wilson, "Sketch of the Religious Sects of the Hindus," As. Res., Vol. XVII., p. 216-29.

troduced, they go on to say, into Tíbet from India viâ Kashmír, in the year 1025 A.D. I cannot believe it accidental that the beginning of the Tibetan era of counting time, about which I shall have occasion to say some words in a later chapter, coincides with the introduction of this system. I am rather inclined to think (though as far as I know, this has not yet been pointed out as particularly important) that the readiness with which this system was received made it appear at once so important, that events were dated from its introduction.

The principal rites and formulæ of mysticism and the theories about their efficacy bear an extraordinary analogy to the Shamanism of the Siberians, and are, besides, almost identical with the Tantrika ritual of the Hindus; for it promises endowment with supernatural faculties far superior to the energy to be derived from virtue and abstinence, and capable of leading to the union with the deity, to the man who keeps in mind that all three worlds exist in the imagination only and regulates his actions accordingly. Its theories are laid down in two series of works, which are known under the collective titles of Dhāranīs (in Tibetan Zung), and Tantras (in Tibetan Gyut). The Dhāranī formulæ may be of considerable antiquity, and it is not unlikely that already the Mahāyāna leaders took some of them into their books. The Tantras are of a more modern date, especially those of them, in which the observance of magical practices is carried to a point which is an extreme even for mysticism in any form. Wilson believes Tantrika notions to have originated in India in the early centuries of Christianity, but the present Hindu ritual seems to him not to date back beyond the tenth century; about at the same time the Tantras were probably introduced also into the Buddhist sacred literature. Their modern origin is proved by the statement of the Tibetan autorities respecting the appearance of the Dus kyi khorlo system, which makes the deliverance from metempsychosis dependent upon the knowledge of the Tantras. So at least says Padma Karpo, a Tibetan Lama, who lived in the sixteenth century, in his description of these doctrines. "He who does not know the Tantrika principles and all such, is a wanderer in the orb of transmigration and is out of the way (path) of the supreme triumphator, Sanskrit Bhagavan Vajradhara."[1] Another and indirect proof of their recent origin is the fact, that there are much fewer works on Tantrika principles existing in the Chinese language; had the Chinese Buddhist pilgrims who travelled in India still during the seventh century A.D. found such treatises (had they existed at all, they would soon have become acquainted with them), they would certainly have brought them home in order to have them translated into the Chinese language; and then, also, in this particular branch the Chinese Buddhist literature would be richer than the Tibetan, whilst the reverse is actually the case. Besides, it is also reported, that the most expert Indian magicians, or Tantrists, did not exist till after the travels of the

[1] The claim that Sākyamuni is their original author, is undoubtedly inadmissable, both on account of their style and contents, as well as of historical dates.

Chinese pilgrims in India, and that the most important Tantras had been translated into Chinese during the reign of the northern Song dynasty which ruled from the years 960 to 1127 A.D.

Kāla Chakra is also the title of the principal work of this system; it stands at the head of the Gyut division of the Kanjur, as well as, the Tanjur, and was explained and repeatedly commented on by several learned men who lived in the fourteenth, fifteenth, and sixteenth centuries, of whom the most celebrated were Puton or Buston, Khetup, and Padmo Karpo.

I have arranged the dogmas propounded by mysticism in four groups.

I. There is a first, chief Buddha, Ādi Buddha, in Tibetan Chogi dangpoi sangye, who is without beginning or end; none of the human Buddhas have arrived at the Buddhaship for the first time, and the Sambhogakāya, or body of blissfulness of the Buddhas has existed from all eternity and will never perish. This first of the Buddhas is called in the Tantras Vajradhara (in Tibetan Dorjechang or Dorjedzin), and Vajrasattva (in Tibetan Dorjesempa).[1] As Vajradhara he is epitheted "the supreme Buddha, the supreme triumphator, the lord of all mysteries,[2] the prime minister of all Tathāgatas, the being who is without beginning or end, the being who has the soul of a diamond (Vajrasattva)." It is he to whom the subdued and conquered evil spirits swear that

[1] Dorjechang and Dorjedzin have the same meaning, "holding the diamond (Vajra)." Sempa (sems-pa) means "the soul."

[2] Sangbai Dagpo, "concealed lord," in Sanskrit Guhyapati.

they will no longer hinder the propagation of the faith of the Buddha, nor in future do any mischief to man. To Vajrasattva the epithets are given of "the supreme intelligence, the chief (Tsovo), the president of the five Dhyāni Buddhas."[1] But Vajradhara and Vajrasattva are also considered as two different beings, as they occur in several treatises both at the same time, the one putting questions, the other answering them. Their respective position may be explained the best by supposing Vajradhara to be too great a god and too much lost in divine quietude to favour man's undertakings and works with his assistance, and that he acts through the god Vajrasattva, who would be to him in the relation of a Dhyāni Buddha to his human Buddha. This explanation is also supported by the epithet of "president of the Dhyāni Buddhas."

By the name of Dhyāni Buddha,[2] "Buddha of contemplation," or by the term Anupadaka, "without parents," celestial beings are designated corresponding to the human Buddhas teaching upon earth, who are called "Mānushi Buddhas." The Buddhists believe that each Buddha when preaching the law to men, manifests himself at the same time in the three worlds which their cosmographical system acknowledges. In the world of *desire*, the lowest of the three to which the earth belongs, he appears in

[1] See Csoma, As. Res., Vol., 20, pp. 496, 503, 549, 550. Journ. As. Soc. Beng., Vol. II., p. 57. Wassiljew, "Der Buddhismus," p. 205.

[2] Respecting the theory of the Dhyāni Buddhas *see* Schmidt, "Grundlehren," Mem. de l'Acad. de Petersb., Vol. I, p. 104. Burnouf, "Introduction," pp. 116, 221, 525, 627. "Lotus de la Bonne Loi," p. 400. The more theistical ideas of the Nepalese about their origin are noknot wn to the Tibetan Buddhists.

human shape. In the world of *forms* he manifests himself in a more sublime form as Dhyāni Buddha. In the highest world, the one of the *incorporeal beings,* he has neither shape nor name. The Dhyāni Buddhas have the faculty of creating from themselves by virtue of Dhyāna, or abstract meditation, an equally celestial son, a Dhyāni Bōdhisattva, who after the death of a Mānushi Buddha is charged with the continuance of the work undertaken by the departed Buddha till the next epoch of religion begins, when again a subsequent Mānushi Buddha appears.[1] Thus, to each human Buddha belongs a Dhyāni Buddha and a Dhyāni Bōdhisattva,[2] and the unlimited number of the former also involves an equally unlimited number of the latter.

Out of this vast number the five Buddhas of the actual period of the universe are particularly worshipped. Four of these Buddhas have already appeared; Sākyamuni is the fourth and the last who has appeared till now; his Dhyāni Buddha is Amitābha, in Tibetan Odpagmed; his Dhyāni Bōdhisattva Avolōkitēsvara, or Padmapāni, in Tíbet generally implored under the name of Chenresi. To the Dhyāni Buddhas of these five Mānushi Buddhas is added, as a sixth and the highest in rank, Vajrasattva. To him or occasionally also to Amitābha who then takes his place, the Tibetans attribute the function of the "God

[1] The Buddhas are men and subjected to the physical conditions established for human creatures; it is in consequence of this principle that the stay of every Buddha upon earth is limited by the laws which fix for the period during which he appears, the life-time of man, which varies from 80,000 to 10 years. When this period had elapsed he dies, or as the Buddhists say, he returns to Nirvāna.

[2] He has, besides, a female companion, a Sakti.

above all." One of these two divine persons is addressed in such ceremonies as are believed to grant success to undertakings, and the belief in the absolute necessity of their assistance is so positive that a Lama told my brother that "a ceremony which does not include an address to Dorjesempa (Vajrasattva) is similar in efficacy to a bird which, with its wings cut, tries to fly."[1]

With reference to the representations of these divine persons in drawings I am able to add the following details.

A picture on canvas received by Adolphe from Thóling, in Gnári Khórsum, represents Vajrasattva with rosy complexion, holding the Dorje in his right hand and a bell in his left; the latter, in Tibetan called Drilbu, is identical in shape with those used in sacred choral songs to mark the pauses. Vajrasattva is surrounded by various groups of gods representing protectors of men against evil spirits.—Amitābha is represented in all the images I have examined, with a vivid red complexion; in a very nicety executed picture from Mángnang in Gnári Khórsum were subjoined beneath the seat the seven precious things, in Tibetan called Rinchen na dun. They are:—Khorlo (Sanskr. Chakra), "the wheel;" Norbu (Sanskr. Mani), "the precious stone;" Tsunpo, "the royal consort;" Lonpo, "the best treasurer;" Tachog, "the

[1] A very powerful prayer is that which concludes the address to the Buddhas of confession, see Plates V *et seq.*—The fact of the frequent imploration of the Dhyāni Buddhas shows that the Tibetan Buddhists differ in this point from those of Nepál, who believe the Dhyāni Buddhas to be absolutely inactive.

best horse;" Langpo, "the elephant;" Maglon, "the best leader."[1]

II. *Worldly* notions or phenomena dare not be selected for contemplation; but from assiduous meditation in which any *religious* object is analysed (Zhine lhagthong, Sankr. Vipasyana), man acquires new faculties, provided he most earnestly concentrates his thoughts upon one object. Such a state of calmness and tranquillity, in Sanskrit Samatha, occasions, however, great trouble, and it is considered as not at all easy to concentrate the mind, this requiring long practice; but if man has once succeeded, aided by preparatory exercises,[2] in bringing himself to meditate with unmoved mind upon the deepest religious abstractions in the four degrees of meditation, Dhyāna (in Tibetan Samtan), he finally arrives at entire imperturbability, Samāpatti (in Tibetan, Nyompa), which has also four gradations. First of all, a perfect absence of all idea of individuality is the result; then secrets and powers hitherto concealed to him become at once unveiled, and he has now entered "the path of seeing," Thonglam; by continued, uninterrupted meditation on the four truths, his mind becomes supernaturally pure, and gradually rises to the most perfect states, called the Top, Tsemo (in Sanskrit Mūrdhan), patience, Zodpa (in Sanskrit Kshānti), and the supreme in the world (in Sanskrit Lokottaradharma).[3]—

[1] Compare about them I. J. Schmidt, "Ssanaug Ssetsen," p. 471.

[2] A Tibetan mode of keeping the thoughts together, shall be noticed in Chapter XV.

[3] See Burnouf, "Le Lotus," pp. 348, 800. Hardy, "Eastern Monachism," p. 270. Wassiljew, "Der Buddhismus," p. 149.

This dogma is in decided contradiction to the Mahāyāna principle that the meditation on *any object whatever* keeps man back from arriving at the highest degree of perfection.[1]

III. The recital of mystical words and sentences, the Dhāranīs (Tib. Zung), bestows upon man every kind of bliss and obtains for him the assistance of the Buddhas and Bōdhisattvas. These Dhāranīs[2] have been decidedly adopted from the generally felt want of incantations as remedies against fear of danger, though the Buddhists believe them to have been delivered by Sākyamuni, or by those Buddhas, Bōdhisattvas, and gods over whom Dhāranīs are supposed to exercise an influence. The number of the formulæ taught by these gods is described in the sacred books as enormous, and each is considered as equally efficacious. But Wassiljew is of opinion that the great number alluded to most likely is to be referred to so many verses (Gāthās) or even single words of the treatises which describe their powers and the ceremonies in the performance of which they are recited. These formulæ are either short sentences or even only a few words, as *e. g.* the names and the epithets of the Buddhas and Bōdhisattvas. There are some Dhāranīs which are equal to the practise of the Pāramitās, others subdue gods and genii, or call for Buddhas and Bōdhisattvas; some impart longevity or accomplish every wish; others cure diseases, &c. It is even assumed, that by a mere

[1] *See* p. 36.

[2] Compare Burnouf, "Introduction," pp. 522—74. Wassiljew, l. c., pp. 153, 193.

uttering of the letters of which the Dhāranī is composed—nay even by their aspect alone—power may be gained over those beings of which they treat, or for such purposes for which they are supposed to grant help.

They dare not be altered when recited or written, as each letter has its own magical power, and it is owing to this belief that they have not been translated into Tibetan, and that the Tibetan alphabet has been adapted to the exact rendering of every Sanskrit letter.[1]

The magical influence of words is deduced from the unreality of all existing objects: all existence being but ideal, the name is just as much as the object itself; consequently, if a man holds sway over a word expressive of anything, he also disposes of the thing itself. The same influence is also attributed to conventional signs formed by a certain placing of the fingers, Chakja, in Sanskrit Mudrā. All objects being identical with reference to their nature, signs which symbolize the attributes of a god produce the same effect as words and offerings.

IV. The reciting of Dhāranīs, if combined with the practise of magical rites and supported by morality and contemplation, leads to superhuman faculties (in Sanskrit Siddhi)—nay, even to the union with the deity. This is a doctrine which, in all probabilitity, has

[1] The Sanskrit names of the Buddhas and Bōdhisattvas have been, however, translated into Tibetan, but these names are rendered as literally as possible. I quote as examples Amitābha and Odpagmed; Manjusrī and Jamjang; Avalōkita and Chenresi; Vajrasattva and Dorjesempa; Vajradhara and Dorjechang.—For the alphabetical scheme of the Sanskrit language when written with Tibetan characters *see* Csoma's Grammar, p. 20.

grown up very recently. The compendious books Tantra treat of this dogma and say, that by magical arts either worldly purposes can be attained, as longevity and riches, or also religious ones, as dominion over malignant spirits, the aid of a Buddha or Bōdhisattva, or the removal by him of any doubt or uncertainty with regard to any of the dogmas. But the chief aim is to obtain final emancipation from metempsychosis, and acquire re-birth in Amitābha's celestial mansion, which latter, by means of such magical ceremonies, can be obtained already in one existence, instead of being the reward of uninterrupted privations in an unlimited series of existences.[1]

[1] The observances in connexion with such magical arts, and the description of magical rites, &c., is given in Chapter XV.

SECTION II

TIBETAN BUDDHISM

CHAPTER VII

HISTORICAL ACCOUNT OF THE INTRODUCTION OF BUDDHISM INTO TÍBET

EARLIEST RELIGION OF THE TIBETANS.—INTRODUCTION OF BUDDHIST DOGMAS INTO EASTERN TIBET.—Era of King Srongtsan Gampo and King Thisrong de tsan.—The reforms of the Lama Tsonkhapa.—PROPAGATION OF BUDDHISM INTO CHINA, LADÁK AND EASTERN HIMÁLAYA.

BEFORE the propagation of Buddhist doctrines in Tíbet the religion of the inhabitants of this country was most probably a kind of worship differing but little from that prevalent among all rude nations, viz. a mingled system of idolatry and sorcery administered by priests enjoying great reputation and power, in consequence of their supposed intercourse with the Gods, and presumed knowledge of the means whereby the divine favour and assistance can be obtained. The first attempt of Buddhist followers to extend their creed to Tíbet doubtless met with general opposition at the hands of both priesthood and people. The latter indeed must have found it far less troublesome to pay a clerical class to obtain a sensual prosperity for them, than by painful discipline, combined with profound meditation, to seek salvation and eternal welfare in a future re-birth and final emancipation from metempsychosis. In order to attain success and the more readily impose upon the tribes they were about to convert to a new religion, the first teachers of Buddhism in Tibet were most probably induced to ascribe to themselves supernatural qualities, and to yield, in minor points of discipline, to some of the ideas of their neophytes. Many suggestions to this effect are to be found in the sacred Tibetan books, as in the Bodhimör, and in the history of Ssanang Ssetsen, which teems with the miraculous and wonderful works performed by early Buddhist priests. Again, it is related that Padma Sambhava's first labour was the subduing of the dreadful demon who rose up in opposition to prevent his entering Tíbet. His scholars are said to have derived from the instructions he gave them on the proper employment of charms, the power of performing most extraordinary deeds.[1] Thus, they caused good harvests, and similar prosperous events, taught the Tibetans some of the arts and sciences which were then practised in the more advanced civilization of China and India (whence they came), but were discreet enough, after a while, to attribute all their successes to the worship of the images and relics of Sākyamuni.

With regard to the introduction of Buddhism into the *Eastern part of Tíbet* we are now in possession of many positive data, though here also the early history is in-

[1] Schmidt, "Ssanang Ssetsen's Geschichte der Ostmongolen," pp. 41, 43, 355. Compare "Forschungen," p. 136.

volved in darkness and myth. The first attempts apparently led to very unsatisfactory results; at least, the monastery which is reported to have been erected in the year 137 B.C. on the slopes of the Kailás range seems to have been soon abandoned and to have fallen into ruins[1] The legends attribute the conversion of the Tibetans to Buddhism to the Dhyāni Bōdhisattva Avolōkitēsvara, the celestial son of Amitābha, whose chosen land is Tíbet; many of the rulers and priests who took an active part in the consolidation of Buddhist faith in this country were regarded by its inhabitants as incarnations of these two sacred persons.

We here give the following as a narrative of some historical facts intimately connected with Buddhism.[2]

In the year 371 A.D. there suddenly appeared five foreigners before the king Thothori Nyan tsan, who instructed him, how he might use for the general welfare

[1] Lassen, "Ind. Alterthumskunde," Vol. II., p. 1072.

[2] See Csoma's Chronological Table, extracted from an historical book written by Tisri, the regent at Lhassa in the year 1686 A.D.; in the notes, Csoma adds further details from other original books. See his "Grammar," pp. 181—98.—Ssanang Ssetsen, "Geschichte der Ostmongolen," aus dem Mongolischen übersetzt von I. J. Schmidt; Chapter III., treats of the history of Tíbet from the years 407 to 1054 A.D. The annotations to Ssanang Ssetsen contain translations from the Bodhimör, and other Mongolian books. "Chronologie Bouddhique, traduite du Mongol," par Klaproth. Fragments Bouddhiques = Nouveau Journal Asiatique, 1831.—The data of these three authors differ as far as the eleventh century, from which period Csoma's and Klaproth's lists agree, saving a constant diversity of two years, which results from the circumstance that the one counts from the Tibetan era, whilst the other brings the data in accordance with the Chinese years (see Chapter XVI.). In the text I have adopted Csoma's dates, with the single exception of the time of Srongtan Gampo's birth, which, it is more probable, took place in the year 617 A.D. (Klaproth and Ssanang Ssetsen), instead of the year 627. See Köppen, "Die Religion des Buddha," Vol. II., p. 54. In the notes I have added the dates given by Ssanang Ssetsen and Klaproth.

of Tíbet four objects, which, in the year 331 A.D.,[1] had fallen from heaven, enclosed in a precious chest, but of the intrinsic value of which no one had hitherto entertained any adequate idea. These instructions being given, the five foreigners at once disappeared. The four precious objects were:—

1. Two hands folded in prayer.
2. A small Chorten.[2]
3. A gem with an inscription of the prayer: Om mani padme hum.[3]
4. The religious work Zamatog, "constructed vessel," a work on moral subjects forming part of the Kanjur.

The king Thothori strictly obeyed the advice received from the five foreigners, and paid great reverence to the said four objects; by their blessing and powerful influence he contrived to live one hundred and nineteen years, during which time universal prosperity and welfare prevailed throughout the kingdom.

Ssanang Ssetsen connects the introduction of Buddhism with the date of this event; but according to Tibetan historians "the earliest period of the propagation of Buddhism," which reached down till the end of the tenth

[1] Ssanang Ssetsen, anno 367, calls this king Lhatotori; Csoma's authorities have Thothori Nyan tsan. The above is the version according to Ssanang Ssetsen; Csoma, p. 194, relates 'that a voice was heard from heaven, saying, that after so many generations (in the seventh century), the contents of the book should be made known'.—It is not stated whence these five men proceeded, but I believe them, for reasons which will hereafter become apparent, to have been Chinese Buddhist priests. *See* p. 68.

[2] About Chortens, *see* Chapter XIII.

[3] See Chapter X.

century A.D., begins with King Srongtsan Gampo, who was born in the year 617 A.D. and died 698.[1] This king is highly extolled by them on account of his successful efforts in propagating Buddhism. He even went so far as to send to India, in the year 632 A.D., his prime-minister, Thumi Sambhota, with sixteen companions, who had orders to study carefully the sacred Buddhist books and the Indian language; the members of this mission were also instructed to bring back to Tíbet a complete system of the alphabet as used in India, with a view to its being hereafter adapted to the Tibetan language.[2] After the safe return of the party from a journey which is described as fraught with incredible difficulties, Thumi Sambhota constructed the Tibetan letters from the Devanāgari alphabet, whereupon King Srongtsan Gampo ordered the sacred Indian books treating on Buddhists doctrines to the translated into Tibetan.[3] At the same time he

[1] Respecting this distinction of the two periods see Csoma's Grammar, p. 196, Note 18.—The year of Srongtsan's death is given on the authority of Ssanang and Klaproth; in Csoma's list it is not mentioned.

[2] A previous mission is said to have been compelled by the malignant spirits to return, after reaching the frontier. For Tibetan accounts of the attempts of Srongtsan to form a Tibetan alphabet, see Schmidt's notes to "Ssanang Ssetsen," p. 326.

[3] Respecting the striking resemblance of the Tibetan capital letters to the ancient Devanāgari characters much interesting information is furnished in the comparative tables given by Hodgson in his "Notices," As. Res., Vol. XVI., p. 420. Schmidt, "Ueber den Ursprung der tib. Schrift," Mém. de l'Acad. de Pet., Vol. I., p. 41. Csoma, "Grammar," p. 204.—Thumi Sambhota is said to be an incarnation of the Bodhisattva Manjusrī. This divine person, in Tibetan called Jamjang, is to be viewed in a double sense. He appears to be an historical personage who taught Buddhist doctrines in Népal in the 8th or 9th century A.D.; but he is also worshipped as a mythological person of the divine nature of a Bōdhisattva (his Sakti is Sarasvatī, Tib. Ngagi lhamo), who is believed to have inspired with his divine intelligence many a person who has much contributed to the propagation of Buddhist theories. He is

issued severe laws with the intent of abolishing once and for ever some of the rude manners of his subjects.

In all these praiseworthy actions King Srongtsan Gampo was most energetically supported by his two wives, one of whom was a Nepalese the other a Chinese princess; both of them, who throughout their life-time proved most faithful votaries to the faith of Buddha, are worshipped either under the general name of Dolma (in Sanskrit Tārā), or under the respective names of Dolkar and Doljang. These princesses are said to have brought with them to Tíbet a variety of valuable religious books, with wonderful miracle-working images, and relics of Sākyamuni, besides building numerous temples and colleges.[1] Attracted by these acts of benevolence, which soon became widely known, many foreign priests settled in Tíbet during the lifetime of these

the God of wisdom, swinging the "sword of wisdom" (Tib. Shesrab ralgri) with a flamed point to dissipate the darkness among men. Chinese books say of his faculties: "When he preaches the great law, every demon is subjugated, every error that may deceive man is dissipated, and there is not a heretic but returns to his duty." Manjusrī is also "the ruler of the year," which epithet refers to the first day of the year being consecrated to him. Foe koue ki, p. 116. Compare Hodgson, "Classification of the Nevars," in Journ. As. Soc. Beng., Vol. XII., p. 216. Burnouf, "Le Lotus," pp. 498-511. Lassen, "Indische Alterthumskunde," Vol. III., p, 777.

[1] In pictures they are both represented in identical attitudes, the right foot hanging down over the throne, the right hand holding the blue lotus Utpala (*Nelumbium speciosum*, "Encyclopædia of India," by Balfour, p. 1291, a plant which occurs in Kashmír and Persia). But the complexion is different; Dolkar is of white colour, Doljang of green colour. Doljang is also implored by women for fecundity, and it is in allusion to this virtue that in a picture of ours a flat dish in which apples are heaped up, is drawn at their feet. The fullest Tibetan account of the legends concerning these deities is found in the Mani Kambum (see p. 84) and in a book mentioned to Adolph to be entitled, "a clear mirror of royal pedigree." A hymn addressed to Doljang is given by Klaproth, "Reise in den Kaukasus," Vol. I., p. 215.

princesses, and thus contributed to a more general knowledge of Buddhism.

Under the successors of King Srongtsan Gampo the religion did not greatly flourish, but under one of them, Thisrong de tsan, who lived in the years 728-786 A.D.[1] Buddhism began to revive, owing to the useful regulations proclaimed by this king. He it was who successfully crushed an attempt made by the chiefs during his minority to suppress the new creed, and it is principally due to him that the Buddhist faith became henceforth permanently established. He induced the learned Pandit Santa Rakshita (Tib. Zhiva tso), commonly called Bōdhisattva, to leave Bengál and settle in Tíbet; and at his recommendation the great Guru Padma Sambhava (in Tibetan Padma jungne, or Urgyen) from Ḳafirịstán (Udyāna), who was famed far and wide for his extraordinary knowledge of Dhāranīs and their application and rites, also changed his residence to become a Tibetan subject. The Indian sages who were now induced to settle in Tíbet for ever superseded the influence of the Chinese priests and the doctrines propounded by them. The latter had been the first Buddhist missionaries in Tíbet, and seem to have taught the principles of Nāgārjuna with the modifications established by the Yogāchārya school; for we learn from the history of Buddhism of the Tibetan Puton or Buston, who wrote in the fourteenth century, that in their system man is not allowed to make any notion the object of his meditation. Padma

[1] Ssánang Ssetsen, 787-845. Klaproth, 778.

Sambhava and subsequent Indian priests, however, explained the law in the sense of the Madhyamika school, which in India at this period had just gained influence over the Yogāchārya system; they insisted upon assiduity in undisturbed meditation. But King Thisrong de tsan, who did not wish two opposing doctrines to be taught, ordered a disputation to take place between the Chinese Mahāyāna (a name evidently symbolical of the system he defended) and the Hindu Kamalasīla. Mahāyāna was defeated and obliged to leave Tíbet, and since this period Indian priests only were called and Madhyamika doctrines taught.[1] King Thisrong built the large monastery and temple of Bima at Samyé, and ordered the translation of the sacred books into the Tibetan language to be carried on energetically.

A later ruler of the name of Langdar, or Langdharma, again tried to abolish Buddhist doctrines. He commanded all temples and monasteries to be demolished, the images to be destroyed, and the sacred books to be burnt; but so intense was the indignation excited by these acts of sacrilege, that he was murdered, in the year 900 A.D.[2] Langdar's son and successor is also said to have died in his 64th year "without religion." Bilamgur Tsan, Langhdarma's grandson, proved, on the other hand,

[1] *See* p. 54.—Wassiljew, "Der Buddhismus," p. 350; comp. pp. 324, 355. Rémusat, Nouv. Journ. As. 1832, p. 44. The Bhodimör designates the two doctrines *s*Tonmin and Tsemin; Georgi, "Alphab. Tibet," p. 222, by Dote (from the *m*Do or Sūtras) and Gyute (from the Gyut or Tantras); these names imply that Tantrika principles had gradually crept into the Madhyamika systems.

[2] Ssanang Ssetsen post-dates this event to the year 925. Langdharma was born, according to Csoma, in 861; Ssanang Ssetsen says 863 and Klaproth 901.

favourably inclined to Buddhism; he re-built eight temples, and died after a glorious reign of eighteen years. With this period we have to connect "the second propagation of Buddhism;" it received, especially from the year 971, a powerful impetus from the joint endeavours of the returned Tibetan priests (who had fled the country under the preceding kings), and of the learned Indian priest Pandita Atisha and his pupil Bromston. Shortly before Atisha came to Tíbet, 1041 A.D., the Kāla Chakra doctrine, or Tantrika mysticism, was introduced into Tíbet, and in the twelth and thirteenth centuries, many Indian refugees settled in the country, who greatly assisted the Tibetans in the translation of Sanskrit books.

Three hundred years from the time of Atisha's death bring us to the period of Tsonkhapa, the extraordinary reformer, who was born in the year 1355 A.D., in the district of Amdo, where is now the famous monastery of Kunbum. Tsonkhapa had imposed upon himself the difficult task of uniting and reconciling the dialectical and mystical schools which Tibetan Buddhism had brought forth, and also of eradicating the abuses gradually introduced by the priests, who had returned to the ordinary tricks and pretended miracles of charlatanism, in order to prove to the crowd their extraordinary mission. Tsonkhapa strictly prohibited such proceedings, and enforced a rigid observance of the laws binding upon the priests; he also distinguished himself by publishing most comprehensive works, in which the principles of the faith of the Buddha are explained from his particular point of view.—Traditions report him to have had some intercourse with a stranger from the west who was remarkable for a long nose. Huc believes this stranger to have been a European missionary, and connects the resemblance of the religious service in Tíbet to the Roman Catholic ritual with the informations which Tsonkhapa might have received from this Roman Catholic priest. We are not yet able to decide the question as to how far Buddhism may have borrowed from Christianity; but the rites of the Buddhists enumerated by the French missionary can for the most part either be traced back to institutions peculiar to Buddhism, or they have sprung up in periods posterior to Tsonkhapa.[1]

Though all the innovations introduced by Tsonkhapa, were never universally acknowledged, yet he obtained numerous followers, whose numbers rapidly increased during the next two centuries, until they predominated in Tíbet and High Asia. The rigour of his ordinances against the priests has been, however, considerably relaxed, and how widely the practice now differs from theory, we may infer from the fact, that the entrance into the clerical profession is an object of general ambition, and that a considerable part of the priestly revenues is derived from rites of an emphatically shaman character, performed at the request of the lay population to drive off the evil spirits.

[1] Csoma, Journ. As. Soc. Beng., Vol. VII., p. 145. Huc, "Christianity in China, Tartary and Thibet," Vol. II., p. 10. Wassiljew, "Notices sur les ouvrages en langue de l'Asie orientale," &c., Bull. hist.-phil. de St. Pet., Vol. XIII., pp. 233, 242. Köppen, "Die Religion des Buddha," Vol. II., p. 117. About the miracles executed by Buddhist priests previous to Tsonkhapa, see Marsden "The travels of Marco Polo," p. 169.

With reference to the introduction of Buddhism into *China Proper*, I will only add, that as early as the year 217 B.C. an Indian missionary is said to have preached in that country, but the Emperor sent him away, and Buddhism in China did not become fully established till the year 65 A.D., when it was received with universal pleasure.[1]

According to Cunningham,[2] Buddhism was introduced into *Ladák* about the year 240 B.C., but its final domestication in the country, seems not to have been anterior to the first century before the Christian era. The historical books concerning the early history of Ladák are said to have been destroyed about at the end of the sixteenth century by the fanatic Mussalmans of Skárdo who invaded the country, burned the monasteries, temples, and religious monuments, and threw the contents of the various libraries into the river Indus. But the reign of the Mussalmans was of but short duration, and the Buddhists have not been oppressed since this period.

In the Eastern Himálaya, in *Bhután and Síkkim*, the conversion of the inhabitants to Buddhism was effected at a comparatively modern date, namely about the sixteenth century of the Christian era.[3] The cir-

[1] Lassen, "Indische Alterthumskunde," Vol. II., p. 1078, Vol. IV., p. 741. W. Schott, "Ueber den Buddhaismus in Hochasien," p. 18. About the fate of Buddhism in China see "Nouveau Journal Asiatique," 1856, pp. 106, 137, 139. C. Gützlaff, R. As. Soc., Vol. XVI., p. 73.

[2] Cunningham, "Ladák," p. 317. When at Leh, my brothers came into possession of several large historical books. A particular value was laid upon two books entitled Gyelrap salvai melong "a true mirror of the Gyelrap," or the genealogy of the Rājas of Ladák, which were obtained from Chigmet Choiki Senge, a descendant of the former Rājas.

[3] Hooker, "Himalayan Journals," Vol. I., p. 127. Köppen, "Die Religion des Buddha," Vol. II., p. 360.

cumstances attending the introduction of the new religion are well known to the lamas of these countries, who are still in possession of many historical books treating of this interesting subject. Of works of this class we have, in our own private library, a manuscript account of "The first arrival of the Lamas in Síkkim," in twelve leaves, written with small characters; besides a printed, "History of the Erection of Colleges," consisting of no less than three hundred and seventy-five leaves. Both of these books were originally contained in the library of Pemióngchi, and were obtained in Síkkim by my brother Hermann.

Buddhist sects in Tíbet.

Sects did not exist in Tíbet previous to the eleventh century; nine are still existing and are considered orthodox, we know, however, but few details about them. The sect founded by Tsonkhapa and its later subdivisions have chosen the yellow colour for their dress; the others wear in preference a red garb. The sects are:[1]

1. The *Nyigmapa* sect is the most ancient, to which the Lamas of Bhután, Gnári Khórsum and Ladák belong. This sect adheres strictly to the ancient rites and ceremonies in the manner probably taught by the earliest Chinese priests, and possesses some pe-

[1] See Csoma's Chronological table, Note 18 in his "Grammar," p. 197; Colloquial phrases, ibid. p. 175; Notices, Journ. As. Soc. Bengal., Vol. VII., p. 146; Cunningham, "Ladák," pp. 367-72; Köppen, "Die Religion des Buddha," *Index*.

culiar symbolical works which have not been embodied in the large compilations of the Kanjur and Tanjur works.

2. The *Urgyenpa* sect (disciples of Urgyen, or Padma Sambhava) is also one of the most ancient, and has its adherents especially in those parts of Tíbet which border on Nepál and the Himalayan provinces of India; but the principal monastery of this sect is at Samyé, in Eastern Tíbet. The Urgyenpas differ from the Nyigmapas in the worship of the incarnation of Amitābha as Padma Sambhava.

3. The *Kadampa* sect, founded by Bromston (born in the year 1002 A.D.), limits itself to the observance of the "precepts" (*b*ka'), and does not care for the acquirement of the higher branches of transcendental wisdom. The followers of this sect wear red dresses.

4. Respecting the sect *Sakyapa*, nothing is known, except that its followers wear a red costume.

5. The *Gelukpa*, or *Galdanpa* and *Geldanpa* sect, a name derived from its principal monastery, called Gáldan, at Lhássa, which had been erected by Tsonkhapa: this sect adheres to his doctrines and institutions. Its members wear a yellow costume, and are now the most numerous sect in Tíbet.

6. The adherents of the *Kargyutpa* sect, "the believers in the succession of precepts," are satisfied with the observance of the Do (Sūtras or aphorisms), and do not care either for the attainment of the esoteric doctrines of the Prājna Pāramitā, or for the transcendental wisdom.

7. The *Karmapa* sect, "the believers in the efficacy of works," seems to be nearly identical with the Karmika sect of Nepál.[1]

8. The *Brikungpa* sect derives its name from the monastery Brikung in Eastern Tíbet. This sect, as well as the two preceding ones (the Kargyutpa and Karmapa), are offshoots of the Gelukpa sect, and also adhere to their rule of dressing in yellow.

9. The *Brugpa* (also Dugpa or Dad Dugpa) sect has established a particular worship of the Dorje (Vajra, or thunderbolt), which descended from heaven and fell upon the earth at Séra in Eastern Tíbet. This sect seems, moreover, to be particularly addicted to the Tantrika mysticism, in which the Dorje is considered as a very important and powerful instrument.

To these nine sects must be still added the *Bon* religion, which has many followers called *Bonpas*, and numerous and wealthy monasteries in Eastern Tíbet. As yet little is known about the Bon religion. Judging from the way in which Tibetan books speak of the followers of this sect, it is probable that the name *Bonpa* was restricted to those who neglected to embrace Buddhism upon its first introduction. By degrees they have, however, adopted Buddhist principles, still rigorously preserving as far as we are able to infer from the meagre information hitherto known about them, the ancient superstitious ideas and rites of the primitive inhabitants of Tíbet. This opinion is also that of Csoma, and is

[1] About these see Hodgson, "Illustrations," pp. 82, 112.

later supported by Hodgson, who has recently published several engravings of their deities; it is further corroborated by the important fact, that to the exorcists of some of the ruder Himálayan tribes, as the Murmis and Sunvars, the name of "Bonpa" is applied even to the present day.[1]

[1] The Bodhimör in Ssanang Ssetsen's history, pp. 351, 367. Csoma, "Geographical Notice of Tíbet," in "Journ. As. Soc, Beng.," Vol. I., p. 124; "Dictionary of the Tibetan language," p. 94. B. H. Hodgson, "Notice on Buddhist symbols," in Royal As. Soc., Vol. XVIII., p. 396. The identity of these Bonpa images with those met with in the temples of the orthodox Buddhists (the only difference existing in the name) is a further corroboration of the close alliance (already examined p. 48) of the Buddhist faith with pagan rituals and ideals.

CHAPTER VIII

THE SACRED LITERATURE

WORKS TRANSLATED FROM SANSKRIT, AND WORKS WRITTEN IN TIBETAN.—THE TWO COMPILATIONS KANJUR AND TANJUR.—TIBETAN LITERATURE IN EUROPE.—ANALYSIS OF THE MANI KAMBUM.—NAMES AND REPRESENTATIONS OF PADMAPĀNI.

THE earlier religious books published in Tibetan are simply translations from the Sanskrit, undertaken by Indian priests, Tibetan translators (Lotsavas), and also Chinese. The work of translation was carried on with remarkable zeal and energy; for the sake of uniformity a vocabulary of the Sanskrit proper names, and of the technical and philosophical terms occurring in the original texts, was prepared, and the latter was ordered to be adhered to.[1] But it is to be regretted that the trans-

[1] The first steps of this undertaking date perhaps from the times of Srongtsan Gampo and Thumi Sambhota. This vocabulary still exists in three editions, varying according to the greater or smaller number of terms contained in them; that of middle size was composed in the time of Ralpachen, or Khiral, who ruled in the ninth century: it is comprised in the Tanjur. Wilson, "Note on the literature of Tibet." Gleanings in science, Vol. III., p. 247. Compare also Hodgson, As. Res., Vol. XVI., p. 434.—For many books the names of the translators have been preserved to us.

lators, instead of supplying us with correct versions, have interwoven them with their own commentaries, for the purpose of justifying the dogmas of their several schools. To these alterations of the genuine text is chiefly owing the obscurity that has so long shrouded the subject and prevented a clear understanding of the principles of the original Buddhism and its subsequent divisions.

Simultaneously with the formation of a Tibetan alphabet, books were also written in the native tongue. The Mani Kambum, which is an historical work attributed to Srongtsan Gampo, is the production of a Tibetan; and, besides this, the "Grammatical Introduction," and the "Characteristic Letters" of Thumi Sambhota, as well as the historical works on Tíbet written by the ancient Tibetan translators, appear to have been composed in the vernacular tongue.[1] From the fourteenth century, beginning with Tsonkhapa, native literature developed itself on a large scale. Tsonkhapa himself published systematic works of a most voluminous character; his principal works are the Bodhi-mur, the Tarnim-mur, the Altanerike, and the Lamrim "a degree to advance," a title which has also been employed by other writers. Many learned Tibetans also used the vernacular in composing their numerous commentaries on Buddhist dogmas and history; and in writing in Tibetan they were followed even by the Mongolians, who were obliged to learn Tibetan because it formed (then, as now) the sacred language of divine service.

[1] Also Csoma, in his paper on historical and grammatical works in Tíbet, does not mention Sanskrit titles for these books, as he otherwise usually does when treating of works translated from Sanskrit.

All the Sanskrit translations were again collected, in the form of compilations, in two large and voluminous works, which contain irrespectively the sacred and the profane publications of different periods. These compilations bear the titles of Kanjur, "translation of the commandments (of the Buddha)," and Tanjur, "translation of the doctrine." The Kanjur consists of one hundred and eight large volumes, which are classed under the following seven principal divisions:—

1. Dulva, or "discipline."
2. Sherchin, or "transcendental wisdom."
3. Palchen, or "association of Buddhas."
4. Kontseg, or "jewel peak."
5. Do, Sūtras, or "aphorims."
6. Myangdas, treating on the doctrine of "deliverance from emancipation from existence."
7. Gyut, "Tantra," treating on mysticism.

Each of these divisions is composed of a greater or smaller number of treatises. The Kanjur is reputed to contain the "word of the Buddha," its principal contents being the moral and religious doctrines originally taught by Sākyamuni and his disciples. The Tanjur comprises 225 volumes, which are divided into two great classes: Gyut and Do. Its content is of a more miscellaneous character; there are also treatises on the different philosophical schools, besides various works on logic, rhetoric, and Sanskrit grammar. In several volumes the subject is the same as in the Kanjur.

The principal works in these collections were translated about in the ninth century, and other articles, especially those in the Gyut division, even much later. For instance, the Kāla Chakṛa, or Dus kyi khorlo, which is contained in the latter, was not introduced into Tíbet previous to the eleventh century; also the translation of the Do class of the Tanjur occupied no doubt a longer period on account of the greater variety of its contents.

Although it still remains impossible to determine exactly the time when these two collections were first compiled yet it is very likely, that the present arrangement of the volumes is not previous to the beginning of the last century; similar compilations may have existed in earlier times, but it is not very probable that they were exactly the same. We owe an abstract of the contents of the Kanjur and Tanjur to Csoma de Körös, whose analysis has been abridged by Wilson. An Index to the Kanjur was edited by the Imperial Russian Academy of St. Petersburgh in the year 1845, with a preface by I. J. Schmidt; a memoir by Schiefner treats of the logical and grammatical works embodied in the Tanjur.[1]

These collections were printed by order of Mivang, regent of Lhássa, in the years 1728-46; the first edition being prepared at Nárthang, a town near Tashilhúnpo, still celebrated for its typographical productions. At the present day they are printed in many of the monasteries;

[1] See about these collections H. H. Wilson, "Note on the literature of Tibet;" Gleanings in science, Vol. III., p. 243. Journ. As. Soc. Beng., Vol. I. Csoma, "Analysis," As. Res., Vol. XX. A. Schiefner, Bull. hist. phil. de St. Pet., Vol. IV., No. 18. Wassiljew, "Notices sur les ouvrages en langue de l'Asie orientale." Bullet. Vol. XIII. Nos. 13. 14.

but the paper as well as the impressions of those copies at least which are sold at Pekin, are for the greater part so bad, and the text is so full of errors, that altogether they are scarcely legible.

For printing Tibetan only capital letters (Tib. Vuchan) are used, as far as I know; for manuscripts small letters (Vumed) are frequently employed, which, for the requirements of running-hand, are often somewhat modified. When Indian letters are employed for Sanskrit sentences, the Ranjā alphabet, called by the Tibetans Lantsa, is used in which also most of the ancient Sanskrit works discovered in Népal are written; this Ranjā, or Lantsa, alphabet is a variety of the Devanāgari alphabet, and is particularly employed for writing the mystical Sanskrit sentences, the Dhāranīs, which must be written without any alteration in order to the preservation of their efficacy; and though the Tibetan letters have been adapted to their exact transliteration, yet we see the Ranjā alphabet preferred in many instances.[1]

Tibetan books are spread all over Central Asia, owing to the great reputation enjoyed by everything that has its origin in Tíbet, the chosen land of Padmapāni. The art of printing, long-known to the Tibetans, and for which they employ engraved wooden blocks, must also have greatly favoured their dissemination. There is no Buddhist monastery which does not contain a series of works in the Tibetan language, and the sums which the Buriats and Kalmuks occasionally pay for the most

[1] Compare: Hodgson, "Illustrations," p. 171; Schmidt, Mém. de l'Acad. des Sciences, Tom. I., p. 41.—Concerning the Tibetan mode of printing, and the technical terms for printing, printers' ink, &c., see Hodgson, As. Res., Vol. XVI., p. 421; Cunningham, "Ladak," p. 393.

sacred of them, as *e. g.* the Kanjur and Tanjur, have amounted in some cases to nearly £2,000.

A great many Tibetan books, as well original as translations from the Sanskrit, have reached Europe and Calcutta through the zealous exertions of Csoma, Schilling von Cannstadt, Hodgson, some English gentlemen residing at the Hill Stations, and the members of the Russian embassy at Pekin. The library and the museum of the India Office, so richly supplied in every branch of scientific and practical objects referring to oriental life, possesses also a great number of important Tibetan works, of which, however, till now no catalogue has been published. The whole of the Kanjur and Tanjur are to be found there. Another copy of the two collections exist in the library of St. Petersburgh, which has, besides, obtained the greatest number of important works on Buddhism written in Tibetan, Mongolian and Chinese. The Imp. library at Paris has the Kanjur only. The Asiatic Society of Bengal has likewise a complete copy of the Kanjur; its copy of the Tanjur is incomplete, or at least was so in 1831. An index of the Tibetan books in the Asiatic Museum of the Imperial Academy at St. Petersburgh, including the works it contained up to the year 1847, was published by I. J. Schmidt and O. Boehtlingk; an appendix by Schiefner registers also the later works sent from Pekin.[1] A new and detailed catalogue is now in progress of publication, and will, no doubt, furnish

[1] Bulletin hist.-phil. de St. Petersb., Vol. IV.; IX.—Concerning the astonishing number of important works so liberally presented by B. H. Hodgson to London and Paris, see Wilson, "Buddha and Buddhism." R. As. Soc., Vol. XVI., p. 234.

many interesting facts connected with Buddhism, and greatly enlarge our knowledge of Tibetan literature in general. Of the Tibetan books contained in the library of the Asiatic Society of Bengal Csoma de Körös had begun to compile a detailed catalogue, when the undertaking was stopped by his death, and has not, I believe, been continued.

The Tibetan language has become known in Europe only of late years, the claims to a detailed and scientific acquaintance put forward by Fourmont, Müller, and Georgi being very exaggerated. The first inquirer who placed the Tibetan language within the reach of European students, was Csoma de Körös, a zealous and indefatigable Hungarian from Transylvania, who had made it the principal object of his long and laborious researches to discover the original seats of the Hungarians (in German *Hunen*), whose native land he expected to find in Asia. Having failed in his attempts in Western Asia, he retired, in 1827, for some months to the monasteries of Zankhar, where he devoted himself to the study of Tibetan literature, and succeeded in nearly completing—though he had to undergo many hardships—a dictionary and grammar of the Tibetan language, which were published (in English) at Calcutta in the year 1832.[1] Later, in 1839 and 1841, I. J. Schmidt published another

[1] See some interesting remarks on his opinions, and an account of his death in the Journ. of the As. Soc. of Bengal, Vol. XI., p. 303; Vol. XIV., p. 323, by Dr. Campbell.—There are two tribes in the mountains who have preserved the designation of "Huns;" the one residing in Gnári Khórsum, who call themselves "Hunia;" the other being the Limbu in Nepál and Síkkim, a large division of whom goes by the name of the "Hungs." Comp. Campbell, Journ. As. Soc. Beng., Vol. IX., p. 599.

Tibetan grammar and dictionary in German, which is likewise based upon original works and Tibetan-Mongolian-Manju dictionaries. The contents of Schmidt's dictionary exceed that of Csoma by about 5,000 words and terms. Further notices on Tibetan grammar have been published by Schiefner in the *Bulletins* of the St. Petersburgh Academy, and more recently by Foucaux in his *Grammaire Tibétaine*. In theyear 1845 Schmidt published the translation of the large Tibetan treatise Dsang-lun, "the wise and the unwise," together with the original text.[1] Foucaux next followed with a translation of the Ryya chher rol pa. In addition to these publications I must still allude to the numerous important translations by Schiefner and Wassiljew.

In connexion with my inquiries about a picture of the goddess Doljang (see p. 66), I also obtained from the Buriat Lama Gombojew an abstract of the Mani Kambum, an ancient historical work the authorship of which is attributed to king Srongtsan Gampo. Schmidt had already drawn attention to the great reputation of this work among the Buddhists of High Asia; he was not, however, so fortunate (in 1829) as to procure for himself the Mani Kambum, which has but recently reached St. Petersburgh. As at present we have nothing but an abstract of the first chapter, by Jähring, the interpreter of Pallas, I give here Gombojew's cursory note on the general contents of this important work, which, short though it is, will at least furnish an idea concerning one of the most ancient historical books of Tibetan literature.

[1] Additions and emendations to Schmidt's edition were published by Schiefner in 1852.

Analysis of the book Mani Kambum.

The book Mani Kambum (a name also softened into Mani Gambum), or literally Mani *b*ka' 'bum, "a hundred thousand precious commandments," contains in twelve chapters a most detailed account of the numerous legendary tales respecting Padmapāni's merits as the propagator of Buddhism in Tíbet, and a statement of the origin and application of the sacred formula, "Om mani padme hum." Some historical events are further added with reference to Srongtsan Gampo (who lived from 617 to 698 A.D.) and his wives, as also a general explanation of the leading doctrines of Buddhism.

Chapter I. begins with a description of the wonderful region Sukhavatī (Tib. Devachan),[1] where Amitābha (Tib. Odpagmed) sits enthroned, and wherein those are received, who have merited the most perfect blissfulness of existence.

Once upon a time Amitābha, after giving himself up to earnest meditation, caused a red[2] ray of light to issue from his right eye, which brought Padmapāni Bōdhisattva into existence; while from his left eye burst forth a blue ray of light, which becoming incarnate in the virgins Dolma (in Sanskrit Tārā, the two wives of king Srongtsan), had power to enlighten the minds of living beings. Amitābha then blessed Padmapāni Bōdhisattva by laying his hands upon him, when, by virtue of this benediction, he brought forth the prayer "Om mani padme hum." Padmapāni moreover made a solemn vow to rescue all

[1] See the following Chapter.

[2] In Pallas' translation, p. 396, this ray is of a white colour.

living beings from existence, and to deliver all the wretched souls in hell from their pains; and, in token of his sincerity, he added the wish, that his head should split into a thousand pieces, did he not succeed. To fulfil his vow, he gave himself up to earnest meditation, and after remaining absorbed in contemplation for some time, he proceeded, full of wisdom, to look into the various divisions of hell, expecting that its former inhabitants had ascended by virtue of his meditations to the higher classes of beings which indeed had taken place. But who can describe his amazement on seeing the compartments of hell again as full as ever, the places of the outgoing tenants being supplied by an equal number of new-comers. This sight, so dreadful and overpowering, proved too much for the unfortunate Bōdhisattva, who considered the cause of this apparent failure to lie in the weakness of his meditations. His head instantly split into a thousand pieces, he fainted, and fell heavily to the ground. Amitābha, deeply moved by the pains of his unfortunate son, hastened to his assistance. He formed the thousand pieces into ten heads, and assured him, for his consolation, as soon as he had recovered his senses, that the time had not yet arrived to deliver all beings, but that his wish should yet be accomplished. From this moment Padmapāni redoubled his praiseworthy exertions.[1]

[1] This legend is somewhat differently given in the Mongolian work Nom Gharchoi Todorchoi Tolli, translated by Schmidt, "Forschungen," pp. 202—206. Padmapāni had vowed not to return to Sukhavatī until all beings, and the Tibetans in particular, should be brought through him to

Then succeeds a history of the creation of the universe and of the animal beings; the twelve acts, the *Dzadpa chugnyi*, of Sākyamuni are enumerated,[1] and an account of the erection of the palace on the top of the mountain Potala is given, followed by a sketch of the propagation of Buddhism from its beginning till the death of Srongtsan Gampo.

Chapter II. gives instructions concerning the prayers to be addressed to Padmapāni, and enumerates the immense advantages offered by the frequent perusal, and recital of the prayer "Om mani padme hum." A discourse on "voidness" forms the conclusion.

Chapter III. gives the meaning of the prayer "Om mani padme hum." Remarks are also made upon the different representations of Padmapāni; it is also explained why he is sometimes represented with three faces and eight hands, again with eighteen faces and

salvation; but when he saw that but the hundredth part of the Tibetans had entered the paths of salvation, the longing to return to Sukhavatī, came upon him; and it was in consequence of this desire that his head clove into ten pieces (not into a thousand pieces as the Mani Kambum has it) and his *body* was divided into a thousand pieces; Amitābha afterwards repaired the corporeal damages.

[1] The Tibetan biographies of Sākyamuni are divided into twelve chapters, taken from his twelve acts, which are as follows: "1. He descended from among the Gods; 2. he entered into the womb; 3. he was born; 4. he displayed all kinds of arts; 5. he was married, or enjoyed the pleasures of the conjugal state; 6. he left his house and took the religious character; 7. he performed penances; 8. he overcame the devil, or god of pleasures; 9. he arrived at supreme perfection, or became Buddha; 10. he turned the wheel of the law, or published his doctrine; 11. he was delivered from pain, or died; 12. his remains were deposited (in a Chorten)." Csoma, "Notices on the life of Shākya." A. R. Vol. XX., p. 285. Compare also Schmidt, "Ssanang Ssetsen," p. 312. Schiefner, "Tib. Lebensbeschreibung Sākyamuni's." Mémoires des sav. étrang., Vol. VI., p. 232.

eight hands, and occasionally even with 1,000 faces and as many hands and feet. Next is related the manner in which Srongtsan Gampo became acquainted with the tenets of Buddhism; in conclusion, some particular facts are given respecting the general propagation of Buddhism in Tíbet and the mission of Thumi Sambhota to India.

Chapters IV. to VIII. are full of information respecting the qualities of Samsāra, and the ethics and religious ordinances of Buddhism. The illiterate state of the Tibetans is lamented; and then follows a short biography of Padmapāni Bōdhisattva during his existence as King Srongtsan Gampo.

A discourse is reported, in which this King enunciates, in reply to a question respecting the faculties of the mind, that happiness and salvation depend upon a man's own energy and conduct, and if one wish to break the fetters of Samsāra he can effect this by reciting the prayer "Om mani padme hum," the power of which is irresistible. Srongtsan takes upon himself to interpret this prayer: he teaches it to his parents and wives, and explains the duties to be observed by those who believe in the truth of the doctrines revealed by the Buddha. These explanations are calculated for practical use,[1] and relate to such topics as ignorance, sins, virtues, and their influence.

Chapters IX. and X. recount the legends which are intimately connected with Buddhist doctrines.

Chapter XI. treats of the end of Srongtsan's life.

[1] Concerning the number of prescriptions to be observed and dogmas to be believed in by the lower classes see p. 103—7.

Chapter XII. speaks of the translation of the Sanskrit books into Tibetan, as also of Thumi Sambhota's mission to India, and of the alphabet he had formed from the Devanāgari.

The Mani Kambum has been translated into Mongolian and into Dsungarian. The latter version was executed, at the command of Dalai Khan, in the seventeenth century, by a Dsungarian Lama who had resided for several years in Lhássa, and was distinguished, on account of his translation, by the honourable title of Pandit.

The Dhyāni Bōdhisattva Padmapāni, or Avalōkitēsvara, who is the subject of this work, is, of all the gods, the one most frequently implored, on account of his being the representative of Sākyamuni and the guardian and propagator of his faith until the appearance of the future Buddha Maitreya, as well as on account of his particular protection of Tíbet.

In order to show the Tibetans the path to ultimate happiness, he has been pleased, they say, to manifest himself, from age to age, in human shape. They believe that his descent and incarnation in the Dalai Lama takes place by the emission of a beam of light, and that he shall be finally born as most perfect Buddha in Tíbet, instead of in India, where his predecessors had appeared.

Padmapāni has in the sacred books a great many of names, and is represented under various figures. Most frequently he is addressed by the name of Chenresi, or more fully Chenresi vanchug, "the powerful, looking with the eyes," in Sanskrit Avalōkitēsvara. To this name, as well as to that of Phagpa Chenresi, in Sanskrit Aryāvalōkita, or Chugchig zhal, "eleven-faced," correspond the representations of him with eleven faces and eight hands. The eleven faces form a pyramid, and are ranged in four rows. Each series of heads has a particular complexion; the three faces which base upon the neck are white, the three following yellow, the next three red, the tenth is blue and the eleventh (the face of Amitābha) is red. Such is the arrangement in all the Tibetan and Mongolian images I had occasion to examine; but in the Japanese images presented in the Nippon Pantheon the eleven faces are much smaller, and are arranged similar to a crown; its centre is formed by two entire figures: the lower one is sitting, the other is standing above it; and ten smaller heads are combined with these two figures in a kind of radial arrangment; six are resting immediately on the forehead, the four other, form the second row above them.

Like Chagtong Khorlo, "the thousand-handed circle," or as Thugje chenpo chugchig zhal, "the great pitier with eleven faces," he has likewise eleven faces, but the number of his hands amounts to a thousand. As Chag zhipa, "four—armed," he is represented with one head and four arms; two are folded, the third holds a lotus-flower, the fourth a rosary or a snare. As Chakna padma karpo (in Sanskrit Padmapāni), "holding in the hand a white lotus," he has two arms, one of which supports a lotus. He is called Chantong, "with a thousand eyes," on account of having "the eye of wisdom" upon each palm of his thousand hands. The name Jigten Gonpo (in Sanskrit Lokapati, or Lokanātha), "lord of the world, protector, saviour," is an allusion to his causing deliverance from sins and protecting against all kinds of evil.

CHAPTER IX

VIEWS ON METEMPSYCHOSIS

Re-births.—Means of Deliverance from Re-birth.—Sukhavatī, the Abode of the Blessed.

Re-births.

When treating the developement of Buddhism, I had repeated occasion to allude to metempsychosis, or the migration of the souls of animated beings, as one of the established laws of Buddhism, according to which man's soul migrates as long as the causes of re-birth have not been taken away from it. The forms under which any living being may be re-born, are sixfold:—

1. The highest class are the Lha, "spirits, highest beings, gods," Sanskr. Deva; they rank next to the Buddhas, and inhabit the six celestial regions (Sanskr. Devalōkas). Two of these regions belong to the earth; but the four others, which are considered as superior mansions, lie in the atmosphere, far beyond the earth.

2. The second class is formed by men, called Mi.
3. The third class are the Lhamayin, "the evil spirits" literally, not a god (in Sanskrit Asuras). They are the adversaries of the Devas, and the most powerful of the evil spirits; they dwell in the regions below the mountain Mēru (Tib. Lhungpo).
4. The fourth class are the brutes (beasts), Dudo, or Jolsong.
5. The fifth class is formed by the Yidags, imaginary monsters representing the state of a wretched being (Sanskrit Prēta). They do not receive food or water, though greatly in want of both. Accordingly they ever remain in a state of extreme hunger and thirst; their mouth has the size of a needle's eye, but their bodies are twelve miles in height.
6. The sixth and lowest class of beings is composed of the wretched inhabitants of the hell, Myalba (Sanskrit Naraka), a place of dreadful punishment for the wicked, who are tormented there most cruelly.

Of the six classes, those of gods and men are styled the good grades, the four others being called the bad conditions.[1]

[1] Respecting these six orders of sentient existence see Burnouf, "Lotus de la Bonne Loi," p. 309; Pallas "Mongol. Völkerschaften," Vol. II., p. 95; Schmidt, "Ueber die dritte Welt der Buddhisten," Mém. de l'Acad. des sciences, Vol. II., pp. 21-39. The Mongolian authorities place the Lhamayin before man, degrading the latter to the third class; but the works consulted by Burnouf, Rémusat, Hardy, &c., classify them in the order given in our text. In many sacred books, however, only five classes are enumerated, the Singhalese, for instance, omitting the class of Asuras. Hardy's Manual,

The class in which any animated being is to be reborn depends upon the actions, or works, "Las," which he has performed, either in the present life, or in a previous existence; they are the destiny (in Tibetan Kalba) of the Buddhists, good works involving re-birth in one of the superior classes, evil conduct in the bad states of existence. The valuation of the works, viz. the determination of the moment in which the present existence has to end, and of the class in which man has to be reborn, is the particular business of Shinje, "the Lord of the dead," also called Choigyal (in Sanskrit Dharma rāja), "the king of the law." Shinje possesses a wonderful mirror, which shows him all the good and bad actions of men; with a balance he weighs both the good and he bad, and, if in this manner he finds that the present existence of an individual has to cease, he orders one of his servants, who are also styled Shinjes, to seize the soul and bring it before him, in order that its future may be announced. It not unfrequently happens, that the messenger seizes a wrong soul by mistake, or in some instances by design, being bought off by offerings. The Lord of death, after revealing by his mirror that the soul brought before him is the wrong one, then dismisses it, and threatens his servant with severe punishment in the event of the mistake proving an intentional one. At the same time, he orders another servant, to bring him the right soul, which, pending the discovery,

p. 37; Burnouf, p. 377. For the description and divisions of hell see Foe koue ki, Engl. Transl., p. 133; Hardy's Manual, pp. 2, 27; Pallas, Vol. II., p. 53.

has remained undisturbed in the body. Hence it appears that the life of a being can be lenghtened by propitiating the servant of the Lord of death.[1]

Means of deliverance from re-birth.

Re-birth is to be regarded in the light of an expiation of sins. The pains to be endured through being subjected to migration are, however, considered so terrible, that the Buddhist faith has offered its votaries the means of atoning, even during their lifetime, for a portion at least of the evil they have committed. Emancipation may be obtained by subduing evil desires, by the assiduous practise of virtues, of Dhāranīs, and Tantras, and by confession. Already in the early history of Buddhism we find confession of sins enjoined by authority. Thus the novices had to perform this rite before they were received into the congregation of the faithful; the predominant character of public worship, also, when performed according to the prescriptions of the book Pratimoksha, is decidedly that of a solemn confession (Poshadha) before the assembly of priests. This renewal of priestly vows was, in fact, the original purport

[1] Shinje answers to the god Yama of the Hindus, about whom compare Coleman, "Mythology of the Hindus," p. 112. The Mongolians call him Erlik Khan, or Yamantāka; Pallas, "Mongol. Völker." Vol. II., pp. 95, 61. "Voyages," Vol. I., p. 553. Pallas was told that the good and bad actions are recorded by two spirits, the one favourable, the other ill-natured. These, by order of Shinje, bring the soul before him and mark the number of its good and bad actions by white and black pebbles, a proceeding which Shinje controls by the book Bealtan Tooli, in which the deeds of every individual are registered.

of confession; the dogma that it confers entire absolution from sins ("from the root, tsava nas") was established by the Mahāyāna schools.[1]

Up to the present day this is also the character of confession amongst the Tibetan Buddhists, who consider it of the greatest influence for a happy metempsychosis and the attainment of Nirvāna. The confession (in Tibetan Sobyong) always includes an open repentence of the sins and the promise to commit no more. Also the solicitation of the gods is indispensable, but various are the modes which may accompany the avowal and the prayers addressed to the deities for abolishment of one's sins. As the most easy may be named the use of the water which has been consecrated by the Lamas in the divine ceremony Tuisol, "entreaties for ablution;" but also the abstinence from food and the tiresome reciting of prayers may be combined with it, a kind of confession which bears the name of Nyungne, "to continue abstinence."[2] Such painful modes of getting rid of sins are, however, not greatly in favour, and the less as a simple address to the gods is considered to be almost equally efficacious.

The gods who have the faculty of delivering from sins, are for the greater part imaginary Buddhas

[1] See Burnouf, "Introduction," p. 299. Csoma, "Analysis," As. Res., Vol. XX., p. 58. Wassiljew, "Der Buddhismus," pp. 92, 100, 291. Pratimoksha is a Manual containing the laws of the Buddhist priesthood. A translation by the Rev. Gogerly appeared in the "Ceylon Friend," 1839; an analysis is to be found in Csoma, l. c., with whom compare Burnouf's "Introduction," p. 300. Hardy gives numerous extracts from its precepts.

[2] 'Khrus, "to be thoroughly washed;" *g*sol, "prayer, entreaty;" *s*nung, "to reduce (in food);" *g*nas, "to continue." For details I refer to Chapter XV.

who are considered to have preceded Sākyamuni; others are the holy spirits equal in power to the Buddhas, such as the Hērukas, Samvaras, &c. From all these deities thirty-five Buddhas are considered the most effectual in taking away sins, and to them accordingly the prayers of the contrite are most frequently addressed. These Buddhas are styled Tungshakchi sangye songa,[1] "the thirty-five Buddhas of confession." Already in the two highly esteemed Mahāyāna compilations, the Ratnakūta and Mahāsamaya, the adoration of these Buddhas is strongly recommended;[2] and beautiful coloured images of them adorn the interior of numerous monasteries, where they take their places by the side of the most celebrated Indian and Tibetan priests and gods. Prayers to these Buddhas are also included in almost every Tibetan liturgy, or compilation of the daily prayers, such as the Rabsal, "principal clearness," and Zundui, "collection of charms." The number of the Buddhas implored has not been, however, limited to thirty-five; in one of these petitionary addresses, the translation of which is the object of Chapter XI, I found their number to be fifty-one; also to the Buriats Tibetan treatises of this kind are known in which more than the original number of thirty-five Buddhas occurs.

One of these Buddhas is also Sākyamuni; he is called in the address just mentioned by his Tibetan name, Shakya Thub-pa, and is the twenty-seventh of the list; it

[1] *Ltung-bshags*, "confession of sins;" kyi (chi) = the genitive case; so-*l*nga "thirty-five."

[2] Wassiljew, "Der Buddhismus," pp. 170, 186.

is said that "if a man once utter this name he shall be purified from all sins committed in anterior existences." In sacred images representing the Buddhas of confession his figure is regularly the central and the most prominent one, the other thirty-four Buddhas being smaller and ranged above his head. In a picture which had been hung up in the temple of Gyungul, in Gnári Khórsum, the images of various sacred persons are added to these thirty-five Buddhas. Amongst the additional figures the persons in the clerical garb of the ancient Indian priests are the sixteen Netan (Sanskrit Stavirās), who are said in the sacred books to have visited Ceylon, Kashmír, and the southern foot of the Kailāsa or Trans Sátlej range already shortly after the first convocation of the Bikshus, held immediately after Sākyamuni's death, and to have spread in these countries Buddhist theories.[1] Six other priests in Tibetan lamaic dress have each some words written beneath them, viz. Je Tsonkhapa; Prulku thongva dondon; Khetup sangye; Jampaijang lhai thama shesrab od; Khetub chakdor gyatso; Grubchen tsulkhrim gyatso. Tsonkhapa, the famous Lama, who was born 1355 A.D., is honoured, by the title of reverence, *r*je; Thongva dondon (prulku, the word preceding his name, means incarnation) was born in 1414; Khetup sangye is probably the Khetup pal-gyi senge of Csoma (born 1535);

[1] See their Tibetan names in A. Schiefner's "Tibetanische Lebensbeschreibung Sākyamuni's," Note 43. Csoma, As. Res., Vol. XX., p. 439, has for several of them other names. The Netans enjoy great reputation amongst the Tibetans, who have recited on various occasions a hymn in their honour, entitled Netan chudrugi todpa "praise of the sixteen Netan." The library of the St. Petersburgh university has a copy of it.

Tsulkhrim gyatso (grubchen = very perfect) is probably the tenth Dalai Lama, who ruled from 1817—35;[1] concerning the other two Lamas I know no particulars.

An additional figure in Chinese dress has the words Genyen darma written at his feet; Genyen (Sanskrit Upāsaka) denotes him to be an adherent to the Buddhist faith, Darma is most probably his proper name. He carries a basket filled with the sheets of a religious book, probably the Prājna Pāramitā; this very ancient mode of using a basket-case for the palm-leaves, which in former times served as paper, is said to be actually still in use in Tíbet, the single volumes of larger works being put together into a common basket. Beneath the throne is represented the goddess Lhamo (Sanskr. Kālādevī), with her attendants; Tsepagmed (Sanskr. Amitāyus), the god of longevity; and the five great kings (in Tibetan Ku nga gyalpo).[2]

Sukhavatī, the abode of the blessed.

Complete deliverance from existence, or from the world in its most general meaning, is comprised under the name of Nirvāna (Tib. Nyangan las daspa, by contraction Nyangdas).[3] The essence of Nirvāna is not clearly pointed out in the sacred books; and this, indeed, is

[1] See Csoma, "Grammar," pp. 181 *seq.*

[2] About Lhamo see p. 112; concerning Tsepagmed see p. 129; about the five great Kings see Chapter XIII.

[3] Respecting the difference between the genuine idea of Nirvāna, and the Tibetan opinion, see Köppen, "Die Religion des Buddha," Vol. I., p. 307.

not possible in a philosophical system in which negation of reality is the fundamental principle;[1] and the sacred Buddhist books also declare at every occasion that it is impossible positively to define the attributes and properties of Nirvāna.

The secondary kind of happiness, to which the Buddha has likewise revealed the path,[2] is the enjoyment of Sukhavatī, the abode of the blessed, into which ascend those who have accumulated much merit by the practise of virtues. Already the entering into Sukhavatī involves the deliverance from metemphsychosis, but not from absolute existence, nor is the perfection of the Buddhas yet attained.

In general, the Tibetans of the present day do not properly distinguish between Nirvāna and Sukhavatī, their highest ideal being attained by liberation from rebirth and the reception into Sukhavatī. My brothers who have had frequent opportunity of consulting Tibetan Lamas, learned that particular stress is now laid upon the complete emancipation from metempsychosis. It is believed, that then they have no feeling whatever about their existence; a Lama once compared them to a healthy man, who, though provided with a stomach, lungs, a liver &c., experiences no feeling of their presence. How greatly freedom from metempsychosis is prized, appears from a conversation, which Hermann once held with a Lama of Bhután. This man who had been at Lhássa during the residence there of the French mission-

[1] See p. 33.
[2] Compare p. 42.

aries, Huc and Gabet, had seen some coloured lithographs representing our Saviour Jesus Christ, and various episodes of Bible history. The Lama alleged against the creed of these missionaries, that it does not afford final emancipation. According to the principles of their religion, he said, the pious are rewarded with a re-birth among the servants of the supreme God, when they are obliged to pass an eternity in reciting hymns, psalms, and prayers, in his glory and honour. Such beings, he argued, are consequently not yet freed from metempsychosis; for who can assert, that, in the event of their relaxing in the duty assigned them, they shall not be expelled from the world where God resides, and in punishment be re-born in the habitation of the wretched.[1] Buddhist doctrines, the Lama concluded, are certainly preferable to this theory: they do not allow a man to be deprived of the fruits of the good works performed during life; and if once arrived at final perfection, he is never again, under any circumstances, subjected to metempsychosis, although, at the same time, if desiring to benefit animated beings, he is at liberty to re-assume the human form, whenever it pleases him, without being obliged to retain it or to suffer from any of its disadvantages.

The happy region Sukhavatī, where thrones Amitābha, lies towards the west.[2] In Sanskrit it is called Sukha-

[1] In the prints seen by the Lama angels were doubtless depicted soaring in the air and hovering round the chief figures of the picture. He must have also heard of the expulsion of the bad angels from heaven.

[2] Genuine Buddhism rejects the idea of a particular locality being appropriated to Nirvāna. In the remarkable treatise entitled Milinda prasna,

vatī, "abounding in pleasures;" in Tibetan Devachan, "the happy;" the Chineses designate it Ngyan-lo, "pleasure;" Kio-lo "the greatest pleasure;" Tsing-tu "pure or glorious land;" and in sacred treatises it is denominated "the pure region, a kind of prosperity." We find an account of this glorious region of Amitābha in many religious books.[1] Sukhavatī is declared to be a large lake, the surface of which is covered with lotus-flowers (Padmas), red and white, with perfumes of rare odour. These flowers form the couches for pious men, whose virtues were the cause of their growth, while yet sojourners upon earth. Such men, after being purified from their sins, soar up into their lotus-flowers. The inhabitants of this paradise are moved to earnest devotion by the beautiful song of paradisiacal birds, and receive food and clothes for the mere wishing, without any exertion on

translated by Hardy in his works on Buddhism, the priest Nāgasena (Nāgārjuna), is said to have replied to the King Milinda of Sangala (who ruled about 140 B.C.; see A. Weber, Indische Studien, Vol. III., p. 121), in answer to his inquiries about the nature, essence, and locality of Nirvāna: "Nirvāna is wherever the precepts can be observed; and there may be the observance in Yawana, China, Milāta, Alasanda, Nikumba, Kāsi, Kōsala, Kāsmira, Ghandhāra, the summit of Mahā Mēru, or the Brahma-lōkas; it may be anywhere; just as he who has two eyes can see the sky from any or all of these places; or as any of these places may have an eastern side." Eastern Monachism, p. 300.

[1] Some descriptions of this region were translated from the Mongolian and Chinese into European languages by Pallas, "Mongol. Völker," Vol. II. p. 63 (his description, however, seems not to have been correctly be rendered from the original text, see Schott); Schmidt, "Geschichte Ssanang Ssetsens," p. 323 (from the Bodhimör); Kowalewsky in his "Mongolian Chrestomathy" (in Russian), Vol. II., p. 319. Schott, "Der Buddhaismus in Hochasien," pp. 50-9. Compare also the analysis of the Sukhavatī vyūha in Burnouf's "Introduction," p. 99, and in Csoma's paper, As. Res., Vol. XX., p. 439. Among other Tibetan books containing a description of it, are the Mani Kambum and the Odpagmed kyi shing kod, "construction of Amitābha's land." The library of St. Pētersburgh has a copy of it in a Mongolian translation, entitled: Abida in oronu dsokiyal.

their part. They have not yet reached the estate of a Buddha, but have entered the direct path which leads to it; they are endowed with the faculty of assuming human forms and descending upon earth; although when doing so, they are not subjected to a repetition of births, but rise again to the region they have left. Re-birth into a Padmaflower of this paradise is obtained by invocations of the Buddhas, and more particularly of Amitābha; a form of devotion, according to the Tsing tu nen, translated by Schott, involving greater merit, than that of offerings and mortifications.

CHAPTER X.

DETAILS CHARACTERISTIC OF THE RELIGION OF THE PEOPLE.

Amount of religious Knowledge.—Gods, Genii and Malignant Spirits. The spirits Lhamayin and Dudpos. The legends about Lhamo, Tsangpa, and Chakdor.—Prayers.

Amount of religious knowledge.

It is evident that a religion containing so much of philosophical speculation and divided into many various systems, schools and sects, cannot be known in its full extent by the lower classes forming the bulk of the population, but only by those of a certain degree of education. Csoma, who paid great attention during his personal intercourse to the general amount of religious knowledge amongst the various classes, gives the following details in his "Notices:"[1]

"The systems Vaibhāshika, Sautrāntika, Yogāchārya, and Madhyamika, are well known to many of the learned

[1] Journ. As. Soc. Beng., Vol. VII., p. 145.

in Tíbet; but there are, on the other hand, many who are acquainted with their names only. The works explanatory of the Yogāchārya and Madhyamika theories can be understood only by the learned, because they deal with too many abstract terms and minute distinctions, while the generality of the religious persons (or the clergy) prefer reading Tantrika works, and of the Kanjur, the Dulva (or discipline), and some tracts of the Do (or Sūtra) class." He adds, that the Tibetans are tolerably familiar with the dogma of the "three vehicles" (Tib. Thegpasum, Sanskr. Triyāna).[1] This dogma, which has been taken from the Mahāyāna schools, is explained in detail in the Tibetan compendiums entitled Lamrim, or the gradual way to perfection, of which the most celebrated was written by Tsonkhapa. The argumentations of these books are taken from the consideration, that the dogmas of the Buddha are intended alike for the lowest, the mean or middle, and the highest capacities; as they contain low, or vulgar, middle, and high principles; thus, from the knowledge of each of these classes a particular degree of perfection is deducible. They then describe what a man must believe according to his capacities, in the following terms:

1. "Men of vulgar capacities must believe, that there is a God, that there is a future life, and that they shall earn the fruits of their works in this, their worldly life.
2. Those that are in a middle degree of intellectual and moral capacity, besides admitting the former

[1] Compare p. 22.

positions, must know, that every compound thing is perishable, that there is no reality in things; that every imperfection is pain, and that deliverance from pain, or bodily existence, is final happiness or beatitude.

3. Those of the highest capacities must know, in addition to the above enumerated dogmas, that from the body, or last object, to the supreme soul, nothing is existent by itself; neither can it be said that it will continue always or cease absolutely, but that every thing exists by a dependent, or causal connexion (or concatenation).

5. With respect to practice, those of vulgar capacity are content with the exercise of the ten virtues. Those of a middle degree, besides fulfilling the ten virtues, endeavour to excel in morality, meditation, and ingenuity, or wisdom. Those of the highest capacities, besides the former virtues, will perfectly exercise the six transcendental virtues."

Also with reference to the *summum bonum* of beatitude or perfection, three degrees are distinguished. Some are already content with a happy transmigration, and limit their wishes to be re-born as gods, men or Asuras. Others hope to be rewarded by a re-birth in Sukhavatī, and to be delivered from pain and bodily existence. A third class wishes not only to attain Nirvāna for themselves, but also to show others the paths leading to it in a future period as most perfect Buddhas.

Such a power, however, can only be gained by those

who enter the priesthood, or, as the Lamas say, who take the vows, Dom. There are many legends illustrating the merits to be acquired by entering the religious order and inculcating the necessity of doing so.[1] The idea at last grew into an undisputable dogma, that laymen cannot gain the Bōdhi in their present existence, but only in a future state; their actual religious occupations will secure the reward of re-birth in a happy condition, or in Amitābha's celestial region, but, with respect to the supreme rank of a Buddha, their attempts are nothing but preparations.

Clear and intelligible as these principles are, they have been found nevertheless, too learned for the lay followers of Buddhism; and for a more general diffusion, a code of eight specific duties was drawn up, forming a practical summary of the laws of the Buddhist faith. The contents of the popular code are given in Csoma's paper as follows:

1. To take refuge only with Buddha.
2. To form in one's mind the resolution to strive to attain the highest degree of perfection, in order to be united with the supreme intelligence.
3. To prostrate one'sself before the image of Buddha; to adore him.
4. To bring offerings before him, such as are pleasing to any of the six senses: as, lights, flowers, garlands, incenses, perfumes; all kinds of edible and trinkable things (whether raw, or prepared);

[1] See p. 27, 38.—I cite as an example Schmidt, "Dsang-lun, der Weise und der Thor," p. 108.

stuffs, cloths, &c. for garments and hanging ornaments.

5. To make music, sing hymns, and utter the praises of Buddha, respecting his person, doctrine, love or mercy, perfections or attributes; and his acts, or performances, for the benefit of all animal beings.
6. To confess one's sins with contrite heart; to ask forgiveness for them and to resolve sincerely not to commit the like hereafter.
7. To rejoice in the moral merits of all animal beings, and to wish that they may thereby obtain final emancipation or beatitude.
8. To pray and entreat all the Buddhas that are now in the world to turn the wheel of religion (or to teach their doctrines), and not to leave the world too soon, but to remain here for many ages, or Kalpas.

Gods, genii, and malignant spirits.

The Tibetan Buddhists believe well-being and misfortune alike to depend upon the action of gods, genii, and malignant spirits.[1] The gods are considered to exist in large numbers; they derive their divine nature from having received a particle of the supreme intelligence, which possesses such power and is of such

[1] Many instances of this belief, common to all the Buddhist races of Asia (Schmidt, "Forschungen," p. 137; "Ssanang Ssetsen," p. 352; Marsden, "The travels of Marco Polo," pp. 159, 163), will be found in the writers on Tibet.

illimitable extent as to allow of a division amongst any number of beings. All gods are, therefore, embodiments and multiplications of one and the same supreme wisdom, created for the purpose of choosing the most suitable way for the salvation of mankind from Samsāra (the world).[1] In the face of all these gods, the Lamas emphatically maintain monotheism to be the real character of Buddhism.

In Tibetan the collective name for deity (god and genius) is Lha, an appellative similar to its Sanskrit equivalent Deva, meaning a god, a divinity. The deities have each their particular names, by which they are worshipped, as also their definite spheres, beyond which they cannot exercise any power, but within which they cannot be influenced by another god. They materially assist man in his undertakings, and remove the dangers with which they may be threatened from natural phenomena—acts in which they feel great delight and pleasure and which they perform in a state of calmness, Zhiva. There exist male as well as female deities, the latter being either the wives of male deities, deriving from the husband the same power of which he is the possessor, or they are endowed with special faculties of their own. Of this kind are the Samvaras (in Tibetan Dechog), and the Hērukas, female genii equal in power to the Buddhas, whose images occur in numerous religious pictures.[2]

[1] Schmidt, in Mém. de l'Acad. de Petersb., Vol. I., p. 119.

[2] Csoma in his Analysis, As. Res., Vol. XX., p. 489, considers these divine beings as two gods or demons, and, in an other passage, p. 491, he calls the Hēruka a deified saint of the character of Siva, and the Samvara a Dākinī. He

The malignant spirits are designated by names expressive of their hostility towards man, as Da, "enemy," Geg, "devil;" the most dreaded are the Lhamayin and the Dudpos.

To *the Lhamayin*, amongst which also man may be re-born (see p. 92), the Yakshas, the Nāgas, the Rākshasas, and many other groups of illnatured spirits are subjected; their particular adversaries are the four Mahārājas (Tib. Gyalchen zhi), who dwell upon the fourth step of the mount Mēru.[1] Amongst these evil spirits those deserve a particular notice who cause the Dusmayinpar chi, or "untimely death." According to the belief of the Tibetans, that is considered an untimely death, which, in opposition to the ordinary course of nature, is accelerated by the evil spirits, such as Sringan, Dechad, Jungpo, and others. As a consequence of premature decease, the "Bardo," is prolongated. This is the middle state between the death and the new re-birth, which does not follow immediately, but there exists an interval, which is shorter for the good than for the bad. The prolongation of this intermediate state is considered as a punishment caused by evil spirits who have only power over sinful men. The soul exists during this interval without any shape whatever, and the

also treats of both in the singular number; but Burnouf, "Introduction," p. 538, doubts whether Samvara be a proper name; and his opinion is supported by the fact that various Samvaras and Hērukas occur in pictures; as well as by the Tibetan treatise Dechogi gyut, in which numerous Samvaras and Hērukas are mentioned. The case appears to be similar to that of Shinje, the judge of the dead (see p. 93), whose assistants, the Dudpos, are likewise styled Shinjes.

[1] See Burnouf, "Introduction," p. 603. Schmidt, in Mém. de l'Acad. de Petersb., Vol. II., p. 33 *et seq.*

wretched ones, who have been seized by the spirits, make earnest efforts but without success to get placed within a body. At such moments they appear to men as a raw, shapeless piece of meat, and such a vision is considered unlucky, boding illness and even death. Dhāranīs and particular offerings are supposed to keep off such dreaded visions, and the wealthy have magical sentences and treatises printed, of which the following are the most frequently met with:[1] Choichi gyalpoi shed dul, "to break the power of Choigyal," an epithet of Shinje; Tamdin gyalpoi sri nanpa, "to subdue the honourable King Tamdin"; Dragpo chinsreg, "the fierce sacrifice;"[2] Jig grol gyi pavo "the hero delivering from the danger (of Bardo)."[3]

The *Dudpos*, the assistants of Shinje, the judge of the dead, and often likewise called Shinjes, inhabit the region Paranirmita Vasavartin ("that exercises a power over the metamorphoses produced by others"), the highest in the world of desire. They try to hinder the depopulation of the world by supporting man in evil desire, and by keeping off the Bōdhisattvas from attaining the Bōdhi; it is they who disturb the devoutness of assembled Buddhists, and put an end to steady meditation by assuming the shape of a beautiful woman, or by suggest-

[1] Untimely death is also enumerated in a Tantra of the Kanjur amongst the objects of fear against which protection is obtained by the Dhāranīs therein mentioned. Csoma, "Analysis," As. Res., Vol. XX., p. 519. Respecting the dogma of the Bardo, see Wassiljew, "Der Buddhismus," p. 110.

[2] Chinsreg is the Tibetan name for the burnt-offering, a description of which is to be found in Chapter XV., No. 2; about Tamdin compare No. 5.

[3] In full title: Bardo phrang grol gyi sol debjig grol gyi pavo zhechava "a petition protecting from the chasm of Bardo, or a hero delivering from the danger (of Bardo)."

ing ludicrous ideas, by asserting that those who do not enjoy the pleasures of life shall be re-born in hell, with many other tricks of a similar nature. But they are also those spirits who, when the time of death has arrived, seize the released soul and bring it before Shinje, their King, to be tried and sentenced according to its works. The apparent contradiction of this function with their tendency to induce man to abandon himself to pleasure in existence, is to be explained from the dogma, "that birth and decay cannot be separated;" whence it results that the gods who cause existence simultaneously bring into action the destructive power, which is the unavoidable consequence of existence.[1]

To subdue the evil spirits, is one of the most important duties of the gods and genii, and they assume a horrible aspect when fighting with the evil spirits; during these such dreadful encounters, they are supposed to become highly inflamed with rage. Though any god is at liberty to subdue any of the evil spirits, yet there exist a particular class who have especially devoted themselves to the extirpation of evil spirits, in the pursuance of which object they are further confirmed by an awful oath deposited in the hands of the Buddha Vajradhara.[2] These gods are called Dragsheds,[3] "the cruel hangmen," and their anger against the evil spirits—so

[1] Foe koue ki, Engl. transl., p. 248. Schmidt, Mém. de l'Acad. de Petersb., Vol. II., p. 24. "Ssanang Ssetsen," p. 310.

[2] See about him p. 50 *et seq.*

[3] From dragpo, "cruel, wrathful," and *g*shed-ma "a hangman." In Mongolia out of this variety of Dragsheds eight are particularly worshipped; they are styled, according to Pallas, "Mongol. Völker," Vol. II., p. 95, Naiman Dokshot.

the legends relate—arose in consequence of the innumerable tricks that had been played off upon them by the latter. There are again subdivisions amongst the Dragsheds themselves. The one called Yab yum chudpa, "the father embracing his mother," in addition to his power of successfully keeping off a legion of evil spirits, is also able to deliver man from his sins, if the latter sincerely repent and confess them prostrate before his image. These representations show them in a curious position, with a female tenderly clasped round their bodies.

As an addition to the number of the legendary tales communicated by Pallas concerning the eight Dragsheds whom the Mongolians predominantly implore, I insert here the legends about Lhamo (Sanskr. Kāladevī), Tsangpa (Sanskr. Brahma), and Chakdor or Chakna dorje (Sanskr. Vajrapāni), having become the adversaries of the evil spirits.

The legend about Lhamo (Sanskr. Kālādevī). The goddess Lhamo[1] was married to Shinje, the king of the Dudpos, who at the time of the marriage had assumed the form of the king of Ceylon. The goddess had made a vow, either to soften her husband's notoriously wild and wicked manners, and make him favourably disposed towards the religion of Buddha, or, failing in her praiseworthy endeavours, to extirpate a royal race so

[1] In a prayer addressed to this goddess, and which is printed on Plate No. III., she is also invoked by the name of Rimate.—The present legend is related in the book Paldan Lhamoi kang shag, "to perform confession before the venerated Lhamo," a treatise which is read when offerings are presented to this goddess. A copy of this book in Tibetan and Mongolian is in the library of the Petersburgh university. The Mongolian edition contains some details in Kalmuk, which are not met with in the Tibetan.

hostile to his creed by killing the children that might issue from the marriage. Unfortunately it was beyond her power to effect an improvement in the evil ways of the king, and, accordingly, she determined to kill their son, who was greatly beloved by his father because in him he had hoped to put a complete end to Buddhism in Ceylon. During a temporary absence of the king, the goddess put her design in execution; she flayed her son alive, drank the blood from out his skull, and even ate his flesh. She then left the palace and set out for her northern home, using her son's skin as a saddle for the king's best horse. On his return, seeing what had happened, the king at once seized a bow, and, with a terrible incantation, shot off a poisoned arrow after his dreadful wife. The arrow pierced the horse's back, in which it stuck fast; but the queen, neutralizing the efficacy of the imprecation, took out the deadly weapon and uttered the following sentence: "May the wound of my horse become an eye large enough to overlook the twenty-four regions, and may I myself extirpate the race of these malignant kings of Ceylon!" The goddess then continued her journey towards the north, traversing in great haste India, Tíbet, Mongolia, and part of China, and finally settling in the mountain Oikhan, in the district Olgon, which is supposed to be situate in Eastern Siberia. This mountain is said to be surrounded by large, uninhabited deserts, and by the ocean Muliding.[1]

[1] A portrait of Lhamo, who is identical with the goddess Okkin Tängri of the Mongolians, and with the Chammo or Lchamu of Pallas (Mongol. Völkerschaften, Vol. II., p. 98), I found added to the picture of the thirty-five Buddhas

The legend about Tsangpa (Brahma). Tsangpa, a follower of the Buddha, who had retired into the woods, was on the point of discovering the secrets of the Buddha doctrine by extraordinary meditation and the practice of virtues, when a Dudpo appeared before him in the shape of a beautiful woman, who offered him exquisite delicacies. Tsangpa incautiously partook of them, was soon drunk, and in his phrensy killed the ram upon which the demon had ridden. By this savage act he lost the merits of the good works which he had accumulated with so much pain and perseverance, and attained no higher degree than that of a common follower, or Upāsaka (Tib. Genyen).[1] Tsangpa was now filled with rage towards the evil spirits, and took an awful oath, in the hands of of the Buddha Vajradhara, vowing to do his utmost to extirpate the pernicious race through which he had lost his position.[2]

The legend about Chakdor (Vajrapāni).[3] Once upon a time the Buddhas all met together on the top of Mount Mēru, to deliberate upon the means of procuring the water of life, Dutsi (Sanskr. Amrita), which lies

of confession described p. 97. There is a similar representation of her in Plate VI. of Pallas's work, beneath the central figure; in Fig. 5, Plate IX., she is represented without the staff and the skull-cup.

[1] I have already stated that these are not virtually admitted to the rank of a Buddha. *See* pp. 28, 38, 106.

[2] This legend inclines me to believe that Manjusrī, a Bōdhisattva, and the god of wisdom (*see* p. 65), did not, when repelling the obnoxious Choichishalba, take the dreadful form of Yamāntaka by order of Sākyamuni, as Pallas was informed (see his Mong. Völker., Vol. II., p. 96), but assumed it of his own free will, and in consequence of a similar snare laid for him.

[3] This legend is given in the book Drimed shel phreng, "spotless garland of crystals." For an image of Vajrapāni see Plate II.

བཛྲ་པཱ་ཎི། ཕྱག་རྡོར།

Vajrapāni or Chakdor, the subduer of the evil spirits.

Reduced from the original, which is cut into a prayer-stone put upon a prayer wall in Sikkim.

ADDRESS

TO THE

GODDESS LHAMO,

IN SANSKRIT KĀLADĒVĪ.

༄༅ བདག་ཉིད་ཀྱི་ཐུགས་ཀའི་ཧཱུྃ་སྔོན་པོའི་འོད་ཟེར་ལྕགས་ཀྱུ་རྣམ་པ་ཅན་བྱུང་ཤར་སྟུ་
ལི་དིང་གི་རྒྱ་མཚོ་ཆེན་པོ་ནས་འདོད་ཁམས་དབང་ཕྱུག་དཔལ་ལྡན་དམག་ཟེར་གྱི་རྒྱལ་མོ་རེ་
མ་ཏི་འཁོར་དང་བཅས་པ་སྐད་ཅིག་གི་གནས་འདིར་སྤྱན་དྲངས།། ། །

concealed at the bottom of the deep ocean. In their benevolence, they intended, as soon as they obtained possession of the water of life, to distribute it amongst the human race as a powerful antidote against the strong poison Hala hala, which the evil demons, at this period, had been using with such mischievous effect against mankind.

In order to procure the antidote they determined to churn the ocean with the mountain Mēru, and so cause the water of life to rise to the surface of the sea. This they did, and delivered the water of life to Vajrapāni, with orders to secure it safely until a future meeting, when they would impart it to living beings. But the monster Rāhu[1] (Tib. Dachan), a Lhamayin, happened to hear of this precious discovery, and having carefully watched Vajrapāni's movements, seized an opportunity, in the absence of the latter, to drink the water of life; not satisfied with this act, he even voided his water deliberately into the vessel. He then hurried away as fast as possible, and had already proceeded a great distance, when Vajrapāni came home, and having perceived the theft, instantly set out in pursuit of the culprit. In the course of his flight Rāhu had passed the sun and

[1] In his "Manual of Buddhism," p. 58, Hardy has extracted from Singhalese books the following mythical measurements of Rāhu's hody: "Rāhu is 76,000 miles high; 19,000 miles broad across the shoulders; his head is 14,500 miles round; his forehead is 4,800 miles broad; from eye brow to eye-brow he measures 800 miles; his mouth is 3,200 miles in size, and 4,800 miles deep; the palm of his hand is 5,600 miles in size; the joint of his fingers 800 miles; the sole of his foot 12,000 miles; from his elbow to the tip of his fingers is 19,000 miles; and with one finger he can cover the sun or moon, so as to obscure their light."

the moon, whom he menaced with vengeance, should they venture to betray him to Vajrapāni. His searches proving fruitless, Vajrapāni betook himself to the sun, and asked him about Rāhu. But the sun replied evasively, saying, that he had certainly seen somebody passing a long time ago, but had paid no particular attention as to who it was. The moon, on the other hand, returned a candid answer, only requesting that Vajrapāni would not repeat it before Rāhu. Upon this information Rāhu was shortly afterwards overtaken, when he got such a terrible blow from Vajrapāni's sceptre that, besides rereceiving many wounds, his body was split into two parts, the lower part of the body with the legs being entirely blown off.

The Buddhas once more held a meeting, in which they deliberated upon the best means of disposing of Rāhu's urine. To pour it out would have been most dangerous for living beings, as it contained a large quantity of the poison Hala hala; they therefore determined, that Vajrapāni should drink it, in just punishment for the carelessness through which the water of life had been lost. Accordingly he was forced to do so, when his fair, yellow complexion was changed by the effects of this dangerous potion into a dark one. Vajrapāni conceived, from his transfiguration, a most violent rage against all evil demons, and in particular against Rāhu, who, notwithstanding his deadly wounds, was prevented from dying by the water of life. This powerful water, however, dropped from his wounds and fell all over the world, numerous medicinal herbs springing up on the spots where it touched the soil. A severe punishment was also inflicted upon Rāhu by the Buddhas themselves; they made a horrible monster of him, replaced his legs by the tail of a dragon, formed nine different heads from his broken one, the principal wounds were made into an enormous throat, and the lesser ones changed into so many eyes.

Rāhu, who had ever distinguished himself from his fellow-beings by his wickedness—in their earliest youth even the other gods had to suffer from his malignity—became, after this transformation, more dreadful than he was before. His rage was turned especially towards the sun and the moon, who had betrayed him. He is constantly trying to devour them, particularly the moon, who displayed the most hostile disposition towards him. He overshadows them whilst trying to devour them, and thus causes eclipses; but owing to Vajrapāni's unceasing vigilance, he cannot succeed in destroying them.[1]

Prayers.

Prayers, in the usual sense of the word, as addresses to the deity imploring assistance, or in the form of

[1] This legend decidedly derives its origin from the Hindus, from whose tales it was taken almost without alteration. According to these, the water of life, Amrita, was also procured by churning the ocean, and was distributed amongst the gods. Rāhu, a monster with a dragon's tail, disguised himself like one of the gods, and received a portion of it; his fraud having been discovered by the sun and moon, Vishnu severed his head; but the nectarean fluid secured his immortality. See Fr. Wilford, "On Egypt and the Nile," As. Res., Vol. III., p. 331, 419; "Essay on the Sacred Isles in the West," As. Res., Vol. XI., p. 141.

thanksgivings and praises for mercies received,[1] are known to genuine Buddhism only in the form of hymns for honouring and glorifying the Buddhas and Bōdhisattvas, for having pointed out to man, by word and example, the right path leading to Nirvāna. But in the Mahāyāna Buddhism man is not directed to perfection by information only, but he may hope to be actually supported by divine assistance; for the Bōdhisattvas, instead of emulating the quietness of the Buddhas, are supposed to wander about in the world and to ensure by their powerful assistance man's attainment of eternal happiness. We here meet with implorations which, in their first stage, however, do not exhibit the character of petitions or thanks, but only express the desires of the votary to attain the same high faculties as the Bōdhisattvas enjoy themselves. Whenever, in the legends, any Buddhist is about to perform a meritorious work, he utters the words: "May I become delivered from pains on account of this work, and may I lead all beings to deliverance by my good example and these works." But in the books belonging to the later Mahāyāna and the mystical schools, we see such wishes very closely allied to the dogma of an unlimited charity of the Bōdhīsattvas towards man. As an example of this I quote a Tantra of the Kanjur, in which seven imaginary Buddhas had each desired, when they were practising a holy life in order to become

[1] Schott, "Ueber den Buddhaismus in Hochasien," p. 58. Wassiljew, l. c., pp. 136, 139, 166. Csoma, "Analysis," As. Res., Vol. XX., p. 508. See also the Address to the Buddhas of Confession in the following chapter.—Concerning the Gēyas, or works in metric form, to the glory of the Buddhas and Bōdhisattvas, see Burnouf's Introduction, p. 52.

Buddhas, that all animal beings (or creatures) that were suffering such and such specified kinds of misery or distress, might, at the time of their becoming Buddhas, enjoy all sorts of prosperity and happiness. In the sacred writings of these systems the mythological Buddhas residing in the various regions beyond the earth are frequently addressed with prayers in the strict sense of the word, and the reciting of prayers is recommended as a most successful expedient for annihilating sins and for removing the impediments which hinder the attainment of final emancipation.

In Tíbet this is also the actual opinion respecting prayers (Tib. Monlam). The general confidence of the Tibetan Buddhists in their efficacy is more especially due to their enjoying the character and possessing the virtue of Dhāranīs; they are endowed with supernatural powers and are considered to exercise an irresistible magical influence over the deity implored. That this is the light in which they are viewed is clearly evident from the form of many prayers, which are frequently little more than mere incantations. Here, for instance, is an address to the goddess Lhamo, which runs thus: "I summon thee hither from the north-eastern region surrounded by the great ocean Muliding, by the blue letter Hum, which is traced upon my heart, spreading with its iron hook a beam of light;—thee, the mighty and powerful mistress and queen Rimate and thy attendants."[1]

[1] For the Tibetan text which Adolphe got written down by a Lama, see Plate No. III.

Other prayers are, according to their form, praises, or hymns, or petitions in which the name of the god addressed is mentioned, as in the prayer: Om Vajrapāni hum; or is at times omitted altogether, as in the celebrated six-syllable prayer: Om mani padme hum, O, the Jewel in the Lotus: Amen. This prayer is an invocation of Padmapāni (see p. 88), who is believed to have delivered it to the Tibetans; it is the most frequently repeated of all prayers, and has on this account excited the curiosity of the earliest visitors to Tíbet. Its real meaning, however, was long involved in doubt, and it is only by the most recent researches that a positive determination has been finally arrived at.[1] The Lotus (*Nymphæa Nelumbo, Linn.*), is known to be the symbol of highest perfection, and is here employed in allusion to Padmapāni's genesis from this flower. To each syllable of the prayer is attributed a special magical faculty,[2] and this theory has perhaps more favoured its general application than its supposed divine origin.

In the plates this prayer occurs in No. IV., which is a print from an original wood-block. In a prayer cylinder[3] which I had the opportunity of opening, I found the

[1] See Klaproth, "Fragments Bouddhiques," p. 27; Schmidt, Mém. de l'Acad. de Pétersb., Vol. I., p. 112; Foe koue ki, Engl. Translation, p. 116; Hodgson's "Illustrations," p. 171; Schott, "Ueber den Buddhaismus," p. 9; Hofmann, in "Beschreibung von Nippon," Vol. V., p. 175.

[2] Schmidt, "Forschungen," p. 200; Pallas, "Mongol. Völkerschaften," Vol. II., p. 90. The power of any sentence or book is increased by being written in red, silver or gold. Red ink *e.g.* is considered to have exactly 108 times more power than black ink. Schilling de Canstadt, in Bull. hist. phil. de Pet., Vol. IV., pp. 331, 333.

[3] Further information about these curious instruments will be given in a subsequent chapter.

THE SIX-SYLLABIC PRAYER "OM MANI PADME HUM."

Taken from a woodcut from Eastern Tibet.

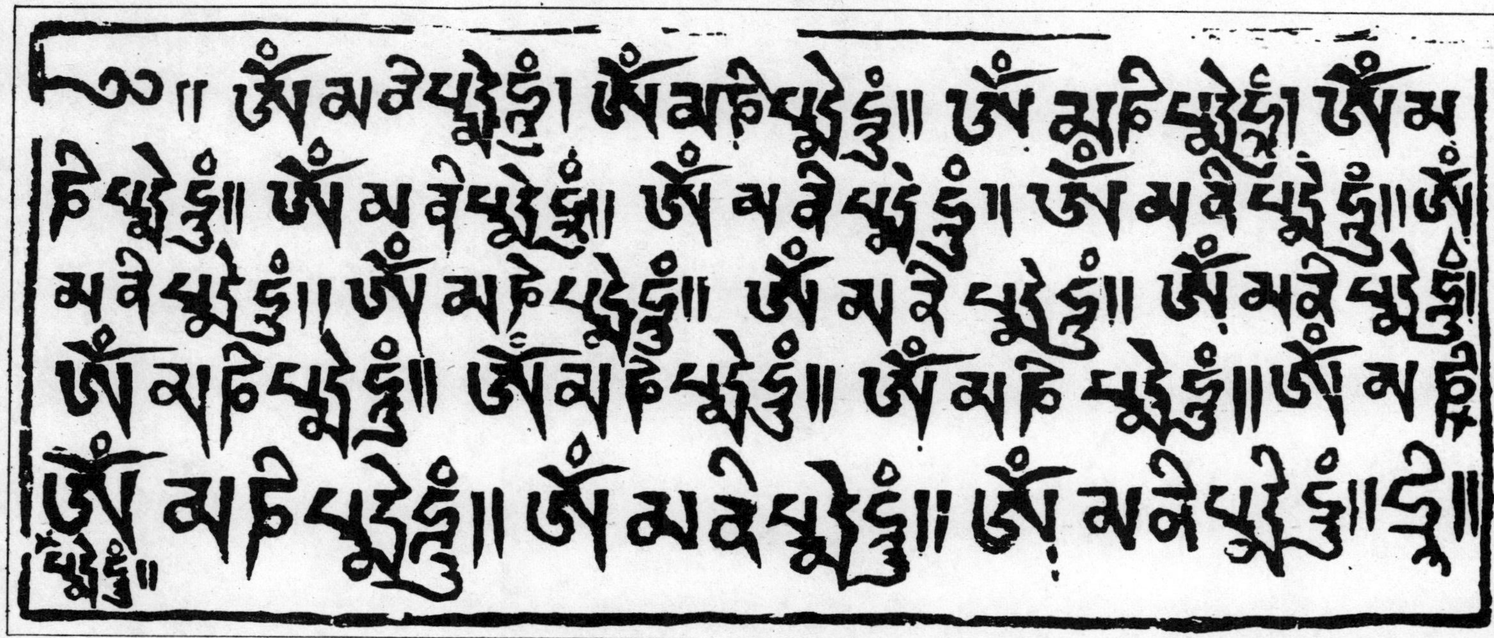

sentence printed in six lines and repeated innumerable times upon a leaf 49 feet long and 4 inches broad. When Baron Schilling de Canstadt paid a visit to the temple Subulin in Siberia, the Lamas were just occupied with preparing 100 millions of copies of this prayer to be put into a prayer cylinder. His offer to have the necessary number executed at St. Petersburg was most readily accepted, and he was presented, in return for the 150 millions of copies he forwarded to them, with an edition of the Kanjur, the sheets of which amount to about 40,000.—When adorning the head of religious books, or when engraved upon the slabs resting on the prayer walls,[1] the letters of the above-mentioned sentence are often so combined as to form an anagram. The longitudinal lines occurring in the letters "mani padme hum" are traced close to each other, and to the outer longitudinal line at the left are appended the curved lines. The letter "om" is replaced by a symbolical sign above the anagram, showing a half-moon surmounted by a disk indicating the sun, from which issues a flame. Such a combination of the letters is called in Tibetan Nam chu vangdan, "the ten entirely powerful (viz. characters, six of which are consonants, and four vowels);" and the power of this sacred sentence is supposed to be increased by its being written in this form. This kind of anagrams are always bordered by a pointed frame indicating the leaf of a fig-tree.

[1] See about them. Chapter XIII.

CHAPTER XI

TRANSLATION OF AN ADDRESS TO THE BUDDHAS OF CONFESSION

TRANSLATION AND EXPLANATORY REMARKS.

In the chapter on "Metempsychosis" I have already alluded to the various means of purification from sins, a very efficacious one, it will be remembered, consisting in the supplication of the deities. I have likewise there referred to the addresses offered up to the Buddhas of confession, which are contained in various compilations of prayers. A sacred treatise of this nature forms the subject of the present chapter. The original I found concealed in a Chorten my brother Hermann had obtained from the Lama at Saimonbóng, in Síkkim;[1] it is written in small characters (the Vumed) on two sheets

[1] The Chorten stood on the altar in the Lama's praying-room already when Hooker was there. See the View of the interior of the house of the Lama at Saimonbóng in his "Himalayan Journals."

of unequal size. The larger is about four feet square, its height being two feet four inches, its breadth one foot nine inches; the smaller has the same breadth, but its height is only six inches, giving a surface of $^7/_8$ square foot. These two sheets were lying one upon the other, but separated by grains of barley interposed between them. They were wound round a wooden four-sided obelisk which filled the central part of the Chorten. The four sides of this obelisk were covered with Dhāranī inscriptions.

As the size of the two sheets does not allow of my reproducing here this invocation of the Buddhas of confession in the form of a facsimile, I preferred giving it transcribed in the head characters in the ordinary form of Tibetan books, at the end of the chapter. The contents of the two parts are separated by a distance left between them; the beginning of the second part is besides also marked in the Tibetan text by the recurrence of the initial sign.[1]

Its full title runs thus: Digpa thamchad shagpar terchoi, "Repentance of all sins, doctrine of the hidden treasure."[2] The words ter-choi were illegible in the sentence at the head of the treatise, and it was only through their occurring at the foot of the larger leaf in connexion with the rest of the phrase that the hiatus could be filled up. Here also the other words preceding them had suffered considerable injury, but the general

[1] In the English translation the words in parenthesis are rather explanatory paraphrases, than literal translations of the Tibetan.

[2] *S*dig-pa "sin, vice;" thams-chad "all;" *b*shags-pa "repentant confession;" *r*, the sign of the locative, is often used in stead of the genetive sign (comp. Foucaux, Gram. Tib., p. 94); *g*ter "a treasury;" chhos "the doctrine."

context and the few letters still decipherable proved sufficient to remove all doubt that the title had been repeated. Another name for the petition, and one which we several times meet with in the text, is Digshag ser chi pugri, "the golden razor which takes away sins,"[1] this designation evidently signifying its extraordinary efficacy in delivering the sinner.

The larger leaf commences with a general laudation of the Buddhas—past, present, and to come—who are considered to have approached nearest to perfection; then fifty-one Buddhas are mentioned each by name; of some the region is stated in which they dwell, to others is added the number of their births from the moment in which they entered the Buddha career down to the time when they obtained the Buddhaship. Sins are said to be annihilated by reading or uttering the names of these Buddhas, and the sins are specified from which each Buddha has the power to purify. The wickedness of the human race, which caused the destruction of the universe, is alluded to, and the prophecy is made that man shall have recourse to this treatise and derive from it great advantages.

The second, smaller leaf, begins with the words: "Enshrined in the sacred box at the time of the uttering of benedictions," which refer to the usual inauguration ceremonies of religious buildings, as also to the blessings pronounced on such solemn occasions. Their effects upon the salvation of man, and the ad-

[1] *G*ser "gold;" kyi, chi, is the sign of the genitive case; *s*pu-gri "a razor."

vantages which the inhabitants of the monastery shall derive from repeating them, are also again noticed. It concludes with four Dhāranīs.

The address styles itself a Mahāyāna Sūtra (in Tibetan, Thegpa chenpoi do), under which we should also have to class it from the nature of its contents.[1] The addressing of imaginary Buddhas and the admission of a magical influence of prayers upon the deity implored is particularly to be mentioned in evidence of its being written in this period of mystic modification of Buddhism.[2] We may also, with equal right, regard it as a translation from an ancient Sanskrit work, on account of the occurring of the title in Sanskrit.

The personal names of the Buddhas, and the Tibetan terms explained in the notes, are given in exact transliteration, and are not reprinted in the GLOSSARY OF TIBETAN TERMS, APPENDIX B., if they occur in the text; the native spelling of the other words may be looked for in this Glossary.

Translation of the first part.

"In the Sanskrit language[3] .... Reverence be to the

[1] For the characteristic signs of a Mahāyāna Sūtra, *see* Burnouf, "Introduction," p. 121.

[2] The Sūtras Phal-po-chhe and Rim-pa-*l*nga which are referred to for particulars concerning several Buddhas, are contained in the Kanjur.

[3] My original is injured in this place, and the Sanskrit name cannot be read.—It is a curious custom, differing from translations in European languages, that books which have been translated from the Sanskrit have frequently two titles, the Sanskrit and the Tibetan one. Some larger works of the Kanjur also receive an additional title in the Tibetan dialect called Dulva zhi, "the basis of religious discipline." See Csoma, "Analysis," As. Res., Vol. XX., p. 44.

very spotless Buddhas, who all came in the same way.[1] In Tibetan: Repentance of all sins" (or *s*dig-pa-thams-chad-*b*shags-par).

"I adore the Tathāgatas of the three periods,[2] who dwell in the ten quarters of the world,[3] the subduers of the enemy, the very pure and perfect Buddhas, (I adore)

[1] In the original, Na-mo-sarva-bi-ma-la-ta-thā-ga-ta-bud-dha; the words are all Sankrit. Tathāgata, in Tibetan De-*b*zhin, or more fully De-*b*zhin-*g*shegs-pa, an epithet of the Buddhas who have appeared upon earth, implying that they have gone in the manner of their predecessors. Comp. pp. 4, 15.—In the sequel I shall translate De-*b*zhin-*g*shegs-pa by its Sanskrit equivalent Tathāgata, the literal rendering of the passage making the phrase inconveniently long.

Similar sentences begin religious treatises; the Kanjur *e. g.* has in the first page three images representing Sākyamuni, with his son on his left, and one of his chief disciples on the right, the following legends being written respectively under each: "Salutation to the prince of the Munis; salutation to the son of Shārikā; salutation to Grachen dzin (Sanskrit Lāhula)." The title-page of the work is followed by the Salutation to the three holy ones. Csoma, "Analysis of the Dulva class of the Kanjur," As. Res., Vol. XX., p. 45. Our historical document relating to the foundation of the Hímis monastery, an abreviated translation of which is appended to the chapter on monasteries, commences with the words: "Hail! praise and salutation to the teachers!"

[2] The three periods are the past, the present and the future; the Buddhas of the past are those who had preached the law and have now returned to Nirvāna; the Buddha of the present time is Sākyamuni, the last of the Buddhas that have yet appeared; the Buddhas of the future time are the Bōdhisattvas, the candidates for Buddhaship. The Buddhas of the *three* periods include all the Buddhas.

[3] In Tibetan phyog*s*-*b*chu. These ten quarters of the world are: north; north-east; east; south-east; south; south-west; west; north-west; the quarter above the zenith; the quarter below the nadir. Each region is inhabited by its own Buddhas and gods, and to know their feelings towards a particular man is considered of the greatest importance. Compare for details Chapter XVII. No. 2.—A totally different meaning must be attached to Sa-*b*chu-pa "the ten earths," a term equivalent to the Sanskrit Dasabhūmi, referring to the ten regions or degrees of perfection which a Bōdhisattva has to pass in succession in order to attain the Buddha perfection. Comp. Csoma's "Dictionary," p. 89; "Analysis," As. Res., Vol. XX., p. 469; 405. Burnouf, "Introduction," p. 438. Wassiljew, "Der Buddhismus," p. 405.

these illustrious beings,[1] each and all. I offer to them and confess my sins."

"I rejoice over the cause of virtue,[2] I turn the wheel of the doctrine,[3] I believe that the body of all the Buddhas does not enter Nirvāna.[4]

"The causes of virtue will grow to great perfection.

"I adore the Tathāgata, the vanquisher of the enemy,[5] the very pure, the most perfect[6] Buddha Nam-*m*kha'-*d*pal-dri-med-*r*dul-rab-tu-*m*dzes;[7]

"I adore the Tathāgata Yon-tan-tog-gi-'od-la-me-tog-padma-vaidhurya'i-'od-zer-rin-po-chhe'i-*g*zugs, who has the body of a god's son;

"I adore the Tathāgata *s*Pos-*m*chhog-dam-pas-*m*chhod-pa'i-*s*ku-*r*nam-par-*s*pras-shing-leg*s*-par-*r*gyan-pa;

[1] In Tibetan *d*pal, a title applied to gods, saints, and great men.

[2] The Tibetan word is *r*tsa-va "root, first cause, origin." The meaning of the phrase is a promise for the practise of virtues.

[3] This is the technical term for *teaching* and *preaching* the laws of the Buddha, though it is also applied by analogy to the *observation* of the precepts of the Buddha. Compare Foe koue ki, Engl. Transl., pp. 29, 171.

[4] This sentence is to be explained by the dogma of the three bodies of every Buddha, concerning which comp. p. 38. When a Buddha leaves the earth, he loses the faculty of embodying himself again in human shape; the Nirmānakāya body (Tib. Prulpai ku) in which he has contributed to the welfare and salvation of mankind in the periods preceding the attainment of the Buddha perfection, dies with him, and does not enter Nirvāna. The Tibetan *g*sol-ba-'deb*s* had, therefore, to be translated by "I believe," though the dictionaries only give "to intreat, to beg" as its signification.

[5] In Tibetan *d*gra-*b*chom-pa, in Sanskrit Arhat (see p. 27).

[6] In Tibetan Yang-dag-par-*r*dzog*s*-pa, in Sanskrit Samyak sambuddha.

[7] This and the following Tibetan terms are the personal names of the respective Buddhas.

"I adore the Tathāgata *g*Tsug-tor-gyi-*g*tsug-nas-nyi-ma'i-'od-zer-*d*pag-med-zla-'od-*s*mon-lam-gyis-*r*gyan-pa,

"I adore the Tathāgata Rab-*s*prul-*b*kod-pa-chhen-po-chhos-kyi-*d*byings-las-*m*ngon-par-'phags-pa-chhags-dang-*l*dan-zla-med-rin-chhen-'byung-*l*dan,

"I adore the Tathāgata Chhu-zla'i-*g*zhon-nu-nyi-ma'i-*s*gron-ma-zla-ba'i-me-tog-rin-chhen-padma-*g*ser-gyi-'du-ni-*m*kha', who has perfectly the body of a god's son,

"I adore the Tathāgata who is sitting in the ten regions, 'Od-zer-rab-tu-'gyed-ching-'jig-*r*ten-gyi-nam-*m*kha'-kun-du-*s*nang-bar-byed-pa,

"I adore the Tathāgata Sangs-*r*gyas-kyi-*b*kod-pa-thams-chad-rab-tu-*r*gyas-par-*m*dzad-pa,

"I adore the Tathāgata Sangs-*r*gyas-kyi-*d*gongs-pa-*b*sgrubs-pa,

"I adore the Tathāgata Dri-med-zla-ba'i-me-tog-gi-*b*kod-pa-*m*dzad,

"I adore the Tathāgata Rin-chhen-*m*chhog-gis-me-tog-grags-*l*dan,

"I adore the Tathāgata 'Jigs-med-*r*nam-par-*g*zigs,

"I adore the Tathāgata 'Jigs-pa-dang-'bral-zhing-bag-chhags-mi-*m*nga'-zhing-*s*pu-zing-zhis-mi-byed-pa,

"I adore the Tathāgata Seng-ge-*s*gra-*d*byangs,

"I adore the Tathāgata *g*Ser-'od-*g*zi-*b*rjid-kyi-*r*gyal-po."

"Whatever human being upon earth writes the names of these Buddhas, or carries them with him, or reads them, or makes a vow (to do so), will be blessed for it: he will become clean from all darkening sins, and will be born in the region *b*De-va-chan,[1] which is towards the west."

"I adore the Tathāgata Ts'he-*d*pag-med[2], who dwells in the Buddha-region *b*De-va-chan;

"I adore the Tathāgata *r*Do-rje-rab-tu-'dzin-pa, who dwells in the Buddha-region Ngur-*s*mrig-gi-*r*gyal-*m*ts'han;

"I adore the Tathāgata Pad-mo-shin-tu-*r*gyas-pa, who dwells in the Buddha-region Phyir-mi-*l*dag-pa'i-'khor-lo-rab-tu-*s*grog-pa;

"I adore the Tathāgata Chhos-kyi-*r*gyal-*m*ts'han, who dwells in the Buddha-region *r*Dul-med-pa;

"I adore the Tathāgata Seng-ge-*s*gra-*d*byang*s*-*r*gyal-po, who dwells in the Buddha-region *s*Gron-la-*b*zang-po;

"I adore the Tathāgata *r*Nam*s*-par-*s*nang-*m*dzad-*r*gyal-po,[3] who dwells in the Buddha-region 'Od-zer-*b*sang-po;

"I adore the Tathāgata Chhos-kyi-'od-zer-gyi-*s*ku-pad-mo-shin-tu-*r*gyas-pa, who dwells in the Buddha-region 'Da'-bar-*d*ka'-ba;

"I adore the Tathāgata *m*Ngon-par-*m*khyen-pa-tham*s*-

[1] In Sanskrit Sukhavatī. This word is the name of the happy mansion where the Dhyāni Buddha Amitābha, or in Tibetan Odpagmed, sits enthroned; it is considered the greatest reward of a virtuous life to be re-born in this world. See the description of this region p. 98.

[2] In Sanskrit Amitāyus. This is another name of Amitābha (Burnouf "Introduction," p. 102) who is so styled when implored for longevity. In images referring to this power of the Buddha, he holds a vase-like vessel filled with the water of life, which he is believed to pour out over those who address him.—Such a figure may be very often seen in every kind of religious representations, paintings as well as plastic objects.

[3] In Sanskrit Vāirōchana, the name of a fabulous Buddha, regarded as the Dhyāni Buddha of the first human Buddha who taught the law in the actual universe. See Burnouf's Introduction, p. 117.

chad-kyi-'od-zer, who dwells in the Buddha-region *r*Gyan-dang-*l*dan-pa;

"I adore the Tathāgata 'Od-mi-'khrug*s*-pa, who dwells in the Buddha-region Me-long-gi-*d*kyil-'khor-*m*dog-'dra;

"I adore the illustrious *s*Nying-po, who dwells in the Buddha-region Padmo, in that pure Buddha-region where abides the victorious, the Tathāgata who has subdued his enemy, the very pure, perfect Buddha Ngan-'gro-tham*s*-chad-*r*nam-par-'jom*s*-pa-'phag*s*-pa-*g*zi-*br*jid-*s*gra-*d*byangs-kyi-*r*gyal-po."

"All these (Buddhas' stories) are contained in the Sūtra Phal-po-chhe."[1]

"I likewise adore the Buddha Shākya-thub-pa, who is known to have been born thirty millions of times;[2]

[1] Comp. p. 125.—In Csoma's Analysis of it Vāirōchana (*r*Nam-par-*s*nang-*m*dzad) is the only Buddha mentioned.

[2] An allusion to the numerous descents of Shākya-thub-pa, or Sākyamuni, the founder of Buddhism, who, in common with all candidates for the Buddhaship previous to their final elevation, has passed through countless probationary stages, during which period greater merit is accumulated by most extraordinary works. The life of the Buddhas in anterior existences is related at large in the sacred books styled Jātakas, not a few of these tales being identical with the fables of the Greek Aesop. Hardy, "Manual of Buddhism," p. 100; Burnouf, "Introduction," pp. 61, 555. The previous re-births of Sākyamuni are in most of the sacred books variously estimated from 500 to 550. Upham, "History and Doctrine of Buddhism," Vol. III., p. 296; Foucaux, "Rgy chher rol pa," Vol. II., p. 34; Hardy, "Manual," *l. c.* But there are also many phrases to be met with tending to establish their infinity, and the Buddha himself is reported to have said: "It is impossible to reckon the bodies I have possessed." Foe koue ki, pp. 67, 348; Hodgson, "Illustrations," p. 86. The number in the text is accordingly an instance rather of the latter belief, and the term khrag might be an abreviation from khrag-khrig, "a hundred thousand millions," which is also used to signify any indefinitely large number. See Csoma's Dictionary, *voce* Khrag-khrig.

once uttering this name, shall purify from all sins committed in anterior existences.

"I adore the Buddha Mar-me-*m*dzad,[1] who has done so eighteen thousand times. Once uttering this name shall purify from the sins committed by pollution with the properties of lower men.

"I adore the Buddha Rab-tu-'bar-ba, who is known (to have been born) 16,000 times. Once uttering this name shall confer absolution, and purify from all sins committed against parents and teachers.

"I adore the Buddha *s*Kar-*r*gyal, who has been born ten million three thousand times. Once uttering this name shall purify from all sins committed by polluting one's self with sacred riches.

"I adore the Buddha Sā-la'i-*r*gyal-po, who has been born eighteen thousand times. Once uttering this name shall purify from all sins of theft, robbery, and the like.

"I adore the Buddha Padma-'phags-pa, who has been born fifteen thousand times. Once uttering this name shall purify from all sins committed by polluting one's self with, and coveting, the riches belonging to Chortens.[2]

[1] In Sanskrit Dīpankara. This name, "the luminous," is applied to an imaginary Buddha who, according to Turner and Hărdy, is said to have been the twenty-fourth teacher of the Buddha law previous to Sākyamuni, to whom he was the first to give a definite assurance of his future Buddhaship. Turner, "Extracts from the Attakata," Journ. As. Soc. Beng., Vol. VIII., p. 789; Hardy's Manual, p. 94. In Hodgson's list (Illustrations, p. 135), however, he is the first Buddha of the actual period and the ninth predecessor of Sākyamuni.—Hardy's texts allege him to have lived 100,000 years; the Nippon Pantheon (by Hofmann in v. Siebold's "Beschreibung von Japan," Vol. V., p. 77) says that his stay upon earth lasted 840 billions of years.

[2] About Chortens see Chapter XIII.

"I adore the Buddha Ko'u-'din-ne'i-rig*s*,[1] who has been born ninety millions of times. Once uttering this name shall purify all sins committed....[2]

"I adore the Buddha,[3] who has been born ninety thousand times.

"I adore the Buddha 'Od-*b*srung,[4] who has been born nine hundred thousand times.

"I adore the Buddha Bye-ba-phrag-ganga'i-*k*lung-gi-bye-ma-*s*nyed-kyi-grang*s*-dang-*m*nyam-pa-*r*nam.

"I adore the Buddha Kun-du-*s*pas-pa-la-sog*s*-pa-*m*ts'han-tha-dad-pa, who has been born a thousand times.

"I adore the Buddha 'Jam-bu-'dul-va, who has been born twenty thousand times.

"I adore the Buddha *g*Ser-*m*dog-dri-med-'od-zer, who has been born sixty-two thousand times.

"I adore the Buddha *d*Vang-po'i-*r*gyal-po'i-*r*gyal-*m*ts'han, who has been born eighty-four thousand times.

"I adore the Buddha Nyi-ma'i-*s*nying-po, who has been born ten thousand five hundred times.

[1] In Sanskrit Kāundinya, one of the earliest disciples of Sākyamuni, who will teach the Buddha law at a very remote period. See Burnouf, "Le Lotus de la Bonne Loi," p. 126; Csoma, "Life of Sākya," As. Res., Vol. XX., p. 293.

[2] In Tibetan follow the two words *r*mos, "ploughed," and *b*skol, "to boil in oil or butter." As these two words have no apparent connexion, I have omitted them in the text.

[3] Here the Buddha is not called by name.

[4] In Sanskrit Kāsyapa, who is viewed as the third Buddha of the actual period, or the immediate predecessor of Sākyamuni; particulars about his nativity, race, age, disciples, &c., are to be found in Csoma's "Analysis," As. Res., Vol. XX., p. 415, and Foe koue ki, p. 180.

"I adore the Buddha Zhi-bar-*md*zad-pa who has been born sixty-two thousand times.

"I adore all these Buddhas, together with the assembly of the Srāvakas,[1] and Bōdhisattvas.[2]

"All these (Buddhas' stories) are contained in the treatise Rim-pa-*l*nga" (a part of the Kanjur).[3]

"I adore the victorious,[4] the Tathāgata, the vanquisher of the enemy, the very pure, the perfect Buddha Rin-chhen-*r*gyal-po'i-*m*dzod. Once to utter this name takes away the sins which would cause one further existence.

"I adore the victorious, the Tathāgata, the vanquisher of the enemy, the very pure, the perfect Buddha Rin-chhen-'od-kyi-*r*gyal-po-me-'od-rab-tu-*g*sal-va. Once to utter this name takes away the sins committed in one existence by polluting one's self with the riches of the clergy.[5]

"I adore the victorious, the Tathāgata, the vanquisher of the enemy, the very pure, the perfect Buddha *s*Pos-dang-me-tog-la-*d*vang-ba-*s*tob*s*-kyi-*r*gyal-po. Once to

[1] In Tibetan nyon-thos, "auditor." By this word is designated in the ancient religious books a disciple of Sākyamuni, as also an earlier adherent to his law. In the later sacred writings it is applied to Buddhists who had abandoned the world and turned ascetics. See pp. 18, 149.

[2] In Tibetan byang-chhub-sems-*d*pa'. The Mahāyāna books apply this name to every follower of the Buddhist faith; the lay members are called "Bōdhisattvas who reside in their houses," the ascetics, "Bōdhisattvas who have renounced the world."

[3] As an example of the contents of such descriptive stories see Csoma's Analysis, As. Res., Vol. XX., p. 415.

[4] In Tibetan *b*Chom-*l*dan-das, in Sanskrit Bhagavan.

[5] In Tibetan *d*ge-'dun, also pronounced Gendun, a general name for the "clergy," respecting whose institutions see Chapter XII.

utter this name takes away the sins committed by violation of the moral laws.

"I adore the victorious, the Tathāgata, the vanquisher of the enemy, the very pure, the perfect Buddha Ganga'i-*k*lung-gi-bye-ma-*s*nyed-bye-ba-phrag-*b*rgya'i-grang*s*-dang-*m*nyam-par-des-pa. Once to utter this name takes away the sins committed in one existence by taking life.

"I adore the victorious, the Tathāgata, the vanquisher of the enemy, the very pure, the perfect Buddha Rin-chhen-*r*do-rje-*d*pal-*b*rtan-zhing-'dul-va-pha-rol-gyi-*s*tob*s*-rab-tu-'jom*s*-pa. Once to utter this name makes one equal in religious merit to him who has read over the royal precepts.[1]

"I adore the victorious, the Tathāgata, the vanquisher of the enemy, the very pure, the perfect Buddha *g*Zi-*b*rjed-nges-par-*r*nam-par-*g*non-pa. Once to utter this name takes away the sins committed in one existence by evil desire.

"I adore the victorious, the Tathāgata, the vanquisher of the enemy, the very pure, the perfect Buddha Rin-chhen-zla-'od-*s*kyab*s*-*g*nas-dam-pa-*d*gra-las-*r*nam-par-*r*gyal-ba. Once to utter this name takes away the sins which would cause the sufferings in the hell *m*Nar-med.[2]

[1] In Tybetan *b*ka'. This word means "precept," and is here to be referred to the rules enacted to the Lamas; the meaning of this reward accordingly is, that the suppliants shall be counted amongst the priests and enjoy the blessings reserved to them. *See* p. 149.

[2] *m*Nar-med is the name of one of the most dreadful divisions of hell. Csoma's and Schmidt's Dictionaries. About the hells see p. 92.

"I adore the victorious, the Tathāgata, the vanquisher of the enemy, the very pure, the perfect Buddha Rin-chhen-*g*tsug-tor-chan. Once to utter this name removes the danger of being born in any of the bad grades of existence,[1] and the most perfect body of a god or man shall be obtained.

"I adore the victorious, the Tathāgata, the vanquisher of the enemy, the very pure, the perfect Buddha *r*Gyal-ba-*r*gya-*m*ts'ho'i-ts'hog*s*-dang-*b*chas-pa-*r*nam. It is said that once to utter this name purifies from the sin of perjury, and from all sins committed by the mind (bad feelings) through lust, deceit, and the like.

"I adore the victorious, the Tathāgata, the subduer of his enemy, the very pure, the perfect Buddha Ts hei-bum-pa-'dzin-pa-*r*nam.

"May these Buddhas, deliver all animal beings from the horrors of untimely death.[2]

"I adore all the victorious, the Tathāgatas, the vanquishers of the enemy, the very pure, the perfect Buddhas, the past, the not arrived (future), and the present Buddhas.[3]

"I adore the protector of the creatures, *k*Lu-*s*grub*s*, the hero; Guru Padma; *d*Pal Na-ro-va; *d*Pal Bi-ma-la-

[1] The Buddhists count six classes of existence. Those in hell, the brute, Asur, and Yidag, are considered as bad existences; those of man and god as the good grades.

[2] See p. 109.

[3] An analogous phrase to one occurring at the commencement of the address; its meaning was explained at p. 126.

mitra; Pandita A-ti-sha,[1] &c.; together with the succession of holy Lamas.[2]

"(This book) *s*Dig-*b*shag*s*-*g*ser-kyi*s*-*s*pu-gri is able to subdue, to burn, to destroy hell. It will be a consolation to the animated beings in that period of distress and misery,[3] when in the (places for the) representatives of the Buddha, of his precepts, and of his

[1] These are Indian priests who were very celebrated for their zeal in the propagation of Buddhism; with the exception of Lugrub, the first of this series, they all took an active part in spreading its doctrines throughout Tíbet. Lugrub, in Sanskrit Nāgārjuna, is regarded as the founder of the Mahāyāna system. See p. 30. Guru Padma is the famous teacher Padma Sambhava, who was sent for by king Thisrong de tsan, and is said to have reached Tíbet A.D. 747. Bimala mitra also came to Tíbet in accordance with an invitation from this king. See Schmidt in "Ssanang Ssetsen," p. 356. Na-ro-va, who is enumerated before Bimala mitra, must doubtless have been contemporaneous with him and Padma Sambhava. Pandita Atisha, the last of the series, has a great reputation for re-establishing Buddhism after the persecutions of its followers under the reigns of Langdharma and his successors (902-71).

[2] The Tibetan *b*la-ma-dam-pa-*b*rgyud, is an honorary title applied to the priests with whom originated a specific system of Buddhism. In a subsequent sentence, and also in the document relating to the foundation of the Hímis monastery, we shall find them called "Foundation-Lamas," in Tibetan *r*tsa-va'i-*b*la-ma.

[3] In Tibetan *b*skal-ba-*s*nyig-ma. According to the notions of the Buddhists, as well as of the Brahmans, the universe, which is without beginning or end, is periodically destroyed and constructed again, these revolutions passing through four different periods, or Kalpas, viz.: the periods of formation, and of the continuance of formation; and those of the destruction, and disappearance of the universe. Here the Kalpa of destruction is referred to, and it is foretold that man shall obtain absolution from his sins by reading this book. The universe is dissolved and consumed by the powers of fire, water, and wind, which effect its entire destruction in sixty-four attacks upon its substance. The moral condition of man previous to the several agencies coming into action is stated as follows: "Before the destruction by water, cruelty or violence prevails in the world; before that by fire, licentiousness, and before that by wind, ignorance. When licentiousness has prevailed, men are cut off by disease; when violence, by turning their weapons against each other, and when ignorance, by famine." Hardy, "Manual of Buddhism," pp. 28-35; Schmidt, Mém. de l'Acad. de Pétersb., Vol. II., pp. 58-68.

mercy,[1] men shall cut stuffs woven of cotton, and work it, when cut, to garments; when there they take meat; when there they buy and trade with goods; when the Gelongs[2] break down inhabited places; when the astrologers[3] invoke good fortune;[4] when the Bonpo[5] carry with them (listen to) the secret mystical sentences (Dhāranīs); when the Gebshi are the commanders in

[1] This phrase is to be understood as a sort of prediction that the temples shall be desecrated by worldly negociations; for it is in the temples that are put up the three reprēsentatives (Tibetan Tensumni) of the Buddha, his precepts, and his mercy.

The Buddha is figured as a statue, a bas-relief, or a picture. The pictures hang down from the cross-beams of the roof, or are traced on the walls; the statues and bas-reliefs show him in a sitting attitude, and are placed behind the altar in a recess. The precepts which he bequeathed to man after his departure from earth, are symbolized by a book, which lies upon a lower step of the altar, or rests upon a shelf suspended from the roof. His mercy, or unlimited charity, which enabled him to obtain the sublime rank of a Buddha, in order to lead man to salvation, is signified by a Chorten, a pyramidal chest containing relics, which always occupies a prominent place upon the altar. See Csoma, "Grammar," p. 173, "Dictionary," *voce* *r*ten;—also Schmidt's Lexicon. For further details about images of gods see Chapter XIV.; for books, see p. 80; Chortens, Chapter XIII. For the place which these objects occupy in temples, I may refer to the Chapter on the temples, and to the view of the interior of the temple at Mangnáng, in Gnári Khórsum, by my brother Adolphe in the Atlas to the "Results of a Scientific Mission."

[2] The term *d*ge-*s*long is applied to ordained priests, who, however, are generally called by the more honourable title of Lama (*b*la-ma), a distinction strictly belonging only to the superiors of convents. The Gelongs must not care for riches or worldly prosperity; their breaking down inhabited places may mean, perhaps, their fighting against other monasteries or against rich men in general.

[3] In Tibetan *s*ngags-pa, *one versed in charms.*

[4] In Tibetan *g*yang-'gug*s*; a ceremony of this nature will be noticed in a subsequent chapter. The allusion here is to the abuse of it as a substitute for prayers.

[5] Bon-po is the name of the followers of the sect which adheres in the closest manner to the superstitious ideas transferred from the earlier Tibetan creed; comp. p. 74.

chief;[1] when the learned and poor (= the priests) live in and preside over the nunneries;[2] when the Zhanglons[3] amuse themselves with their daughters-in-law; when men destroy (eat) the meat destined for the manes of the dead; when the head Lamas eat the meat prepared for offerings;[4] when men cut themselves off from the vital principle (commit suicide[5]); when bad actions increase upon earth; when the song Mani shall be returned in answer;[6] when the calves of the Dzo[7] breed shall devastate (the fields); when men covet the goods of others; when the saints[8] travel and establish trade;

[1] *D*ge-*b*shes, abreviated from *d*ge-bai-*b*shes-*g*nyen, in Sanskrit Kalyānamitra, meaning a learned priest, a friend to virtue. It is hardly necessary to say that the functions of a military chief do not agree very well with the clerical character.

[2] The priests are not allowed to have intercourse with women, but the violation of this precept is but too probable by their dwelling under the same roof with nuns.

[3] Zhang, "a maternal-uncle;" *b*lon, "a magistrate, an officer, a nobleman;" the two words in connexion designate a man of superior rank.

[4] The Tibetan has zan, which is explained in the dictionaries as "meat, a kind of thick potage, dough, or paste made of the meal or flour of parched grains." As an instance of its use for food in general see the details in Hermann's "Glossary," *s. v.* Zánkhar, in Vol. III., of the "Results," &c., and R. A. Soc., 1862.

[5] Deliverance from existence is only the consequence of good actions; but suicide is also in the opinion of the Buddhists a bad action, and has a re-birth in a lower degree as one of its consequences, since the sins for the expiation of which the present existence had to be endured, are not yet atoned for, and also a new crime is committed. In the period of misery alluded to in the text, however, also this moral law will be overlooked.

[6] By Mani the famous six-syllable prayer Om mani padme hum, "O, the Jewel in the Lotus: Amen," is to be understood; the allusion in the text refers to its conversion into a popular song.

[7] *m*Dzo, a mixed breed, the offspring of a Yak (*bos gruniens*) and a common common Indian Zhebu cow; in the language of the Himálaya tribes it is called Chubu. The Dzos are one of the few mixed species which are capable of propagation, and they outnumber in some valleys the pure Yaks.

[8] In Tibetan nal-jor, in Sanskrit Yogāchārya, "a saint, a devotee," is also the name of a religious sect, which enjoyed the most favour in India until the seventh century A.D.—Respecting its history and religious tenets, see Chapter V.

when fraud is committed with measure[1] and weight; when the Chinese trade with little children (which they would obtain from the Tibetans); when under the gates (of the temples) illusory miracles (sorcery) shall be practised; when men eat and drink and care but for this actual existence; when there shall be no more gratuities; when the time shall arrive that old customs are disturbed (changed); when men shall be given up to the ravages of war and the enemy; when frost, hail, and drought shall spread (make general) famine;[2] when men and animal beings shall have to suffer from bad actions:[3] then, in this period of distress and misery this *s*Dig-*b*shags-*g*ter-chhos will be an ablution for every kind of sin which has been accumulated in the meantime; all animated beings shall read it, and on account of it all sins shall be wiped away."[4]

Translation of the second part.

"Enshrined in the sacred box at the time of the uttering of benedictions.[5]

"In this period of distress and misery, when many

[1] The Tibetan bre, also pronounced pre, is, according to Csoma's Dictionary, "a dry measure, the twentieth part of a Tibetan bushel."

[2] Some words are here illegible.

[3] For the Buddhist theory on the influence of good and bad actions upon well-being, see p. 93.

[4] The last four lines of the original text have been so much injured that only a few of the words could be deciphered, enough, however, remaining to give a clue to the meaning.

[5] With reference to the religious rites and ceremonies connected with the erection of Chortens, see Chapter XIII.

living beings shall suffer and sigh for deliverance, these benedictions shall afford great advantages to sinners. The sins which arise from discord and dispute among the inhabitants of this monastery[1] shall be taken away through them.

"These blessings, if recited on the 8th, 15th, and 30th of every month, purify most surely from the five great crimes,[2] and from all sins, and deliver from the six kinds of hell. The 84,000 great emblems of the essence of the sublime doctrine shall be the same with every being.[3] The mind of man shall become unchangeably directed towards attaining the sanctity of a Buddha; he shall gain the energetic will of the Buddha, and shall in the end obtain the advantages of a Buddha himself.

"This is the end of the Mahāyāna Sūtra *s*Dig-*b*shags-*g*ser-gyi*s*-*s*pu-gri.

"All beings be blessed!"

[1] The name of the monastery is not given in the original, which only says, *d*gon-pa "a monastery".

[2] The five great crimes of the Buddhists are: 1. The taking of life; 2. Theft; 3. Adultery; 4. Lying; 5. Drunkenness. See Burnouf, "Lotus de la Bonne Loi," p. 447; Hardy, "Manual of Buddhism," Chapter X., p. 488.

[3] This phrase refers, as may be seen from the sequel, to the inferior signs of a Buddha's beauty. They are generally stated to be 80 in number, but other books, as *e. g.* the Rgya-chher-rol-pa (translated by Foucaux, Vol. II., p. 108) give 84, which, in the present treatise, have been multiplied by 1000. The number of 84,000 is a most favourite one in Buddhist cosmogony and seems to be used in the same way as Khrag-khrig, "a hundred thousand millions" (p. 130), and the Chinese Wan, or 10,000 (Ideler, "Ueber die Zeitrechnung der Chinesen," p. 10), as the designation of an infinite number. The extent, thickness, and diameter of the sakwalas can always be divided by 8; the prolongation of the age of mankind continues for 84,000 years. See Hardy, "Manual," Chapter I.; Foe koue ki, p. 127.

(Three Dhāranīs, in corrupt Sanskrit, now follow. The first Dhāranī is a mystic invocation of Dorjesempa, Sanskrit Vajrasattva (see p. 50); in the second Dhāranī is condensed the belief in the four truths (see p. 16); the third Dhāranī is recited at the inauguration of the temples; now the text continues:[1]

"By means of these invocations the creatures become perfect in the two collections;[2] they shall be purified from their sins and blessed with the dignity of a most perfect Buddha.

(A fourth Dhāranī follows).

"This (Dhāranī) is raised (granted) as a favour[3] to the wanderers in the orb for not having paid reverence to parents—instead of thankfully remembering favours received—nor to the holy Foundation-Lamas,[4] who have obtained perfection by virtues.

"All sins committed by taking life, together with the transgressions accumulated in previous existences, the sins of lying, envy, and wickedness which proceed from the mind—all these sins are abolished by this sublime doctrine.

"Most perfect Sages, be gracious and clement, if I should not have rendered rightly the letters of the

[1] The transcription of these three Dharānīs has been omitted from considerations of brevity.

[2] In Tibetan ts'hogs-gnyis; by this term is understood the combination of the highest perfection in the practice of virtues, and the highest degree of wisdom, both of which are reserved for the Buddhas; but simple men can attain this sublimest rank by following the path revealed by Sākyamuni and his acknowledged predecessors.

[3] It delivers from the sins specified.

[4] In Tibetan *r*tsa-vai-*b*la-ma; in a foregoing passage they were styled *b*la-ma-dam-pa-*b*rgyud. See p. 136.

alphabet.[1] Mi-*r*gan-*s*de-*g*sal-*r*do-rje has written it. Praised be this sheet, that he may gain entire deliverance from his sins. This *s*Dig-*b*shags-*g*ser-gyis-*s*pu-gri has been completed in two days."

[1] For explanation of this sentence I refer to p. 56.

DIGPA THAMCHAD SHAGPAR TERCHOI,

AN ADDRESS TO THE BUDDHAS OF CONFESSION.

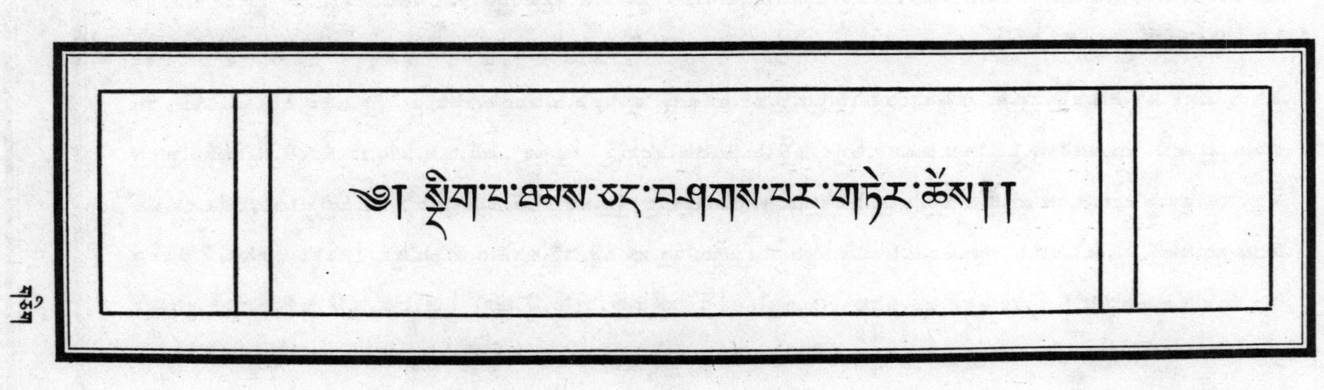

༄༅། །རྒྱ་གར་སྐད་དུ།···།ན་མོ་སཏྲ་ཡེ་མ་ལ་ཏ་ཐ་ག་ཏ་ཧྲད་ཏྱཱ། བོད་སྐད་དུ། སྡིག་པ་ཐམས་ཅད་བཤགས་པར···། ཕྱོགས་བཅུ་དུས་གསུམ་
དེ་བཞིན་དགྲ་བཅོམ་པ་ཡང་དག་པར་རྫོགས་པའི་སངས་རྒྱས་སོ་སོ་དཔལ་ཐམས་ཅད་ལ་ཕྱག་འཚལ་ལོ་། མཆོད་པ་འབུལ་ལོ། སྡིག་པ་བཤགས་སོ།
དགེ་བའི་རྩ་བ་ལ་རྗེས་སུ་ཡི་རང་ངོ་། ཆོས་ཀྱི་འཁོར་ལོ་བསྐོར་རོ། གསོལ་ལོ། སངས་རྒྱས་ཐམས་ཅད་ཀྱི་སྐུ་མྱ་ངན་ལས་མི་འདའ་བར་
བཞུགས་སུ་གསོལ་བ་འདེབས། དགེ་བའི་རྩ་བ་རྣམས་བྱང་ཆུབ་ཆེན་པོར་བསྔོའོ། དེ་བཞིན་གཤེགས་པ་དགྲ་བཅོམ་པ་ཡང་དག་པར་རྫོགས་པའི་སངས་
རྒྱས་ནམ་མཁའ་དཔལ་དྲི་མེད་རྣལ་རབ་མཛེས་ལ་ཕྱག་འཚལ་ལོ། དེ་བཞིན་གཤེགས་པ་ཡོན་ཏན་ཏོག་གི་འོད་ལ་མེ་ཏོག་པད་མ་བཻཌཱུརྱའི་འོད་ཟེར་རིན་
པོ་ཆེའི་གཟུགས་ལྷ་བུའི་སྐུ་དང་ལྡན་པ་ལ་ཕྱག་འཚལ་ལོ། དེ་བཞིན་གཤེགས་པ་སྤོས་མཆོག་དམ་པས་མཆོད་པའི་སྐུ་རྣམས་པར་སྤྲས་ཤིང་ལེགས་
པར་རྒྱན་པ་ལ་ཕྱག་འཚལ་ལོ། དེ་བཞིན་གཤེགས་པ་གཙུག་ཏོར་གྱི་གཙུག་ནས་ཉི་མའི་འོད་ཟེར་དཔག་མེད་ཟླ་འོད་སྒྲོན་ལམ་གྱིས་རྒྱན་པ་ལ་ཕྱག་
འཚལ་ལོ། དེ་བཞིན་གཤེགས་པ་རབ་སྣང་བཀོད་པ་ཆེན་པོ་ཆོས་ཀྱི་དབྱིངས་ལས་མངོན་པར་འཕགས་པ་ཆགས་དང་ལྡན་ཟླ་མེད་རིན་ཆེན་འབྱུང་ལྡན་
ལ་ཕྱག་འཚལ་ལོ། དེ་བཞིན་གཤེགས་པ་རྒྱ་ཟླའི་གདོན་ཏུ་ཉི་མའི་སྒྲོན་མ་ཟླ་བའི་མེ་ཏོག་རིན་ཆེན་པད་མ་གསེར་གྱི་འདུ་ནི་མཁའ་ལྷ་བུའི་སྐུ་དང་
ལྡན་པ་རྣམ་པར་སྣང་མཛད་ལ་ཕྱག་འཚལ་ལོ། དེ་བཞིན་གཤེགས་པ་ཕྱོགས་བཅུ་ན་བཞུགས་པའི་འོད་ཟེར་རབ་ཏུ་འགྱེད་ཅིང་འཇིག་རྟེན་གྱི་ནམ་
མཁའ་ཀུན་ཏུ་སྣང་བར་བྱེད་པ་ལ་ཕྱག་འཚལ་ལོ། དེ་བཞིན་གཤེགས་པ་སངས་རྒྱས་ཀྱི་བཀོད་པ་ཐམས་ཅད་རབ་ཏུ་རྒྱས་པར་མཛད་པ་ལ་ཕྱག་
འཚལ་ལོ། དེ་བཞིན་གཤེགས་པ་སངས་རྒྱས་ཀྱི་དགོངས་པ་བསྒྲུབས་པ་ལ་ཕྱག་འཚལ་ལོ། དེ་བཞིན་གཤེགག་ས་དྲི་མེད་ཟླ་བའི་མེ་ཏོག་གི་བཀོད་པ་
མཛད་ལ་ཕྱག་འཚལ་ལོ། དེ་བཞིན་གཤེགས་པ་རིན་ཆེན་མཆོག་གིས་མེ་ཏོག་གྲགས་ལྡན་ལ་ཕྱག་འཚལ་ལོ། དེ་བཞིན་བཤེགས་པ་འཇིགས་མེད་རྣམ་

པར་གཟིགས་ལ་ཕྱག་འཚལ་ལོ། དེ་བཞིན་གཤེགས་པ་འཇིགས་པ་དང་བྲལ་ཞིང་བག་ཆགས་མི་མངའ་ཞིང་སྤུ་ཟིང་ཞེས་མི་བྱེད་པ་ལ་ཕྱག་འཚལ་ལོ། དེ་བཞིན་གཤེགས་པ་སེང་གེ་སྒྲ་དབྱངས་ལ་ཕྱག་འཚལ་ལོ། དེ་བཞིན་གཤེགས་པ་གསེར་འོད་གཟི་བརྗིད་ཀྱི་རྒྱལ་པོ་ལ་ཕྱག་འཚལ་ལོ། . སངས་རྒྱས་ཀྱི་མཚན་འདི་དག་ནི་སེམས་ཅན་གང་ལ་ཞིག་གིས་ཡི་གེ་བྲིས་འམ། འཆང་ཞིང་ཀློག་འམ། ཡི་དམ་དུ་བྱས་ནས་སེམས་ཅན་ཐམས་ཅད་ཅན་གྱི་དོན་དུ་བསྔོས་ན་སྡིག་པ་སྒྲིབ་ཐམས་ཅད་བྱང་ཞིང་དག་ནས་ནུབ་ཕྱོགས་ཀྱི་བདེ་བ་ཅན་དུ་སྐྱེ་བར་འགྱུར་རོ། སངས་རྒྱས་ཀྱི་ཞིང་བདེ་བ་ཅན་ན་ཡོད་པ་ན་དེ་བཞིན་གཤེགས་པ་ཚེ་དཔག་ཏུ་མེད་པ་ལ་ཕྱག་འཚལ་ལོ། སངས་རྒྱས་ཀྱི་ཞིང་ངུར་སྨྲིག་གི་རྒྱལ་མཚན་ན་དེ་བཞིན་གཤེགས་པ་རྡོ་རྗེ་རབ་ཏུ་འཛིན་པ་ལ་ཕྱག་འཚལ་ལོ། སངས་རྒྱས་ཀྱི་ཞིང་ཕྱིར་མི་ལྡོག་པའི་འཁོར་ལོ་རབ་ཏུ་སྒྲོག་པ་ན་དེ་བཞིན་གཤེགས་པ་པད་མོ་ཤིན་ཏུ་རྒྱས་པ་ལ་ཕྱག་འཚལ་ལོ། སངས་རྒྱས་ཀྱི་ཞིང་རྡུལ་མེད་པ་ན་དེ་བཞིན་གཤེགས་པ་ཆོས་ཀྱི་རྒྱལ་མཚན་ལ་ཕྱག་འཚལ་ལོ། སངས་རྒྱས་ཀྱི་ཞིང་སྒྲོན་ལ་བཟང་པོ་ན་དེ་བཞིན་གཤེགས་པ་སེང་གེ་སྒྲ་དབྱངས་རྒྱལ་པོ་ལ་ཕྱག་འཚལ་ལོ། སངས་རྒྱས་ཀྱི་ཞིང་འོད་ཟེར་བཟང་པོ་ན་དེ་བཞིན་གཤེགས་པ་རྣམས་པར་སྣང་མཛད་རྒྱལ་པོ་ལ་ཕྱག་འཚལ་ལོ། སངས་རྒྱས་ཀྱི་ཞིང་འདའ་བར་དཀའ་བ་ན་དེ་བཞིན་གཤེགས་པ་ཆོས་ཀྱི་འོད་ཟེར་གྱི་སྐུ་པད་མོ་ཤིན་ཏུ་རྒྱས་པ་ལ་ཕྱག་འཚལ་ལོ། སངས་རྒྱས་ཀྱི་རྒྱན་དང་ལྡན་པ་ན་དེ་བཞིན་གཤེགས་པ་མངོན་པར་མཁྱེན་པ་ཐམས་ཅད་ཀྱི་འོད་ཟེར་ལ་ཕྱག་འཚལ་ལོ། སངས་རྒྱས་ཀྱི་ཞིང་མེ་ལོང་གི་དཀྱིལ་འཁོར་མདོག་འདྲ་ན་དེ་བཞིན་གཤེགས་པ་འོད་མི་འཁྲུགས་པ་ལ་ཕྱག་འཚལ་ལོ། སངས་རྒྱས་ཀྱི་ཞིང་པད་མོའི་དཔལ་གྱི་སྙིང་པོ་ལ་ཕྱག་འཚལ་ལོ། སངས་རྒྱས་ཀྱི་ཞིང་སྟོང་ཕྱོགས་དག་པའི་གནས་ན། བཅོམ་ལྡན་འདས་དེ་བཞིན་གཤེགས་པ་དགྲ་བཅོམ་པ་ཡང་དག་པར་རྫོགས་པའི་སངས་རྒྱས་ངན་འགྲོ་ཐམས་ཅད་རྣམ་པར་འཇོམས་པ་འཕགས་པ་གཟི་བརྗིད་སྒྲ་དབྱངས་ཀྱི་རྒྱལ་པོ་ལ་ཕྱག་འཚལ་ལོ། འདི་རྣམས་

མདོ་ཞལ་པོ་ཆེ་ནས་གསུངས་སོ། ཡང་སངས་རྒྱས་ཤཱཀྱ་ཐུབ་པ་ཞེས་བྱ་བ་ཏ་ཐཱ་ག་ཏ་བྱེ་བ་ཁྲག་ཁྲིག་སུམ་བཅུ་འབྱུང་བ་ལ་ཕྱག་འཚལ་ལོ། འདིའི་མཚན་ལན་གཅིག་བརྗོད་པས་སྐྱེ་བ་སུམ་ཅུའི་སྡིག་པ་ཐམས་ཅད་བྱང་བར་གསུངས་སོ། སངས་རྒྱས་མར་མེ་མཛད་ཅེས་བྱ་བ་ཁྲི་བརྒྱད་སྟོང་ལ་ཕྱག་འཚལ་ལོ། འདི་ལན་གཅིག་བརྗོད་པས་མར་མེ་དཀོར་ལ་འབགས་པའི་སྡིག་པ་ཐམས་ཅད་བྱང་བར་གསུངས་སོ། སངས་རྒྱས་རབ་ཏུ་འབར་བ་ཞེས་བྱ་བ་ཏ་ཐཱ་ག་ཏ་ཁྲི་དྲུག་སྟོང་ལ་ཕྱག་འཚལ་ལོ། འདི་ལན་གཅིག་བརྗོད་པས་ཕ་མ་དང་སློབ་དཔོན་ལ་བསྐུར་པ་བཏབས་པ་དང་ཉེས་པ་བྱས་པའི་སྡིག་པ་ཐམས་ཅད་བྱང་བར་གསུངས་སོ། སངས་རྒྱས་སྐར་རྒྱལ་ཞེས་བྱ་བ་ཏ་ཐཱ་ག་ཏ་བྱེ་བ་ཕྲག་གསུམ་སྟོང་ལ་ཕྱག་འཚལ་ལོ། འདི་ལན་གཅིག་བརྗོད་པས་ཆོས་ལ་དཀོར་ལ་འབགས་པའི་སྡིག་པ་ཐམས་ཅད་བྱང་བར་གསུངས་སོ། སངས་རྒྱས་ཟླ་བའི་རྒྱལ་པོ་ཞེས་བྱ་བ་ཏ་ཐཱ་ག་ཏ་ཁྲི་བརྒྱད་སྟོང་ལ་ཕྱག་འཚལ་ལོ། འདི་ལན་གཅིག་བརྗོད་པས་མ་བྱིན་བླངས་ལ་སོགས་པའི་སྡིག་པ་ཐམས་ཅད་བྱང་བར་གསུངས་སོ། སངས་རྒྱས་པད་མ་འབགས་པ་ཞེས་བྱ་བ་ཏ་ཐཱ་ག་ཏ་ཁྲི་ལྔ་སྟོང་ལ་ཕྱག་འཚལ་ལོ། འདི་ལན་གཅིག་བརྗོད་པས་མཆོད་རྟེན་གྱི་དཀོར་ལ་འབགས་པ་དང་ཚེམ་སེམས་བྱས་པའི་སྡིག་པ་ཐམས་ཅད་བྱང་བར་གསུངས་སོ! སངས་རྒྱས་ཀོཎྜ་འདི་ནེའི་རིགས་ཞེས་བྱ་བ་ཏ་ཐཱ་ག་ཏ་བྱེ་བ་ཁྲག་དགུ་བཅུ་ལ་ཕྱག་འཚལ་ལོ། འདི་ལན་གཅིག་བརྗོད་པས་རྨོས་བསྐོལ་བྱས་པའི་སྡིག་པ་ཐམས་ཅད་བྱང་བར་གསུངས་སོ། སངས་རྒྱས་སྟོང་ཕྲག་དགུ་བཅུ་ལ་ཕྱག་འཚལ་ལོ། སངས་རྒྱས་འོད་བསྲུང་ཞེས་བྱ་བ་ཏ་ཐཱ་ག་ཏ་སྟོང་ཕྲག་དགུ་སྟོང་ལ་ཕྱག་འཚལ་ལོ། སངས་རྒྱས་བྱེ་བ་ཕྲག་གདུགའི་ཀླུང་གི་བྱེ་མ་སྙེད་ཀྱི་གྲངས་དང་མཉམ་པ་རྣམས་ལ་ཕྱག་འཚལ་ལོ། སངས་རྒྱས་ཀུན་ཏུ་སྣང་བ་ལ་སོགས་པ་མཆེད་བ་དང་བ་སྟོང་འབྱུང་བ་ལ་ཕྱག་འཚལ་ལོ། སངས་རྒྱས་འཛམ་བུ་འདུལ་བ་ཞེས་བྱ་བ་ཏ་ཐཱ་ག་ཏ་སྟོང་ཕྲག་ཉི་ཤུ་ལ་ཕྱག་འཚལ་ལོ། སངས་རྒྱས་གསེར་མདོག་དྲི་མེད་འོད་ཟེར་ཞེས་བྱ་བ་ཏ་ཐཱ་ག་ཏ་དྲུག་ཁྲི་ཉིས་སྟོང་ལ་ཕྱག་འཚལ་ལོ། སངས་རྒྱས་དཔང་

པོའི་རྒྱལ་པོའི་རྒྱལ་མཚན་ཞེས་བྱ་བ་ཁྲ་སྟག་བརྒྱད་ཁྲི་བཞི་སྟོང་ལ་ཕྱག་འཚལ་ལོ། སངས་རྒྱས་ཉི་མའི་སྙིང་པོ་ཞེས་བྱ་བ་ཁྲ་སྟག་ཁྲི་ལྷག་ལྔ་བརྒྱ་ལ་ལ་
ཕྱག་འཚལ་ལོ། སངས་རྒྱས་ཞི་བར་མཛད་པ་ཅེས་བྱ་བ་ཁྲ་སྟག་དྲུག་ཁྲི་ཉིས་སྟོང་ལ་ཕྱག་འཚལ་ལོ། སངས་རྒྱས་དེ་དག་ཐམས་ཅད་ཀྱི་ཉན་ཐོས་དང་
བྱང་ཆུབ་སེམས་དཔའི་ཚོགས་དང་བཅས་པ་ཐམས་ཅད་ལ་ཕྱག་འཚལ་ལོ། འདི་རྣམས་མདོ་སྡེ་རི་མ་པ་ལྔ་ནས་གསུངས་སོ། བཅོམ་ལྡན་འདས་དེ་བཞིན་
གཤེགས་པ་དགྲ་བཅོམ་པ་ཡང་དག་པར་རྫོགས་པའི་སངས་རྒྱས་རིན་ཆེན་རྒྱལ་པོའི་མཛོད་ལ་ཕྱག་འཚལ་ལོ། འདིའི་མཚན་ལན་གཅིག་བརྗོད་པས་ཆེ་
གཅིག་ལ་བསྐྱོན་པ་ཞོམ་པའི་སྡིག་པ་དག་གོ། བཅོམ་ལྡན་འདས་དེ་བཞིན་གཤེགས་པ་དགྲ་བཅོམ་པ་ཡང་དག་པར་རྫོགས་པའི་སངས་རྒྱས་རིན་ཆེན་འོད་ཀྱི་
རྒྱལ་པོ་མེ་འོད་རབ་ཏུ་གསལ་བ་ལ་ཕྱག་འཚལ་ལོ། འདིའི་མཚན་ལན་གཅིག་བརྗོད་པས་ཆེ་གཅིག་ལ་དགེ་འདུན་གྱི་དཀོར་ལ་འཕགས་པའི་སྡིག་པ་དག་གོ།
བཅོམ་ལྡན་འདས་དེ་བཞིན་གཤེགས་པ་དགྲ་བཅོམ་པ་ཡང་དག་པར་རྫོགས་པའི་སངས་རྒྱས་སྨྲས་དང་མེ་ཏོག་ལ་དབང་བ་སྟོབས་ཀྱི་རྒྱལ་པོ་ལ་ཕྱག་འཚལ་
ལོ། འདིའི་མཚན་ལན་གཅིག་བརྗོད་པས་ཚུལ་འཁྲིམས་འཆལ་བའི་སྡིག་པ་དག་གོ། བཅོམ་ལྡན་འདས་དེ་བཞིན་གཤེགས་པ་དགྲ་བཅོམ་པ་ཡང་དག་པར་
རྫོགས་པའི་སངས་རྒྱས་གདུགས་ཀྱི་གླིང་གི་བྱེ་མ་སྙེད་བྱེ་བ་ལྷག་བརྒྱའི་གྲངས་དང་མཉམ་པར་ངེས་པ་ལ་ཕྱག་འཚལ་ལོ། འདིའི་མཚན་ལན་གཅིག་བརྗོད་པས་
ཆེ་གཅིག་སྲོག་གཅོད་པའི་སྡིག་པ་དག་གོ། བཅོམ་ལྡན་འདས་དེ་བཞིན་གཤེགས་པ་དགྲ་བཅོམ་པ་ཡང་དག་པར་རྫོགས་པའི་སངས་རྒྱས་རིན་ཆེན་རྡོ་རྗེ་
དཔལ་བརྟན་ཞིང་འདུལ་བ་པ་རོལ་གྱི་སྟོབས་རབ་ཏུ་འཇོམས་པ་ལ་ཕྱག་འཚལ་ལོ། འདིའི་མཚན་ལན་གཅིག་བརྗོད་པས་རྒྱལ་བའི་བཀའ་ཆར་གཅིག་
བཀླགས་པ་དང་བསྐོར་ནམས་མཉམ་མོ། བཅོམ་ལྡན་འདས་དེ་བཞིན་གཤེགས་པ་དགྲ་བཅོམ་པ་ཡང་དག་པར་རྫོགས་པའི་སངས་རྒྱས་གཟི་བརྗིད་ངེས་
པར་རྣམ་པར་གནོན་པ་ལ་ཕྱག་འཚལ་ལོ། འདིའི་མཚན་ལན་གཅིག་བརྗོད་པས་ཆེ་གཅིག་འདོད་ལོགས་སྤྱད་པའི་སྡིག་པ་དག་གོ། བཅོམ་ལྡན་འདས་དེ་

བཞིན་གཤེགས་པ་དགྲ་བཅོམ་པ་ཡང་དག་པར་རྫོགས་པའི་སངས་རྒྱས་རིན་ཆེན་ཟླ་འོད་སྐྱབས་གནས་དམ་པ་དགྲ་ལས་རྣམ་པར་རྒྱལ་བ་ལ་ཕྱག་འཚལ་ལོ།
འདིའི་མཚན་ལན་གཅིག་བརྗོད་པས་དཀྱིལ་བ་མནར་མེད་དུ་སྐྱེ་ངེས་པའི་སྡིག་པ་དག་གོ། བཅོམ་ལྡན་འདས་དེ་བཞིན་གཤེགས་པ་དགྲ་བཅོམ་པ་ཡང་དག
པར་རྫོགས་པའི་སངས་རྒྱས་རིན་ཆེན་གཙུག་ཏོར་ཅན་ལ་ཕྱག་འཚལ་ལོ། འདིའི་མཚན་ལན་གཅིག་བརྗོད་པས་སེམས་ཅན་གང་གིས་ཐོས་པ་དེ་ངན་སོང
དུ་མི་སྐྱེ་ཞིང་ལྷ་དང་མི་ལུས་ཕུན་གསུམ་ཚོགས་པ་ཐོབ་པར་འགྱུར་རོ། བཅོམ་ལྡན་འདས་དེ་བཞིན་གཤེགས་པ་དགྲ་བཅོམ་པ་ཡང་དག་པར་རྫོགས
པའི་སངས་རྒྱས་རྒྱལ་བ་རྒྱ་མཚོའི་ཚོགས་དང་བཅས་པ་རྣམས་ལ་ཕྱག་འཚལ་ལོ། འདིའི་མཚན་ལན་བརྗོད་པས་དམ་ཚིག་ཉམས་ཆགས་དང་གསོ་སྦྱོང་བྱས་པ
ལ་སོགས་པའི་སྡིག་པ་ཐམས་ཅད་བྱང་བར་གསུངས་སོ། བཅོམ་ལྡན་འདས་དེ་བཞིན་གཤེགས་པ་དགྲ་བཅོམ་པ་ཡང་དག་པར་རྫོགས་པའི་སངས་རྒྱས
ཚེའི་ཕྲམ་པ་འཛིན་པ་རྣམ་ལ་ཕྱག་འཚལ་ལོ། འདིས་སེམས་ཅན་ཐམས་ཅད་དུས་མ་ཡིན་པར་འཆི་བའི་འཇིགས་པ་ལས་ཐར་པར་འགྱུར་རོ། བཅོམ
ལྡན་འདས་དེ་བཞིན་གཤེགས་པ་དགྲ་བཅོམ་པ་ཡང་དག་པར་རྫོགས་པའི་སངས་རྒྱས་འདས་པ་དང་མ་བྱོན་པ་དང་། ད་ལྟར་བཞུགས་པ་ཐམས་ཅད་ལ
ཕྱག་འཚལ་ལོ། འགྲོ་བའི་མགོན་པོ་ཀླུ་སྒྲུབ་དཔའ་བོ་དང་། གུ་རུ་པདྨ་དང་། དཔལ་ན་རོ་པ་དང་། དཔལ་བི་མ་ལ་མིཏྲ་དང་། བརྟེན་ཨ་ཏི་ཤ
ལ་སོགས་པ་བླ་མ་དམ་པ་བརྒྱུད་པར་བཅས་པ་རྣམས་ལ་ཕྱག་འཚལ་ལོ། སྡིག་བཤགས་གསེར་གྱིས་སྦྲུ་གྲི་ཞེས་པར་དཀྱིལ་བ་འཇོམས་པའི་སྨིག་བཏར་འདི
བསྐལ་བ་སྙིགས་མའི་སེམས་ཅན་སྙིང་རྗེ་བ་སྐུ་གསུང་ཐུགས་ཀྱི་རྟེན་ལ་རས་ཆོད་དང་ཐབ་གཙོད་བྱས་ནས་ཟས་སུ་ཟ་བ་དང་། གོས་སུ་གྱོན་པ་དང་།
སྐུ་གསུང་ཐུགས་ཀྱི་རྟེན་ལ་ཉོ་ཚོང་བྱེད་དུ་བྱེད་པའི་དུས། དགེ་སློང་གྲོང་ཆོག་བྱེད་པའི་དུས། སྔགས་པ་གཡང་འགུགས་བྱེད་པའི་དུས། བོན་པོས
གསང་སྔགས་ཁྱེར་བའི་དུས། དགེ་བཤེས་དམག་དཔོན་བྱེད་པའི་དུས། ཆོས་མཁན་འཁོངས་འགྲིམ་པའི་དུས། ལྷ་ཁང་བུད་མེད་འཛིན་པའི་འདུས།

ཞང་བློན་མནའ་མ་ལ་དགའ་བའི་དུས། སྐྱེས་པ་མཚུན་གྱིས་བཀུམ་པའི་དུས། གནས་ཆེན་དགོར་ཟན་ཟ་བའི་དུས། རང་སྲོག་རང་གི་གཅོད་པའི་དུས། ལས་ངན་ནམ་ས་མང་བའི་ཚེ། རང་བཙུན་རང་ལ་བྱེད་པའི་དུས། མ་ཧེ་གླུ་ཙ་ལན་པའི་དུས། མཛོ་སྦུ་གུ་རྡོག་པའི་དུས། གཞན་གྱི་ཛས་ལ་འདོད་ཁ་སྐྱེ་བའི་དུས། རྣལ་འབྱོར་པ་འགྲོ་འགྲོ་རྒྱུ་འདེབས་པའི་དུས། སྔེ་དང་སྤང་ལ་གཡོ་སྒྱུ་བྱེད་པའི་དུས། རྒྱ་དང་ཚོང་ལ་ཁྲེ་ཐོགས་བྱེད་པའི་དུས། སྒོ་ལ་རྫུ་འཕྲུལ་འགྱུར་བའི་དུས། ཆེ་བྱེ་མ་མི་འདོན་འདི་ག་བསམ་པའི་དུས། དུས་・・・དུས་ཀྱི་མ་ལན་ལས་ངན་བསགས་པས་ལན། དུས་མི་འགྱུར་དེ་མི་རྣམ་འགྱུར་བས་ལན། ས་ཊོ་ལ་དམག་གནོད་སད་སེར་ཐན་པ་སྦུ་གེ་དར་བའི་དུས། པ་ལ་མནར་・・・・དུ་སྐྱེ་བའི་སེམས་ཅན་ལས་ངན་ཅན་ལ་དང་པོ་ཡོད་པའི་དུས། ・・・・རྣམ་ཀྱི་ནང་ན་བསགས། ・・・・དགའ་ཡོད་པས་སྡིག་བཀགས་གཏེར་ཆོས་・・・པར་ཤོག། ཅེ・・・ཀྱིས་སྨྲོན་ལམ་བཏབ་པ་ལགས་སོ། འདི་བསྐལ་པའི་སྙིགས་མའི་སེམས་ཅན་ཐམས་ཅད་ཅན・・・གླིག་དང་། ཁ་དོན་བྱས་ན་སྡིག་པ་ཐམས་ཅད・・・・། གྱེར་དེའི་སྡིག་པ་ཐམས་ཅད་བྱང་བར་གསུངས・・・གཏེར་ཆོས་・・・ས་སླིག་མ་ཚེལ་・・・།། ||

༄༅། །བའི་འོག་ཏུ་གཏེར་དུ་སྦས་ནས་སྨོན་ལམ་བཏབ་སྐད། བསྐལ་པ་སྙིགས་མའི་སེམས་ཅན་ལས་ངན་ཅན་སྙིང་རྗེ་བ་མང་པོ་ཡོད་པས་དེ་རྣམས་ཀྱི་ནང་ནས་ལས་འཕྲོ་ཅན་འགའ་ཡོད་པས་དེ་རྣམས་ཀྱི་འགྲོ་དོན་ཐུགས་མེད་དུ་སྡིག་པ་ཅན་རྣམ་ལ་ཕན་པར་གྱིས་ཤིག །འདི་དགོན་པར་བཞུགས་ན་སྡེ་འཁྲུགས་བྱས་པའི་སྡིག་པ་ཐམས་ཅད་བྱང་བར་གསུངས་སོ། འདི་ཀ་དང་། གནམ་སྙིང་དང་། ཆེས་བརྒྱད་གསུམ་ལ་ཚར་བདུན་གློགས་ན་འཆམས་མེད་ལྔའི་སྡིག་པ་དང་སྒྲིབ་པ་ཐམས་ཅད་བྱང་བར་ཐེ་ཚོམ་མེད་དོ། དཔལ་པ་རིགས་རྒྱུག་ལ་འཁོར་མི་དོ། ཆོས་ཀྱིས་སྐྱང་པོ་བརྒྱད་ཁྲི་བའི་སྙིང་རྣམ་

ཕྱག་རྒྱ་ཆེན་པོའི་སེམས་ཉིད་གཅིག་ལ་ལུས། དོན་དོ་སང་་སེམས་ཉིད་འགྱུར་་པ་མེད་པར་་མངོན་པར་་འཚང་རྒྱ། སངས་རྒྱས་ཀྱི་དགོངས་པ་མཐར་་ཕྱག་
ཡིན། ཕྱི་མ་འབྲས་བུ་སངས་རྒྱས་འགྲུབ་པར་་ཤོག། སྡིག་བཤགས་གསང་་གྱིས་སྦྱ་གི་ཉེས་བྱ་བ་ཐེག་པ་ཆེན་པོའི་མདོ་རྫོགས་སོ། སེམས་ཅན་ཐམས་
ཅད་དགེ་བའི་བཀྲ་ཤིས། ཨོཾ་བཛྲ་སཏྭ་ས་མ་ཡ། མ་ནུ་པ་ལ་ཡ། བཛྲ་སཏྭ་ཏེ་ནོ་པ་ཏིཥྛ། དྲྀ་ཌྷོ་མེ་བྷ་ཝ། སུ་ཏོ་ཥྱོ་མེ་བྷ་ཝ། སུ་པོ་ཥྱོ་མེ་བྷ་ཝ། ཨ་ནུ་
རཀྟོ་མེ་བྷ་ཝ། སརྦ་སིདྡྷི་མྨེ་པྲ་ཡ་ཙྪ། སརྦ་ཀརྨ་སུ་ཙ་མེ་ཙིཏྟཾ་ཤྲེ་ཡཾ་ཀུ་རུ་ཧཱུྃ། ཧ་ཧ་ཧ་ཧ་ཧོ། བྷ་ག་ཝཱན་སརྦ་ཏ་ཐཱ་ག་ཏ་བཛྲ་མཱ་མེ་མུ་ཉྩ་བཛྲཱི་བྷ་ཝ་མ་
ཧཱ་ས་མ་ཡ་སཏྭ་ཨཱཿ། ཨོཾ་ཡེ་དྷརྨཱ་ཧེ་ཏུ་པྲ་བྷཱ་ཝཱ་ཧེ་ཏུནྟེ་ཥཱན་ཏ་ཐཱ་ག་ཏོ་ཧྱ་ཝ་དཏ྄་ཏེ་ཥཱཉྩ་ཡོ་ནི་རོ་དྷ་ཨེ་ཝཾ་ཝཱ་དཱི་མ་ཧཱ་ཤྲ་མ་ཎ་ཡེ་སྭཱ་ཧཱ། ཨོཾ་སུ་པྲ་ཏི་
ཥྛ་བཛྲ་ཡེ་སྭཱ་ཧཱ། འདི་ལ་འབྲེལ་ཐམས་ཅད་ཚོགས་གཉིས་རྫོགས་སྒྲིབས་གཉིས་སྦྱངས་ནས་རྫོགས་པའི་སངས་རྒྱས་ཀྱིས་གོ་འཕང་ཐོབ་པའི་ཕྱིར་
བསྔོ་བའོ། པྲུཾ་བྲུ་བྲི་སྲུ་སརྦ་ཛ་ག་ཏི། དམ་ཆོས་འདི་བཞེངས་པའི་དགེ་ཐོབ་སྨན་པའི་ཕྱིར་་། རྩ་བའི་བླ་མའི་སྐུ་དྲིན་འཁོར་་བ་དང་་། ཕ་མ་གཉིས་
ཀྱིས་ལུས་དྲིན་ཆེས་ཀྱིས་མ་འཇལ། བདག་བཞིན་འཁོར་་བ་ཆེ་ར་བ་ཏུ་མ་ནས་བསགས་པའི་སྡིག་སྒྲིབ་ཉམས་ཆགས་ལུས་་གྱིས་མགོ་ནས་སྲོག་གཅོད་པ་
དང་་། ངག་གི་མགོ་ནས་རྫུན་སྨྲས་པ་དང་་། ཡིད་ཀྱིས་མགོ་ནས་རྣམས་སེམས་ཅན་གནོད་སེམས་ལོག་ལྟ་འཛིན་སེམས་གནོད་གིས་སྒྲོད་སེམས་ཐམས་
ཅད་བཤགས་སོ། ཡི་གེ་ཚུ་ལ་མེད་ཀྱང་མཁས་པ་རྣམ་ཀྱིས་བཟོད་པ་ཞེས་པ་བཞུ། མི་ཤད་སྲེ་གསལ་རྫ་རྫེ་གྲིས་པའོ། བཀྲ་ཤིས་པར་་ཤོག །སྡིག་
བཤགས་གསང་་གྱིས་སྦྱ་གིའི་སྡིག་པ་ཀུན་ཀྱང་སྦྱངས་པའི་ཕྱིར་། — ཉིན་ཕྱུང་གཉིས་ལ་འགྲུབས་པ་ཡིན།། ||

PART II

PRESENT LAMAIC INSTITUTIONS

CHAPTER XII

THE TIBETAN PRIESTHOOD

Materials contained in Reports of European Travellers.—Fundamental Laws.—Hierarchical System.—Organisation of the Clergy.—Principles of its constitution.—Revenues.—Grades amongst the Lamas.—Number of Lamas.—Occupations.—Diet.—Dress.

Reports of European Travellers.

By Lamaism Europeans designate that peculiar form of Buddhism which developed itself from Tsonkhapa's institutions in Tíbet and soon spread over all Central Asia, where it took deep root. Our knowledge of this most modern form of Buddhism is also of no long date; for to penetrate into Tíbet was always a matter of great difficulty, both on account of the impediments presented by the general great elevation of the country, as also by the jealous and hostile feelings of the natives towards foreigners. The supremacy gradually obtained by the Chinese Government has but increased the difficulty;

even quite recently it has proved its hostile disposition, notwithstanding the treaties signed after the last war in China.[1]

The first Europeans who penetrated into Tíbet were Christian missionaries. In the year 1624 a Jesuit, Pater Antonio de Andrada, travelled as far as Chábrang, the capital of the Gúge district of Gnári Khórsum, the Rāja, or Gyalpo, of which was very favourably inclined towards him. The first who reached Lhássa, the centre of the Lamaic church, were the Jesuits Albert Dorville and Johann Gruber, who, in 1661, returned from China viâ Tíbet and Hindostán to Europe. The next who followed them were the Capucine patres Josepho de Asculi and Francisco Maria de Toun, who started from Bengál in the year 1706 and safely reached Lhássa. In 1716 the Jesuit Desideri again penetrated up to Lhássa from the west, through Kashmír and Ladák. The most important event for our knowledge of Tibetan Buddhism was the Capucine mission under the superintendance of Horačio de la Penna, who, with five companions, arrived at Lhássa in the year 1741; their efforts to propagate the Christian faith had but little success, though they were kindly received by the Tibetan authorities. They collected much valuable information concerning the geography of the country and the history, religion, manners and customs of the inhabitants. Horacio de la Penna was particularly distinguished by an ardent zeal in the cause of Christianity;

[1] I allude to the case of Capt. Smyth, for whom no passports could be obtained; and of Capt. Blackiston, who was obliged to return in the first weeks after his setting out from the shores of China to reach Tíbet through China.

he translated into Tibetan a catechism of the Christian faith, the Doctrina Christiana of Cardinal Belarmino, the Thesaurus Doctrinæ Christianæ of Turlot, and he also compiled a Tibetan-Italian dictionary. The materials brought home by this mission, which a few years afterwards was obliged to leave Lhássa, were examined by Pater Antonio Georgi, who in his curious "Alphabetum Tibetanum," Romæ 1762, undertook to prove by comparative philology the opinion entertained by the missionaries, that Lamaism was a corrupted form of Christianity.

In the year 1811 Manning, according to Princep, made an attempt to pass through Tíbet into China; but he was stopped at Lhássa, and not being permitted to go any farther, he was obliged to turn back.[1] In 1845 two Lazarist missionaries, Huc and Gabet, again reached Lhássa from Mongolia; but after a short stay, they also had to leave this capital, and were escorted to Macao by a Chinese officer.

Since the commencement of this century various journeys have been undertaken into Bhután, Síkkim, and the western districts adjoining the British territories. Particularly precious are also the publications of Pallas,

[1] Ritter, "Die Erdkunde von Asien," Vol. II., pp. 439-64. H. Princep, "Tibet, Tartary and Mongolia," London 1852, p. 17. For an interesting collection of the views of various missionaries on this subject see Marsden's note to "Marco Polo's Travels," p. 240. The Popes had hoped the Capucine mission would prove of very great importance for the propagation of Christianity in Central Asia, and had supported them in every way. Pope Clemens IX. issued a particular Breve concerning Tíbet (Ritter, l. c., p. 459), and the nomination of a Vicarius apostolicus for Lhássa still takes place. The "Annuario Pontificio," Roma 1862, p. 243, gives as the gentleman in charge of this office Monsignore Giacomo Leone Thomine Demazures, nominated March 27, 1846; he is at the same time the Bishop in *partibus infidelium* of Sinopolis in Cilicia.

detailing the information obtained by him in Russian Mongolia; and those of Klaproth—his translation of the description of Tíbet by a Chinese officer, as well as the results of his investigations connected with his travels in the regions of the Kaukasus. All the various narratives treat principally of the hierarchical system, the regulations and social habits of the clergy and the religious establishments; the notices on religious ceremonies are very rare. In addition to the above-mentioned sources of information, which have been laid under contribution in my endeavour to define, in the following chapters, the nature and characteristics of the Tibetan priesthood and the institutions connected therewith, I have also been enabled to turn to good account the observations made by my brothers during their travels in the Eastern Himálaya and in Central and Western Tíbet, in the years 1855 to 1857.

Fundamental laws.

It is very probable that in the earliest periods of Buddhism all those who embraced this religion, abandoned the world and assisted their master, as much as lay in their power, in propagating his faith. Those who, after having heard Sākyamuni explain his doctrines, desired to become Buddhists, were first obliged to make an explicit declaration to that effect, whereupon the teacher proceeded to cut off their hair and beard, and then invested them with the religious garments, whereby they were received into the community of the faithful. Later, when the number of Buddhists had increased, the neophite was placed for instruction under the charge of an elder disciple, a practice which became general after Sākyamuni's death. The distinction between lay brothers and priests, and the important dogma that only the latter, as having renounced the world, can obtain Nirvāna, was certainly not introduced till after Sākyamuni's death, although he himself had recognized *mendicants*, the receivers of alms, who are forbidden to eat other food than that which has been received under certain conditions (one being that it has been given in the form of alms); and *householders*, the givers of alms, who thereby gain merit; but by him both these classes were admitted with equal rights to the advantages promised to his followers. But already the earlier schools (the Hīnayāna sect) excluded lay brothers from attaining to the perfection of an Arhat, and to Nirvāna; the Mahāyāna system admits them, but the present sects of Tíbet again raised that strongly marked barrier between the laity and the priests, denying to the former the possibility of attaining to the rank of a Buddha; they may attain Nirvāna, but they cannot become "a blessing to the world."[1] The ascetics are styled in the sacred books Bhikshus, Sramanas, Srāvakas, Arhats; and the lay followers, the devotees, Upāsakas (in Tibetan Genyen); in the Mahāyāna Sūtras the latter are also called "Bōdhisattvas who reside in their houses," the former "Bōdhisattvas who have renounced the world."

[1] See pp. 27, 38, 106. Compare also Hodgson, "Illustrations," p. 98. Hardy, "Eastern Monachism," p. 12.

The early disciples of Sākyamuni are generally represented as wandering about with their royal master; others, in consequence of his frequent exhortations to lead a solitary life, are said to have retired to the forests and woods which surround the settlements, or to have lived in solitary and forsaken houses, which they only left on certain periods in order to betake themselves to Sākyamuni and listen to his words. Large regular assemblies, which probably date back as far as Sākyamuni himself, took place when the rainy season was over; during the rains Sākyamuni himself, as well as his immediate followers and the hermit-disciples, had taken up their abode in the houses of well-intentioned persons, and had devoted themselves to meditations on such parts of the doctrine as they had not yet clearly understood; they also employed part of their time in the instruction of their entertainers. At the assemblies above mentioned the Bhikshus reported their success in gaining neophites, discussed various dogmas, and requested a solution of any doubts with which they may have been troubled.

Originally such assemblies were held in the open air; the Vihāras, in the sense of monasteries, in which they might otherwise have taken place, did not come into existence till a much later period. The word Vihāra, according to its etymological derivation, denotes a place where the Buddhists assembled; and it is in this sense that this term is used in the Sūtras, or books considered to contain the words of Sākyamuni, which always begin thus: "When Sākya happened to be (viharati sma) at a place;"

but later this name was applied to those houses in which the priests met, and where strangers and the ascetics (who went about collecting alms) found an asylum. The meaning of the word became more restricted still, and was subsequently given to monasteries only, or to those religious establishments, in which those who once enter them are bound to remain for life. It is impossible to determine exactly the various periods during which Vihāras took the form of meeting-houses or, later, of monasteries. In the Hīnayāna books on discipline they are mentioned only as an appendix to the chapter on the seats, and they were probably erected later than the temples, the first of which is said to have been built in the period of Upagupta, who lived in the third century B.C. The violent attacks of the Brahmans must soon have convinced the Buddhist clergy of the advantages to be derived from association; rules were then drawn up for life in community and for subordination, and the beginning of monastic institutions was thus made, which latter were, however, in India, even in their final perfection, widely different from those of Tibetan monachism at the present day. In earlier times each Vihāra had its own administration and its own chief, and was independent of the others; and it was so even in the seventh century, when Hiuen Thsang resided in India; a hierarchy so thoroughly organized as we now find in Tíbet, was never known in India.[1]

[1] See Burnouf, "Introduction," pp. 232 *seq.*, 279 *seq.*, 286; Hardy, "Eastern Monachism," Chapter III., IV., XIII.; Wassiljew, "Der Buddhismus," pp. 45, 96. Compare also Barthélmy St. Hilaire, "Le Bouddha

Hierarchical system.

The first organisation of the Tibetan clergy dates from King Thisrong de tsan (728—86 A.D.), of whom the Bodhimör says that "he gave the clergy a firm constitution and divided it into classes."[1] But the development of the present hierarchical system, which was independent of these ancient institutions, dates from the fifteenth century. In 1417 the famous Lama Tsonkhapa founded the Gáldan monastery at Lhássa, and became its superior; the great authority and reputation he had enjoyed, devolved upon his successors in the abbotship of this monastery, who, down to the present day, are believed to have been men of particular sanctity. But these abbots were soon superseded in influence by the Dalai Lama[2] at Lhássa (now the highest in rank of the Tibetan priesthood), and by the Panchen Rinpoche at Tashilhúnpo,[3] who are both considered to be of divine

et sa religion," p. 299. Wilson, "Buddha and Buddhism," p. 251. The principal cave temples were probably excavated in the period from the commencement of the Christian era to the fifth century after it. It needs hardly be added that the sacred books which represent Sākyamuni himself to have felt the necessity of instituting head priests are interpolated.

[1] Schmidt, "Ssanang Ssetsen," p. 356; comp. p. 67.

[2] Dalai Lama is the title which the Mongolians give to him; Dalai is a Mongolian word meaning *ocean*, Lama or correctly *b*lama, is the Tibetan word for a *superior*. Schott, "Ueber den Buddhaismus in Hochasien," p. 32. The Europeans became familiar with this term from the works of Georgi, Pallas and Klaproth.

[3] Tashilhúnpo, or in exact transliteration: "*b*khra shis lhun po," is the neighbouring city of chiefly ecclesiastical establishments, about a mile to the south east of Digárchi, "the four-housed (top?)" (in Tibetan written *b*zhi-ka-*r*tse, in Nevari zhi-kha-chhen), the capital of the province Tsang, of Chinese Tibet. See the map of Turner, "Embassy;" Hooker, "Himalayan Journals," Vol. II., pp. 125, 171. Hodgson, "Aborigines of the Nilgiris." Journ. As, Soc. Beng., Vol. XXV., p. 504.

origin, and are, consequently, regarded more in the light of gods than of mortal beings. This assumed divine origin gives them a character totally different from that of the Pope of the Roman Catholic church; but then, on the other hand, neither of them has such a widely-spread acknowledged supremacy as that enjoyed by the Pope of Rome.

The *Dalai Lama* is viewed as an incarnation of the Dhyāni Bōdhisattva Chenresi, who is supposed to effect his re-incorporation by a beam of light which issues from his body and enters the individual whom he selects for his re-descent.[1] The *Panchen Rinpoche* is considered to be an incarnation of Chenresi's celestial father, Amitābha.[2] There is a story relating that Tsonkhapa himself had ordered his two principal disciples to take upon themselves a mortal form in an uninterrupted series of rebirths, and to watch over the propagation of the Buddhist faith and the maintenance of its purity;[3] and according to this account, it was Tsonkhapa who created these two principal clerical dignities. But we learn from Csoma's Chronological Tables, that Gedun Grub (born 1389 A.D. died 1473) was the first, who assumed the title of Gyelva Rinpoche, "His precious Majesty," which is applied to the Dalai Lama only; Gedun Grub is, therefore, to be considered the first Dalai Lama, and not the Dharma Rinchen, the successor of Tsonkhapa in the chair of the Gáldan monastery. In the year 1445 he

[1] "Description du Tubet," Nouv. Journ. Asiatique 1830, p. 239. Comp. p. 88.
[2] See about the dogma of Dhyāni Buddhas and Bōdhisattvas, p. 51.
[3] "Arbeiten der russ. Mission in Peking," Vol. I, p. 316.

also built the large monastery of Tashilúnpo, whose abbots assumed the title of Panchen Rinpoche, "the great teacher-jewel," and who claimed with much success the same divine nature and temporal power as that till then enjoyed by the Dalai Lama alone. He shares an equal authority and sovereignty as the Dalai Lama, but in ecclesiastical affairs, even in his own territories, his words are considered less divine, his faculties inferior to those of the Dalai Lama.

The fifth Gyelva Rinpoche, Ngagvang Lobzang Gyamtso, a most ambitious man, sent to the Koshot Mongolians, who had settled in the environs of the lake Kuku Nor, and requested their assistance against the Tibetan king then residing at Digárchi, with whom he was at war. The Mongolians conquered Tíbet, and are said to have made a present of the same to Ngagvang Lobzang. This event took place in the year 1640, and it is from this moment that we must date the extension of the *temporal government* of the Dalai Lamas over all Tíbet.[1]

The Dalai Lamas are elected by the clergy, and up to the year 1792 these elections had taken place uninfluenced by the Chinese government; but since this time the court of Pekin, to whom the Dalai Lama is a very important personage in a political as well as a religious point of view, has taken care that the sons of such per-

[1] Csoma, "Grammar," pp. 192, 198. Ritter, "Asien," Vol. III., pp. 274-86. Köppen, "Die Rel. d. Buddha," Vol. II., pp. 129-52. Cunningham, "Ladak," p. 389, has understood Csoma's account as if in the year 1640 the *first* Dalai Lama had been established, but Csoma decidedly only alludes to the uniting of the temporal government with his ecclesiastical sovereignity.

sons only as are known for their loyality and fidelity shall be elected to this high dignity.[1]

The next in rank to these sublime Lamas are the superiors of several larger monasteries, of whom some are considered as incarnations, others as common mortals; in either case head Lamas of so high a rank are styled Khanpos.[2] My brothers saw Khanpos at the monasteries of Láma Yúru in Ladák, and at Thóling in Gnári Khórsum. They were natives of Lhássa, and had been appointed by the Dalai Lama's government for periods of from three to six years, at the expiration of which time they would return to Lhássa. The abbots in smaller monasteries are elected for life by the monks; but the election has to be submitted for approval to the Dalai Lama, who can either sanction or reject it.

Other persons superior in rank to the common monks are the Budzad, the superintendent of the choral songs and music during the divine service; and the Gebkoi, who has to maintain discipline and order. These dignitaries are also elected by the monks, and constitute, with the abbot, the council which regulates the affairs of the monastery. Some other dignities which are occasionally

[1] Compare for details Huc, "Souvenirs," Vol. I., p. 292. Köppen, l. c., p. 247.

[2] In Bhután the incarnated Khanpos had profited by political circumstances to make themselves independent of the Dalai Lama. The relations between the ruler of Bhután proper, the Dharma Rinpoche (called by the Hindus Dharma Rāja), and Lhássa seem to be very loose; and the abbots of the monasteries in the southern valleys have also set up principalities almost independent of the Dharma Rinpoche. These Lamas, styled Lama Rājas by Hermann's companions, are very jealous of their power, and endeavoured most energically to prevent Hermann from entering Bhután, by abducting his servants.

found in larger monasteries are mere posts of honour, having no direct influence upon the administration.[1]

The title of Lama, written in Tibetan *b*lama, is applied by right to the superior priests only; but just as the Arabic word Sheikh, and other titles of honour and rank in European languages, so also the word Lama has come to be regarded as a title which courtesy requires one to give to every Buddhist priest.[2]

A particular class of Lamas are the astrologers, the Tsikhan (occasionally also styled Kartsi-pa, or Chakhan = fortune-teller, Ngagpa = one expert in charms), who are allowed to marry and to wear a peculiar phantastic dress. These people are professional fortune-tellers, who are officially authorized to conjure and to exorcise evil spirits, on behalf of and to the profit of the clergy. Common tricks, such as vomiting fire, swallowing knives, &c., are not openly practised, nor would they be allowed, though in other things these conjurers are permitted to play upon the credulity of the ignorant multitude to any extent, and derive as much profit therefrom as they can. The instruments which they most frequently employ in their incantations, are an arrow and a triangle upon which supposed talismanic sentences are inscribed.[3] Amongst these astrologers, the Lamas called Choichong, who are said to be all educated at the Garmakhyá monastery at

[1] Compare Pallas, "Mongol. Völker," Vol. II., pp. 117-37. Huc, "Souvenirs," p. 297.

[2] Compare Hardy, "Eastern Monachism," p. 11. Gerard, "Koonawur," p. 119, states that he heard the head priests of the monasteries styled Gelong or Guru.

[3] For particulars concerning certain ceremonies in which these things are used, see Chapter XV.

Lhássa, enjoy the greatest reputation, because the god Choichong, or Choichong gyalpo, is supposed to become incorporated in one of the Lamas belonging to this monastery as often as he descends upon earth. His re-descent becomes manifest by the frequency of miraculous deeds performed by a Lama, who is then considered as the favourite instrument chosen by king Choichong. He soon becomes the object of universal worship, which is most lucrative to the monastery; for Buddhists from all parts of High Asia come as pilgrims to Lhássa to receive his benediction; and they consider themselves happy if the valuable presents they offer as an equivalent, are accepted by the incarnate Choichong.—In the monasteries beyond Tíbet Choichong astrologers are not frequent; and though the images of king Choichong are met with in most monasteries of Western Tíbet and the Himálaya, my brothers never saw a Lama Choichong.[1]

The god Choichong is but one of the "five great kings," in Tibetan Ku nga gyalpo. These five mythological persons are considered to protect man most efficaciously against the evil spirits and enable him also to attain the accomplishment of every wish. Their names are Bihar gyalpo; Choichong gyalpo; Dalha gyalpo; Luvang gyalpo; Tokchoi gyalpo. Of Bihar I know particularly that he has chosen the protection of monasteries

[1] Compare "Description du Tubet," Nouv. Journ. As., Vol. IV., pp. 240, 293. The offerings which are the most agreeable to these kings, and the conditions under which they are to be presented, are detailed in the Tibetan book entitled Ku nga gyalpoi kang shag, "to make confession to the five great kings." Of Choichong in particular treats the book Prulku choichong chenpoi Kang shag "to make confession to the incarnation of the great Choichong."

and religious establishments; of Dalha that he is the tutelary god of warriors. The images of the five gods are very generally met with in temples and in the private praying-room of laymen: amulet-boxes also not unfrequently contain such representations. They are also added to an image of the thirty-five Buddhas of confession (see p. 97), in which they are drawn riding phantastic animals. Bihar is riding a red tiger; Choichong a yellow lion; Dalha a yellow horse (Khyang); Luvang, the god of the Nāgas (see p. 31), a blue crocodile; Tockchoi a yellow deer. In other pictures, in which one of these gods is the *principal* object, this very one is drawn on a larger scale than the surrounding figures. Such a picture, bought by Adolphe at Mángnang, in Gnári Khórsum, shows Choichong extremely fat and three-headed, riding a white lion with a blue mane; the figure is surrounded by flames." His side heads are blue and crimson, the central one is, like the body, of flesh-colour. His broad hat and some arms, the symbols of his activity, are gilt; his dress is a tiger's skin; of which the feet are tied round his neck. In the upper part of the picture various domestic animals are sketched, alluding to the great merit to be derived from consecrating to him an animal, which then is no more allowed to be killed for private use, but after some time is delivered to the Lamas, who may eat it. Below him are traced three other defenders of man against the mischievous spirits, viz.: Damchan dorje legpa, riding on a camel; Tsangpa, in Sanskrit Brahma (see p. 114), riding a ram; Chebu damchan, riding a goat.

Organization of the clergy.

The principles of its Constitution. The number of observances to be followed, at the present day, by the Lamas, has increased, from precepts plain and brief, to an ample code of laws, which contains two hundred and fifty rules, in Tibetan Khrims: they are detailed in the first, or Dulva division of the Kanjur, and have been explained in the well-known works of Hardy and Burnouf.[1] But of this mass of precepts, I direct the attention chiefly to those of celibacy and poverty (which Tsonkhapa enacted anew), because they have been of great importance in forming the present character of the Tibetan priesthood.

The violation of the ordinance of celibacy, or even sexual intercourse, is severely punished; nevertheless it is not unfrequent, particularly in the case of Lamas who do not live in the monasteries. Besides, we know of two instances in which, from considerations of public interest, the Dalai Lama has granted indulgences to marry to Lamas of royal pedigree. The one instance is reported by Dr. Campbell, who says that a prince of Síkkim obtained this permission; another analogous case is noticed by Moorcroft concerning the Rāja of Ladák.[2] The vow of

[1] Hardy, "Eastern Monachism," London 1850. Burnouf, "Introduction," pp. 234-335. Comp. Csoma's "Analysis," in As. Res., Vol. XX., p. 78.

[2] Journ. As. Soc. Beng., Vol. XVIII., p. 494. Travels, Vol. I., p. 334. There is a sect in Chinese Tíbet which P. Hilarion calls Sa zsya; it allows its priests to marry, and to beget a son, whereupon they abandon their wives and retire into the monasteries. "Arbeiten der russ. Mission," Vol. I., p. 314.

poverty is one of those institutions which seriously affect the public welfare in Tíbet, as the monks, so very numerous in every Buddhist country, have to live from the contributions of the lay population. Though the single Lama who has renounced the world is not allowed to possess any thing besides the articles permitted by the code of discipline, the Lama convents may possess landed property, houses, and treasures, and its members may enjoy the abundance of its well-filled store-houses.

The *revenues* are derived from the collecting of alms, from voluntary offerings, from the remunerations for the performance of sacred rites, from the rents of properties, and even from commercial enterprises.

Alms are more particularly collected at harvest time, when a number of Lamas are deputed to visit the villages for the purpose of begging for grain. When Hermann was at Hímis (in Sept. 1856) more than one half of the Lamas were out in the country. Of voluntary offerings the most considerable are those presented to an incarnated Lama, or given at the annual festivals.[1] The greater number of smaller ones are obtained by those monasteries situated along the principal passages over the mountains, as it is the custom for every traveller to repeat some prayers in the temples he meets with, and to leave a small present. The remunerations for attending at births, marriages, illnesses, death, &c., are generally regulated by the officiating priest himself in proportion to the means of those requiring their service. These consist generally in natural products, which appear

[1] See an example in Turner's Embassy, p. 345.

to be given in advance.[1] The landed property, which is sometimes even very considerable, is either tilled by the dependents, or is let at a high price. The making and selling of images, charms, &c., is another source of considerable income for every Lama; their trading with wool, and in Eastern Tíbet with musk, is mentioned by several travellers.[2]

Grades amongst the Lamas. In Tíbet the clergy, besides living at the public expense, are also in most districts free from taxes[3] and contributions for public works; and it is on account of these and other advantages that the condition and dignity of a Lama are every where so sought after. It is the custom in Eastern, as well as in Western Tíbet, to make the elder son of a family a Lama, and restrictive regulations, analogous to those mentioned in the ancient religious books, seem to have lost their force; for all travellers report that any one can become a member of the religious order; the only restriction I know of is this, that in Bhután the father who wishes his son to be received as a novice must ask the permission of the Deba and the Dharma Rāja, and pay a fee of 100 Deba rupees.[4] When any one declares his wish to enter the priesthood, or when he desires to make his son a Lama, the faculties of the novice are examined. In most cases the novices

[1] As an instance of this custom I mention the ceremonies connected with the driving away of the evil spirits from the burial-ground (see Chapter XV., No. 9). See also Huc, "Souvenirs," Vol. II., p. 121.

[2] See Turner, l. c., pp. 200, 312. Moorcroft, "Travels," Vol. II., p. 61; "Mansaraur Lake," As. Res., Vol. XII., p. 432.

[3] In Ladák, however, the monasteries as such are taxed with considerable sums by the Kashmír government; Cunningham, "Ladak," p. 273.

[4] Pemberton, "Report," p. 118. Burnouf, "Introduction," p. 277. Turner, "Embassy," p. 170 Moorcroft, "Travels," Vol. I., p. 321.

are boys, and if they are found intelligent enough, they are allowed to take the vows (Tib. Dom), viz. to observe the religious duties connected with the priesthood; and then they become "candidates for orders," Genyen (an equivalent to the Sanskrit Upāsaka).[1] The Lamas who have charge of the instruction of the novices, seem not always to treat their scholars well, for several travellers have witnessed rudeness and even cruelty in punishments.[2] The grade next to the Genyen is that of Getsul; an ordinated priest is styled a Gelong; the grades are conferred by a council, before which the candidate has to prove in a public disputation his experience in the sciences he has been taught hitherto.[3]

Women are also allowed to embrace the monastic life, and we read of female mendicants, the Bhikshunīs, who have devoted themselves already in the earliest youth of Buddhism with the permission of the founder to an ascetic life. The nuns are styled Gelong-ma in Tibetan; in Western Tíbet, however, and in the Himálaya they cannot be very numerous, for my brothers never saw any great number of them.[4]

The clergy are monastic; the greater part of the priests reside in monasteries, others are allowed to live as clergymen in the villages for the convenience of the population, who so frequently require their assistance.

[1] See p. 149.

[2] See Dr. Hooker, "Himalayan Journals," Vol. II., p. 93. Huc, "Souvenirs," Vol. I., p. 299.

[3] Compare p. 21.

[4] Burnouf, "Introduction," p. 278. Hardy, "Eastern Monachism," p. 150. Gerard, "Kanawur," p. 120, was told that it is mostly the ugliest women who, having but little chance of getting husbands, retire to convents.

Hermits also are not rare: they inhabit the highest parts of the valleys, and live from the charity of passers-by. It is characteristic of them that they allow the hair and beard to grow; and the custom is so general that the typical representation of a hermit is always that of a man with long uncut hair and beard. Each chooses a particular rite, and believes he derives from the frequent practice of the same supernatural assistance. A rite very often selected, though I am unable to state for what reason, is that of Chod, "to cut, or destroy," the meaning of which is anxiously kept a profound secret by the Lamas. The recluses are believed to be exposed to repeated attacks on the part of the evil spirits, the enemies of earnest and assiduous meditation; but the beating of a drum is regarded as a most efficacious means of keeping them at a distance.[1]

On certain days those isolated Lamas, the village priests as well as anachorites, are required to revisit the respective

[1] See Moorcroft, "Mansaraur." As. Res., Vol. XII., pp. 458, 465. Their living in seclusion is also alluded to by the name of Rikhrodpa, which means "one who lives on or amongst hills," and also "a hermit." Csoma and Schmidt's Dictionaries. In pictorial representations of a recluse a drum is a frequent object in one of his hands, while the other very generally holds a cord, typifying the wisdom granted him by the deity as a reward for his strong mind and perseverance.—With reference to the encouragement given by Buddhism in its early days to anachoretism, I wish to remark (see also p. 6, 150) that Sākyamuni himself, as well as all the founders and supporters of the various systems of Buddhism, urgently exhorted to energy in the practise of meditation, as the most efficacious means of becoming emancipated from existence; and that they recommended for these religious exercises the choice of out-of-the-way places little likely to be visited by any one in pursuit of worldly pleasure or gratification. Sākyamuni himself had set the example by retiring to remote places previous to obtaining the Buddhaship, and it was not only duly followed by his early adherents, but is also practised by the modern Tibetans.

monasteries to which they belong; and they are punished if they fail to present themselves to submit to this sort of control. In every monastery there is a list of all the monks forming part of the clerical community.[1]

Number of Lamas. With reference to the number of Lamas I here present the following data.

For Eastern Tíbet Dr. Campbell gives a list of twelve principal convents at *Lhássa* and in its vicinity, inhabited by a total of 18,500 Lamas.[2] Surprising as this number is, it is far from representing the entire number of Lamas spread over all the country of Eastern Tíbet.

In Western Tíbet Cunningham has estimated the lay population of *Ladák* at 158,000, the Lamas at 12,000, which gives one Lama to every thirteen laymen. In *Spíti* the lay population was computed by Major Hay, in 1845, to number 1414, the Lamas 193, or about one Lama to seven laymen.[3]

For the Buddhist countries of the Eastern Himálaya I can give no numbers at all, but only offer some general remarks. In *Bhután*, the number of Lamas in proportion to the lay population in extremely great. In Tassisúdon (*b*kra-shis-chhos-grong, *the holy town of the doctrine*) 1,500 to 2,000 live in the palace of the Dharma Rāja alone; and their number must be considered as one of the chief causes of the poverty of the inhabitants. Pemberton

[1] Compare Moorcroft, "Travels," Vol. I., p. 339. Pemberton, "Report," p. 117. Huc, "Souvenirs," Vol. I., p. 203. Schmidt, in Mém. de l'Acad. de Petersb., Vol. I., p. 257.

[2] "Notes on Eastern Tíbet," in the Journal of the As. Soc. Beng., 1855, p. 219.

[3] Cunningham, "Ladak," p. 287. "Report on the valley of Spíti," in the Journal of the As. Soc. of Beng., Vol. XIX., p. 437.

says that the expenses for the maintainance of this privileged class have repeatedly been made the subject of earnest discussion.[1] In *Sikkim* also the monasteries and Lamas are described by Hooker as being very numerous and influential.[2]

For comparison I add some data for countries beyond the limits of High Asia. Amongst the Kalmuks it was calculated, when Pallas visited their country in the last century, that there was one lama to every 150 to 200 tents.[3]

In the environs of Pekin there are about 80,000 Buddhist monks.[4]

Ceylon has about 2,500 priests, a number which gives for a total population of two millions one priest to 800

In Bérma there is one priest to every thirtieth soul.

Occupations. The monks, notwithstanding the religious duties they have to perform, would have plenty of time for the cultivation of larger tracts of land; but the only thing they do in this way is to keep in the best possible condition the gardens surrounding their monasteries, which greatly contribute to their support and comfort: these same gardens are also very often the only places for miles round where fruit-trees, chiefly apricots, are met with. In general the Lamas are an idle set of people, disinclined to either bodily or mental exertion, the

[1] Turner, "Embassy," p. 83. Pemberton, "Report," p. 117.

[2] "Himalayan Journals," Vol. I., p. 313.

[3] Pallas "Reisen," Vol. I., p. 557. (French edition).

[4] Wassiljew, "Der Buddhismus," p. 18.

[5] The data for Ceylon and Bérma are taken from Hardy, "Eastern Monachism," p. 309. Compare p. 11 about the census of Ceylon.

majority passing the greater part of the day in revolving prayer-cylinders, or counting the beads of rosaries, though occasionally some are found who are very skilful in carving blocks of wood and making images of gods, as well as in painting and sculpture. The cleverest Lamas, however, as my brothers were frequently told, are generally summoned to Lhássa.[1] Although every Lama can read and write, yet these accomplishments form no favourite occupation among them; and with reference to the slowness of their mode of writing, I may mention that the Lama who copied the document concerning Himis (see p. 183) spent about six hours over it. The illiterateness of the Lamas has often been regretted. Many were asked for an explanation of the six-syllabic prayer Om mani padme hum, of whose magical influence upon the welfare of man so many religious books treat; and it was not till after repeated inquiries that at last a satisfactory answer was obtained. Schmidt was much surprised at the answers which the Nepalese Buddhists gave Hodgson. "A Tibetan or Mongolian Lama," he says, "would not have answered his questions so well." Both Csoma and Huc have observed that the Lamas are not very well acquainted with their sacred literature; Huc says that they excuse their ignorance by urging the profoundness of their religion; and again: "a Lama who knows Tibetan and Mongolian is styled a sage, or wise

[1] Compare Turner, "Embassy," p. 316. The activity of the Ladaki Lamas in the cultivation of land, which Moorcroft, "Travels," Vol. I., p. 340, notices, is actually confined to their gardens.—There was a very skilful carver in wood residing in Spíti at the time of Trebeck's visit to that province, and his works are highly praised by this traveller.

man; and if he has also a slight knowledge of Chinese and Mandshu literature, he is viewed as of more than human nature."[1] My brothers also were often puzzled by the confused answers they received from the Lamas to any questions either on natural phenomena, or concerning their religion or history. The Lamas always preferred talking about matters connected with mystical theology, and it was a comparatively easy affair to obtain from them explanations of the supposed magical properties of particular charms.

The *Diet* of the Lamas is that usual in the country.[2] They may eat whatever is offered them in alms, but are not allowed to drink intoxicating liquors: these are, however, taken under the pretext of "being medicine."[3] Animal food is not forbidden, Sākyamuni himself is said in Singhalese legends to have died from eating pork,[4] but it is considered as an impediment to the attainment of perfection, as man should view all animated beings as his brethern and relations, and not kill them; there is

[1] Mém. de l'Acad. de Petersb., Vol. I., p. 93. Csoma, Journ. As. Soc. Beng., Vol. VII., p. 14. Huc, "Souvenirs," Vol. I., pp. 56, 299. Compare also Turner, "Embassy," p. 316.

[2] About the food of the Tibetans in general; see Turner, "Embassy," pp. 24, 48, 82, 126, 129, 136, 195, 220, 245, 343. Pemberton, "Report," p. 156. Moorcroft, "Travels," Vol. I., pp. 182, 208, 232, 243, 291, 309, 328-332; Vol. II., p. 77; "Mansaraur," As. Res., Vol. XII., pp. 394, 396, 444, 446, 486. Huc, "Souvenirs," Vol. II., p. 258. Cunningham, "Ladak," p. 305.

[3] Wassiljew, "Der Buddhismus," p. 94. Moorcroft, "Travels," Vol. II., p. 12, remarks, that he saw at Láma Yúru the Lámas take Chong, the national liquor, during their religious service. Also the fermented drink of the Lepchas, made of millet, is taken in great quantities by the Lamas in Sikkim.

[4] Hardy, "Eastern Monachism," p. 92. In the Tibetan biographies he is reported to have died from affection of the spine. Schiefner, "Tibet. Lebensbeschreibung." Mém. des Savants étrangers. Vol. VI., p. 292.

even a proverb which says—"To eat flesh is equal to eating one's relations."[1] Laymen, however, eat meat of any kind: according to my brother Robert, however, they abstain—in Spíti at least—from partaking of fish, although no satisfactory reason could be alleged by them for their so doing. In order that the monks may not inordinately indulge their appetite for meat, there exist a great many regulations; on certain days no animal food whatever is allowed; the monks are also obliged to abstain from it as often as confession is made, as also at those periods when very sacred religious ceremonies are performed.

The principal food consists in rice, wheat, or barley, flour, milk, and tea. The rice is boiled or roasted; the flour is mixed with milk and tea, or formed into unleavened cakes and seasoned with salt. Such cakes have a taste similar to that of the unleavened bread of the Jews. The tea is made in two different ways; first as an infusion with hot water, as in Europe, and this preparation is called Cha-chosh "tea water;"[2] secondly in a very peculiar manner, which I will describe in detail from a recipe obtained by my brothers at Leh:—

The tea—loosened brick-tea,[3]—is mixed with nearly half its volume of soda, in Tibetan called Phuli. The mixture is then thrown into a kettle filled with the necessary quantity of cold water, the proportion varying

[1] Comp. Wassiljew, l. c., p. 134.

[2] This and the following terms, Phuli and Gurgur, do not occur in the dictionaries.

[3] Brick tea is the commercial name of this peculiar kind of tea; it refers to its having a form not unlike that of a brick. It obtains its shape and at the same time its consistency by being pressed into a form.

as in our mode of making tea. When the water is about to boil, the mixture of tea leaves and soda is stirred, an operation continued four to six minutes after the boiling of the water. The kettle is then removed from the fire and the tea is filtered through a cloth into a round, wooden cylinder about three to four inches in diameter and two to three feet high; the tea-leaves are generally considered as useless and are thrown away. The tea is vigorously querled in a wooden tub (called in Tibetan Gurgur), like chocolate; a large amount of clarified butter is then added (generally double the quantity of the brick tea), and some salt; when the operation of querling is continued. Finally the tea is again thrown into a kettle, mixed with milk, and heated anew, as it has generally greatly cooled down during all the operations just described. This tea, called "Cha," strongly resembles a kind of gruel, and is taken, together with meat or pastry, at dinner or supper; but it is not allowed to be taken during the performance of religious ceremonies, when tea-water alone, Cha-chosh, is handed round as refreshment.[1]

On certain occasions the Lamas give grand dinners. To one of them my brother Robert was invited at Leh; it had been arranged in honour of the visit of a high Lama from Lhássa. Tea was given in the place of soup, and was handed round all dinner time. A particular honour was shown to the guests by care being taken that their

[1] As yet this brick tea is used almost exclusively, though it is to be hoped that the exertions of the Indian Government to introduce tea grown in the Himálaya and in Assam into Tíbet will ere long meet with success.

cups should never become quite empty. There were various kinds of meat, some roasted, some boiled, and even some as a kind of pie. No wine was served, but the cooking was really much superior to that generally met with in the country, and much better than could have been expected. On inquiry Robert learned that the dinner had been cooked by the high priest's own cook, whom he had brought with him from Lhássa.

Dress. The original precepts laid down by Sākyamuni for regulating the dress of the priests had been well adapted to the warm climate of India; later, however, when his faith extended over more northerly and, consequently, rougher climates, he himself is said to have allowed the use of warmer clothing, of stockings, shoes, &c. The principal advantage of dress, as taught by Sākyamuni, is to cover the shame of the priest; besides which, it has also other benefits, such as protection from the cold and the attacks of mosquitoes, &c., things which cause disturbance of the mind.[1]

The various parts of the dress of a Tibetan Lama are: a cap or hat, a gown, an inner vest, trousers, a cloak, and boots.[2]

Caps and hats. The caps are made of double felt or cloth, between which are put charms; in the rainy

[1] Hardy, "Eastern Monachism," Chapter XII.

[2] In the Himálaya districts and in Western Tíbet the predominant colour of the objects of dress is a more or less brillant red; yellow is met with among the sects enumerated p. 72.—About the dress in general notices are also found in Turner, "Embassy," pp. 32, 86, 242, 314. Moorcroft, "Travels," Vol. I., p. 238. Pemberton, "Report," pp. 108, 153. Dr. Campbell, in the Journ. of the As. Soc. of Bengal, Vol. XVIII, p. 499. Huc, "Souvenirs," Vol. II., p. 141. Cunningham, "Ladak," p. 372.

districts of the Himálaya the Lamas wear during the summer large hats of straw. The shape of the caps varies considerably, but it is curious that they are all of Chinese or Mongolian fashion, whilst the form of the robes has been adopted from the Hindus. The mode of salutation is also the Chinese as the Tibetans always take off their hat, whilst the Hindus, as a sign of reverence, approach their masters not bare-headed, but bare-footed. Most of the caps are conical, with a large lap, which is generally doubled up, but is let down over the ears in cold weather (see plate XVI. where the laps are let down). The head Lamas wear a particular sort of cap, generally low and conical, similar to those worn by Padma Sambhava[1] and mythological deified persons of particular influence upon man's welfare, as King Bihar; this form is called Nathongzha. Some head-priests of Western Tíbet have an hexagonal hat formed of paste-board, and showing four steps diminishing towards the top; or in some cases a kind of mitre of red cloth ornamented with flowers of gold worked in the stuff. This latter kind of cap bears a remarkable resemblance to the mitres of Roman Catholic bishops. Occasionally, if the weather allows it, the Lamas in Eastern Tíbet, in Bhután and also in Síkkim, go bare-headed.

The gown reaches to the calves and is fastened round the waist by a slender girdle; it has an upright collar and is closely buttoned up at the neck. In Síkkim the Lamas occasionally wear, slung round the shoulders, a kind of red and yellow striped woollen stole. In general

[1] See the plates in Hooker, "Himalayan Journals," Vol. I., p. 328.

the gown has sleeves, except in the Bhután Duárs, a country where the mean temperature does not go down even in the coldest mouth, in January, below 22° or 18° Fahrenheit.

The *inner vest* has no sleeves, and reaches to the haunches. It is not at all cut to the form of the body of the individual but hangs down quite straight. In Ladák, most of the Lamas wear it over the gown instead of underneath.

The *trousers* are fastened to the waist by a sort of lace running in a drawing hem. The two legs are equidistant throughout, also in their inner side, as in Fig. *a*, and not in *b*. During the winter the trousers are worn over the larger gown as a better protection against the cold. In Bhután the Lamas, according to Turner,[1] wear, instead of trousers, philibegs hanging down nearly as far as the knee.

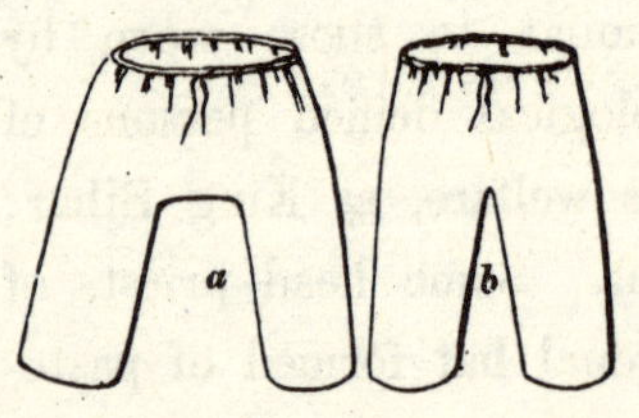

The *cloak*, in Tibetan Lagoi, "the upper garment," is the distinctive ecclesiastical dress of the monks, in which also the Buddhas, Bōdhisattvas and sacred Lamas are represented. It is a long but narrow shawl of wool or sometimes even of silk, ten to twenty feet long, and two

[1] "Embassy," p. 86.—The wearing of trousers is a very ancient custom; see the most interesting and complete work of Weiss, "Kostümkunde," Vol. II., pp. 545-674, who gives many drawings in which the races who in ancient times inhabited Northern and Eastern Asia, are represented with trousers. It is altogether remarkable to see their dress but little differing from what they wear now.

to three feet broad; it is thrown over the left shoulder and passed under the right arm, so as to leave bare the right arm. Perhaps the custom of having the right arm uncovered may be explained from the rejection of the castes by Sākyamuni; for the border of the shawl describes a line across the breast just as the triple cord does, which according to the laws of Menu, the three higher castes alone are allowed to wear; whilst the shawl had been worn by all priests, from whatever caste they may have sprung.[1]

The *boots* are made of stiff felt, either white or red, and are ornamented with perpendicular blue stripes. They reach up to the calves. The soles are of double-felt, sometimes furnished, besides, with a sole of leather. These soles form a very solid and unyielding support for the foot, protecting it very well against sharp stones, much better than do the shoes worn by the Turkistanis, the sole of which consists of thin leather only, which gives neither protection against the roughness of the ground nor support to the foot; the advantages of the Tibetan boots are, however, sometimes secured by thick felt-stockings.

My brothers have seen *shoes* in use but very rarely, and then only amongst the superiors of the monasteries.

To complete the description of the appearance of a Lama I have still to notice various smaller articles generally worn. From the girdle which keeps together

[1] Menu, Chapter II., pp. 42, 44. On ancient sculptures the Buddhas not unfrequently wear nothing but the three strings; see the drawings in Crawfurd's Archipelago, Vol. II., and in Foucaux's Rgya chher rol pa, Vol. II., Plate I.

the gown, hang a knife-case and several purses or little pockets containing various articles, such as a tooth-brush, a tongue-scraper and an ear-pick, steel and tinder, tabacco or betel-nut, dice used in foretelling future events; a prayer-cylinder and a Chinese metal pipe are also almost always to be found among the articles fastened to it.

The *rosaries*, in Tibetan Thengpa, indispensable instruments for counting the due number of prayers, are generally fastened to the girdle, or sometimes worn round the neck.[1] The beads amount to 108, which answer to the number of the volumes of the Kanjur; but most of those used by the lay population have a much smaller number of beads, about thirty to forty. The beads are of wood, pebbles, or bones of holy Lamas; the latter have a very high price; the rosaries of the head Lamas are not unfrequently of precious stones, particularly of nephrite (the Turkistani Yashem) and of turquoise. To most rosaries are fastened a pair of pinchers, needles, an ear-pick, and a small Dorje.[2]

The *amulet-boxes*, in Tibetan Gaũ (in the Lēpcha language of Síkkim Koro, and Kandum, if of wood), are likewise worn round the neck; and it is not unfrequent to see several fastened to the same string. Most of the

[1] Compare Pallas, "Reisen," Vol. I., p. 563. Turner, "Embassy," pp. 261, 336. I. J. Schmidt, "Forschungen," p. 168. While travelling the Lamas are loaded with many other objects. See Hooker, "Himalayan Journals," Vol. II., p. 142.

[2] Pinchers are in use even amongst the rudest tribes, who go almost naked; for they need them to draw out thorns. I add as another instance of the ancient use of pinchers, that we have found them also in the oldest graves in the Franconian Hills, in Bavaria.

boxes are pointed, imitating the form of a fig-leaf; but they are also square or circular. The outside is either embossed or painted.

Wooden boxes are closed by a slide, which has not unfrequently a space cut out to allow the image of the chosen tutelary god to be seen. Those of brass have the two parts fitting together like the cover and the lower part of boxes; but hinges are replaced by rings, of which one at least must be connected with each part. A string or a piece of leather can be passed through, and serves to hang up the object as well as to keep it together.

The things put into such cases are relics, images of deities, objects which are believed to be dreaded by the evil spirits, and charms.[1] I had occasion to examine the following different sorts:—

1. A square wooden box from Gyúngul, in Gnári Khórsum; the box was bound in brass. In the interior were carved on one side one of the goddesses Dolma (see p. 66), who are supposed to protect against emaciation, having on her left Chenresi (see p. 88) and Amitābha (see p. 53) on her right. The opposite side shows Sākyamuni with the same deities.

2. A leaf-shaped wooden box painted yellow, with red clouds. It contained a figure of Shinje (see p. 93) of tinted clay; at the bottom of the case lay a little medal of hardened barley-paste representing Tsonkhapa

[1] Compare about the kind of charms, Csoma, "Journ. As. Soc. Beng.," Vol. IX., p. 905.

(see p. 69); it is half an inch in diameter, and was wrapped in paper covered with charms.

3. A circular box of brass with charms and a similar medal of Tsonkhapa, covered with gold paint.

4. Three conical brass boxes fastened to one string. The central box enclosed a gilt figure of Tsepagmed (= Amitābha, see p. 129), who is supposed to grant longevity. Also a piece of copper formed to represent a thunderbolt was wrapped in a piece of red cloth as a protection from the effects of lightning. In the smallest box several slips of paper were covered with seals of the Dalai Lama printed in red, which are supposed to protect against death by drowning. I found there also grains of barley and earth. The third box contained several figures of Lha Dolma, and Tsonkhapa (all carefully wrapped in pieces of red silk) alternating with charm-papers.

The charms were all written in small characters, or running hand, but by the friction against the images and grains the papers had been almost reduced to loose fibres. All objects were strongly perfumed with musk, and had besides, like every sacred article fabricated in monasteries, an unpleasant greasy odour.[1]

[1] Drawings of the different sorts of rosaries, as well as of the amulet boxes described above, from originals obtained by my brothers, will be given in a plate accompanying the "Results of a Scientific Mission to India and High Asia."

CHAPTER XIII

RELIGIOUS BUILDINGS AND MONUMENTS

Ceremonies preceding the Erection.—Monasteries.—Historical Document Relating to the Foundation of the Monastery of Hímis.—Temples.—Religious Monuments. 1. Chortens. 2. Manis. 3. Derchoks and Lapchas.

Ceremonies preceding the erection.

The erection of every new religious building is preceded by a benediction of the ground and by various other ceremonies. The Lamas of the neighbourhood come together, and the highest in rank presents offerings to the deity selected as tutelary god, it being the custom to dedicate every building to a particular god, who is supposed then to protect it against mischievous spirits as well as malignant men, and to bestow every kind of happiness upon its frequenters. A god very often chosen as patron, is King Bihar (Bihar gyalpo) one of the five great kings.[1] An image which my brother Adolphe obtained in Gnári Khórsum represents Bihar in an upright attitude, standing upon the "seat of diamond," Tib. Dorje-dan, Sanskrit Vajrasāna, formed of Lotus leaves. He is trampling upon four human beings of black, red, white and yellow colour; the skulls also of which his necklace is composed are of these colours. His gown is of blue silk (Tib. Darzab), with various ornaments; his cap, of the form I have described (p. 171) as Nathongzha, and his shawl are red. His right hand wields the Dorje, in his left is the Phurbu. The picture is meant to represent a statue placed in a box the four sides of which form a frame separating it from the surrounding figures, which are: the fabulous kings Dalha, Luvang, and Tokchoi gyalpo, and three highly revered Lamas.

The prayers accompaning the inaugurative ceremonies are read for the prosperity of the edifice. At the ceremony of laying the first stone prayers are recited for the prosperity of the new temple or place of worship; these are then written down and deposited with other prayers and certain forms of benediction (Tib. Tashi tsig jod, "blessing speeches"), together with relics and other sacred objects, in a hollow in the foundation stone. When the building is finished, the Lamas again assemble to perform the rites of consecration.[2]

The restoration of a ruined building is also preceded

[1] See p. 157.

[2] A volume treating of these ceremonies, in which Vajrasattva (p. 53) is addressed, is mentioned by Csoma in his Analysis of the Kanjur, As. Res., Vol. XX., p. 503. Concerning the objects usually enclosed in the Chortens, see Cunningham, "Ladak," p. 309.

by religious ceremonies, which bear the name of Argai choga, "ceremony of presenting offerings."

Monasteries.

The monasteries, in Tibetan Gonpa,[1] "a solitary place," are mostly at some little distance from the villages, and very frequently even on the summit of hills, in a commanding position. Each monastery receives a religious name, in allusion to its being a centre of Buddhist faith: thus the monastery at Hímis, near Leh, in Ladák, is called in the historical document relating to its foundation, Sangye chi ku sung thug chi ten, "the support of the meaning of the Buddha's precepts." Other instances are Darjíling, in Síkkim, "the far-diffused island (of meditation);"[2] Tholing, in Gnári Khórsum, "the high-floating (monastery);" Mindoling,[3] "the place of perfection and emancipation." Occasionally the monastery is more ancient than the village, which has sprung up afterwards in its immediate vicinity; in this case, the name of the monastery is transferred to the village, as in Darjíling; whilst in the opposite case, the monastery takes the name of the village, as at Hímis.

The architecture of the monasteries is that employed

[1] It is written *d*gon-pa. The descriptive designations for monasteries which occur in religious books, such as "house of science" (*g*tsug-lag-khang), and similar ones, are not in use in ordinary every-day language; and the word chhos-*s*ne, which Cunningham, "Ladak," p. 376, mentions as being given to monasteries was scarcely ever heard by my brothers.

[2] Dar-*r*gyas-*g*ling. In its complete form the name is preceded by *b*sam, meaning "thought, meditation."

[3] Quoted in Csoma's and Schmidt's Dictionaries, *voce s*min-pa. Tholing is spelled *m*tho-lding.—For further details of these names see my brother Hermann's Glossary, in R. As. Soc., 1859.

for the houses of the wealthier population of the country; but they are loftier, and are adorned with a greater number of flags and prayer-cylinders on the roof. The approach to a monastery is also distinguished by a number of religious monuments, as Chortens, Manis, &c.[1]

The materials used in the construction of monasteries vary in different districts. Thus, in the Himálaya, where wood is plentiful, they are built almost entirely of timber; and in Síkkim and Bhután, where the bamboo abounds, they are often constructed of this material, which is occasionally interlaced so as to form a lattice-work. It is a very general custom in these latter countries to build the monasteries upon piles, in order to prevent the lower floor from getting wet or damp in the rainy season; while the roofs are constructed in the Chinese style, being mostly of the pyramidal or prismatic form, not flat, and projecting considerably over the sides of the building. In Tíbet, where trees are very scarce, the walls are made either of stone—which for larger buildings are regularly shaped—or of unburnt, sun-dried bricks, which are cemented with most imperfectly made lime, or even with clay only. In Ladák and Gnári Khórsum, the roofs of the monasteries are flat, and they are constructed like the ceiling of the

[1] Concerning the houses of the Tibetans in general, see: for *Bhután*, Turner, "Embassy," pp. 50, 61, 93, 142, 177, 180; Pemberton, "Report," p. 154; for *Síkkim*, Gleanings in science, Vol. II., p. 179; Hooker, "Himalayan Journals," in many passages; for *Lhássa*, Huc, "Souvenirs," Vol. II., Chapt. II.; for *Gnári Khórsum*, Moorcroft, "Lake Mansaraur," As. Res., Vol. XII., pp. 426, 442, 456, 479; for *Ladák*, Moorcroft, "Travels," Vol. I., p. 315; Cunningham, "Ladak," p. 312. See also various representations in the "Panoramas and Views" accompanying the "Results of a Scientific Mission," by my brothers.

different stories, of small beams of willow or poplar. They are then covered with sprigs of willow, straw, and leaves, and plastered together with clay to render the whole a somewhat compact mass. The roofs of the houses of the head Lamas are, besides, surmounted by the form of a regular cube, terminating in a cone covered with gilt tiles.

Numerous prayer-flags are set up round the roof, as also cylinders about five feet high and two feet in diameter, supporting a crescent surmounted by a pinnacle similar to the pointed end of a spear. Some cylinders are covered with black cloth, round which are sewn horizontally and vertically white ribbons, so as to form the figure of a cross; in other cases the colours are respectively red and yellow.

The entrance to the monasteries looks towards either the east or the south, the latter position being probably chosen as affording protection against the north winds. The entrance-door is six feet, or sometimes even more, above the ground, with steps leading up to it.

The monasteries sometimes consist of one large house several stories high, with occasionally a covered gallery running round outside and used as a promenade. Sometimes they are composed of several buildings, containing respectively the temple, house of assembly (also used as refectory), the dwelling of the Lamas, storehouses for provisions, and the like. These various establishments extend in larger monasteries, such as Thóling, in Gnári Khórsum, over a large surface, and are enclosed by a common wall, which, as Cunningham was told, is intended to serve as a means of defence; but my brothers observed, that at present it is, in most instances, too weak to lay claim to the name of a fortification, particularly if the establishment is an old one, as Thóling for instance, which is mentioned in Ssanang Ssetsen's "History of the Eastern Mongolians" to have been built 1014 A.D.[1]

The ground-floor is without windows, and is used as a receptacle for provisions; it is generally a little broader than the upper stories. These latter have large windows and balconies. The windows have no panes of glass, but are closed by black curtains, upon which are sewn figures of a Latin cross, formed of white stripes of stuff.[2] The cross denotes quietness or peace, and is well known in this quality to the Europeans who visit Japan, where the loop-holes of the forts are covered with such curtains in time of peace; when a war breaks out they are all removed.[3] The upper stories are reached either by a staircase or by a broad, sloping beam, in which incisions are made to serve in lieu of steps. Each story is divided off into large compartments, in which several Lamas live together; small cells, each appropriated to a single person (as is the custom in Roman Catholic monasteries), are not known in Buddhist establishments. The furniture is most plain; the chief articles are low tables and benches (in the dining room); bed-steads of rough-hewn planks, with blankets and cushions, and different vessels. All these articles are generally of very inferior workmanship. Stoves

[1] Ssanang Ssetsen, ed. by Schmidt, p. 53.

[2] See the plates in Turner, and the View of Hímis by Hermann de Schlagintweit, l. c.

[3] From an oral communication from Captain Fairholme, R. N.

or chimneys are unknown in Tíbet, and fire is made on the ground where the form of the house allows of it. The smoke, like in the châlets of the Alps, escapes through an opening in the roof.

There is no monastery without a temple, and this latter occupies the centre of the building; in large monasteries, where more temples than one exist, the central one is the principal.

Each monastery is surrounded by a well-cultivated garden, in which flourish, owing to the care bestowed upon it by the Lamas, groups of poplar and willow trees, as well as apricots. The Lamas have succeeded in growing trees in localities far beyond the ordinary limit of such kind of vegetation. Thus it happens that at Mángnang, in Gnári Khórsum, at a height of 13,457 feet, fine poplars are found.

Historical Document relating to the Foundation of the Monastery of Hímis, in Ladák.

The following summary of a curious document of foundation is now published for the first time. The original, which is carved on a broad stone slab, 24 ft. high, was seen by my brother Hermann on the occasion of his visit to the monastery of Hímis, in September 1856, and he got an exact copy of it made, of which the following is an approximate translation. The occurrence of terms not explained in the dictionaries, and a spelling different from tha temployed in the sacred writings, made it impossible to give here a literal translation, as has been done with the address to the Buddhas of confession (Chapter XI.); yet all the importants facts could be deciphered which had reference to the time of the erection of the monastery, to the persons who ordered the building, and to those who constructed the edifice.[1] The document is divided into two paragraphs, which are distinguished in the original, printed on Plate IX., by a blank space between them.

First paragraph. This begins with a hymn to the Buddhist triad, viz. the Buddha (the author of the doctrine), the Dharma (his law), and the Sangha (the congregation of the faithful).[2]

"Hail! praise be and benediction! Salutation to the teachers! To the most perfect, eminent Buddha, who has the characteristic signs and proportions; to the excellent law, which reveals the entire truth; to the congregation of the faithful, who endeavour to become delivered: all honour be to these three Supremacies after a prosternation at the feet of the superiors" (here called *b*la-ma, comp. p. 156).

The remainder of this paragraph relates, in the usual

[1] In specimens of modern Tibetan, as *e. g.* in the treaty between Adolphe and the authorities of Dába (see Chapter XVI., 2), and in geographical names, we find words used which are not met with in literary language; and, more frequently still, terms presenting a most unexpected orthography. Perhaps we must account for this by phonetic corruption and the gradual formation of dialects; but we must not lose sight of the fact that but few people in Tíbet know how to write correctly—an art which, for that matter, was not very general in Europe either but a short time ago, when schools were limited to monasteries.

[2] "The protection derived from these three gems is said to destroy the fear of reproduction, or successive existence, and to take away the fear of the mind, the pain to which the body is subject, and the misery of the four hells." Hardy, "Eastern Monachism," p. 209.

bombastic style, the faithful adherence to Buddhism of Dharmarāja Senge Nampar Gyalva, and his father,[1] and the universal reverence paid by the Ladakis to the holy triad. It is stated that Senge Nampar ordered to be built on a magnificent style, and in his residences,[2] the "Vihāra of the three gems," the Sangye chi ku sung thug chi ten, *i. e.* the support of the meaning of Buddha's precepts, "whence the sun of the doctrine arose in this country brilliant as the dawn of the day." This monastery is said to be "the place where originated the entirely victorious (translators) of the three secrets," in Tibetan *g*sang *g*sum, which latter is probably to be referred to the book Gyatoki sangsum, which Jamya Namgyal ordered to be copied in letters of gold, silver, and copper (red).

It is further reported, that in the reign of this monarch many most learned and powerful Lamas had come to Ladák and taught the doctrine; we find the following names:

"*d*Pal-*m*nyam-med-'brug-pa = the master of incomparable happiness, the thunderer, who has spread Buddhist

[1] Dharmarāja, in Tibetan Choichi gyalpo, or by contraction Choigyal, "king of the law," is a title applied to the rulers and mythological persons who have furthered the cause of Buddhism.—This king is called by Cunningham, "Ladak," Chapter XII., Sengge Namgyal; his father is named Jamya Namgyal. Jamya had been dethroned and emprisoned by Ali Mir, a fanatic Mussalmán ruler of Skárdo, who had invaded Ladák and destroyed both the temples and the sacred images and books of the Buddhists. But later, when Jamya was re-established in his kingdom, he sent a mission to Lhássa with precious presents, and showed himself in many other ways a very faithful believer in Buddhism.

[2] The word here translated "residences," in Tibetan pho-brang-*r*nams, seems, on account of the plural particle *r*nams, to mean "territories, lands."

doctrine with the greatest energy throughout 'Dzam-bu-*g*ling,[1] but more particularly in this country.

"*r*God-ts'hang-pa,[2] whose titles are the victorious holding the Dorje, the beloved son of the patron of creatures.[3]

"*s*Tag-ts'hang-ras-pa-chhen, the great Bhikshu of the tiger nest, the greatly venerated, who disposes of magical power, and before whom many Lamas have prostrated themselves.[4]"

Second paragraph. The erection of the convent was entrusted to "*d*Pal-*l*dan-*r*tsa-va'i *b*la-ma = the illustrious Foundation Lama—who had dwelt in numerous monasteries, and had become firm and strong in the ten commandments.[5]

The edifice was begun in the month Voda, in Sanskrit Uttaraphalgunī (the second month), in the male water-horse year, and finished in the male water-tiger year, when the Lama performed the ceremony of consecration, the sign of completion. In the male iron-dog year the

[1] In Sanskrit Jambudvīpa; it is the name given to that quarter of the globe in which India lies.—Concerning the Brugpa sect see p. 74.

[2] The construction of the name makes it very probable that this Lama came to Ladák from the monastery God-tsang in Eastern Tíbet, to the name of which would then be added the particle pa.

[3] In Tibetan 'gro-va'i-*m*gon-po, from 'gro-va "a creature," and *m*gon-po "a patron;" a title indicating, that the person so styled is "a saint, a god." Perhaps we ought to take *r*God-ts'hang-pa as an incarnation of Chenresi (see p. 88), as well as grovai gonpo as one of his surnames; he is also styled Jigten gonpo, in Sanskrit Lokanātha, "the patron of the world."

[4] Cunningham, l. c., heard that this Lama had travelled through India, China, Kafiristan and Kashmir, and had made, and then consecrated an image of Maitreya in Tamosgang, in Ladák.

[5] With respect to the meaning of the term *r*tsa-va'i *b*la-ma see p. 141.—Concerning the ten commandments see Burnouf, "Le Lotus de la Bonne Loi," p. 446; Csoma, "Dictionary," p. 69.

monastery was encircled with "a hedge of the 'spen' shrub, and outside the Lion entrance were put up along the walls and the enclosure 300,000 Manis (or prayer-cylinders)." The document concludes by alluding to the merits which the king, the workmen (*i. e.* the masons, carpenters, porters), and in fact all engaged in the construction of this monastery, had derived from their assistance, and mentions in particular the salutary influence which the monastery will exercise in future upon the welfare and salvation of the inhabitants of Ladák.

When endeavouring to refer the years which I have given in the preceding part with their Tibetan denomination, to the corresponding years of the Christian era, it must be kept in mind that Senge Ṇampar Gyalva reigned, according to Cunningham, from 1620-70. Now, calculating by a cycle of 60 years, we obtain the following years for the dates occurring in this document:—

The erection was commenced in 1644;
The monastery was finished in 1664;
The 300,000 Manis were put up in 1672.

Calculating by a cycle of 252 years, we find the respective dates to be 1620, 1640, 1648. Also the latter years would not be excluded, as they would admit the supposition that the Hímis monastery was amongst those which his predecessor Jamya Namgyal had left unfinished at his decease; but in the present case we must adopt the years 1644-72, since for history it is the cycle of 60 years and not the cycle of 252 years which is used in Tibetan literature. As an instance confirming this I quote Csoma, who, in his Chronological Table, applied the cycle of 60 years to Tisri's designations, and obtained results sufficiently in accordance with those derived by Schmidt and Klaproth from Mongolian and Chinese works.[1]

Temples.

The exterior of the Buddhist temples in Tíbet differs in generally widely from that met with in other countries where Buddhism prevails. Whoever has had occasion to see the magnificent temples of Bérma, with their curious architecture, will be greatly disappointed on beholding a temple in Tíbet; for, with the exception of Lhássa, Tashilúnpo and Tassisúdon, scarcely any Tibetan temple presents extraordinary dimensions or a particularly imposing appearance.

The temples are called in Tibetan Lhakhang, and are most generally in immediate connexion with the buildings of the monasteries. There are, however, villages which have a temple only, without a monastery, and in this case the temple stands beside the houses; in hamlets without a temple, where nevertheless a solitary Lama resides, there is a room fitted up in his dwelling-house for the performance of the different rites and ceremonies. The architecture of the temples is simple. The roofs are now flat, now sloping, with square holes serving as windows and skylights, which are shut by a curtain being drawn across them.

The walls of the temples look towards the four

[1] Concerning the various systems of reckoning time see Chapter XVI.

Plate IX. HISTORICAL DOCUMENT RELATING TO THE FOUNDATION

OF THE

MONASTERY OF HÍMIS, IN LADÁK.

Copied from a large stone fixed in the wall.

༄༅།། །། ཨོཾ་སྭསྟི། །ན་མོ་གུ་རུ་བྷྱ། །མཚན་དཔེས་གསལ་རྫོགས་ཡང་དག་རྫོགས་སངས་རྒྱས། །བདེན་པ་མ་ལུས་སྟོན་ལ་
དམ་པའི་ཆོས། །གྲོལ་བ་དོན་གཉེར་འཕགས་ཚོགས་འདུས་པའི་སྡེ། །མཆོག་གསུམ་བླ་མའི་ཞབས་ལ་གུས་པས་འདུད། །དེ་ཡང༌། །
གསང་གསུམ་རྒྱལ་བ་ཀུན་གྱིས་འབྱུང་བའི་གནས། །རྒྱལ་བ་ཐམས་ཅད་ཀྱི་མངོན་པར་དབང་བསྐུར་ཞིང༌། །སྲིད་པའི་ཀུན་གྱིས་མཆོད་
ཅིང་མངོན་པར་མཆོད་འོས་ཆེན་པོའི་བདག་ཉིད་དཔལ་མཉམ་མེད་འབྲུག་པ་ཞེས་ཡོངས་སུ་གྲགས་པ་སངས་རྒྱས་ཀྱི་བསྟན་པའི་སྙིང་པོ་
ཡང་དག་པས་ནམ་ཁའི་མཐས་ཅན་ཡངས་པོར །ཁྱབ་ཅིང་ལྷུག་པར་འཛམ་བུ་གླིང་གིས་གནས་དང་གནས་ཁྱད་པར་ཡོངས་ལ་དར་ཞིང་
རྒྱས་ལ། །དེ་སྙིང་གི་གདུལ་བྱ་རྣམས་ཀྱང་སྨིན་སྨིན་ཅིང་གྲོལ་བའི། ལམ་ལ་བཀོད་པའི་མཛད་པའི་འཕྲིན་ལས་བསམ། ཀྱི་མི་ཁྱབ་
པའི་ས་གསུམ་དུ་བསྟན་པ་འཛིན་པ་ཀུན་ལས་ལྷག་པར་བཀྲིན་ཆེ་བར། །སྐུ་ཆེན་དམ་པ་རྣམས་ཀྱང་ཆེར་དུ་བསྔགས་བརྗོད་བླ་མ་མེད་པར་
མཛད། །ཞིང་འདིར་ཡང་བརྩེ་འགྲོ་བའི་མགོན་པོའི་ཐུགས་སྲས་རྗེ་རྗེ་འཆང་རྒྱལ་བ་རྒོད་ཚང་པ་ཡབ་སྲས་ཀྱིས་བྱིན་གྱིས་རླབས་མེད་ད།
སྤྲུལ་པའི་ཉིང་དེ་འཛིན་ལ་བཞུགས་དུས་མ་དང་མཁའ་འགྲོ་སྤྲིན་ཚོགས་སྐར་འདུ་ཞིང་མཆོད་ཅིང་བསྐོར་བ་ན་དཔལ་ཧེ་རུ་ཀ་ཡིས་ཀྱི་
ཁོར་ལོ་སོགས་གནས་ཉེར་བཞི་དང་མཚུངས། །རིམ་པའི་མཚན་ལྡན་གྱི་བླ་མ་སྐྱེས་ཆེན་འགའ་ཡང་བྱོན། །ཁྱད་པར་མཆོག་གིས་བསྔགས་
པའི་གྲུབ་དབང་སྟག་ཚང་རས་པ་ཆེན་པོའི་ཞབས་ལ། །ཆོས་ཀྱི་རྒྱལ་པོ་སེངྒེ་རྣམ་པར་རྒྱལ་བ་ཡབ་སྲས་རྗེ་བློན་འཁོར་དང་བཅས་པས་
མི་ཕྱེད་པའི་དད་པས་སྤྱི་བོས་མཆོད་ཅིང་བསྟེན་པའི་ཐུགས་གཉིས་ཀྱི་དཔལ་འབྱོར་ཕུན་སུམ་ཚོགས་པར་བསྟེན། །གདན་ས་ཆེན་པོ་མ་
ཐུ་རྣམས་དང༌། །རྒྱལ་པོའི་སོ་བྱང་རྣམ་སུ་ཡང་སངས་རྒྱས་ཀྱི་སྐུ་གསུང་ཐུགས་ཀྱི་རྟེན་གསུམ་རིན་པོ་ཆེ་གཙུག་ལག་ཁང་སོགས་བྱེ་དང་
དུ་རྒྱ་ཆེར་ཀུན་པས་བསྟན་པའི་ཉི་མ་ཤར་བ་ལྟར་བྱུང༌། །སྐྱབས་རྗེ་ཡབ་རིན་པོ་ཆེ་མི་ཕམ་འཇམ་དཔལ་མཐུ་སྟོབས་རྡོ་རྗེའི་སྒྲ་རིང་
ལ། །རིགས་ཀྱི་བདག་པོ་དཔལ་མཉམ་མེད་རྗེ་འབྲུག་པ་ཐམས་ཅད་མཁྱེན་པ་ཆེན་པོ་ངང་སེམས་དམ་སྨིན་གྲོལ་དམ་པའི་ཆོས་ཀྱི་རྗེ་སུ་
གཟུང་ཞིང་བྱིན་གྱིས་རླབས། །རྗེ་མཉམ་མེད་བསྟན་འགྲོའི་མགོན་པོ་སྐྱབས་ཀུན་དུས་ཞལ་དཔལ་རིག་པ་འཛིན་དབང་ཆེན་པོས་རིམ་སུ་
མ་ཆད་པའི་བསྟན་འགྲོ་སྤྲོ་དང་ཕྱི་ནག་ལྗོངས་འདིར་རས་ཁྲུས་ཀྱི་བསྟན་པ་དང་འགྲོ་བའི་བདེ་སྐྱིད་ལ་དགོངས་པའི་བཀའ་དང་ཐུགས་རྗེས་
ཁོ་བོ་ལ་འདང་སྐལ་ལྡན་གྱི་སྐྱེས་བུར་རྗེ་སུ་བཟུང་ནས་མཚན་མི་ཕམ་ཆོས་དབང་འཕྲིན་ལས་བསྟན་འཛིན་མི་འགྱུར་རྡོ་རྗེ་ཞེས་དབང་བསྐུར་
གནང་བས་བྱིན་གྱིས་རླབས་ནས་སངས་རྒྱས་ཀྱི་བསྟན་པ་དགེ་འདུན་ལ་རག་ལས་པའི་འཕགས།། ||

༄༅། །དགོན་པར་ཚུན་འདུས་སྡེ་རྣམས་ལ་སྐྱབས་གསུམ་གྱི་སྡོམ་ཁྲིམས་ལ་གནས་ནས་དགེ་བ་བཅུའི་སྤང་བླང་འཛེམ་མེད་དུ་སྤྱོད་རྒྱུའི་
ཕྱག་རྒྱ་དང་བཅས་བཀའ་ཤོག་ཏུ་སྩལ་ཞིང༌། དེར་བརྟེན་རང་ངོས་ནས་ཀྱང་རྗེ་བཙུན་དཔལ་ལྡན་རྩ་བའི་བླ་མ་ཡབ་སྲས་ཀྱི་བཀྲིན་
ཡིད་ལ་བཅངས་ནས་དགོངས་པ་རྫོགས་བྱེར་སྟར་ལོ་ཆུ་མོ་སྟག་གི་དཔོ་ཟླ་དཀར་བརྩེགས་ཚེ་མོ་ཧའི་ཡོར་གཙུག་ལག་ཁང་ལེགས་པར་
གྲུབ་ཏུ་གནས་བཀྲ་ཤིས་མངའ་གསོལ་དགའ་སྟོན་རྒྱ་ཆེ་བ་གྲུབ་པའི་ཐོག །ལྷུགས་པོ་ཁྲིའི་ལོར་སེངྒེ་སྒོམ་པའི་ཕྱིར་རིམས་པའི་མན་ཐང་
སོ་སོའི་དོན་སུ་མ་ཉེ་འབུམ་གསུམ་ཡོད་པ་སྙིན་བང་དང་བཅས་པ་ཕྱི་ནང་ཀུ་ན་ཏུ་བཀོད་པ་པོ་ཕྱག་མཛོད་བཀྲ་ཤིས་ཀྱིས་བླ་མ་མཆོག་
གསུམ་ལ་གུས་ཤིང་ལྷག་པའི་བསམ་སྦྱོར་རྣམ་པ་དཀར་བས་ཞབས་ཏོག་ཕུལ་དུ་ཕྱུང་བ་ཕུན་མེད། ལས་སུ་སྦྱོལ་པོ་ལྷ་ཐུར་ཤེས་
རབ་ཆེ་དབང་སོགས་དང༌། ལས་མི་མིང་མཁན་རྩིག་བཟོ་བ་རྣམས་དང༌། མཐའ་ན་ཕྱི་ལག་གི་ལས་མི་ཐམས་ཅད་ཀྱི་ཀྱང་དད་པ་དད་པ་
ཆེན་པོའི་བསམ་སྦྱོར་རྣམ་དག་གི་ངང་ནས་བསྒྲུབས་པ་ཡིན་པས། དེ་གེ་བ་རྒྱ་ཆེན་ཐག་མེད་ཏུས་པའི་མཐུས། །སྐྱབས་ཀུན་འདུས་པའི་
བླ་མའི་ཞབས་པདྨ་བརྟན་ཅིང༌། །སྨིན་གྲོལ་ཆོས་ཆར་འཛམ་གླིང་ཁྱབ་པ་དང༌། །བསྟན་པའི་སྦྱིན་བདག་ཆོས་རྒྱལ་རྗེ་འབངས་བཅས།
།བདེ་སྐྱིད་ཡར་ངོའི་དཔལ་ལ་སྤྱོད་པ་དང༌། །དགྲས་མཐའི་དམག་དཔུང་བསམ་སྦྱོར་ངན་པའི་ཚོགས། །མ་ལུས་ཀུན་ཞི་བདེ་སྐྱིད་དགའ་
བདེ་དང༌། །ཐུགས་མཐུན་ཆོས་བཞིན་བསྐྱབ་ལ་བརྩོན་གྱུར་ནས། །རྒྱ་སྐྱོར་ཡོད་ཀྱི་འཕེལ་ཐོགས་ཐོགས་ཅད་ཀྱང༌། །རྣམ་ཀུན་ཆོས་
སྤྱོད་བཅུ་ལ་འབད་པའི་མཐུས། །ཀྱོགས་བཅུར་བཀྲིས་ཆར་ཆུ་དུས་སུ་འབབ། །ལོ་ཕྱུགས་ཏག་ལེགས་རྫོགས་ལྡན་བཞིན་སྤྱོད་ནས། །
སངས་རྒྱས་གོ་འཕང་མྱུར་ཐོབ་རྒྱུར་གྱུར་ཅིག། །།སརྦ་མངྒ་ལཾ།། །།ཛེ་ཡ་ཛེ་ཡ་སུ་ཛེ་ཡ།། །།

quarters of heaven, and each side should be painted with a particular colour, viz. the north side with green, the south side with yellow, the east side with white, and the west side with red; but this rule seems not to be strictly adhered to, as my brother saw many temples with all sides either of the same colour, or simply whitewashed.

The interior of the temples which my brothers had occasion to see[1] consisted of one large square room, with an entrance-hall in the front; occasionally also entrance-halls—but then smaller ones—are found along the other three sides of the temple. The inside surface of the walls is whitewashed or covered with a kind of plaster. They are then generally decorated with paintings representing episodes taken from the life of the Buddhas, or images of gods of dreadful countenance. My brothers were told, that the art of fresco painting is practised by a particular class of Lamas, called Pon, who reside in Lhássa when their services are not required for country temples.

In the side halls of the temple is generally situated the library, the volumes being regularly arranged on shelves, and wrapped in silk. In the corners are placed tables bearing numerous statues of deities; and the religious dresses, the musical instruments, and other things required for the daily service, are hung up on wooden pegs along the walls. Benches are also placed

[1] As an example of their construction see the interior of the monastery of Mángnang, in Gnári Khórsum, by Adolphe in the "Atlas of Panoramas and Views." The interior of the Singhalese temples is very similar to that of the Tibetan temples. See Hardy, "Eastern Monachism," p. 200.

in the temple, upon which the Lamas take their seat, when assembled for prayer.

The roof of the temples is supported by two rows of unornamented wooden pillars painted red, and dividing it into three parallelograms; large silken fans, called Phan, striped white and blue and with unravelled fringed edges,[1] together with musical and other instruments, are suspended to these pillars; while from the cross-beams hang numerous Zhaltang, or pictures of deities, each fastened to two red sticks, and generally covered with a veil of white silken cloth. The altar stands in the central gallery, and consists of differently sized wooden benches, beautifully carved and richly ornamented; the smaller ones are set upon the larger before a partition of planks on which hang fans of the five sacred colours (viz. yellow, white, red, blue and green) held together by a crescent, the convex side of which was turned upwards. Upon these benches are ranged the offering vessels, statues of Buddhas and gods, and some instruments and utensils used in religious worship; amongst the latter is always seen the mirror Melong which is used in the ceremony Tuisol; then some bells and Dorjes, together with a Chorten containing relics and having occasionally a niche with the statue of some deity; also a vase with peacock feathers and a sacred book is never wanting. The offering vessels are of brass, and similar

[1] These fans are to be understood as tokens of reverence paid to the gods, and answer to the silken scarfs inscribed with sentences which Tibetan politeness requires should be offered by visitors or enclosed in letters. These scarfs are called in Tibetan Khatak, or Tashi Khatak, "scarf of benediction."

in shape to the Chinese tea-cups; they are filled with barley, butter, and perfumes, in summer with flowers. Beside the altar is a small bench upon which the officiating Lama ranges the offerings to be consumed in the burnt-offering, and the ritual instruments he requires in particular ceremonies.—At the end of the gallery stands, in a recess, the statue of the *genius loci* to whom the temple is consecrated; in some temples his head is shaded by a canopy of cloth, the form of which may be seen from Plate X.; from its central part called Dug (literally umbrella) extend some horizontal ribands, Labri, at the ends of which hang vertical flags, Badang, Sanskrit Patāka.

In the entrance-hall, at both sides of the door, and also in the interior of the temple, are several large prayer-cylinders, which are perpetually kept revolving by the attending Lama. The walls are not unfrequently decorated with views of sacred cities and monasteries,[1] executed in colours upon paper; these are much ruder than their drawings of gods; they have no perspective, and the houses are traced in front view, but very incorrectly. A vertical plan of Lhássa, which the Tibetan Lamas honour with the name of a landscape, is almost always amongst these representations of sacred spots; it resembles somewhat the older plans of European cities, drawn from a bird's-eye view.

[1] Also Turner, "Embassy," p. 158, mentions having seen some in the temple of Wandeechy, in Bhután.

Religious monuments.

Buddhism has erected various religious monuments, amongst which are particularly to be mentioned the Chortens, the Manis, and the Derchoks and Lapchas.

1. *Chortens.*

The motive for the erection of these monuments is identical to that which gave rise to the frequent erection of the Stūpas, or Chāityas of ancient Buddhism in India, of which so great a number have been recently discovered in India and Afghanistán and carefully examined.[1] But a peculiarity of the Chortens is the use which the Tibetans make of them: The name of Chorten denotes at once their nature and object, for its component words *m*chhod, and *r*ten signify "an offering" and "to keep, a receptacle." The Tibetan mode of spelling this word would imply that its pronunciation was Chodten, but the "d" before "t" is suppressed, and the "r" is heard, although, according to grammatical rules it should be mute. The Tibetans of Gnári Khórsum, however, pronounce Chogdan; Gerard[2] writes Chosten or Chokten, a designation which appears

[1] Concerning the ideas connected with Stūpas, and the reports about their construction and the objects which have been digged out, see the works of Ritter, "Die Stūpas," Berlin 1834. Wilson, "Ariana antiqua," London, 1841. Cunningham, "The Bhilsa Topes," London, 1854. Sykes, "On the miniature Chaityas," R. A. S., 1856; and "Account of Golden Relics," R. A. S., 1857. Compare also Burnouf, "Introduction," p. 346. Respecting their age Wilson, "Buddha and Buddhism," R. A. Soc., p. 249, is of opinion that the custom of erecting Stūpas is somewhat posterior to that of excavating temples and constructing Vihāras, or monasteries; the Stūpas in the North-west of India were most probably erected in a period commencing with the first years of the Christian era and terminating in the sixth century.

[2] "Kanawur," p. 124.

to be a dialectical modification. Both he and Cunningham[1] also mention the name Donkten or Dungten for those Chortens in which relics are deposited—a name which seems not frequently used.

The ancient Stūpas were originally meant as receptacles for relics of either the Buddhas or the Bōdhisattvas and the kings who encouraged the propagation of the Buddhist faith. But already in the early periods of Buddhism Stūpas were constructed *ex voto* as symbolical substitutes for a tomb with a sacred relic, either for marking the spot where remarkable incidents in the sacred history had taken place, or for decorating the Vihāras and temples. Their erection is considered as an act of devotion and reverence paid to the Buddhas, and was recommended already in the ancient legends as a most meritorious work.

The Tibetan Chortens also serve as *relic repositories*, as they enclose remains of revered Lamas, sacred writings, consecrated objects, &c., deposited therein already at their erection. Chortens containing bones or ashes in a box are erected in the burial grounds; Chortens with writings are of smaller size, and are ranged upon the altars; they typify the Buddha's mercy.[2] But the predominant idea connected with the Chortens is that of their being *offering receptacles*,[3] for no Tibetan passes them without depositing some sort of oblation, either on the

[1] "Ladak," p. 377.

[2] See p. 137.

[3] Also the Singhalese believe the protection of Buddha not to be obtained by simply going near a Dagopa (= Stūpa) or other sacred place, if the passer-by performs no particular act of worship. Hardy, "Eastern Monachism," p. 210, compare also p. 223.

steps, or in the interior by a small opening leading to a shrine. The objects deposited are chiefly the Satsas, or Tsatsas, which are very generally made on the road by kneading a portion of clay between the fingers; they are conical, in imitation of the form of a Chorten. Other Satsas represent Buddhas, or have a sacred sentence pressed upon by means of moulds; the latter are bought from the Lamas.[1] The quantity of Satsas is really astonishing; it not unfrequently happens that the steps are nearly hidden by the heaps of Satsas.

The form of the Chortens varies much more than that of their prototypes, the Stūpas. The base of the Stūpa is a cylinder or cube, upon which a body shaped like a cupola is set up. Stūpas which have been broken down have been found to be solid buildings, with a little shrine in the centre only, in which had been deposited the burnt bones of a human being, together with coins, jewels and inscribed slabs. The bones are sometimes enclosed in small cases made of the precious metals.

In the Tibetan Chortens this form has in general undergone considerable modifications; the unaltered ancient type has remained limited to the smaller Chortens put up in the temples. The principal difference between a Stūpa and a Chorten is that in the latter the cupola is either surmounted by a cone, or that it is inverted. The most general style is the following: The base is a cube, upon which rests the inverted cupola; this cupola is the principal part; it encloses the objects enshrined, and in it is

[1] In Mongolia, the name Satsa, by Pallas called Zaga, is applied to the cones of clay only: *see* his "Mongol. Völker," Vol. II., pp. 108, 211.

the hole leading to the space for the offerings. A graduated pinnacle rises above it, and this is either a cone of stones or a wooden spire; it is surmounted by a disk placed horizontally and a pear-shaped point, or, instead of it, by a crescent supporting a globe and the pear upon that. Chortens of this form occur in every Tibetan district. They are exclusively used in Bhután and Síkkim, and are also met with in the plans of sacred temples; but in other parts of Tíbet several other forms are seen. Of these I mention the following: In Ladák a moderately high cone, similar to the roof of a building, and projecting over the border of the inverted cupola, forms its top; it either rests immediately upon the cupola, or a cube of smaller dimensions is interposed between them. This cone ends in a wooden point similar in shape to the point of a spear, or there is a slender pole the size of which diminishes with the scarcity of wood. Originally a flag with prayers printed upon it was fastened to every pole; but in most cases only rags are left, or the flags have been blown away entirely. In Gnári Khórsum some Chortens are more like a tower; upon a cube as base is placed a body square at the base and slightly pyramidal in form, which, after diminishing a little and again increasing in width, is surmounted by a bell-shaped projecting top, or a bell resting upon a little tower. When new or in good condition it is surmounted by a pole embellished with a flag. The Chortens in the environs of Thóling are plainly pyramidal, consisting of five to six steps; the upper end is a small cube covered by a conical roof. Others can be described in reference to their principal parts as a cube notched into several steps, supporting an angular bell-shaped body: these Chortens are very similar to the ancient Stūpas.

The materials used for the Chortens in the open air are rough stones, bricks,[1] or clay; they are almost all of solid masonry. The outer surfaces are thickly plastered with mortar, which is coloured red with the dust of pounded bricks. Grooves are formed similar to the panels on European doors, and simple ornaments are delineated in the mortar. Only once, at Gyúngul, in Gnári Khórsum, my brother Adolphe saw a hollow tower-chorten, which was constructed of planks. It stood close to the monastery, and was perhaps but an enclosure for smaller Chortens, similar to those which Gerard had seen in Kanáur,[2] where they are open in front; this is not the case with the Chorten at Gyúngul, which has four walls and no entrance.

The height of the Chortens is in general from 8 to 15 ft., though a few considerably exceed this latter height, attaining to as much as 40 ft. Those set up in the temples are moulded from metal, or more generally from clay mixed with chopped straw; occasionally they are carved of wood; but such Chortens scarcely ever exceed four feet; they are often not higher than as many inches.

2. *Manis.*

Mani, originally a Sanskrit word meaning "a precious stone,"[3] which became naturalised in Tibetan, is used to

[1] The custom of hardening the bricks in the sun originated in the powerful insolation, combined with the very small amount of humidity in the atmosphere.

[2] Gerard, "Kanawur," p. 124.

[3] The prayer cylinders are also called "Manis."

designate walls of about six feet in height and four to eight feet in breadth, but their length varies much more considerably. The largest hitherto known is that which is situated on the road from the banks of the Indus to Leh; according to Cunningham it has a length of 2200 ft.[1] Two others at Leh itself Hermann found to be respectively 459 and 386 ft. in length. He also measured one at Mándang, near Darjíling, in Síkkim, which was 90 ft.: another at Narigún was 244 ft. in length.

The Manis are constructed in the higher valleys of loose stones only; whilst in the lower ones, where mortar is not so expensive an article, lime is used. Some of the large Manis have a kind of tower at both their ends, occasionally in the form of a Chorten, with a sacred image in front; if, as is sometimes the case, the Mani is made longer, the old tower remains and a new one is added at the end of the prolongation. Large poles, to which flags with prayers are attached, are also not unfrequent at the ends of the Manis.

Rough, irregularly rectangular stone slabs greatly differing in size, and bearing inscriptions in Tibetan or Lantsa characters,[2] or adorned with images of deities, lean against the upper part of the wall or are laid down on the roof of the Mani. The most frequent inscription met with in the stone slabs is the six-syllabic prayer: Om mani padme hum;[3] or adorations of Vajrasattva, as:

[1] "Ladák," p. 378.

[2] See p. 80.

[3] This sentence was traced in enormous characters, formed by blackish stones, on the slope of the mountain opposite Láma Yúrru, and was visible at a great distance.

Om, ah, hum; vajra guru padma siddhi hum; of Vajrapāni, as: Om Vajrapāni hum; or mystical ejaculations, as: Om, ah, hum. Amongst the names of deities engraved on the stone slabs, we frequently find Sākyamuni, Padmapāni, Padma Sambhaba, Vajrapāni (see Plate II.), and different recluses. The slabs are, according to Cunningham, votive offerings made for the purpose of obtaining the fulfilment of particular wishes. Travellers, when passing along the Manis, leave them on the left hand, in order to follow the succession of the letters of the inscriptions.[1]

3. *Derchoks and Lapchas.*

Almost every building is decorated with flags, attached to a pole set up before the edifice, such flags being considered efficacious in preventing the evil spirits from doing mischief. Single flags are also met with in front of religious buildings, and along the road; those before large monasteries are often of considerable height; the two largest which my brothers saw were planted in front of the entrance to the monastery of Hímis;[2] one was 45, the other even 57 ft. in height, and as there is no tree in Tíbet attaining such a height, these poles

[1] Gerard, in his "Kanawur," p. 123, remarks that passers-by always leave the Manis to their right, and expresses his belief that superstition is the reason for their doing so; but my brothers never saw their people pass them in this way, but always so as to leave the Mani on the left hand; and they were told by several Lamas that the reason for this was, that in so passing by they could follow the characters, instead of having to spell backwards.

[2] See my brother Hermann's "Views of the monastery of Hímis," in the Atlas to the "Results of a Scientific Mission."

must have been transported with great difficulty, across the Himálaya. The upper part of these poles was decorated with three concentric rings of black yaks-hair suspended at some distance from each other; whilst in general the poles have but one tuft of yaks-hair surmounted by a gilt spear-end.

The flags are called Derchok (the Durchut of Gerard), the heap of loose stones to support the pole, Lapcha; both terms are doubtless words of popular origin, not occurring in the Dictionaries. The "der" in Derchok might be explained from dar, *silk*, a stuff sometimes used for flags. Lapcha is very probably a modification of lab-tse, "a heap," which also occurs in geographical names, either in the form of Labtse, as in Lábtse Nágu and Lábtse Chhu, in Gnári Khórsum, or as Lápcha.[1]

Some flags are of a regular shape, and prayers and incantations (such as "Om mani padme hum"), invocations of the airy horse (in Tibetan Lungta), the magical figure Phurbu, and others, are printed upon them. These printed flags are fastened to the pole on the longest side, and are prevented from loosely hanging down and folding by horizontal red sticks. Other flags are mere rags of every size and material; such rags are chiefly added by travellers to the Lapchas found along the route, in order to obtain "a happy journey." Nowhere are Lapchas more numerous than on the highest point of a pass, and not unfrequently one is surprised to find a Lapcha even on

[1] For details I refer to Hermann's "Glossary of Geographical names," *s. v. Lápcha* which forms Part. II. of Vol. III. of the "Results."

high spots situated out of the regular road; the reason is that the frontiers of provinces are likewise marked by irregular heaps of stones,[1] and thus, even on the top of the Gunshankår, in Gnári Khórsum, which attains a height of 19,699 ft., my brothers found a Lapcha. Their Buddhist companions were always most eager to add new flags wherever they passed, or to erect a new Lapcha by making a large heap of stones, in the middle of which they set up one of their almost indispensable mountain-sticks, which was then decorated with flags, partly made from my brothers' handkerchiefs, partly from the bags in which they had kept their provisions, and from pieces of their very dress. When every one had made his contribution to the Derchok, they walked solemnly round the heap whispering prayers.

[1] Comp. Georgi, "Alphabetum Tibetanum," p. 508.

CHAPTER XIV

REPRESENTATIONS OF BUDDHIST DEITIES

Deities Represented.—Methods of executing sacred Objects. Drawings and paintings.—Statues and bas-reliefs.—**Characteristic Types.**—General attitude of the body and position of the fingers.—Buddhas.—Bōdhisattvas.—Priests, ancient and modern.—Dragsheds. **Illustrations derived from Measurements.**

Deities represented.

We learn from the ancient legends, that already in the earliest periods of Buddhism relics and images of the Buddha had been highly honoured; the religious works recommend them to be worshipped, as also the monuments in which the relics are deposited; and we find it mentioned that the images which were sent to royal persons at their desire, were previously inscribed with the sacred dogma "Ye Dharma," &c., and similar formulæ, in order to make them acquainted with Buddhist doctrines.[1] Such were the earliest objects of worship; the mode of worship was also very simple; prosternations were made before the images of the Buddha, flowers and

[1] Burnouf, "Introduction," p. 337-51. Schmidt, "Grundlehren." Mém. de l'Acad. de St. Petersb., Vol. I., p. 238. For the Sanskrit and Tibetan text see Plate I.

perfumes were offered, and prayers and hymns recited for their glorification. The same simplicity of rite prevailed still in the seventh century A.D., as we learn from Hiuen Thsang, though the objects of adoration and worship had increased in number; for Hiuen Thsang mentions, that the principal disciples of Sākyamuni were then worshipped, as also the Bōdhisattvas who had excelled in virtue and in the sciences, as Manjusrī; the Mahāyāna schools, he says, have adored even all Bōdhisattvas without any further distinction.[1]

At the present day, besides the things and persons just mentioned, the mythological Buddhas preceding Sākyamuni as well as those who will follow him, their corresponding Dhyāni Buddhas and Dhyāni Bōdhisattvas, are worshipped, and a host of gods, spirits, and deified priests enjoying a local reputation for sanctity. In order to furnish an idea of their immense number, I mention, that the Tibetan collection of Buddhist images, known under the name "Gallery of Portraits," contains the drawings of more than three hundred Buddhas, saints, &c., each having his name added beneath.[2]

Methods of executing sacred objects.

Modern Buddhism, in order to facilitate the worship of its many deities, has made representations of

[1] Barthélemy St. Hilaire, "Le Buddha et sa Religion," p. 288-297.

[2] This "Gallery of Portraits" is similar to the Japanese collection of Buddha figures, entitled "the Buddha Pantheon of Nippon," which was compiled 1690 and consists of 631 drawings. Prof. J. Hofmann at Leyden has published it and illustrated it by annotations in Siebold's "Nippon, Archiv zur Beschreibung von Japan," Vol. V.

them in prodigious quantities. Copies are met with everywhere, not a temple but contains lots of them; they are set up in the private houses and in the open air; and title-pages of printed books, nay even the headings of each chapter are frequently embellished either by a black figure, or by a coloured one. This astonishingly frequent application of representations has probably sprung from the belief, that the image, by being consecrated, becomes "animated," amilakho in Mongolian, viz. endowed with the powers of the God whom it represents; addresses, therefore, may be directed not only to the God himself, but also to his respective image.[1]

The images are manufactured exclusively by the Lamas, who excel herein like their masters the Chinese (who first introduced the images of the Buddha into Tíbet), and from whom they afterwards learned how to overcome many of the technical difficulties connected with the manufacture.[2] The monopoly now exercised by the Lamas has chiefly resulted from the belief that prayers directed to representations are efficacious only when they have been executed under prescribed forms and ceremonies, which the clergy alone know how to perform. The ceremonies to be observed are most numerous and various; there are certain days proper for the commencement of a particular picture, and others again on

[1] See Schmidt, "Ssanang Ssetsen," p. 330. I refer the reader to the legends about the alleged influence of the pictures brought to Tíbet by the wives of Srongtsan Gampo on the spreading of Buddhism and the welfare of the Tibetans. *Ibidem* p. 345.

[2] With reference to Chinese art compare Nott and Gliddon, "Indigenous Races," p. 302.

which alone the eyes are to be painted, these being considered the most important part of the whole picture; besides which during the various stages of progress of each picture other ceremonies and prayers are requisite. Thus, benedictory ceremonies[1] have to be performed immediately after the entire completion of the image, in order that in the meantime no malignant spirit (which beings are considered to be always on the watch to do mischief to man) may take possession of it, whereby the prayers would be rendered utterly valueless.

Plastic objects, such as statues and bas-reliefs, are not less numerous than drawings and paintings.

Drawings and paintings. The patterns for drawings are called Sagpar, and are made by desribing the outlines of an original drawing with numerous pin-holes, and by rubbing coal-dust into these holes the outlines are transmitted to paper or canvass, prepared with lime and flour-paste; the stratum when dry and hard, is carefully polished with stones before being used.[2] The lines are then traced with China ink, and the different parts of the picture covered with colours of a uniform tint; only few ornaments are shaded. The picture, when completed, is bordered by several strips of silk, called Thonka, generally three in number, blue, yellow, and red; occasionally also irregular rags of other colours are sewed to its borders. As they have no glass, they

[1] A work embodied in the Gyut division of the Kanjur also treats of the ceremonies to be performed on such occasions. See Csoma, "Analysis," As. Res., Vol. XX., p. 503.

[2] The Kalmuks and also the Mongolians print the outlines with woodcuts. Pallas, "Mongol. Völker," Vol. II., p. 105.

use for protection against dust silk vail-like coverings; and the only part corresponding to the frame of our pictures, is represented by two round wooden sticks, one of which is passed through the upper border, the other through the lower one; they facilitate the hanging up of the picture and at the same time keep it stretched when hung up. The lower stick is also used to roll the picture upon when sent about.

Statues and bas-reliefs. In the construction of these things moulds are used which are filled out with various plastic materials, such as clay, or a kind of papier-maché, or bread-dough; the positive objects are then generally dried in the sun. Metal figures are but rarely made. The statues are often painted or slightly gilt. As a peculiarity I must mention that even butter is used; it is tinted with different vegetable colours before being put into the mould; the head, the feet, and the hands are filled out in the mould with yellow butter, the garments with red, and so on. They remain put up before the sacred images till the butter, by decomposition, becomes intolerable; they are then thrown away.[1] The sharpness of the statuettes and medaillons, even of the smallest, is quite surprising.

The most esteemed plastic figures are those in which are enclosed relics (as ashes, bones, hair, rags of the garments of saints), or grains first offered to the Buddhas in divine worship. The grains, before being put into the figures, are consecrated again by a particular cere-

[1] Compare also Huc, "Souvenirs," Vol. II., p. 95. In Ceylon temporary images are made of rice. Hardy, "Eastern Monachism," p. 202.

mony, called Rabne zhugpa. Relics and grains are either mixed with the material of which the figure is composed, or they are enshrined in a small hole at the bottom or back, the hole being called Zung zhug, "Dhāranī place," from the Zungs or Dhāranīs read during the ceremonies of the consecration. The hole is closed again by a seal, in order to prevent the objects from falling out or from being taken out without the fact being discovered, for then the figure is supposed to have lost all its beneficial influence. Figures containing such sacred objects, are styled Satsa, or Tsatsa, a name which is also given to the chorten-like cones moulded from clay by travellers.[1]

In the drawings, as well as upon the sculptures a variety of symbolical signs occur. Hodgson has drawn attention in several of his papers to these signs as a means of determining that ruins showing such symbols are certainly Buddhist remains; he has recently published a collection of 110 symbols, which were extracted from Nepalese Buddhist images, books, and engravings on stone—a collection highly important for tracing the extent of Buddhism in earlier periods. In these papers Hodgson points out in several instances the identity of Buddhist symbols with those upon images of Sivaitic deities; but by closely examining their meaning with the Buddhists, he came to the conclusion "that the things typified are always more or less, and generally radically, different;" and his opinion is highly supported by Hofmann, who

[1] Comp. p. 194.

made analogous researches about Japanese writings and images.[1]

Characteristic types.

A comparison of the images of various sacred persons shows at once a strongly marked difference in attitude, features, dress, and emblems between the various groups, particularly between the Buddhas, the Bōdhisattvas, the priests (ancient and modern), and the Dragsheds.

General attitude of the body and position of the fingers. The artist who makes a representation of any god, is not allowed to follow his own idea or to make any alteration in the original design. But many of the gods may be represented in several attitudes recalling some of the glorious and important moments of their life. Thus, *Sākyamuni*, with one hand uplifted, denotes his character as a teacher; a sitting attitude, with one hand holding the alms-bowl, the other hanging down over the knee, is chosen to represent him plunged in meditation; a recumbent position means his having left the world for ever. *Padmapāni's* eleven faces and thousand hands and feet refer to the legend about the cleaving of his head. *Melha*, the God of fire, when driving away the evil spirits, rides a red ram, and has a most horrible countenance; whilst in representations not having for object

[1] Hodgson, "Illustrations," p. 209. Journ. of the R. A. Soc., Vol. XVIII., p. 393; thirty-three symbols derived from coins have been omitted from considerations of cost. See instead of them the series of 168 compiled by Wilson, Plate XXII., in his "Ariana antiqua."—Hofmann, "Nippon Pantheon;" remarks annexed to Fig. 163, 432.

to show his wrath, his attitude and type are those of a Buddha.

The positions of the fingers, also (in Tibetan Chakja, literally *an emblem, a seal,* in Sanskrit Mudrā), have an allegorical meaning. Thus, the right hand hanging down over the knee, with the palm of the hand turned outwards, symbolizes charity, and is called Chagye chin, "the right hand of charity."

The attitude Rangi nying gar thalmo charva, *i. e.* "uniting the palms of the hands on one's heart," is the following:—The two hands uplifted, a finger of the right hand touching one or two fingers of the left hand, like a man accustomed to use his fingers in explaining his meaning. This attitude typifies "the unity of wisdom with matter," in Tibetan Thabshes, or Thabdang shesrab, or the assuming of the material forms by the Buddhas and Bōdhisattvas for the purpose of spreading the right understanding amongst animated beings. It is certainly not accidental that none of the Buddhist gestures are identical with those made by the Brahmans when performing the ceremonies of their creed.[1]

The *Buddhas* are men, but men of the most perfect form, endowed with thirty-two superior beauties, and eighty or eighty-four secondary ones.[2] It is in strict conformity with these characteristics, that the Buddhas are represented with soft and smiling features, which are

[1] These have been collected in Mrs. S. C. Belnos' folio work, "The Sundya, or daily prayers of the Brahmans." London 1851. For *Buddhist* gestures see the plates of Hofmann's "Buddha Pantheon."

[2] See concerning these, Burnouf, "Le Lotus de la Bonne Loi," Appendix VIII. Hardy, "Manual of Buddhism," p. 367.—Compare also p. 140.

also given to Maitreya, the future Buddha, who in the other attributes is likewise equal to the Buddhas who have already appeared. These, the Mānushi Buddhas, are of gold or yellow complexion; both colours are identical, the latter being but the cheaper substitute for gold. The ears are large, the laps rest upon the shoulders; the arms are long; there is a single hair on the forehead, called in Sanskrit Urnā; on the crown of the head is a cylindrical elevation, in Sanskrit Ushnīsha, in Tibetan Tsugtor, and from this rises a conical ornament called in Tibetan Progzhu, or Chodpan, "a head-ornament, a crown, diadem," which is almost always gilt. The Buddhists view the Ushnīsha as an excrescence of the skull, an interpretation, however, which is not supported by the etymology of the name, which would restrict its meaning to "a turban," or "dressed hair." I believe this curious protuberance to have resulted from the way of dressing the hair practised by the Brahmans, which is decidedly very ancient, and is found to be the same as that on the oldest figures we know. The Brahmans cut away the hair, except that on a circular space on the crown, which they twist into a knot. It is most probable that the Buddhist have conferred upon their sublime masters this prerogative of the highest Indian caste.[1]

[1] Burnouf, "Lotus," p. 558, believes this hair-dress to have been adopted as a protection against the dangerous influence of the sun.—A trace of the original view has also been retained in the Tibetan term Tsugtor for Ushnīsha, which is explained in the Dictionaries to mean "a tuft of hair," as well as "a sort of excrescence on the crown of the head." A Nepalese Buddha priest, also, speaking of Vajrasattva's image at Buddha Gayah, says: "The lock on the crown of the head is twisted into a turban." Hodgson, "Illustrations," p. 206.

The Dhyāni Buddhas and the mythological Buddhas have a white, red, green or blue complexion. The Dhyāni Buddhas are, besides, distinguished by a third eye on the forehead—the eye of wisdom, in Tibetan Shesrab chan; in those images of Padmapāni in which he is represented with a great many hands, this eye is also traced in the palm of his hands.

All Buddhas are dressed in the religious shawl, the Lagoi, which is generally folded round the body and over the left shoulder, with a small end coming up over the right shoulder also.[1] The heads are encircled by a glory, typifying a leaf of the sacred fig-tree (*ficus religiosa*), under whose shadow Sākyamuni had obtained the supreme intelligence; in ancient figures this glory is sometimes pointed and oval, like such a leaf, but in modern representations it has universally a circular form.[2]

The right hand of the Buddhas is always represented empty, while in the left is often seen the alms-bowl, in Tibetan Lhungzed, in Sanskrit Pātra. The predominant posture is the sitting one, the legs being crossed and the soles of the feet turned upwards; it is called Dorje kyilkrung. This is said to have been Sākyamuni's attitude in his mother's womb. Images with one foot hanging down over the throne, are not frequent; the European fashion of sitting should be given to Maitreya,

[1] For a description of the Lagoi see p. 172.

[2] See Ritter, "Die Stūpas," p. 232, 267. Concerning the origin of the worship of the fig-tree, compare Hardy, "Eastern Monachism," p. 212. Each Buddha has his peculiar tree, Ibid. p. 215, and "Manual of Buddhism," p. 94.

for this mode is called after him Chamzhug, sitting-like Champa (Maitreya); but in the images in our possession he is figured cross-legged like the others.

The Buddhas, whenever they occupy the central part of a picture,[1] are seated upon "the throne of lions," in Sanskrit Simhāsana, in Tibetan Sengti, or Senge chad ti, "the seat of eight lions." The throne is so called from the eight lions which support it; in the drawings, however, two lions only are seen in front. Over the throne a cloth is spread called "the upper cover," Tib. Tenkab, one end of which hangs down, and is decorated with symbols or the figure of a god; on both sides of this Tenkab are not unfrequently seen the heads of two animals, which Hodgson has called "supporters."[2] As each Buddha and Bōdhisattva has his peculiar animals, they most materially facilitate the determination of the subject of the picture. In images of Sākyamuni, *e. g.*, two peacocks are frequently drawn at the sides of the Tenkab, the form of their long neck being an allusion to the grass Kusa, of which he had made the cushion he sat down upon under the Bōdhi-

[1] The Tibetans like to group together into the same picture several gods, some of whom are represented in formidable attitudes, whilst the others display a smiling countenance. The principal figure is the central one; of the surrounding persons some may have a connexion with him, others have decidedly none. The central figure is very frequently sitting in the middle of a landscape representing the ocean bordered by steep shores beneath him; two snowy mountains rise to the left and right of him; and a dark blue, clouded sky, with the sun and the moon typified by two bright circles, extend above him. Compare Pallas, "Mongol. Völkerschaften," Vol. II., p. 105.

[2] "Illustrations," p. 43. The mystical signs upon the Tenkab he calls "cognizances, or mudrās." W. v. Humboldt, "Kawi Sprache," Vol. I., p. 137, compares them with a heraldic crest and its supporters.

tree in order to obtain supreme wisdom. The throne has a richly ornamented frame, composed of fantastic animals, of which the lower ones are represented lying down, the upper ones standing on the heads of the animals below and raising the fore-feet. On the top of the frame figures very generally the mythological bird Garuda.[1] The interior of the frame is called Jabyol, "back curtain," and is most frequently of a dark colour. The cushion which is upon the throne is a lotus-flower.

The *Bōdhisattvas,* the Dhyāni Bōdhisattvas as well as those of human origin, are represented like the Buddhas, with a smiling countenance and with a glory; their hair is not unfrequently pushed backwards from the forehead and done up into a cone rising above the head, and occasionally showing the curling of the hair; it is embellished with several gold galloons. They sit upon a lotus-flower, but the throne of lions is not accorded to them; in images where the figures are represented in a standing position the lotus pedicle grows out of the water. Several segments of a circle beginning at the feet and joining the glory, serve as frames for these pictures. The Bōdhisattvas are never represented with the large religious shawl Lagoi; their dress is a kind of philibeg, which is wound round the legs in the fashion adopted by the modern Hindus. A large piece of cloth is rolled round the waist, one end of which is passed under the leg and then drawn up and fastened to the

[1] Already in ancient statues these are met with; see Crawfurd, Lit. Soc. of Bombay, Vol. II., p. 154, reprinted in his "Archipelago." Pillars with sculptures of mythological animals are also a frequent ornament in Hindu architecture; I quote as an instance the principal temple at Tanjór.

girdle. This mode of covering the privy parts is very ancient, for we find it represented in numerous ancient figures;[1] it is altogether remarkable how little alteration Asiatic dress and fashion have undergone in thousands of years, whilst in a space of ten centuries Europe has experienced so many variations. A large shawl falls down from the shoulders, the ends floating in the air. The neck, ears, and feet are ornamented with necklace-like ornaments and rings.

The objects which the Bōdhisattvas hold in their hands have reference to their functions, so frequently mentioned in the legends. Thus, Manjusrī, the god of wisdom, holds a book and a sword, in allusion to his dissipating the darkness of the mind. The lotus-flower (Padma) in Padmapāni's hands has reference to his birth out of this flower. An object frequently found in the hands is a snare, in Tibetan Zhagpa, wherewith, in a typical sense, to catch men in order to impart to them supreme wisdom. There is an interesting explanation of this symbol given in the Nippon Pantheon,[2] in connexion with an image of Padmapāni:—

"He disseminates upon the ocean of birth and decay the Lotus-flower of the excellent law as bait; with the loop of devotion, never cast out in vain, he brings living beings up like fishes, and carries them to the other side of the river, where there is true understanding."

Priests, ancient and modern. The disciples of Sākyamuni and the later Indian priests are always represented

[1] See Cunningham, "The Bhilsa Topes," Plate XII.

[2] Nippon Pantheon, Fig. 96.

with the head uncovered and their hair cut short: a characteristic attribute of the former class is the alarm-stick Kharsil, in Sanskrit Hikilo, with which the Indian Buddhist mendicants made a noise when collecting alms, by shaking it and rattling with the metal rings which were passed round the stick and were prevented from being lost by a frame of metallic wire imitating the outlines of a leaf.[1] The figures of the Tibetan Lamas are distinguished by pointed caps.

The *Dragsheds*, or the gods who protect man against the evil spirits, are always represented with a formidable countenance and a complexion very often quite dark;[2] the third eye, the eye of wisdom, upon the forehead has its longer axis in a vertical position. Lha Doljang,[3] the deified consort of King Srongtsan Gampo, has it also traced in her hands and on the soles of her feet; these marks have even a surprising accidental resemblance to the nail marks of our saviour. Some are even figured as fantastic beings, with the head or tail of animals. The glory gives place to flames typifying destruction.[4]

[1] See Schiefner, "Tib. Lebensbeschreibung," Mém. des savants étrangèrs, Vol. VI., p. 323; and Foe koue ki, pp. 92, 355, for a description of the staff of Sākyamuni. In the Kanjur, Do division, Vol. XXVI., we meet with a treatise in which the use of this staff is explained. Csoma, As. Res., Vol. XX., p. 479. The Kharsils engraved upon the official seals of the head Lamas of monasteries end in a trident instead of having a leaf-shaped metallic frame.

[2] Compare p. 111, and Pallas, "Mongol. Völkerschaften," Vol. II., p. 105.

[3] See p. 66.

[4] Also in the curious manuscript volume on Bĕrmese mythology, presented by Dr. G. v. Liebig to the Munich library (Cim. 102), an analogous ornamental use of flames for the ornaments of the head and of the bracelets is repeatedly met with, even parts of their dress floating away in the wind terminate in flames.

They are almost naked; the tiger's skin, with its feet tied under the chin, hangs down behind from the shoulders, and its lower end is the cushion of their seat; they also wear a necklace of human skulls, and foot and arm rings.

Dragsheds represented standing have the legs in a straddling position, the feet not unfrequently resting upon men; some are seated on animals, generally horses or lions; but camels, yaks, deer, and even crocodiles, also occur, though never elephants. The colour of these animals often deviates from the natural one; for green and yellow horses are met with, as well as lions with a green mane, and blue crocodiles.

The instruments in the hands of the Dragsheds are for the greater part symbolic of their power over the evil spirits. These instruments are:—

1. The *Dorje*, in Sanskrit Vajra. It may best be compared with four or eight metallic hoops joined together so as to form two balls; their central axis is a cylindrical staff, the points of which project. In drawings, however, only two hoops are seen, the two others, for want of perspective, absolutely coincide with the axis. Dorjes of one ball only are also met with in drawings, which, for the sake of distinction, I call, in those places where they occur, "half Dorjes."

2. The *Phurbu*, "the nail," three of which are generally united into a triangle, which is attached to a handle terminating in a half Dorje.

3. The *Bechon*, "the club or heavy stick," a staff about as high as a man, with the trident, Tsesum,

in Sanskrit Trisula, at one end, and a half Dorje at the other.

4. *Zhagpa*, "a snare," to catch the evil spirits.

5. The drinking vessel *Kapāla*, a human skull filled with blood, out of which Lhamo drinks the blood of her son. Such skulls are also used as offering vessels in some religious ceremonies.

Illustrations derived from Measurements.

In connexion with the enumeration of the beauties of the Buddha we are naturally led to think of the plastic forms actually given to the representations of the Buddhas and the sacred personages of inferior order. In Tíbet such considerations are the more worthy our attention as the country is inhabited by a race of men so widely differing in form from the Indian races.

My brothers had made it a particular object of their ethnographical researches to take facial casts,[1] moulded by a mechanical process from the living individuals; and to define by minute measurements of the different parts of the body the general physical character of the various tribes; and they were also allowed to take measurements of the statues of the Buddhas and of other pieces of sculpture representing divinities, &c., set up in the temples. These measurements proved a

[1] The entire series comprizes 275 facial casts, published in a metallic edition by J. A. Barth, Leipzig. In this reproduction four principal shadings of colour are distinguished, corresponding to the principal variations of complexion.

very welcome fund of material to me, as the same, together with the analysis of images and the examination of the Buddhist speculations respecting the exterior appearance of their royal founder, gave me the opportunity of entering into an examination of the ethnological characteristics of the various classes of deities represented.[1]

The artistic representations in human form of divinities and figures of heroes we find to be, in every nation, the reproduction of its peculiar type of features,[2] unless history has somewhat modified this otherwise natural course. Instances of this latter case are, however, much less frequent than we might anticipate. The principal causes why history has not a greater influence on the adoption and employment by art of foreign types are, it may be supposed, the following:—Firstly, that the employment of images of a foreign type is but temporary; the peculiar bodily proportions of a people being constantly before the eye of the artist, they are soon taken again as the leading models; and secondly, that the bodily proportions have shown so little variety for periods of unexpected length. Did not the type of a nation remain

[1] The ethnographical materials collected by my brothers during their travels will be the object of Vol. VIII. of the "Results of a Scientific Mission to India and High Asia." Those of the numeric values which were wanted here for the comparison of the measurement of the sculptures with the mean proportions of the Brahmans (the purest caste of the Hindus) and of individuals of the Tibetan race, have been already calculated.

[2] The mental and artistic faculties of a nation undergo modifications in the course of time, and act in a corresponding manner upon its productions, the same either being improvements upon the old models or showing a falling off in the execution of such works.

comparatively unchanged during a long period of time, then indeed the retaining or not of foreign elements in art could not be judged of at all. As a peculiarly striking instance of the constancy of national type I mention the results obtained from the inspection and comparison of works of Egyptian sculpture;[1] they show, although somewhat disguised under the monumental form, the features of the present inhabitants of those regions, as well as of the various neighbouring nations with whom their ancestors had come into contact.

A tendency to adopt in religious images the figure peculiar to the artist's own nation is observed wherever foreign images have been introduced together with foreign worship; the images display the characteristics of the nation now executing them, the proportions of the body and the features may become somewhat idealized;[2]

[1] As the principal works which treat of these interesting and delicate questions I quote "Types of mankind," and "Indigenous races," by Nott and Gliddon.—As another phenomenon in corroboration of the comparative invariability of the original type, may be quoted the Jewish colonies in India, whose members have preserved the Semitic type, and even the fair complexion, wherever they have abstained from intermarriages with natives; but have become assimilated in shape to the native settlers after sexual intermingling has taken place.

[2] As a curious and till now isolated instance of an apparent deviation in sculpture from the *natural* proportions, I may here mention that Hermann observed in the Niniveh sculptures that the foot was considerably longer than the ulna; whilst arbitrary deviations in this respect from nature in plastics most generally show the opposite error. It must be added, however, that as yet it appears impossible to decide whether this deviation is based upon a real anatomical feature or not, as no human remains from those countries nor portraits of the Ninivites by other nations which would corroborate it are to be seen even in the rich oriental museums of London. Perhaps the continued researches and important discoveries in these regions made by Sir Henry Rawlinson, to whom my brother had occasion to communicate his remark, will soon assist in deciding the question.

but garments, ornaments, arms, and the like, remain recognizable as of foreign origin.

But it is a peculiarity of the religious representations of Tibetan Buddhism that they display two well-defined co-existing types, the one showing the Tibetan features, the other having retained the marks of Indian origin. To an eye practised in the examination of minor features in ethnography, the respective geographical origins of the two prototypes present themselves distinctly enough; and even intelligent natives, on their attention being directed to the leading characteristics soon learn how to distinguish the types. Nevertheless great precaution is necessary in touching on so delicate a consideration. Questions of ideal modifications have to be discussed and settled, here as in nearly every analysis of artistic works, before one enters upon a comparison of positive data; and this probably has been the obstacle to the explanation of forms at first sight appearing altogether unusual as well as arbitrary.[1]

The Bhot race, belonging to the Turanian family, has been so often described in detail that I shall confine myself, in my remarks on this people, to what is absolutely necessary. The Bhots are characterised by broad features, strong malar bones, and oblique eylids, the orbits and eyballs, however, being unaffected thereby; I may add as other features less striking perhaps, but not less typical,

[1] I limit myself here almost exclusively to Tibetan Buddhism. China, Japan, and Ceylon, as also the Indian Archipelago, have gods of their own, and these latter show, as was to be expected, types different from those of Tibetan representations.

that in the Bhot race the ear is comparatively longer, the mouth broader, and the lower jaw with the chin decidedly weaker. Now in all the representations of the Buddhas and Bōdhisattvas we meet, on the contrary, with features reminding us of the type of the Indian races of Arian origin—the high and open forehead, and a broad, symmetric and prominent chin. The analytical remarks in reference to the measurements will also prove that the body, too, of the Buddhas presents many other not accidental analogies with the bodily proportions of the Arian family of mankind. Dragsheds, Genii, and Lamas show the Tibetan character.

Before entering into details, however, I desire to say a few words on the form in which the numeric material is presented. In order to facilitate an immediate comparison, the values given here are the *proportional values:* the absolute dimensions are referred, by division by the total height, to this as unit; and they can be re-obtained at once by multiplying the respective number with the total height which before was used as divisor: its mean value for the Brahmans measured is 5 Engl. ft. 6 inches, for the Bhots 5 ft. 4 inches. For the statues the absolute values are of much less importance; here it was particularly necessary to keep in view that objects of coarse workmanship and of very small dimensions were avoided, as such things could not be considered to present a fair average. As an approximate mean value of absolute height I may name 3 to 4 feet for Group C, and 2 to 3 feet for Group D. Group C includes, besides, two statues from Bérma exceeding

10 ft.,[1] which were made a present to Hermann by Dr. Mouatt, who obtained them when accompaning the army in the expedition against Rangún. The measurements of these two statues were only taken into calculation because a careful comparison with Buddha-figures measured in Tíbet had proved them to have almost identical proportions, and had, besides, the advantage of furnishing by their size, well-defined values.

The first and second columns, of the following table, contain the means of the different measurements of the human body. The Brahman dimensions are based upon five high-caste individuals of perfectly pure race; the Bhot upon twenty-seven men, limited also to persons of pure (Tibetan) type, although they include natives of the tract of country extending from the Eastern Himálaya to Western Tíbet. The third column of the tables shows the mean measurements of plastic representations, partly also of pictorial ones, the latter being of Buddhas and Bōdhisattvas. The

[1] Buddha sculptures of enormous dimensions are not rare either in Bérma or in Tíbet. An album of 96 photographs by Col. Tripe, of which the Madras Government ordered several copies to be taken for official distribution, contains numerous instances of Buddha monuments varying from 20 to 40 ft. in height; the figures are partly in a sitting, partly in a standing attitude. The Buddhas are represented either in human shape, or as animals, in allusion to the remarkable pious acts which the legends report them to have performed in the form of such beings. In Tíbet my brothers saw an unusual large figure set up in the temple at Leh; the statue represents the Buddha in meditation (in a sitting attitude), and is a little higher than the temple itself, a part of the head going through a hole in the roof into the open air. The execution of this statue is not less curious than its dimensions: the body is a frame of wood dressed with draperies of cloth and paper, the head, the arms, and the feet are the only parts of the body moulded of clay. An allusion to a similar figure of extraordinary size is the sitting Buddha at the head of the figures carved in the wood-cut printed on Plate XVI.; the cone above the roof appears to be a part of his head-ornament.

fourth column gives the same for Dragsheds, genii, and Lamas.

The quantity of objects measured in living individuals was limited to such parts of the body as by a most varied and detailed examination had been found to be the characteristic.[1] Besides, in the comparison with statues, such parts of the body had still to be excluded the limits of which cannot be well defined in clothed or draperied sculptures.

In reference to the terminology used in the bodily dimensions a few words will be sufficient in explanation.

By vertex is to be understood the junction of the principal cranial bones coinciding with the whirl of the hair.

The diameter antero-posterior is the line connecting the central part of the forehead with the junction of the head and neck.

The distances from the crown of the head to the trochanter, and from the trochanter to the ground, give together the total height of the man. The trochanter is the prominent exterior part of the thigh bone near its upper end.

The total span is the distance from the tip of one middle finger to that of the other, the arms being stretched out to their full length in a horizontal position. In statues the total span had to be obtained by adding the length of hands and arms to the breadth of the torso at the shoulders.

[1] For the anatomical definition of the parts measured and of the instruments employed, see also Hermann de Schlagintweit's Memoir in Bär and Wagner, "Bericht über die anthropologische Versammlung in Göttingen," 1861.

The ulna is the elbow-bone; its ends are marked by the elbow and the prominence of the wrist joint on the side of the little finger.

It is evident that in comparing the relative values the amount of difference has not the same importance for all the parts measured; for if the object in itself is already very small, a small difference is in such a case of the same value as a much larger one in others.

1. *Dimensions of the head.*

(Total height of the body = 1).

Objects measured.	A. Brahmans.	B. Bhots.	C. Buddhas, Bōdhi-sattvas.	D. Dragsheds, Genii, Lamas.
Periphery round the forehead	0·322	0·345	0·350	0·420
From the vertex to the orbital margin.......	0·103	0·111	0·110	0·131
From the vertex to the base of the nose	0·126	0·131	0·140	0·150
From the vertex to the mouth..............	0·133	0·140	0·150	0·152
From the vertex to the chin	0·145	0·149	0·166	0·160
Diameter at the temples..........	0·078	0·083	0·088	0·100
Diameter antero-posterior	0·105	0·114	0·114	0·130
Eyes—exterior distance	0·055	0·065	0·071	0·087
» interior distance..........	0·021	0·022	0·023	0·030
» length of the eye..........	0·017	0·022	0·024	0·029
Malar bones, breadth............	0·064	0·078	0·081	0·090
Nose, breadth	0·022	0·023	0·025	0·029
Mouth, length..................	0·029	0·033	0·035	0·033
Ear, length....................	0·035	0·040	0·110	0·070

The numbers of the table show that *all* the dimensions of the head are greater in both groups of the figures than in the groups of the living beings: the figures have the head in general much *too large* in proportion to their height, but the deviations are not the same in each group. The most arbitrary form is that of the ear, also by the ear-lap being perforated for the reception of ornaments, and being extended to an unusual length, sometimes reaching down to the shoulders. Also the eyes are extremely large, and have in both groups a decided though unequally strong Bhutian type; they show the outer angles raised, the horizontal axis inclined, and a great length; the effect of these dimensions becomes still more striking by the eyes being very often only partly opened. The periphery round the forehead, the diameter at the temples, and particularly the diameter antero-posterior, are much less increased in the Buddha figures, group C, than in those of the Dragsheds and Lamas, group D. The parts least differing in the different types are the mouth, the malar bones, and the breadth of the nose between the eyes as well as at its base; Group D has these parts, however, a little larger.

When defining the general character of the head in the respective groups, we find in Group C the the vertical length of the head comparatively more considerable and the head of a more oval form. Group D has the head horizontally elongated, a form characteristic also of the Bhot race, Group B; in both these the forehead is low and the jaw-bone weak. The distance from the vertex to the orbital margin and to the base of the nose is greater in Group D than in Group C; the distance from the vertex to the chin, on the contrary, is considerably less in Group D: it exceeds the distance to the mouth by 0·016 in Group C, and only by 0·008 in Group D. The pure Brahman type, A, has the respective difference 0·012.

2. *Dimensions of the body.*

Objects measured.	A. Brahmans.	B. Bhots.	C. Buddhas, Bōdhi-sattvas.	D. Dragsheds, Genii, Lamas.
Total height	1·000	1·000	1·000	1·000
Crown of the head to trochanter	0·446	0·449	0·430	0·410
Trochanter to ground	0·554	0·551	0·570	0·590
Total span	1·025	1·069	1·080	1·117
Length of arm	0·433	0·451	0·449	0·430
» of ulna	0·165	0·164	0·149	0·155
» of hand	0·107	0·110	0·110	0·111
Foot, length	0·144	0·145	0·140	0·144
» breadth	0·057	0·058	0·050	0·051

In reference to the dimensions of the body we see, as a peculiarity of the figures, that the upper part of the body is too short: I found this to be more frequently the case with comparatively small figures than with the larger ones. The total span is too large, less on account of a disproportionate dimension of the arms—which in Group D have even a tendency to be below the average—than on account of a great and somewhat exaggerated breadth of the chest. The ulna is decidedly too short; the hand, when well executed, differs but very little, but in badly executed figures it is occasionally somewhat too long. The foot is tolerably well-proportioned both in length and breadth, though in small figures it is very frequent that its dimensions exceed the mean proportion, particularly as regards the length; but these must be considered arbitrary, as dimensions below the average are scarcely less frequent in large-sized figures.

CHAPTER XV

WORSHIP OF THE DEITIES, AND RELIGIOUS CEREMONIES

DAILY SERVICE. Offerings. Musical instruments. Prayer-cylinders.—PERFORMANCE OF RELIGIOUS DRAMAS.—SACRED DAYS AND FESTIVALS.—Monthly and annual festivals. The ceremony Tuisol. The ceremony Nyungne.—RITES FOR THE ATTAINMENT OF SUPERNATURAL FACULTIES.—PECULIAR CEREMONIES FOR ENSURING THE ASSISTANCE OF THE GODS. 1. The rite Dubjed. 2. The burnt-offering. 3. Invocation of Lungta. 4. The Talisman Changpo. 5. The magical figure Phurbu. 6. The ceremony Thugdam Kantsai. 7. Invocation of Nagpo Chenpo by moving the arrow. 8. The ceremony Yangug. 9. Ceremonies performed in cases of illness. 10. Funeral rites.

Daily service.

THE ordinary daily service, instituted for the praise of the Buddha, consists in the recital of hymns and prayers in a manner intermediate between singing and reading. The service is accompanied by instrumental music; offerings are presented, and perfumes are burnt. This kind of service is celebrated by the Lamas three times a day, at sunrise, noon, and sunset; and lasts each time about half an hour. Laymen may be present, but they take no active part in the performance; those who are present are required to make three prostrations, touching the ground with their forehead, when they receive from the Lamas the benediction. On certain days more time is spent in the religious services; the prayers and ceremonies have then reference to the festival of the day; public processions not unfrequently precede the solemnities which take place in the temples, and on some few occasions, even religious dramas conclude them.

Offerings. Blood forms no part of these: they consist chiefly of flour, clarified butter, and tamarind-wood, Ombu in Tibetan. To some particular gods flowers are offered, or, if they cannot be obtained, grain, which is thrown into the air so as to fall down upon the image. To the Buddhas and Bōdhisattvas cones of dough, Zhalsai, literally "meat, food," are offered, similar in shape to the Tsatsas (*see* p. 194), but differing from them in this respect, that they contain no relics or other sacred objects; also the feathers of a peacock are set up in narrow-necked vessels before some of these gods.

Musical instruments. Of all the instruments used by the Tibetans for their service, such as drums, trumpets, flageolets, and cymbals, the trumpets are certainly the most remarkable, being generally made of human bones. Thigh bones give the finest trumpets; they sound very deep. To the top of the bone is fastened a mouth-piece of brass, while the other end is ornamented by brass wire, or leather rings; and the instrument (the construction of which requires but a very trifling outlay) is ready for use. Besides this kind of trumpets, there are still larger ones of copper, from 6 to 7 feet long, which are only made in Lhássa, and which are very expensive.

The flageolets are of wood, and are generally double ones, each tube having seven holes along the upper side and a larger one underneath for the thumb.

The drums are hemispherical, joined on their convex side; upon the skin sacred sentences are frequently written. The drums are beaten in a very curious manner. There are two small leather balls attached to a rope of some length fastened to the drums at the point of their junction; the drums are taken in the hand and shaken in such a manner as to cause a swinging motion of the two balls, which are thus brought into contact with the drums, and cause no little noise. The large tambourines, which are fixed upon a stick about three feet long, are beaten with a bamboo cane, which, on account of its elasticity, strikes the skin often, but not very heavily. The cymbals are very similar to those used in Europe; they are kept in boxes of twisted bast.

All Tibetan music is slow, sounds deep, and is far superior to that of the Hindus of India. Although it cannot be asserted that there is much melody in Tibetan music, yet the instruments employed produce a certain harmonious combination and rythmical succession of sounds.

Prayer-cylinders. An instrument peculiar to the Buddhists, and very characteristic of their religious notions, is the prayer-cylinder, in Tibetan called Khorten, also Mani, or Mani chos khor.[1] The use of these instruments may probably have originated in an exhortation to a frequent reading of the holy books and to the recital of sacred sentences, in order to the attainment of a knowledge of the tenets of the Buddhist doctrine. In the course of time the mere reading or copying of the holy books and writings had come to be regarded as a work of merit, and as one of the most efficacious means for becoming purified from sin and delivered from metempsychosis.[2] Few men, however, knew how to read at all, and those who did were prevented by their occupations from doing so frequently; and therefore, as I believe, the Lamas cast about for an expedient to enable the ignorant and the much-occupied man also to obtain the spiritual advantages attached to an observance of the practice mentioned; they taught that the mere turning of a rolled manuscript might be considered an efficacious substitute for reading it.

The cylindrical cases, in which the prayers to be turned are enclosed, are generally of metal; but envelops of wood, and leather, or even of coarse cotton, are not rare. They are from three to five inches high and two to three inches in diameter. A wooden handle passes through each cylinder and forms its axis. Round this axis long strips of paper or pieces of cloth are rolled, with printed sacred sentences; all these rolls are again covered by an un-printed piece of cotton stuff. To facilitate the turning of the cylinders, a small pebble or a piece of metal is fastened to

[1] Mani "a precious thing;" chhos "the doctrine;" khor, from 'khor-ba "to turn;" *b*rten "to hold, support."

[2] See the Address to the Buddhas of confession, or Confessor Buddhas, Chapter XI.

it by a string, so that a very gentle movement of the hand maintains a steady and regular revolving motion.

Besides the prayer-cylinders of these ordinary dimensions there are some of very large size permanently fixed near monasteries. A man is employed to keep them constantly in motion, or occasionally they are turned by water, like mills, and revolve day and night. Numbers of smaller ones are also ranged at the entrance of monasteries, along the walls, and are turned by passers-by or by those who enter the temple. They are generally so close to each other that anyone going by may easily cause all to revolve one after the other without interruption, by gliding over them with the hand. The number of these prayer-cylinders set up in one single monastery is quite astonishing; thus, the inscription relating to the foundation of the monastery of Hímis, in Ladák (see p. 183), states that 300,000 prayer-cylinders were put up along the walls of the monastery. Though this is an exaggeration in oriental style, the actual quantity is nevertheless very considerable.

Each revolution of the cylinder is considered to be equal to the reading of as many sacred sentences or treatises as are enclosed in it, provided that the turning of the cylinder is done slowly and from right to left; and the effect is made dependent upon a strict observance of these two rules. A slow motion is enjoined because those who turn the cylinders must do so with a faithful, quiet, and meditative mind. The motion from right to left was adopted in order to follow the writing, which runs from left to right. Some of the larger prayer-cylinders are so constructed that a stroke of a bell indicates each single revolution.

The prayer inscribed is most generally simply Om mani padme hum, repeated as often as the space allows of it. The papers rolled up in the larger cylinders are, however, more generally covered with the contents of many of their sacred books.[1] The Lamas have particular books which detail the advantages to be derived from turning these cylinders; I mention especially the Khorloi phanyon, "the advantage of the wheel," which also treats of the prayers and books to be put inside, and of the mode of turning these cylinders.

Prayer cylinders were amongst the very first objects which became known in Europe, through missionaries; but in reference to the religious dramas and the ritual to be observed in particular ceremonies, which shall be now detailed, I was limited for the greatest part to the materials and the native information before me. I may be allowed to allude to this circumstance, in order to request that it may be taken into consideration, in case the interpretations should not be found so complete as the importance which the Tibetans connect with it might seem to require.

Performance of religious dramas.

On certain days of the year religious dramas are performed by the Lamas, who call them Tambin shi,[2]

[1] Compare p. 120.

[2] It is spelled: *b*stan-pa "to show, instruction, the doctrine;" 'i, the genitive case; shi*s*, "a blessing, bliss; blessed."

"the bliss of instruction." My brother Hermann, when at the monastery of Hímis, was fortunate enough to witness the representation of such a drama performed expressly for him; it was as follows:—

The *dramatis personæ* are Dragsheds (the deities who defend man against the evil spirits; see p. 111), malignant spirits, and men. The actors of every group are plainly distinguished by the peculiar kind of masks (Tib. Phag) they wear, and much less by their dresses, which are surprisingly uniform and non-distinctive gowns. The Dragsheds and malignant spirits wear over their clerical dress beautiful large silken gowns of rich showy colours; some few Dragsheds have besides a gilt cuirass and arms. Even the party representing the men are furnished with a uniform particular dress where the means of the monastery allow it.

The *masks* of the first group, those of the Dragsheds, are of enormous size and ferocious aspect; the hinder part of the head is covered by a triangular piece of cotton or silk, and also on the front a similar piece is fastened to the chin and falls down to the breast. The second group, the evil spirits, wear masks of brown or some other dark colour, of dimensions somewhat larger than seems exactly suitable, and their garments are well wadded, so that they feel but little the blows showered upon them. The actors of this group and the following are either neophites, or are taken from among the lay population. The third group, finally, represents the men, who wear their usual dress, but also have their faces covered by a mask of natural size and colours; under their clothes they carry heavy wooden sticks, with which at times, during the performance of the drama, they threaten the evil spirits.

The *drama* is preceded by the recital of hymns and prayers and by a very noisy music. The actors are seen on the stage as follows: The Dragsheds occupy the centre, the men are placed to their right, the evil spirits to their left. At short intervals, the men and the evil spirits, execute slow dances, each group for itself. At last, an evil spirit and a man step forth. The evil spirit then tries, in a well-made speech, to induce the man to do wrong by violating some precepts of morality or religion; other evil spirits approach and assist their comrade in this speech. The man, though at first firm in his resistance to all these entreaties, gradually becomes weaker, and is just about to yield to the temptations of his would-be seducers, when he is joined by other men, who endeavour to lissuade him from listening to evil suggestions. He is now closely pressed by the two different parties, and it takes considerable time before he yields to the exhortations of his human companions. The men render thanks to the Dragsheds, to whose assistance they ascribe the victory (although the Dragsheds have as yet taken no part in the action), and implore them to punish the evil spirits. The Dragsheds are but too ready to do so. Their head god, who is distinguished from the others by an unusually large yellow mask, called by the Lamas Gonyan serpo, "the yellow borrowed head," advances surrounded by about a dozen of followers, representatives of the most powerful Dragsheds. Amongst these was, at the performance at Hímis, Lhamo (see p. 112), with a mask of dark complexion and large tails of Yak's-hair; Tsangpa (*i. e.* Brahma, see p. 114), had put on a cuirass. Several men wore three-eyed red masks, and were styled Lhachen, "the mighty gods;" another group, with masks of green complexion and high conical caps of white cutton stuff upon which three eyes are traced, represented the "sons of the gods;" they were styled Lhatug.[1] The other Dragsheds now rush out too from the back-ground, shoot arrows upon the evil spirits, fire upon them with muskets, throw stones and spears; whilst at the same time the men belabour them heartily with their sticks, hitherto concealed. The evil spirits run away, but the Dragsheds follow them, and drive them into houses, holes, &c., where they are safe from further molestation. The drama is then concluded; all the actors, Dragsheds, men, and evil spirits, return and sing hymns in honour of the victorious Diagsheds.

During the performance, which lasts from one to two hours, most ridiculous mistakes occasionally occur, on account of the large masks which, in certain positions, deprive the wearers of the use of their eyes; thus it sometimes happens, that a Dragshed strikes another Dragshed, or that he—such a powerful god!—falls down at full length upon the ground, where he is then illtreated by the evil spirits till he is again on his feet.

[1] Drawings of these masks, taken from the originals obtained by Hermann, will be given in the Atlas accompanying the "Results of a Scientific Mission."

These dramas remind us of the "Mystères" and "Moralités" of the Middle Ages;[1] but the noisy music, the firing of musketry, and the final fray, produce an effect still less in accordance with a religious act than the comical and burlesque intermezzos of the *Mystères* and *Moralités*, which were intended to amuse the audience and somewhat unbend their minds in the intervals between the serious and heavier parts of the play, calculated to excite their feelings of devotion and appeal to their moral sense.

The subjects of the religious dramas represented in Arrakán have a remarkable analogy to those of Tíbet; I quote the following description from Hardy's "Eastern Monachism."[2] "Lines are drawn upon the ground, in an open space, and dancers are introduced. These lines are regarded as the limits of the territory belonging to different Yakās and Dēvas; and the last is appropriated to Buddha. One of the dancers advances towards the first limit, and when he is told to what Yakā it belongs, he calls out the demon's name in defiance, uttering against him the most insulting language; and declaring that in spite of all the opposition that can be brought against him, he will cross the limit, and invade the territory of its infernal possessor. Then, passing the limit in triumph, he acts in the same manner towards all the other demons and divinities who have had divisions assigned to them, until

[1] Compare Alt, "Theater und Kirche." Berlin 1846. Chapter 26, 27. The "Passionsspiele," which are still kept up in Oberammergau, in Bavaria, have, at present, assumed a thoroughly serious character.

[2] Page 236.

at last he approaches the limit of Buddha. Still he professes to be equally fearless, and bids defiance to the woolly-headed priest who carries the alms-bowl from door to door like a common mendicant; but the moment he attempts to pass the limit, he falls down as if dead; and as he is regarded as suffering the punishment of the blasphemy he had dared to utter, all who are present applaud the greatness of him whose prowess is thus proved to be superior to that of all other beings."

Sacred days and festivals.

Monthly and annual festivals.

The *monthly festivals* are in some countries four in number, connected with the phases of the moon; in others only three of these days are celebrated, those of the first quarter of the moon, of full moon and of new moon. On these days no animal food should be taken nor any animal killed; and those who do so are threatened with severe punishments in a future existence. To abstain from worldly occupations is, however, not enacted, and as the Buddhist laymen in the Himálaya and Western Tíbet are not very fond of passing the whole day in prayers and in the temples,[1] these holy days are not particularly marked in the habits of the population. But the Lamas spend more time in the temples; they perform the ceremony Tuisol, for the taking away of

[1] The northern Mongolians show in this regard much more devotion. See Pallas, "Reisen," French translation, p. 562.

sins, and they make confession in a more solemn way. The confession of sins is preceded and followed by the reading and reciting of passages from sacred books, which occupation is sometimes continued for days, during which time the taking of food and drinking are reduced to a minimum. These austerities, for the deliverance from sins, bear the name of Nyungne, or Nyungpar nepai choga. Every layman is allowed to undergo the hardships connected with this kind of confession, but as less painful modes have, in their opinion, the same effect,[1] the Tibetans—priests as well as laymen—submit to them only so and so many times a year, and not, as they ought properly to do, three times a month. In general, the Lamas do no more than read certain books and celebrate the ceremony Tuisol; the laymen make prostrations before the images of particular gods, and repeat more sentences than on other days.

Annual festivals. In almost every month a particular religious festivity is celebrated, and public amusements are got up on such days; the festivities—religious as well as public—are the most varied at the following periods, which are regarded as the most sacred: About the first of February the festival of the New Year is celebrated; on the fifteenth of the fourth moon (about the beginning of May) honour is done to "Sākyamuni's having entered the womb of his mother;" on the fifteenth of the seventh moon (in August), before the cutting of the grain, solemn processions are made into the fields, where prayers are offered up and thanksgivings repeated

[1] Compare p. 95.

for the blessings of harvest; the twenty-fifth of the same month is the anniversary of the death of Tsonkhapa. For the particular festivals of these days, which are very grand and diversified in character in places where incarnated priests reside, I refer the reader to the "Description du Tubet," translated from the Chinese, and Huc, Pallas, and Klaproth.[1] My brothers, however, were not present at any of them, and I therefore restrict myself to quoting the works where descriptions of them may be found; but I now give the details which my brothers obtained concerning the ceremonies Tuisol and Nyungne.

The Ceremony Tuisol.

The Tuisol, "to pray for ablution,"[2] ranks amongst the most sacred of the Buddhist rites, and is performed at every solemn assembly for the washing away of sins. Water is poured out from a vessel similar to a teapot, called Mangu, and also Bumpa, over the vessel's well-cleaned cover, called Yanga, or a particular metallic mirror, Melong, which is held so, that it reflects the image of Sākyamuni which stands on the altar. The water falls down into a flat vessel, called Dorma,[3] placed

[1] Nouv. Journ. As., Vol. IV., p. 140. Pallas, "Mongol. Völker," Vol. II., pp. 190-215. Klaproth, "Reise in den Kaukasus," Vol. I., p. 193. Huc, "Souvenirs," Vol. I., pp. 96, 291, Vol. II., p. 95. Compare Köppen, "Die Rel. des Buddha," Vol. II., pp. 309-15.

[2] *b*Krus, part. pret. from 'khrud-pa, "thoroughly washed, ablution;" *g*sol, "to pray, beg for entreaty."

[3] The terms Mangu, Yanga, Dorma, appear to be local designations, as I could not find them in the dictionaries. In Síkkim the Mangu vessel was called by the Lepcha Lamas Guri, and the vessel for the reception of the water Thepshi.

upon a tripod. The Lamas of Gnári Khórsum informed my brothers that they put into the vessel a bag filled with rice, which they called Brakhug, "rice bag."[1]

The Ceremony Nyungne, or Nyungpar nepai choga.

This ceremony is performed in its full rigour only once or twice a year; its name means "to continue to abstain," or "ceremony of continued abstinence."[2] It occupies four days; the prayers and passages of books read during them are chiefly in honour of Padmapāni in his quality as Jigten Gonpo, "the protector of the world," for his efforts to release mankind from the miseries of life.[3] Any layman is allowed to take part in these ceremonies; he has to present himself in the afternoon at the monastery, well washed and in clean garments, with a rosary, a cup called Thor, and a bottle filled with pure water for washing.

The first day, "the introductory exercises," in Tibetan called Tagom,[4] are performed, preparatory to those of the following day; prayers are recited and passages from sacred books are read under the direction of a learned Gelong, who has been deputed by the head Lama. The second day is taken up with Chorva, "the preparations."[1]

[1] The Mongolians, according to Pallas, "Mongolische Völker," Vol. II., pp. 161, 177; perfume the water with saffron, and sweeten it with sugar.

[2] *s*Nyung-par "to reduce (in food);" *g*nas-pa "to continue;" chho-ga "ceremony."

[3] Comp. pp. 88, 120.

[4] *l*Ta "to view, theory;" gom "step;" a literal translation gives: "step to the theory."

The devotees are called at sunrise, and wash and prostrate themselves several times before the image of Padmapāni. The head Lama then admonishes them no more to violate their vows, and to renew promises previously made; he commands them to confess their sins, and seriously to meditate upon the evils which result from them. He reads with his attendants for about an hour extracts from several books, an act which is called Sobyong, "confession, amendment of the vicious life." The book Nyungpar nepai choga is then read till ten o'clock, when tea is taken (Cha-chosh, not Cha[2]). After this the reading of books and the recital of prayers is continued till two o'clock, when a dinner is served, consisting of vegetables and pastry; animal food is not allowed. After this scanty dinner, prayers and readings are continued till late at night; but at intervals, tea is handed round. Before retiring to rest, the head Lama specifies the various duties of the assembly for the following day, and orders them, as a penance, to sleep according to "the mode of the lion," Sengei nyal tab,[3] viz. to lie on the right side, to stretch out the feet, and to support the head with the right hand.

The following day is the principal one; it is styled Ngoishi, "the substance, the reality." The day is passed in rigorous abstinence from meat and drink—nay, it is not even allowed to swallow one's saliva; every one has

[1] 'Byor-ba, literally "to come, to arrive," referring to the purification of sins resulting from these exercises.

[2] See p. 168.

[3] Seng-ge "the lion;" nyal "to sleep;" *stabs* "mode." In this attitude Sākyamuni is believed to have entered Nirvāna.

a vessel before him which he uses as a spittoon. Weak persons, who are unable to endure for any length of time this painful operation, are occasionally refreshed with some drops of water, and are brought for some moments into the open air. Not a word is allowed to be spoken, and should any body utter one, he is punished by having to sing some hymns at the height of his voice. All prayers are to be recited in silence, and sinful actions have to be again repented of. The abstinence from food and drink is continued till the sun-rise of the next day; the head Lama then asks the assembly, whether there are any devotees willing to continue in like manner till the next morning—an operation which is considered a very efficacious means for obtaining deliverance from all sins; it is, however, extremely rare that any one feels strong enough to continue. The head Lama therefore gives permission, to eat and drink, whereupon the assembly rise, leave the temple, and partake of a substantial meal, which the pious crowd have prepared for them outside.

Rites for the attainment of supernatural faculties.

The confidence in the powerful influence of prayers and ceremonies is so common among all Buddhist tribes of High Asia, that every undertaking is begun by them with the recital of incantations and the performance of certain ceremonies by which to appease the wrath of the demons; they, moreover, believe that by virtue of the strict observance of the duties connected with such rites, they will in time acquire a miraculous magical energy, called Siddhi, and finally become liberated from metempsychosis. This view is not opposed to the principles of Buddhism, which declare that faculties superior to those with which nature has endowed man can be obtained by meditation, abstinence, the observation of moral duties, and true repentance for sins. This exhortation to a moral life, the consequences of which we see illustrated in the sacred books by numerous parables, is well adapted for exercising a favourable influence in mitigating the barbarous customs of the nations professing Buddhism; but, by errors involved in the misunderstanding of the real aim of virtue, by the non-admittance of a supreme, all-dominating deity, and by the viewing of existence as the cause of all misery, Buddhism was rendered incapable of producing a civilization so general as that developed by Christianity.[1]

The books in which the magical arts are the most systematically treated are the Tantra Sabāhupariprichchā, and the Lamrim of Tsonkhapa, in which every thing having reference to the theory as well as to the practical application is explained in full. In the Sabāhupariprichchā[2] Vajrapāni describes to the Bōdhisattva Sabāhu, in the usual form of a dialogue, the mode of performing various ceremonies, and indicates the prayers and incantations to be used during their performance, in order to acquire

[1] A very interesting dissertation on Buddhism is contained in Barthélemy St. Hilaire's "Le Bouddha et sa religion," Chapter V. Comp. also M. Müller, "Buddhism and Buddhist Pilgrims," pp. 14-20.

[2] The abstract of its contents quoted here has been published in Wassiljew's "Buddhismus," pp. 208-17. See also Burnouf's remarks on the acquirement of magical powers in his "Lotus de la Bonne Loi," p. 310.

the Siddhi. The book points out the obstacles met with, and specifies the signs from which is perceived that Siddhi will be soon obtained; it also defines its essence and qualities.

Eight classes of Siddhi are distinguished:—

1. The power to conjure.
2. Longevity.
3. The water of life, or the remedy (amrita).
4. The discovery of hidden treasures.
5. The entering into Indra's cave.
6. The art of making gold.
7. The transformation of earth into gold.
8. The acquiring of the inappreciable jewel.

Of the highest character are the Siddhis Nos. 1, 3, and 5; the degree of perfection to be attained is fixed by the dignity of the man.

Those desirous of acquiring Siddhi must renounce the vanities of life, they must strictly observe the moral law, and confess their sins; they also must apply for an able teacher, in order that nothing be forgotten; when they proceed to perform the rites, they must be shaved, washed, and cleaned. Of particular importance for the success is the scene of their performance. It must be a place not calculated to distract the mind by a variety of objects more or less attractive, or by the possible appearance of wild beasts. The most favourable spots are those where Buddhas and Bōdhisattvas or Srāvakas dwell. The place must be well swept and otherwise cleaned, and fresh earth must be thrown upon it, in order to make its surface even and smooth. A magical circle of the five sacred colours must be drawn, in order to overcome the impediments, the "Vināyakas," opposed by the demons; for these latter do all in their power to prevent the devotee's efforts and the incantations from exercising their full effect. Within the circle an altar is erected, upon which various vessels are ranged filled with bread, grain, and perfumed water. The ceremonies consist in the reciting of incantations and in the presentation of offerings to the kings of magical power, to the genii, and to demons. A Vajra (Dorje) is held during the recital of the incantations; the material of which this is made varies according to the kind of Siddhi sought. The incantations must be repeated a fixed number of times, as *e. g.* 100,000 times a day; the number is counted by means of a rosary of 108 beads. They must be recited slowly and distinctly, without raising or lowering the voice; nor is it allowed to make any addition or omission; the most earnest attention must be devoted to the recital, otherwise the end aimed at cannot be attained.[1] The thoughts must be predominantly directed to the tutelary deity (Tib. Yidam) selected for bestowing success upon the incantations, offerings, &c.; even the way of placing and holding the fingers, the Mudrās,[2] is important; such positions have to be chosen as typify the attributes of the patronal god. Amongst the offering ceremonies the burnt offering, in Tibetan Chinsreg or Sregpa, in Sanskrit Hōma, is the most im-

[1] The description of a rite considered most excellent for concentrating the thoughts, is given further on, in No. 1.

[2] Concerning the Mudrās *see* p. 56.

portant; it must be performed with a minute observance of the rules laid down for it.[1]

The approach of the moment when the devotee attains the possession of supernatural qualities is indicated by various signs, such as agreeable dreams, the diffusion of sweet odours, &c. Particular offerings must then be made to the Buddhas; only a minimum quantity of food is allowed to be taken for two, and even for four days; and certain Sūtras must be read. If, however, notwithstanding the strict observance of all these rules, no marks reveal the approach of the Siddhi, it is a positive token, that unknown reasons have hindered it, which the patronal deity is supposed to reveal to the devotee in his dreams.

The rites and Dhāranīs vary according to the deity, whose patrocination is implored; each deity has its particular Dhāranīs, Mudrās, magical circles, offerings, and attributes. Avalōkitēsvara, Manjusrī, Vajrapāni, and numerous other persons, are reported to have made known to the Buddha their wish to defend his religion, and to grant their assistance to those who implore it; but the Dhāranīs and ceremonies which are suitable for each of these persons, and the instructions as to their application are not always clear, satisfactory, and complete; explanatory commentaries, have, therefore, been written by famous magicians, which do not, however, always exactly agree; hence, numerous methods, "Lugs," of celebrating the rites, are in practice.

[1] For a description of these offerings see p. 248.

Peculiar ceremonies for ensuring the assistance of the gods.

For most of the ceremonies the performance by a Lama is considered indispensable to its due effect; but even if this is not the case, a Lama is charged with it in cases of importance, as the efficacy of any rite is supposed to become increased by the services of a priest; this assistance, however, causes the laymen considerable expense, as the officiating priests tax them according to their means.[1] The execution by a Lama is not required for the usual libations to the personal genii, nor to those of the house, the country, &c., in whose honour it is the custom to pour out upon the ground some drink or food, and to fill one of the offering vessels ranged before their images before eating or drinking one'sself.[2] Also the putting up of prayer-flags (the Derchoks and Lapchas), and the offerings on the sacred spots met with on travels, can be done without the Lamas, who are likewise not required for the efficacy of the mystical sentences of magical power, the Dhāranīs.

1. *The rite Dubjed.*

This rite, the name of which means "to make ready" (*viz.* the vessels), is intended to concentrate the thoughts. Those who are about to devote themselves to profound meditation, place before them a vase-like vessel called Namgyal bumpa, "the entirely victorious vessel," and a flat vessel

[1] Compare p. 160.

[2] This is done very generally in all countries of Asia and South Eastern Europe. See Pallas, "Reisen," Vol. I, p. 561.

called Lai bumpa, "the vessel of the works.[1] The Namgyal bumpa typifies abstraction of the mind from surrounding objects, the Lai bumpa perfection in abstract meditation. These vessels are not put upon the earth, but upon a cloth or a paper on which an octagon frame is drawn, called Dabchad, "octagon;" the vessels are filled with water perfumed with saffron, and strips of the five sacred colours are twisted round them; flowers also, or kusagrass are put into them.[2] The devotee, fixing his eyes upon these two vessels, reflects upon the benefit to be derived from meditation, and is exhorted to intense concentration of the mind.

The frame Dabchad has nine compartments, of which each is separated from the next by ornaments representing clouds. In each compartment is inscribed the name of a Dākinī or Yōginī, in Tibetan Khado, or also Naljorva; in the central division are words denoting that it is meant for "the chief of the Dākinīs," who is called in the religious books Sangye Khado in Tibetan, Buddha Dākinī in Sanskrit. In a Dabchad obtained by Hermann in Síkkim, the central words are *d*bus-byas-*m*khro',[3] and mean, "Dākinī occupying (done in) the centre," the word *m*khro' being decidedly an abbreviation from Khado, which is spelled *m*kha'-'gro, and is literally "walking in the air." The Dākinīs are female spirits countless in number who evince the greatest kindness towards man. They

[1] These vessels are not unfrequently traced upon the cushions upon which the Lamas sit during the public religious services.

[2] Of this kind was also the grass of which Sākyamuni had piled up his seat when sitting down under the Bōdhi tree.

[3] *d*Bus "centre," byas "done."

are addressed in a religious treatise translated by Schmidt with surnames of sanctity, as *e. g.* Sarva Buddha Dākinī, and their head is styled Bogda Dākinī, Bogda meaning "divine nature." This highest Dākinī is also the female companion, the Sakti of Vajradhara, and is endowed with faculties equally great with those of her husband.[1]

2. *The burnt-offering.*

By the burnt-offering (in Tibetan Chinsreg, or Sregpa,[2] in Sanskrit Hōma) the offerer seeks to be endowed with the faculty of obtaining happiness, wealth, and power, of becoming purified from sins, and of being protected against "untimely death" and the pains connected therewith. It consists in the burning of tamarind-wood, Ombu, and cotton, with coals and perfumed oils in a kind of stove, Thabkhung,[3] made of clay or bricks. The shape and colour of the stove depends upon the purpose for which it is used; in one case it is square, in the others semi-circular, or circular, or triangular. These stoves are about one foot high and two feet broad; they have straight sides, and the bottom is formed by a plate of burnt clay, which projects about two inches beyond the sides; upon the projecting border half-dorjes[4] are stamped, and a mystical sign is cut in the centre of the bottom of the stove,

[1] Schmidt, "Geschichte Ssanang Ssetsens," pp. 468, 75, 76, 81. About Vajradhara see p. 50.

[2] *s*Byin (chin), "alms;" sreg-pa, "to destroy by fire."

[3] Thab, "fire place;" khung, "a hole." In the Tantra Subāhupariprichchā (Wassiljew, "Der Buddhismus," p. 212) 10,000 grains of wheat, sesame, mustard, lotus, &c., are among the offerings required to be burnt.

[4] See p. 215.

symbolizing either the earth, or fire, water, or the air, according to the shape of the stove.

The offerings must be burnt by a Lama, who wears a large gown of the respective colour of the stove, interwoven with numerous characters of the element engraved upon the bottom. He ranges on a side-table, with prayers beginning with the respective appellation of the particular element, the offerings to be burnt, which he puts into the stove, but only in small quantities at a time, as their combustion must be a slow one. He keeps the offerings burning by dropping upon them perfumed oil with two brass spoons; with the larger one, called Gangzar,[1] he takes the oil out of a small brass vessel, and pours it into the smaller spoon, called "Lugzar,"[2] from which he lets it fall, drop by drop, upon the offerings.

This ceremony has four particular names, according to the aim of its celebration:—

1. *Zhibai Chinsreg*, "sacrifice for peace," to ward off calamity in the shape of famine, war, &c., to weaken or totally neutralize the effects of malignant influences, and to abolish sins. The stove is square, the lower part of a red colour and the upper part white. On its bottom "lam" is designed, the symbol of earth.

This offering ceremony is very generally performed after a person's death, because the sins of the deceased are supposed to be gathered into the stove by virtue of the Dhāranīs repeated by the officiating Lama, and

[1] 'Gang, "to make full, to fill," *g*zar, "a ladle, a large spoon.
[2] *b*Lug, "to pour out."

by the power of Melha, or Mẹlhai gyalpo, "the lord of the genii of fire," who is always implored on such occasions; it is believed that with the combustion of the offerings the sins disappear for ever. The address to Melha runs thus:—"I adore thee and present to thee the offerings "for the deceased, who has left this world and has en-"tered the circle, for him who dwells in the assembly of "the three merciful deities, who are now in calmness "now in wrath.[1] Pray purify him from his sins and "any violations of the law, and teach him the right way. "Sarva-agne-dzala-ram-ram."

This prayer is given in Plate X., which is an impression from an original woodcut from Eastern Tíbet;[2] it is placed beneath the image of Melha in a state of calmness. Here he is sitting crosslegged upon a Lotus-flower, holding the blue lotus Utpala (*Nelumbium speciosum*), with joined hands. His head is shaded by the

[1] It is difficult to understand what deities are meant. The phrase would lead us to the three Isvaras, viz. Brahma, Vishnu, and Siva (Schmidt, Mém. de l'Acad. de St. Pétersb., Vol. II., p. 23), about whom we might suppose, from the legend concerning Brahma (see p. 114), that they all three place a check upon the doings of evil spirits. If this be the right interpretation, they would become wrathful in the case of activity, according to the views of the Tibetans (see p. 111). But I cannot perceive for what reason the deceased, in general, should, as it is here stated, ascend to the region where reside these gods so highly esteemed and so extremely superior to simple man and ordinary gods; for Shinje (see p. 93), before whom the deceased is brought, dwells in an inferior region.

[2] As the intersyllabic points are not in the original woodcut, I give the address here in Roman characters, rendering the intersyllabic points which are omitted by horizontal lines:—

Yangs-pa-*g*sum-zhi-khro'i-lha-ts'hogs-dang-gar-*d*vang-thug*s*-*r*je'i-chen-po'i-drung-pu-'jig-*r*ten-'di-na-pha-rol-du-ts'he-las-'das-pa-*d*kyil-'khor-la-phyag-ts'hal-lo-*m*chhod-pa-'bul-lo.

*s*Dig-*s*grib-*s*byang*s*-du-*g*sol; *g*nas-so-rab-tu-*g*sol; lam-*b*stan-du-*g*sol.
Sarva-agne-dza-la-ram-ram.

Dug (umbrella), to which are added the horizontal ribands Labri and the flags Badang.

2. *Gyaspai*[1] *Chinsreg*, "the rich sacrifice," to obtain a good harvest, riches, &c. The stove is hemispherical, and of a yellow colour; on its bottom is figured the word "yam," the symbol of air.

3. *Vangi*[2] *Chinsreg*, "the sacrifice for power," to obtain influence, power, and success in war. The stove is of a red colour and circular, a form symbolical of the Lotus-flower; it bears on its under side "bam," the symbol of water.

4. *Dragpo*[3] *Chinsreg*, "the fierce sacrifice," to obtain protection from "untimely death," as well as to bring down punishment upon the evil spirits who have caused such a dreaded misfortune. The stove is triangular and of a black colour; the character on its bottom, "ram," is the symbol of fire.[4]

Plate No. XIV., Lit. a, gives—immediately transferred upon paper, as if it were a woodcut intended for printing—the surface of a rectangular oblong piece of wood, in which four holes are made, into which bread, paste, butter mixed with grains or similar objects, are pressed and sacrificed as a substitute for the burnt-offering. The characters in the centre are the symbols of the four elements, and the holes show the form of the stoves in which the offerings are burnt. In addition to these figures and symbols there is represented on the woodcut

[1] *r*Gyas-pa, "ample, copious."
[2] *d*Vang, "power."
[3] Drag-po, "fierce, cruel."
[4] Concerning untimely death see p. 109.

IELHAI GYALPO, THE LORD OF THE GENII OF FIRE.

Plate X. From a woodcut from Eastern Tíbet.

the officiating Lama, holding in his left hand the two spoons, emblematical of those used in this ceremony.

3. *Invocation of Lungta.*

Lungta, "the airy horse, the horse of wind,"[1] occurs in the list of the seven precious things under the name of Tachog, "the best horse of its kind." This horse is praised in the legends for its extraordinary swiftness. "When the king of the golden wheel, the governor of the four continents (in Sanskrit Mahā Chakravartin Rāja), mounts it to traverse the world, he sets out in the morning and returns at night without having experienced any fatigue." The Norvu phrengva reports, that it passes over immense tracts in one moment.[2]

The Lungta is the symbol of "harmony;" for it unites in harmony the three conditions of human existence, upon the union of which happiness depends; it strengthens these conditions, so as to cause a union salutary to man. These three conditions of existence and welfare are: Srog, Lus, and Vang.

Srog, the vital principle, "breath," is the basis of existence.

Lus, "body," means the due development of the organic formation of the body.

Vang, "power," means the moral energy enabling man to abstain from such actions as injure the vital

[1] *r*Lung, "wind;" *r*ta, "horse."

[2] Rémusat, in Foe koue ki, p. 128. Schmidt, Ssanang Ssetsen, p. 471. About the seven precious things, see p. 53.

principle and the organs of the body, and produce illness and death. It indicates, at the same time, the faculty of averting the dangers which arise from the natural hostility of the elements.[1]

Another faculty of Lungta is the power of depriving the constellations of the planets hostile to man of their obnoxious influence. Moreover, the efficacy of any Dhāranī, or mystical sentence, for happiness in this existence is supposed to become more certain by the presence of Lungta, and from this belief it has become customary to add to such Dhāranīs a horse supporting the precious stone Norbu, or a figure allegorical of the horse, or at least an address directed to Lungta.

The plates brought home by my brothers, exhibit specimens of this practice. The Dhāranīs are Sanskrit, and are written with Tibetan, and occasionally also with Lantsa characters. The purposes aimed at, and the deities implored by them vary; in most of them, however, we meet with "Om mani padme hum," and "Om Vajrapāni hum," Dhāranīs meant for Padmapāni and Vajrapāni.

The horse stands in the centre of plate No. XI., and bears the precious stone Norbu. In other copies it is running towards the left border, whilst the letters run as usual from left to right; in the present plate

[1] As often as the element which at a person's birth occurred in the denomination of the year comes in contact in "the cycles of years" with a hostile element, the years in which this takes place are unlucky ones; health is endangered and failure in one's undertakings may be expected. This idea refers to the belief of the Tibetans in an influence of the elements upon the welfare of man. See Chapter XVII.

MYSTICAL SENTENCES, WITH THE FIGURE OF THE AIRY HORSE.

The letters are here inverted, the same having been cut in the block itself in their positive form.

Plate XI.

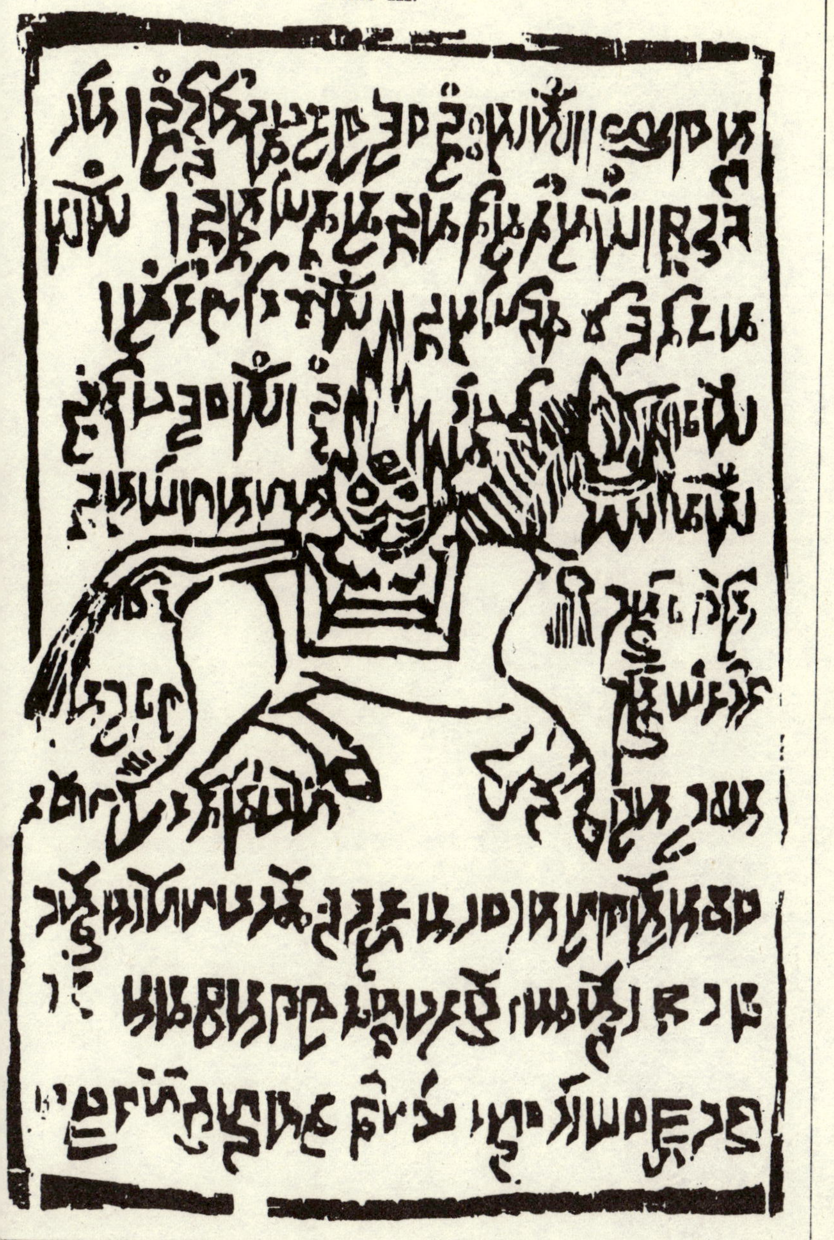

FORMS OF INVOCATIONS OF LUNGTA, THE AIRY HORSE.

1. Print from a Tibetan woodcut, from Síkkim.

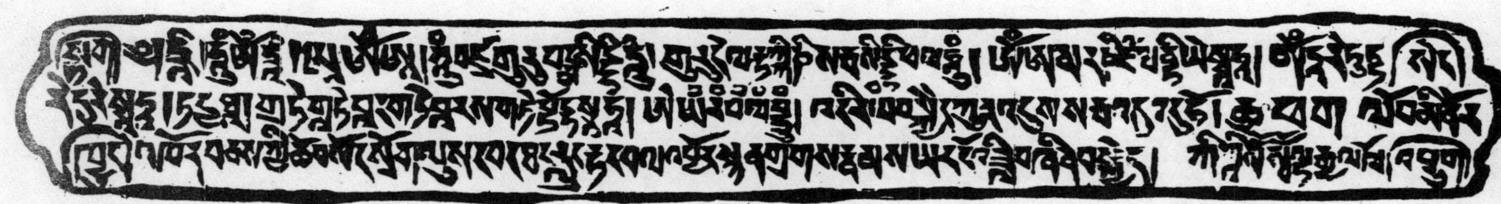

2. Copies of Formulæ, obtained at the monastery of Hímis, in Ladák.

༄༅། མི་ནོར་འཁོར་བཅས་ཀྱི་ཚེ་དཔལ་སྲོག་ལུས་དབང་ཐང་རླུང་རྟ་རྣམས་ཟླ་བ་ཡར་ངོ་བཞིན་དུ་བསྐྱེད་དུ་གསོལ། །

༄༅། སྟག་སེང་འཁྱུང་འབྲུག་འདིར་ཡང་བསྐྱེད། ། ཀུན་འདུས་སརྦ་འདུ་འདུ་ཧོཿ། །

Plate XII.

every thing has the opposite direction, the maker decidedly not taking the trouble to invert his own work. Such irregularities are not very unfrequent, particularly if the plates are not intended to be printed on paper, but only to make impressions on articles of food. As allegorical signs occasionally substituted for the figure of the horse we sometimes find the anagrammatic form of the prayer Om mani padme hum in Lantsa characters, or the Lantsa letter Om, encircled in either case by a glory, with the characters Ba and Bam at its sides. Other invocations of Lungta have no central ornament.

The addresses directed to Lungta personally are generally limited to the lower part of the table; a most potent imploration of it is the one printed on Plate XII., No. 2; it runs thus: "Wealth, the friend of sharpness, Lungta of breath, of body, of power, may you increase and grow like the new moon." In tables on which are inscribed this prayer, the four corners of the image are almost always filled out with the figures or with the names of a tiger (Tib. Tag), a lion (Senge), a bird (Khyung), and a dragon (Brug); and a Dhāranī is frequently inserted before the imploration of the Lungta, running thus: "Tiger, lion, bird and dragon, may they too co-operate to a complete union; sarva-du-du-hom."

In order that the Lungta produce its proper effect, the colour of the cloth or paper upon which it is printed, is also of importance; the rules concerning the modalities are, however, very simple; and if the right colour is not at hand, it may be supplied by rags of the required colour, which are cut into triangles (indicating that they are Phurbus), and fastened along the lower border of the table. The implorations of Lungta do not require the performance by a Lama, neither do the ceremonies more complicated still which have been established for increasing the probability of success,[1] and this belief may also be one of the reasons of the frequent application to Lungta.

4. *The Talisman Changpo.*

This talisman, which means "the keeper, the holder," is believed to protect man from the machinations of the evil spirits and to enable those who hang it up in their houses, or who wear it as an amulet, to resist the temptations to sin prompted by these demons. The form of this talisman is circular, as seen in Plate XIII. In the centre is a smaller inner circle; in a second, larger circle is traced a star, and along the inner side of this circle and in the eight intersectional compartments formed by the corners of the star are inscribed the names of hostile spirits. Outside the circles are seen a male and a female, the arms of the one figure tied with chains to the feet of the other.

This Plate is a print from a woodcut; the block had been so much used that the original sharpness was quite gone, and the wood had become cracked.

[1] There are several books in which is detailed what may be done besides.

THE TALISMAN CHANGPO.

From Dába, in Gnári Khórsum.

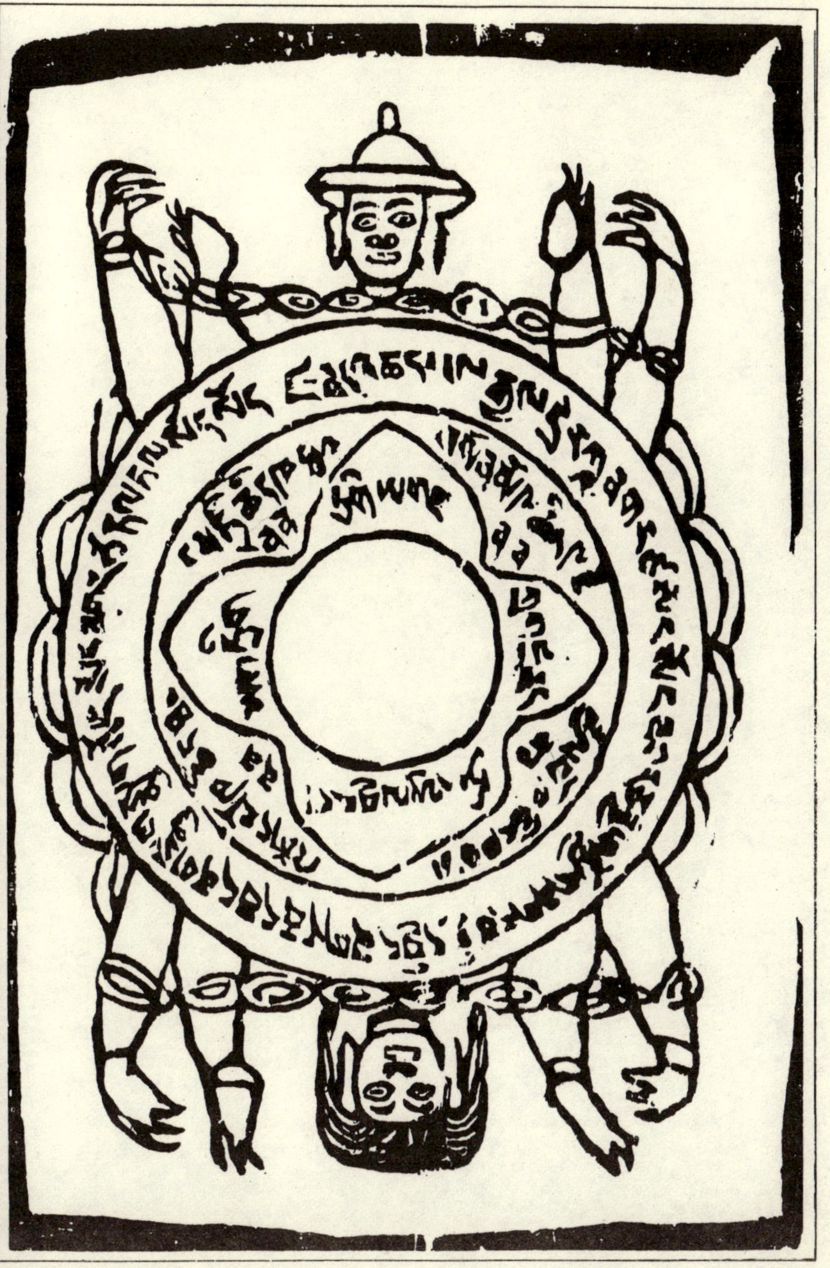

5. *The magical figure Phurbu.*

The Phurbu, literally "a peg," "pin," or "nail," is drawn as a triangle upon paper covered with charms; the handle has the form of a half-dorje. The Buddhists attribute to the Phurbu the faculty of preventing the evil spirits from inflicting mischief, or of expelling them, in case they have already begun to exercise their baneful influence. It is believed, that even the mere presence of the *word* Phurbu prevents the evil spirits from entering the houses and from injuring those who carry it as an amulet; the sentence Phurbui-dab-vo, "I cast thee with the nail," is therefore repeated in many books[1] which treat of the evil spirits; the point of a Phurbu, if directed towards the side where evil spirits dwell, drives them away, and brings them to ruin.

Generally, three Phurbus, enclosed by flames, are traced upon the same paper; this is fixed on paste-board or thin boards. In case of an illness, or when any mischief has been done which is supposed to have originated with evil spirits, the head of the family—or if he is wealthy enough to engage a Lama, the Lama—accompanied by the family and relatives, goes round the house, turning the point of the Phurbu in all directions, and uttering incantations at the height of his voice.

[1] **In the book Dug karchan, "provided with a white umbrella," this sentence is added to the name of the twenty evil spirits who are mentioned there.**

The accompanying woodcut shows the arrangement of the Phurbu. The two Tibetan characters in the central part of the figure stand for *d*Gra (pronounced Da), which means "enemy," and for *b*Geg*s*, pronounced Geg, "evil spirit." The human face between the smaller Phurbus is that of Tamdin, in Sanskrit Hayagrīva. Tamdin is a Dragshed who is considered to take a very prominent part in protecting man against the evil spirits. A dorje projects from his head; and under the chin is inscribed the mystical syllable Ah.

The oblong rectangle next his face and the hexagon contain a Dhāranī several times repeated, which threatens all the "evil spirits who dwell above the earth." The Dhāranīs in the following rectangle are directed against the Geg who inhabit the east, Shar, the south-east, Sharlho, and the south, Lho. The Dhāranīs in the joint of the triangle and at the beginning of the first large line in the triangular part keep off the evil spirits occupying the south-east, Lhonab. Each Dhāranī finishes with the words "destroy, bring to ruin." The Dhāranīs are Sanskrit, written with Tibetan characters.

On the handles of the two smaller Phurbus is inscribed the mystical syllable hum.

The other charms in the triangle begin with "Ah Tamdin," a mystical form of imploring this god. They keep off the evil spirits who dwell in the north-east, Nubjang, in the north, Jang, and in the other quarters of the world;[1] and it is declared that the wearing of such a Phurkha,[2] "sharp Phurbu," serves as a protection against all mischief originating in any of these quarters. Each of these Dhāranīs is Sanskrit, which, like numerous other charms, cannot well be translated in detail, and terminates with the syllables hum phat, a charm, of which the chief of the Dākinīs says, in the Norvu phrengva, "Crying with the voice of concealment *hum* and *phat*, I shall keep in order the innumerable legion of Dākinīs."[3] At the end of the inscription it is said that this Dhāranī is particularly directed against the spirits inhabiting the air, and against that class especially called *r*Gyal-po-*r*gyas-'gong-shin-dre-sron-dre.

The Dhāranīs inscribed on the handle, and the joint of the triangle, are always addressed to Tamdin; those with which the triangle itself is filled may vary, as any one who orders a Phurbu may have Dhāranīs directed against such evil spirits as he considers particularly hostile towards himself.

Those Phurbus are considered the most efficacious to which Dalai Lama and Panchen Rinpoche have composed

[1] Concerning the quarters of the world, which are ten in number, *see* p. 126.

[2] Kha, "bitter," here in the sense of sharp.

[3] Schmidt, "Geschichte der Ostmongolen," p. 468.—Compare also p. 247.

the Dhāranīs; such Phurbus as can prove this claim fetch a high price.

The Phurbus also form an important article of trade for the Mongolian pilgrims returning from Tíbet, who never fail to assert that the Dhāranīs on their Phurbus are the composition of the Dalai Lama.

6. *The Ceremonies Thugdam kantsai.*[1]

Whenever the assistance of any one of the many Dragsheds is sought by ceremonies, the prayers recited and the offerings made to him, must follow in a certain order:

1. The ceremonies with hymns praising the power of the god implored, and enumerating his attributes. This is called Ngontog,[2] "to cause the eminent understanding."

2. The region where the god dwells is described, the technical term being Chandren, "to cite."

3. The offerings are laid on the altar; Chodpa "the sacrifice."

4. Prayers are spoken imploring the remission of sins; an act called Shagpa, "repentance, confession."

5. Kantsai, the presentation of objects "to make content." The mode of offering consists in the consecration of the objects to the gods, which, hereafter, can no more be used for worldly purposes.

The offerings are, in some cases, weapons and living animals, one of the chief objects being an arrow, to which

[1] Thugs-dam "prayer;" *bs*kang "satiate, to make content;" *r*dzas "substance, wealth."

[2] *m*Ngon "clear, eminent;" *r*tog*s* "understanding."

five silken strips of the five sacred colours are fastened, called Darnai janpa, "ornament of five strips of silk,"[1] as well as a disk of brass, called Melong, "a mirror," upon which the mystical syllables om, tram, ah,[2] hri, hum are inscribed as here follows:—

om

tram ah hri

hum

ཨོཾ༔ ཏྲཾ༔ ཨཱཿ༔ ཧྲཱིཿ༔ ཧཱུྃ༔

Feathers, also, are attached to the arrow; they must be selected from such birds as are known favourites of the Dragshed implored; thus, to Lhamo the arrow presented is ornamented with the feathers of the raven, to Gonpo (Mahādeva) with those of a kite. Between the feathers small strips of paper are inserted on which are written certain charms, which are also inscribed upon the point and the shaft of the arrow.

When the act of imploration is over, the arrow is stuck perpendicularly into the ground, a position from which it can only be removed by the astrologers.

7. *Invocation of Nagpo Chenpo, by moving the arrow.*

Nagpo Chenpo, in Sanskrit Mahākala, is supposed to grant success in undertakings and to protect from the hostility of mischievous spirits in general; but the cere-

[1] Dar "silk," *sna* "end, strip," *lnga* "5;" *rgyan-pa* "ornament;" the nga "5," was suppressed in the pronounciation.

[2] Csoma, "Grammar," p. 105, explains *om* to be a mystical interjection, denoting the essential body or person of a Buddha, or any other divinity. *Hri* is a mystical very powerful imploration of Chenresi.

mony of "moving the arrow," is also performed for the purpose of discovering the perpetrators of a theft.

The head Lama of the monastery in which the ceremony has to take place begins it, amidst the loud sound of cymbals, drums, and pipes, with the reading of certain passages from a book which treats of Nagpo Chenpo's faculties, of the Dhāranīs communicated by him to man, of his hatred towards the evil spirits, and of the offerings which are most agreeable to him. The Lama concludes this lecture by threatening the malignant spirits with Nagpo Chenpo's wrath, if they do harm to those who have ordered the performance of this ceremony. He then hands to a novice a large and heavy arrow trimmed with feathers, strips of silk, and slips of paper inscribed with invocations to Nagpo Chenpo. The novice, who has taken a seat upon a carpet of white felt, holds this arrow with one hand, the point resting perpendicularly upon the palm of the other; by a slight shaking and turning he brings this point into motion, and gradually lets the arrow fall on the ground; his shakings become more violent as soon as the point has left the palm of his hand and moves on to the ground; he then seizes it with both hands, and by convulsive shaking he keeps it constantly moving. But the spectators believe the arrow to go on by its own power, and the shakings and tremblings of the priest to be the natural consequences of its spontaneous motion.

The novice continues to turn the arrow for several hours, during which he has perhaps walked over as many miles, and he only ceases to move it, when his hands show blisters or when his strength is exhausted. The halt of the arrow is taken as an unmistakeable manifestation that the evil spirits have been driven away; or if the arrow has been moved for the discovery of a theft, that its perpetrator is to be looked for in the direction pointed out. The novice then returns with his arrow to join the Lamas, who in the meantime have been engaged in singing hymns, and reciting the prescribed prayers; some concluding hymns are sung, and the arrow is solemnly handed over to him who had ordered the ceremony.

8. *The Ceremony Yangug.*

The aim of this ceremony, Yangug or Yangchob, "to call for luck, to insure luck,"[1] is to implore Dzambhala or Dodne vangpo,[2] the god of wealth, to grant riches. An arrow is offered similar to that used in the purchase of the assistance of the Dragsheds (No. 6), but the disk attached to it has a central perforation and four groups of lateral ones, as substitutes for the mystical syllables; the feathers on the shaft of the arrow are those of a black eagle, and round the five strips of silk is wrapped a band of white cloth covered with some Dhāranīs, and terminating in two loops.[3] These notices also present additional illustrations of the address to the Buddhas of confession (Chapter XI.). Every contribution to its explanation was the more welcome to me. as the novelty

[1] *g*Yang "luck," 'gugs "to call;" *s*kyob*s* "to protect."

[2] *g*Dod-nas "from the beginning;" *d*vang-po "ruler, the entirely powerful."

[3] The arrow I have also seen traced on an astrological table.

of the object so considerably increased the difficulty of entering into the full particulars. We found it mentioned there (see p. 137), that in the period of the destruction of the universe the performance of the ceremony Yangug will be more frequent than the pious acts which afford purification from sins.

The representations of Dzambhala show him generally surrounded by the eight other gods granting riches, who are styled Namthosras, in Sanskrit Vaïsravanas; these personages are always represented holding in the left hand a rat with a jewel in its mouth, a supposed symbol of fertility. Dzambhala himself is in all pictures represented riding upon a white lion with a green mane, his right hand supporting the Gyaltsan, in Sanskrit Dhvaja, a kind of banner with a floating cloth which typifies victory. His eight companions bear in the right hand the following objects: 1. A precious thing, in Tibetan Rinchen; 2. The flat vessel Lai Bumpa (see p. 247); 3. A small house several stories high, Khangtsig; 4. A pick-axe, Dungtsi; 5. A sword, Ralgri; 6. The precious stone Norbu; 7. A sword, Ralgri; 8. A clasp-knife, Digug.—A detailed account of the doings of these gods and of the meaning of the articles they hold, is given in the book Gyalpo chenpo namthosras chi kang shag, of which the St. Petersburg Academy has a copy.

My brothers once saw an image in which the mythological Buddha Dīpankara, (*see* p. 131), in Tibetan Marmedzad, and a "Buddha of medicine," in Tibetan Manla, were associated with Dzambhala instead of his eight companions.

9. *Ceremonies performed in cases of illness.*

The remarks offered here are partly taken from the Tibetan book on medicine published by Csoma, and partly based upon observations made by my brothers.

The Tibetan book[1] enumerates three principal and four secondary causes of diseases. The three principal causes are: 1. Lust, or desire; 2. Passion, or anger; 3. Dullness, or ignorance. By the first wind is caused; by the second bile; by the last phlegm. The four causes of a secondary nature are: 1. Season, with respect to cold and heat; 2. Any evil spirit; 3. Wrong use of food; 4. A bad course of life. The book contains useful hints, as to the course to be pursued in order to remain free from illness, and also gives a number of rules with respect to food, occupation, conduct of life in conformity with the different seasons, &c. The symptoms of diseases are indicated, and the questions are given which are to be addressed by the physician to the patient respecting his food, occupation and the circumstances how the disease first arose, its progress, and the pain felt. The several remedies prescribed against diseases are enumerated, 1,200 in number, which may be reduced to four classes: medicine, manual labour, diet, and manner of life.

[1] It is entitled Gyut zhi, "the tract in four parts," and is declared by Csoma to be the principal work on medicine in Tíbet. For an analysis of it see Journ. As. Soc. Beng., Vol. IV., p. 1-20. It is not introduced into the large collections of the Kanjur and Tanjur, which contain several other works on medicine; see Wilson, Journ. As. Soc. Beng., Vol.. I., p. 4. Gleanings in Science, Vol. III., p. 247. For further notices on medicine, compare also the "Description du Tubet," in Nouv. Journ. As., Vol. IV., p. 257. Trail, "Kamaon," As. Res., Vol. XVI., p. 222. Pallas, "Mongol. Völker," Vol. II., p. 338.

My brothers had never seen or heard of any medicine having been taken, or any surgical operation undertaken, which was not preceded and again followed by addresses to the Buddhas of medicine, in Tibetan Manlas, "the supreme physicians," and by the performance of certain ceremonies supposed to increase the sanative power of the medicine. The Manlas are eight in number; they are the imaginary Buddhas who are believed to have created the medicinal plants. When men set out to collect such plants they implore the assistance of the Manlas, and their names are uttered when the medicine is prepared and taken; their names or images are also generally printed at the commencement of books treating on medicine. The greatest number of prayers are addressed to them when the pills "Mani" are prepared, which are employed only in cases of very serious illness. The ceremonies accompanying the preparation of these pills are styled Manii rilbu grub thab, "preparation of the pill Mani."[1] The Manis are made of a particular kind of bread-paste, with which particles of the relics of a saint have been mixed in the form of powder or ashes. This paste is moistened with consecrated water, and kneaded up with ordinary bread-paste, from which are then made the smaller pills to be taken by sick persons.[2] The vessel with the water and paste is put upon a circle divided into six sections and a smaller central circle; in this centre stands the syllable "hri," a mystical and very powerful imploration of Chenresi; in each

[1] Mani "a precious stone," ril-bu "a globular figure, a pill;" grub "to have done; made ready;" thabs "means, method."

[2] These pills are identical with those mentioned by Huc, "Souvenirs," Vol. II., p. 278, as highly esteemed.

of the six sections is inscribed a syllable of the prayer Om mani padme hum. As long as the paste remains in the water (the prescribed time ranges from one to three weeks) some Lamas (who are not allowed to eat meat during this period) recite all day long particular prayers in honour of the Manlas.

With reference to diseases caused by ghosts and evil spirits, the 73rd. Chapter of Part IV. of the book mentioned enumerates twelve kinds, the 77th. eighteen. The causes, symptoms, and remedies are also enumerated. About these kinds of diseases and the methods of curing them my brothers learned the following particulars.

Each malignant spirit causes some particular disease. Thus Rāhu[1] inflicts palsy, in Tibetan Zanad; fifteen other devils, called Donchen Chonga,[2] "the fifteen great evil spirits," cause children to fall sick, &c. When the Lama physician who has been called to a sick man, has determined the illness to have been occasioned by a malignant spirit, he proceeds to examine into the circumstances, in order to detect the causes which have allowed the spirit to gain influence over the patient, and the means he employed to make him sick. When the illness is insignificant, as in cases of cold, hoarseness, light wounds, &c., it does not take, according to the belief of the Tibetans, much trouble to drive away the evil spirit; the remedies consist either in charms, which the patient has to wear, to affix to the door, or to read; or a noisy music is performed, before which the evil spirits are supposed to

[1] See p. 115.

[2] *g*Don "an evil spirit;" chhen "great;" *b*cho-*l*nga "fifteen."

yield; or the very Dragshed who is the particular enemy of the offending evil spirit is implored, and his image is hung up after having been carried in procession round the house; or the Phurbu is applied. These are the most common methods employed for the recovery of health; but it lies in the nature of this matter that these rites should vary considerably.

In cases of serious illness, particularly when the sick man is no more able to rise, the evil spirit is supposed to have crept into the house in the shape of an animal, and to dwell in this form near the sick man. The first business of the Lama then is to find out the form which the evil spirit has assumed, in which endeavours he finally succeeds by various ceremonies very much of a character akin to juggling. An animal is formed of clay or bread-paste by means of a wooden mould, of which he carries with him a variety for selection,[1] and the soul of the spirit is compelled to leave the assumed brute form, and to enter into the representation of it; for this purpose magical circles are traced and incantations recited for some time. When the evil spirit has been confined, by these means, the Lama reads passages out of certain books, and hands the moulded animal over to the patient to burn or to bury it; prints of it are also pasted on various parts of the house and are only removed when the disease has disappeared. If this means is not attended with success, and the sick man dies, it is averred that the illness was a punishment for immoral actions committed in some former existence.

[1] Specimens of such blocks are given in Plates Nos. XIV. to XVI.

PRINTS FROM SLIPS OF WOOD USED IN TÍBET AS A SUPPOSED PROTECTION AGAINST EVIL SPIRITS.

No. 1; from Sikkim.

a.

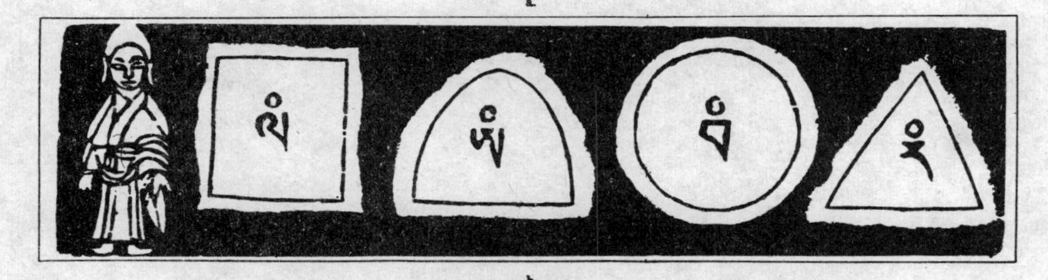

b.

c.

d.

PRINTS FROM SLIPS OF WOOD USED IN TÍBET

No.

UPPOSED PROTECTION AGAINST EVIL SPIRITS.

kkim.

PRINTS FROM SLIPS OF WOOD USED IN TÍBET AS A SUPPOSED PROTECTION AGAINST EVIL SPIRITS.

No. 3; from Síkkim.

a.

b.

c.

10. *Funeral rites.*

The funeral (Tib. Shid) of a layman generally terminates, where circumstances allow of it, in the burning of the body, although the practice of exposing the corpse on the hills as a prey to wild animals, formerly a very common one, is even now sometimes resorted to on account of the scarcity of wood.[1] The ceremony of burning the body is performed upon an altar of a cubical form; in larger towns several of these are kept ready for immediate use; thus there are twelve such altars at Leh, surrounding the burial ground. In countries where wood is plentiful, as in Bhután and Síkkim, enough is employed to render the combustion complete, nothing remaining but ashes; but in Tíbet it often happens that quantities of the bones remain unconsumed, which are then carefully collected, together with the ashes, and buried.[2]

The bodies of the Lamas are not burnt: they are

[1] For descriptions of various kinds of funerals see Nouv. Journ. Asiat., Vol. IV., p. 254. Huc, "Souvenirs," Vol. II., p. 347. Cunningham, "Ladák," p. 308.

[2] Concerning the mode of collecting the ashes in Eastern Bengál and Assám my brother Hermann gave me the following details:—A cloth about three feet square is fastened at its four ends to canes about three to four feet high, which are driven into the earth; into this cloth, thus forming a sort of trough, the ashes, bones and remaining pieces of charcoal are gathered, and left to be dispersed by the wind, or gradually decomposed by the rain and heat. The tribes of the Khássia hills, where the amount of rain exceeds that of any known country, although it is limited to a duration of three to four months, have a most curious practise of keeping their dead till the rainy season is over; as long as the heavy rains last no combustion in the open air would be possible. They put the corpse into trunk of a hollow tree, and fill this up with honey, a process which prevents decomposition for several months, even in these hot and moist regions.

buried in a reclining attitude (not exactly in a sitting posture), with the knees brought up to the chin, and the whole corpse laced together into as small a space as possible; occasionally they are put into a cloth bag. In general, the graves are not dug; the grave-yard being selected in places abounding with stones, the corps is simply laid down on the ground and concealed beneath a heap of stones. The erection of Chortens over the dead is limited to exceptional cases. With the remarkable toleration so characteristic of Buddhism, my brothers were allowed to open and examine some of the graves near Leh, and they even induced a Lama to undertake the boiling of some corpses for the purpose of cleaning and preparing the skeletons, though the latter process had to be concealed from the population in general. The corpses taken out of their graves were not decomposed; the great dryness of the atmosphere had caused the flesh to shrink to a hard leathery substance covering the bones, and this yielded but very slowly to the action of the boiling water. The length of several corpses compressed in the way just described was found to be from 2½ to 3 feet.

During the process of combustion and interment prayers are recited and various ceremonies performed; offerings are presented to the god of the fire, Melha; the Zhiba Chrinsreg, to obtain the remission of the sins of the deceased,[1] is also performed. A ceremony which precedes the interment consists in the purchase of the burial-ground from the *lord of the ground*, in Tibetan

[1] For its description see p. 249.

Sadag gyalpo. The lord of the ground, and the mischievous spirits obeying him, are supposed to do mischief, from innate malice, to the dead in his future existence, as well as to his surviving relatives in their present one. The lord of the ground can be pacified by the purchase of the burial ground, while the other malignant spirits are banished by charms and rites, in which reverence is paid to the three gems, viz. to Buddha, Dharma, and Sanga.[1] These rites are said to have been taught to man by Manjusrī, the god of wisdom. The relatives of the deceased inform the astrologers, who are considered to have intercourse with Sadag, of the amount they propose to pay to Sadag, either in the form of cattle or money, and request them to persuade him to be satisfied therewith. Invariably the answer is returned, that Sadag, who is represented as insatiable, wants more for his pacification than the amount offered. When, finally, the necessary sum has been settled, the grave is marked out, and the astrologers proceed to expel Sadag and all the other malignant spirits in the following terms:

"Lord of the ground, and you Mahōragas,[2] hear my command and order, which I issue with the ceremonies prescribed by the sacred law of the god Manjusrī and of the three gems. I drive the arrow not into the eyes, not into the feet, not into the bowels of the evil spirits, Lord of the ground, but into the earth, in order to

[1] See p. 184, Note 2.

[2] Mahōragas, in Tibetan Tophye chenpo, are terrestrial dragons superior to man. See Foe koue ki, Engl. transl., p. 133.

render propitious the inferior mischievous spirits. Genii, if you do not obey my order, I will break your heads with my dorje. Hear my order: hurt neither the deceased (his name is here repeated) nor his surviving relatives. Do them no damage, neither injure them, nor teaze them, nor bring misfortune upon them."[1]

The Lama then drives the arrow into the ground, where it remains until the dead person is buried.

[1] From an oral communication from a Lama.

CHAPTER XVI

THE SYSTEMS OF RECKONING TIME

1. Calendars and Astrological Tables.—2. The various Modes of Chronology. The cycle of 12 years. Counting back from the current year. The cycle of 60 years. The cycle of 252 years.—3. The Year and its Divisions.

1. Calendars and astrological tables.

The Tibetans received their astronomical science from their neighbours in India and China; the Chinese also becoming their teachers in the art of divination. Their acquaintance with the astronomical and calendrical systems of these nations coincides with the propagation of the Buddhist religion by the Chinese and Indian priests, to whom they are also indebted for the respective systems of defining the year.[1] Both systems are based upon a

[1] In the "Description du Tubet," translated from the Chinese by Klaproth in Nouv. Journ. As., Vol. IV., p. 138, the Chinese consort of King Srongtsan Gampo and her suite are stated to have brought the Chinese system into Tibet in the seventh century A.D.

unit of sixty years, differing, however, in the modes of denominating the years. The Indian denomination is called in Tibetan Kartsis, "white mathematics;" the Chinese method, on the other hand, goes by the name of Naktsis, "black mathematics," a term also extended to the "black art," or the science of divination and of astrological calculations.[1]

The Tibetan designations for almanacs are Leutho,[2] Lotho, or Ritha; they are sketched by the Lamas.

It is a very general custom to append to the almanacs various tables for astrological purposes. These additional tables differ widely in contents as well as in size; they are rarely wanting for the following purposes:

Gabtsis,[3] "the concealed calculations," are tables framed upon the common calendrical system, the occasions for which they are consulted being most various.

Grubtsis,[4] "the perfect astronomy," for deciding the character and influence of the planets.

Tserab las-tsis[5] is the name of the calculations for the duration of life, and of the fate of man.

Bagtsis[6] are the tables consulted in cases of marriage.

Shintsis[7] are those used to find an answer to inquiries respecting the form in which the dead shall be re-born.

[1] Nag, "black;" *r*tsis, "mathematics;" *d*kar, "white." These names have decidedly originated from the Tibetan names for India and China, which are called respectively "white plain," Gya-gar, and "black plain," Gya-nag. Kartsis, however, is also used for "Astronomy," or "Astrology," but it is then spelt *s*kar-*r*tsis, from *s*kar, a star.

[2] The name Dalow for calendar, occurring in Turner, "Embassy," p. 331, is probably a dialectical modification of this word.

[3] Gab, "a shelter; concealed, dubious;" *r*tsis, "mathematics."

[4] Grub, "perfect."

[5] Ts'he, "time, lifetime;" rab*s*, "genealogy;" las, "work, fate."

[6] Bag, "a bride." [7] *g*Shin, "a corpse."

Naktsis, which also designates the art of divination in general, is predominantly applied to tables by means of which the lucky and unlucky times affecting a particular individual, with the reasons of their being so, can be determined. Several tables of this kind will be described in a subsequent chapter.

Tables relating to particular classes, such as Rājas, Lamas, and the like, are less frequently met with.

2. The various modes of chronology.

The various systems of reckoning time have already been the object of the most learned and successful researches by Csoma and Ideler. I give an abstract of their results on account of the connexion of the calendrical systems with the interpretation of the astrological calculations; this affords me, at the same time, the opportunity of combining with it the informations which Hermann obtained from natives during his stay in Síkkim.

1. When any thing is to be defined referring to a period not too distant from the present time, it is not the practice to use a standard unit of sixty years, but a cycle of twelve years is employed instead, each year bearing the name of an animal,[1] which names are invariably repeated in the following order:—

[1] Respecting the origin and introduction of this cycle which is generally called "the Tatar," see Ideler, "Ueber die Zeitrechnung der Chinesen," pp. 75, 78. He believes it to have first arisen in Western Asia. Klaproth finds it mentioned for the first time in Chinese books in the year 622 A.D. Nouv. Journ. As., Vol. XV., p. 145.

1. Ji, the mouse.
2. Lang, the ox.
3. Tag, the tiger.
4. Yos, the hare.
5. Brug, the dragon.
6. Brul, the serpent.
7. Ta, the horse.
8. Lug, the sheep.
9. Prel, or pre, the ape
10. Ja, the bird.
11. Chi, the dog.
12. Chag, the hog.

Thus, when a particular year is to be specified, the Tibetan term for year, Lo, is added to the name of the animal, and it is called Ji-lo, "mouse year;" Lang-lo, "ox year," &c.[1] When the date of an event which has taken place previous to the present duodecimal era is to be indicated, the number of cycles that have passed since the time in question is first put down, and by adding to it the number of the animal year the entire sum of years is accurately arrived at.

2. In books, as well as generally in conversation, the dates of past events are not unfrequently determined by counting back from the current year. For instance, the present year being 1863, the birth of Tsonkhapa, which occurred in 1355 A.D., would be said to have taken place 508 years ago. This method is also applied in the Baidūrya Karpo, from which Csoma has extracted his highly important chronological table.[2]

3. A cycle of sixty years seems to have been in very general use in Tíbet a long time ago.[3] As a novelty,

[1] Csoma, "Grammar," p. 147.

[2] Csoma, "Grammar," p. 181; Huc, "Souvenirs," Vol. II., p. 369.

[3] It is curious that the present generation of Tibetans are unacquainted with the historical data of its origin and antiquity. They account for the introduction of this cycle by the supposition that the idea had been taken from the average length of human life. Such, at least, was the assertion of Chibu Lama, the political agent of the Rāja of Síkkim, and of several other Lamas.

it was ordained, probably in the eleventh century A.D., that the cycles of sixty years should be counted from the year 1026, which is the year next to 1025, in which the Kāla Chakra system had been introduced into Tíbet (see p. 47). The year 1026 being the first year of the first cycle, 1086 became the first year of the second cycle. If the number of the cycles that have already elapsed were regularly added in books and documents to the definition of the current year, this system would be as precise as our way of counting by centuries; but the number of the cycle being omitted before the year to be determined,[1] the reader frequently finds it no easy task to assign the correct era by weighing and comparing dates of an indirect nature.

The year 1026 was also the first year of the contemporaneous Indian cycle, and thus the identity of the Tibetan and the Indian order of years within the cycle became possible. The first, second, third year, &c., of any Tibetan cycle is consequently the first, second, third year, &c., of an Indian cycle; the number of cycles, however, do not accord with each other, the Indian not dating from the year 1026, but from one, or even two other and anterior epochs.[2]

It is already long ago, at least under the dynasty Han, or 206 B.C., that the Chinese began to measure time by cycles of sixty years, a period formed by the combinations of a decimal and a duodecimal series. But

[1] As an example see the historical document relating to the Hímis monastery, p. 183; and the Dába document, p. 278.

[2] See Csoma, "Grammar," p. 148.

between the Chinese cycle and that of the Indo-Tibetan the coincidence was not perfect, a third year of the Chinese cycle being coeval with the first of the Tibetan cycle, and so on. This difference, however, remained without any influence upon Tibetan chronology so long as China possessed no political weight in the country; but when the Chinese government, in 1718,[1] made Tíbet a dependency, it soon followed that the inhabitants were obliged to adapt the cyclic order of their years to that of the Chinese, and this could only be effected by advancing the number of the year throughout by two. Thus two years are virtually cancelled from the Tibetan calendar, so that the cycles commence two years earlier than before the change; *e. g.* in 1864 instead of 1866. The altered chronology is used at present in all official matters, and is generally adopted for private business.

In support of this explanation I quote the document from Dába.[2] It is dated from the sixth month (month

[1] Köppen, "Die Religion des Buddha," Vol. II., p. 196.

[2] It is styled Lam-yig-dang-ming-dang-yar-na, "Road prescription, and also denomination how far up," and was made at Nyugcháng, a halting place about eight miles south of Dába. Adolphe engaged to pay a sum of "six *Srang* (ounces) of gold" (= about £60) to the Chinese officer residing at Dába, if he or his brother Robert should cross the Sátlej river; his head man, called Bara Mañi, or also simply Mani, pledged himself to pay this sum. The treaty was written by the Chinaman himself, who added, instead of his signature, the official seal; Adolphe, having no seal at hand, stamped it with the but-end of his riding-whip.—The Lama Gombojew transcribed the original into capital letters, in which it is also printed on Plate XVII. But here again (comp. p. 183) occur so many deviations from the terminology of the sacred books, that it was impossible to arrive at a translation. Prof. Schiefner, who had kindly looked for analogous documents in modern dialects in the St. Petersburg libraries, did not find any which would have afforded the means of detailing quite literally either the Dába or the Hímis document.

TREATY

BETWEEN ADOLPHE SCHLAGINTWEIT

AND

THE CHINESE AUTHORITIES OF DÁBA.

This was in reference to the Routes he and his brother Robert should be allowed to take in Gnári Khórsum.

ལམ་ཡིག་དང་མིང་དང་ཡར་ན།

༄༅ ཤིང་ཡོས་ཟླ་བ་དྲུག་པའི་ཚེ་ལང་ཆུ་གཉིས་གོང་མ་ཁྲིམས་འདག་པ་རིན་པོ་ཆེ་ཞབས་
དྲུང་དུ་ཞུས་པ་ལམ་ཡིག་གུང་ཐམ་པས་བློས་གླང་བས་མ་རྒྱུར་བས་གས་ཆོག་རྩང་མ་ཡུལ་
གཉེར་པ་འདེས་ལོ་སྐྱེ་གླིང་པོར་སམ་ནས་འདེང་རྒྱུར་བླ་སྐྱུན་གནངས་སོང་འདི་ཕེབས་མི་གྲོལ་
ཞུས་པ་ང་མི་སྐྱོར་གཉིས། ད་འགྲུ་སྣང་ཐོག། ལས་གཅིག་རྩེར་གཉིས། གྲུན་ཏབ་ལས་སྐྱོལ་
གཏོག་མ་བཏོགས་ལོགས། གཡས་ལག་གཡོན་གཉིས། གོང་ཆོག་ལ་འགལ་ཚོས་ཁྲིམས་
ཞབས་རིན་པོ་ཆེ་ལ་སེར་སྣང་ཐུ་སྐྱུལ་ཆེད་ཞུལ་རྒྱུར་དོ་དག་སྐྱིའི་བློས་གླང་པ་ཡས་སལ་གྱི་
ཞེན་ནར་གྱིས་གནང་ལ་གུ་ཚམས་གཉིས་ཀྱིས་དག།། །།

of July) of the wood-hare year. This year is the fifty-second in the cycle. If fifty-one is added to 1806 (not fifty-two, because 1806 is the first year of a new cycle, the fourteenth of the Indo-Tibetan chronology), we obtain the year 1857; but my brothers were in Dába in 1855, which year can only be found by deducting two years (compare p. 287).[1]

Within these cycles of sixty years the single years are denominated differently in the Indian and in the Chinese manner. According to the *Indian principle*, each year is called by a particular name; these Sanskrit terms the Tibetans have simply translated into their own language.[2] In imitation of the *Chinese mode*[3] of reckoning time the sixty years of the cycle are designated in the following way. The twelve animals already mentioned are five times repeated in the order given above, and are coupled with the five elements, each of the latter being introduced

[1] Csoma, though alluding to a difference between the Indo-Tibetan and Chinese cycles ("Grammar," p. 148) does not take into consideration the predominant use of the Chinese system, when he says that the year 1834 is the 28th of the current cycle. From the reasons given above, the 30th will be found the correct number. In Cunningham's example ("Ladak," p. 395) the Indo-Tibetan cycle is also applied.—I must further observe that Csoma was misinformed, when he speaks of the difference between the commencement of the Chinese and the Indo-Tibetan cycle as one of three years instead of two, saying that "the Tibetans give the designation of first to the fourth year of the Chinese cycle."—I may still draw the attention to another deviation, which is easily made by Europeans when counting the years in the cycles. In calculating the difference between any given year and the first of the respective cycle, the two numbers are to be taken inclusive; if, *e. g.*, a cycle begins in 1806, the year 1851 is not the forty-fifth, as Cunningham reckons it (p. 396), but the forty-sixth year of the series.

[2] Csoma, "Grammar," pp. 148, 150, where the sixty names may be found.

[3] For this method see the memoir of Ideler, "Ueber die Zeitrechnung der Chinesen." Berlin, 1839.

in the series twice in immediate succession. We obtain, therefore, sixty combinations each differing from the other. The years are then distinguished in two ways; they are either called by the names of the element and animal combined, or by the names of the colour of the element and the animal combined. A combination of the one form is, *e. g.*, water-hog year; and the same combination, in the second form, blue-hog year. Water-hog or blue-hog year stands for the 60th of the Indo-Tibetan cycle. If the names of the years are given in full detail, a gender is also added to the combinations of element and animal, this being represented alternately by pho, a particle denoting the masculine gender, and mo, the feminine particle; and the gender of every combination is, therefore, defined by its very position in the cycle. The year beginning the cycle has the element and animal masculine, the next year has the same element and the successive animal both feminine; and the same alternations of the gender being kept up throughout, it results that every year the numeral of which is an odd number, as 1, 3, 5, &c., must be masculine, while the years represented by the even numerals 2, 4, 6, &c., are feminine. It must be noticed that a distinctive power is not conferred by the addition of these particles, as at first might appear to be the case.—The natives employ the mode of counting by colours when pointing out a year in an almanac, because the elements are there represented by colours and symbolical signs, and not by words;[1] on all other occasions the

[1] Schmidt, preface to Ssanang Ssetsen's history, p. 20.

name of the element is more usually resorted to. The following table shows the succession of the elements and their colours, from which no deviation is made in counting time.

Tibetan name.	Translation.	Colour.
Shing	wood	green
Me	fire	red
Sa	earth	yellow
Chag	iron	white
Chu	water	blue.[1]

In order to facilitate the determination of our era in Tibetan terms, I append, as an example, the following table, which contains the Tibetan mode of counting and the numbers now used in compliance with the Chinese prescription. The table is, at the same time, selected so as to embrace seventy-five years belonging to three different cycles.[2]

[1] When the animals constituting the cycle of sixty years are traced for astrological purposes, and not for the mere reckoning of time, the succession of the colours corresponding to the elements is given differently from that mentioned above, in order to avoid a coincidence with the colour given to the animals. Their order is given in the next chapter.—The Lamas have many works to explain the system upon which the chronology by the cycle of sixty years is based. A very comprehensive and at the same time detailed hand-book on this subject is the work Yangsal Domi (as it is generally pronounced), meaning "a clear-burning lamp for luck." The number of its leaves somewhat exceeds 500 and it also contains notices of the astrological arts. A copy of this book is also to be found in the St. Petersburg library.

[2] In China the cycles date back to a period so remote, that I cannot here enter into any details respecting this part of the subject; and I simply confine myself to the remark, that the cycle 1864 to 1923, which is No. XV. in the modified Tibetan chronology, is in China Proper No. LXXVI. See Ideler's "Zeitrechnung," p. 60.

TIBETAN CHRONOLOGICAL TABLE

of the cycle of sixty years.

Year of the Christian Era.	Tibetan Era.				
	Counting from 1026.		Modified so as to bring it into correspondence with the Chinese numbers of the years within the cycle.		
	Nos. of the cycle.	Nos. of the year within the cycle.	Nos. of the cycle.	Nos. of the year within the cycle.	Tibetan denomination, corresponding to the present number of the year within the cycle.
1852	(XIV.)	47	(XIV.)	49	Water-Mouse.
1853		48		50	» Ox.
1854		49		51	Wood-Tiger.
1855		50		52	» Hare.
1856		51		53	Fire-Dragon.
1857		52		54	» Serpent.
1858		53		55	Earth-Horse.
1859		54		56	» Sheep.
1860		55		57	Iron-Ape.
1861		56		58	» Bird.
1862		57		59	Water-Dog.
1863		58		60	» Hog.
1864		59	XV.	1	Wood-Mouse.
1865		60		2	» Ox.
1866	XV.	1		3	Fire-Tiger.
1867		2		4	» Hare.
1868		3		5	Earth-Dragon.
1869		4		6	» Serpent.
1870		5		7	Iron-Horse.
1871		6		8	» Sheep.
1872		7		9	Water-Ape.
1873		8		10	» Bird.
1874		9		11	Wood-Dog.
1875		10		12	» Hog.
1876		11		13	Fire-Mouse.
1877		12		14	» Ox.
1878		13		15	Earth-Tiger.
1879		14		16	» Hare.
1880		15		17	Iron-Dragon.
1881		16		18	» Serpent.
1882		17		19	Water-Horse.

TIBETAN CHRONOLOGICAL TABLE.

(Continued.)

Year of the Christian Era.	Tibetan Era.				
	Counting from 1026.		Modified so as to bring it into correspondence with the Chinese numbers of the years within the cycle.		
	Nos.		Nos.		
	of the cycle.	of the year within the cycle.	of the cycle.	of the year within the cycle.	Tibetan denomination, corresponding to the present number of the year within the cycle.
1883	(XV.)	18	(XV.)	20	Water-Sheep.
1884		19		21	Wood-Ape.
1885		20		22	» Bird.
1886		21		23	Fire-Dog.
1887		22		24	» Hog.
1888		23		25	Earth-Mouse.
1889		24		26	» Ox.
1890		25		27	Iron-Tiger.
1891		26		28	» Hare.
1892		27		29	Water-Dragon.
1893		28		30	» Serpent.
1894		29		31	Wood-Horse.
1895		30		32	» Sheep.
1896		31		33	Fire-Ape.
1897		32		34	» Bird.
1898		33		35	Earth-Dog.
1899		34		36	» Hog.
1900		35		37	Iron-Mouse.
1901		36		38	» Ox.
1902		37		39	Water-Tiger.
1903		38		40	» Hare.
1904		39		41	Wood-Dragon.
1905		40		42	» Serpent.
1906		41		43	Fire-Horse.
1907		42		44	» Sheep.
1908		43		45	Earth-Ape.
1909		44		46	» Bird.
1910		45		47	Iron-Dog.
1911		46		48	» Hog.
1912		47		49	Water-Mouse.
1913		48		50	» Ox.

TIBETAN CHRONOLOGICAL TABLE.
(Continued.)

Year of the Christian Era.	Tibetan Era. Counting from 1026. Nos. of the cycle.	of the year within the cycle.	Modified so as to bring it into correspondence with the Chinese numbers of the years within the cycle. Nos. of the cycle.	of the year within the cycle.	Tibetan denomination, corresponding to the present number of the year within the cycle.
1914	(XV.)	49	(XV.)	51	Wood-Tiger.
1915		50		52	» Hare.
1916		51		53	Fire-Dragon.
1917		52		54	» Serpent.
1918		53		55	Earth-Horse.
1919		54		56	» Sheep.
1920		55		57	Iron-Ape.
1921		56		58	» Bird.
1922		57		59	Water-Dog.
1923		58		60	» Hog.
1924		59	XVI.	1	Wood-Mouse.
1925		60		2	» Ox.
1926	XVI.	1		3	Fire-Tiger.

4. Another method of counting is that based on a cycle of 252 years; it was made known for the first time in Georgi's "Alphabetum Tibetanum," and again reported by Huc.[1] From the above mentioned elements and animals a cycle of 252 years is formed by imputing to the masculine and feminine particles a discriminating power, and thus multiplying the combinations. The first

[1] Huc, "Souvenirs," Vol. II., p. 368. The combination of the animals with the elements, as given by Georgi in his "Alphabetum Tibetanum," pp. 464-69, is altogether arbitrary, for by this way the elements follow each other twelve times, whilst in all these modes of chronological combination every element is taken but twice and then followed by the next.

twelve years of this cycle are counted by the names of the twelve animals only; the next sixty years (13-72) by coupling them with the five elements (each being introduced twice, as described in the preceding table); the period from 73 to 132 is denominated by affixing the masculine particle "pho" to the combinations; that from 133 to 192 by appending the feminine particle "mo." The years from 193 to 252, as Abbé Huc concludes, are distinguished by the alternate employment of *pho* and *mo* till the end of the cycle. This is not quite clear. If it were to be understood that, in this last series, a male combination alternates with a female combination, we should obtain only those terms which are already contained in the periods from 73 to 192. As one combination which would provide the addition of the 60 years required for completing the sum of 252 without a repetition, and which could be brought into final accordance with Huc's words, I might suggest the uniting of elements and animals of different genders. According to this mode, the year 193 has the element male and the animal female, 194 has the same element female, the animal male, 195 has the next element male and the animal female, 196 the same element female and the animal male, and so on; while in the previous series the entire combination is of the same gender in both its parts. In this, however, there is a theoretical disadvantage which ought not to be overlooked. When *completely* worked out, it would not conclude with 252, but would proceed as far as 312; for sixty more combinations, differing from those already obtained, are at once formed, if we continue the series by now making the first *element* female and the first *animal* male, and then the same element male and the next animal female, &c.

Perhaps the following combination may not be unworthy of our attention, since it equally excludes repetitions, and has besides the advantage of not extending the series beyond 252. In the group from 13-72 the genders of the elements are undecided, the animals also have no particle appended; failing this, however, usage warrants us in regarding them as males. This supposition is confirmed by the representations wherever they are distinct enough; moreover, in verbal explanations the male nouns are almost exclusively used, as, *e. g.* ram in stead of sheep, &c. In the concluding sěries from 193 to 252 the gender of the elements might also be considered to remain undefined, while the animals might all be taken as females. The combination of two parts of diverse gender rather seems not to be in contradiction with what we may suppose to be intended in Huc's words; and the combination of the elements with *female* animals, besides, derives probability from its being that particular connexion which properly *completes the series in form as well as in number.*

As an illustration of the combinations resulting, I add a list of all the years in the cycle of 252 in which the mouse, the first of the series of animals, occurs.

Year 1. Mouse.
„ 13. Wood-mouse.

Year 73. Male wood-mouse.
„ 133. Female wood-mouse.
„ 193. Male wood, female mouse. (*Huc*).
Wood, female mouse. (*Schlagintweit*).

This cycle of 252 years is not in general use; Csoma heard nothing at all about it, neither did Cunningham; nor did my brothers find it actually employed. As an instance, I may mention that the date wood-hare year of the Dába document gives, according to the 252 years cycle, the year 1845, if we begin with 1026 as the first,—1843, if we correct it for the modifications recently introduced; while it must be 1855 (see p. 277). This cycle may, however, be expected to be in use in the very centres of the Lamaic institutions, such as Lhássa, Tashilúnpo, &c.[1] At some distance from Lhássa it seems to be no longer known, even if it were ever employed; the Lamas in Síkkim were not acquainted with it.

3. The Year and its Divisions.

The year with the Tibetans is a lunar one, *i. e.* the phases of the moon regulate the duration of the month, and twelve such months—after the lapse of which nearly the same season begins to return—are the basis of the definition of the annual period. Twelve of these lunar

[1] The cycle may, however, perhaps be tried when examining older documents. The historical document relating to the foundation of the monastery of Hímis allows at all events of an interpretation by applying the 252 years cycle, compare p. 187; but it appears to be the more general custom to denominate the years also in historical treatises by the cycle of 60 years.

months are equal to 354 days, 8 hours, 48 min., 36·6 sec.—a total which is less than the solar year by 10 days, 21 hours, 0 min., 11 sec. The Tibetan year nominally amounts to 360 days; and in order to bring it into accordance with the moon, one day,[1] from time to time, is not counted at all. But as this does not occur with exact regularity, the months and years do not always begin on the same day as the Chinese months and years.[2]

The difference between the lunar and the solar year is compensated by the Tibetans by inserting, for every period of nineteen years, seven intercalary months (Tib. Dashol); the error then remaining is not more than about two hours for this period, for seven lunar months give 206 days, 17 hours, 8 min., 20 sec., and the inferiority of the lunar year for 19 years is altogether 206 days, 15 hours, 3 min., 29 sec. It is only after about two centuries that the error amounts to one day.[3] With respect to the principle which is followed in the intercalation of the seven months I am not in possession of any details. Csoma says, that generally one month is inserted every third year.[4]

The year begins in February with the appearance of

[1] "Description du Tubet," in Nouv. Journ. As., Vol. IV., p. 137. In his Souvenirs (Vol. II., p. 370) Huc states that, owing to the belief in lucky and unlucky days, many are omitted altogether, and are then counted by the number of the preceding days.

[2] See Ideler, as quoted above, p. 165.

[3] In the Julian calendar the difference is much greater, amounting in 128 years to a whole day. Mädler, Populäre Astronomie, p. 522.

[4] Csoma, l. c., p. 148, and Nouv. Journ. As., Vol. IV., p. 137.

the new moon.[1] The twelve months, in Tibetan Dava, are called the first, second, third month, &c., from one to twelve, or also by the names of the cyclic animals with the word "Dava" added.[2] The months are subdivided into thirty days, in Tibetan Tsei, which are quoted by their numerals, and into weeks, in Tibetan Gungdun. Within the week the days bear the names of the sun, moon, and five planets.[3] Certain symbolical signs are also connected with the different days, as in the following enumeration:

Number of the day within the week.	Celestial body.	Tibetan name.	Symbolical sign.
1	The sun.	Nyima.	A sun.
2	The moon.	Dava.	A waning moon.
3	Mars.	Migmar.	An eye.
4	Mercury.	Lhagpa.	A hand.
5	Jupiter.	Phurbu.	Three nails.
6	Venus.	Pasang.	A garter.
7	Saturn.	Penpa.	A bundle.

The days are subdivided into twenty-four hours, each hour into sixty minutes, in Tibetan Chusrang.

[1] So my brother Hermann, the Chinese description of Tíbet, and Huc. Turner, however, was informed that the first month was January; "Embassy," p. 321.

[2] Cunningham's "Ladak," p. 396. Csoma and Schmidt, Dictionaries *sub voce* zla.

[3] In the Chinese description of Tíbet it is said that the five elements are introduced in the denomination of the days of the week, but I have found nothing at all tending to confirm the statement.

CHAPTER XVII

DESCRIPTION OF VARIOUS TABLES USED FOR ASTROLOGICAL PURPOSES

Importance attributed to Astrology.—I. Tables for indicating lucky and unlucky Periods. 1. The elements and cyclic animals. 2. The spirits of the season. 3. Figures and oracles for determining the character of a given day.—II. Tables for direction in important Undertakings 1. The square tortoise. 2. The circular tortoise.—III. Tables of Destiny in cases of Sickness. 1. The human figures. 2. Allegorical figures and dice.—IV. Tables of Marriage. 1. Table with numerals. 2. Table with cyclic animals.—V. A Soothsaying Table with numerous Figures and Sentences.

Importance attributed to astrology.

The Tibetans, like all primitive nations, attribute to the position of the sun in reference to the constellations, to the planets, to the direct active interference of gods and spirits, and such like, a very considerable influence upon the welfare of man in this and in future existences. To their priests, the Lamas, they ascribe the faculty of deciding what circumstances are to be considered as favourable, and what unfavourable, for counteracting the effect of influences prejudicial to man, and for obtaining the assistance of benevolent spirits. These ends they seek to attain by the performance of certain ceremonies and the presentation of various offerings; and nearly every individual case requires to be accompanied by a ceremony,[1] the efficacy of which does not, however, depend upon its being performed by any particular Lama, although the services of a Lama in great repute for sanctity are considered to increase the chances of the ceremony's producing the desired effect. But with respect to the science of "divination," having for object the determining of the character of a day, the residence for the time being of the gods, &c., the Lamas are not held to be equally endowed, one as the other. Those who have made a particular study of astrology, are applied to in all important cases having reference to the public welfare, as well as on such occasions as the marriage or the death of men of rank and wealth; whilst for subjects of minor importance every Lama is considered well-informed enough to give the required decision. In every monastery there is at least one divining Lama, who is then styled "the astrologer;" and larger ones even have one of the famous Choichong astrologers.[2] These latter have a particular school in the monastery Garmakhyá at Lhássa, whilst the ordinary astrologers are instructed in the science by an elder priest; the principal part of their preparatory labours is the profound study of numerous mystical works.

The decisions of the astrologers are pretended to be

[1] Some of the ceremonies considered the most efficacious, and therefore the most frequently performed, have been described in Chapter XV.

[2] See p. 156.

the result of mathematical calculations, combined with due observation of the phenomena to be taken into consideration for the case in point. The corresponding phenomena and their value vary considerably; there are, however, certain rules respecting the different modalities, and the explanation of these rules forms the subject of numerous books on astrology. The deference paid to the Lamas in such things depends to a great extent upon the observance of secrecy with reference to the combinations employed and the ceremonies performed; these things are kept a perfect secret to Tibetans as well as to Europeans; and even Chibu Lama, who, in his intercourse with Europeans, had laid aside many a superstition, showed great reserve in communicating to my brother Hermann the clue to symbolical designs, or such like; although neither Chibu nor any other Lama ever showed any particular hesitation to sell such objects, when no detailed explanation was demanded. The St. Petersburg libraries, also, contain but few in which the rules for their interpretation are given. Even the different provinces have each its own peculiar principles of divination, and are but indifferently acquainted with the operations practised by, and the formularies in use among their neighbours. Many of the tables and symbolical diagrams described further on proved quite a novelty to the Lama Gombojew, when he was requested to transcribe for me into capital letters those sentences which in the original were written in the small characters.

To the difficulties of obtaining information was added that arising from the vagueness with which all natives speak when attempting any explanation, even of subjects far less mystical than astrology and divination. This may be offered as an excuse for the following details not being so complete and satisfactory as might be desired. And, besides, I could not well alter them much, as in their existing state they were best calculated to make us acquainted with the notions of the Tibetans concerning the natural phenomena and the functions of their gods.

Tables used for the following purposes shall be described:

1. Tables for indicating lucky and unlucky periods.

2. Tables of direction, to determine towards what part of the compass the face of a man is to be turned when praying, and what direction his feet must take when he is about to set out on an important undertaking.

3. Tables of destiny, consulted in cases of illness.

4. Tables of marriage, employed to arrive at a knowledge of the chances of happiness afforded by some proposed matrimonial alliance.

5. A soothsaying table, with numerous figures and sentences.

I.

TABLES FOR INDICATING LUCKY AND UNLUCKY PERIODS.

1. *The elements and cyclic animals.*

Rules and regulations connected with or having reference to the calendar, as is the case with the table here described, are mostly combinations of the figures used in chronology, viz. the twelve cyclic animals and the five elements. The technical term for such a table is Gabtsis (see p. 274). In the present case their divinatory combination forms part of a large roll not unlike in form to the documents of classical antiquity, on which are also delineated most of the diagrams subsequently described. It came from Lhássa, and Hermann, meeting with it at Darjíling, seized the opportunity and bought it. The Gabtsis is composed of eight lines.

Line	
1.	30 elements.
2.	Colours of the elements.
3.	60 cyclic animals.
4.	Three rows of numerals.
5.	
6.	
7.	Sentences, now rubbed off.
8.	Heads of the animals.

Total length: 2 Engl. ft., 1 inch; breadth: 4 inches.

The *first and second lines* are each subdivided into thirty compartments; the upper line contains the conventional figures for the elements,[1] the lower their colours. The series of these figures and colours, and the objects represented are the following:

[1] The same figures are also used to symbolize the names of the sixty years adopted from India.—A detailed explanation of these signs is contained in the astronomical book Yangsal Domi, about which see p. 281.

No. curr.	Figures in the first line.	Colours in the second line.	Elements designated.
1	A cone of sacrifice.[1]	White.	Iron.
2	Flames.	Red.	Fire.
3	A tree, the symbol of the vital principle.[2]	Green.	Wood.
4	A basin[3] filled with fruits.	Yellow.	Earth.
5	A cone of sacrifice.	White.	Iron.
6	Flames.	Red.	Fire.
7	Waves.	Blue.	Water.
8	Ornaments upon the basis of a Chorten.	Yellow.	Earth.
9	A conch.[4]	White.	Iron.
10	A tree.	Green.	Wood.
11	A river in a defile.	Blue.	Water.
12	A fortified temple.	Yellow.	Earth.
13	Flames.	Red.	Fire.
14	A tree.	Green.	Wood.
15	A river in a narrow bed.	Blue.	Water.
16	Nails (the Phurbu[5]).	White.	Iron.
17	Flames on an altar.	Red.	Fire.
18	A tree.	Green.	Wood.
19	Two altars.	Yellow.	Earth.
20	A cone of sacrifice within a basin.	White.	Iron.
21	Flames.	Red.	Fire.
22	A waterfall.	Blue.	Water.
23	The lower part of a Chorten.	Yellow.	Earth.
24	Two swords crossed.	White.	Iron.
25	A tree.	Green.	Wood.
26	A plate with food.	Blue.	Water.
27	Slopes of mountain with shrubs.[6]	Yellow.	Earth.
28	Flames.	Red.	Fire.
29	A tree.	Green.	Wood.
30	A waterfall.	Blue.	Water.

We see from this list, that in four instances the same element returns after having been succeeded by three

[1] It represents either a Satsa (see p. 194), or a Zhalsai (see p. 228).

[2] This tree occurs again on the table described under No. IV, 2, where some details will be given.

[3] This basin is meant for the Pātra, or alms-bowl, carried by the Buddhas and priests in representations. See p. 210.

[4] By a conch the Lamas are convoked to prayers.

[5] Concerning the Phurbu, see p. 257.

[6] This is the usual foreground in the landscapes within which are figured gods. See p. 211.

others, and in two instances this is the case after it had been followed by six.

The *third line* shows the twelve cyclic animals in the form of human figures, standing upright and clad in the religious garment; but the head is that of an animal. The colours of the head, garment, and girdle are the following:

No. curr.	Name of the animal.	Colour of the		
		head.	garment.	girdle.
1	The mouse.	Blue.	Green.	Green.
2	The ox.	Yellow.	Green.	Blue.
3	The tiger.	Green.	Red.	Green.
4	The hare.	Green.	Red.	Yellow.
5	The dragon.	Yellow.	Yellow.	Green.
6	The serpent.	Red.	Yellow.	Blue.
7	The horse.	Red.	White.	White.
8	The sheep.	Yellow.	White.	Red.
9	The ape.	White.	Blue.	Green.
10	The bird.	White.	Blue.	Blue.
11	The dog.	Yellow.	Green.	White.
12	The hog.	Blue.	Green.	Red.

The colour of the head is important for the luckiness and unluckiness of days; if it be the same with the colour of the birthday, the day is an unlucky one, but the probability of misfortune can be counteracted by offerings to the tutelary genii.

The *fourth, fifth and sixth lines* contain Tibetan numerals in compartments tinted with the colours belonging to the respective numbers. 180 numbers are inscribed, 60 in each horizontal series. They follow each other in the order here given:—

198765432198765432198765432198765432198765432198765
432198765432198765432198765432198765432198765432198
765432198765432198765432198765432198765432198765432

Each number has a colour which is not a different one for every one of the nine numbers, but which is never changed for the same number; 1 is white; 9 is red; 8 is white; 7 is red; 6 is white; 5 is yellow; 4 is green; 3 is blue; 2 is black. These numerals so coloured are called "the nine blots," in Tibetan Meba gu, in Mongolian Mangga.[1] The succession of the Mebas is considered as important in many respects; its chief use is to indicate the years particularly dangerous to existence, which, according to the notions of the Tibetans return every tenth year; these are the years, they say, in which "the birth-meba has to consolidate." As birth-meba is taken that number in the fifth line (the second line of the series here detailed), which happens to be just beneath the animal in the sign of which a man has been born; and in the arrangement described this Meba returns every tenth year, and is also the central number of nine compartments, the single numbers of which are exactly identical with those of a group ten, twenty years, &c., distant. The dangers of these critical years, coinciding with the "consolidations of the birth-meba," can be averted by the ceremony Ruibal chenpoi dokjed, "to turn back (the evils) in the name of the great tortoise,"[2]

[1] *s*Me-ba, "a blot, blotch;" *d*gu "nine." Comp. Pallas, "Mongol. Völker," Vol. II., p. 229.

[2] Rus-*s*bal, "tortoise;" chhen-po'i, "of the great;" *b*zlog, "to turn back;" byed, "to do." About the ideas respecting the tortoise, details will be found at No. II., 1.

which the rich generally have performed for them by the Lamas in such years.

In the *seventh line* thirty sentences had been written, but they had been almost entirely blotted out already when Hermann got the original.

In the *eighth line* the heads of the sixty animals are repeated, two in one compartment, to indicate the phases of the moon.

Another table for the same purpose obtained by Adolphe in Gnári Khórsum has the form of a square; round a tortoise in the centre are grouped three times the twelve cyclic animals; in the first series each is repeated once, in the two other series they are repeated five times, to constitute the number of sixty. As a curious deviation from the list of the animals given above, I have to mention that, instead of the ox, we meet an elephant. Between the two spaces filled with the animals are traced the 180 compartments, tinted with the colour of the Mebas and containing the corresponding numerals. In other divisions of the square the symbols of the sun, the moon, and the planets Mars, Mercury, Jupiter, Venus and Saturn (see p. 289) are added, alternating with squares containing the nine Mebas.

2. *The spirits of the season.*

Amongst the causes of the luckiness and unluckiness of days are included the periodical migrations of the spirits inhabiting the regions above the earth. The two kinds of spirits, the good and evil ones, are supposed to shift their abodes, partly every day, partly contemporaneously with the phases of the moon, the commencement of a new season, &c. They perform their migrations with unequal velocity, and therefore, the combination of the spirits varies for every day. It is very important to man, as is believed, to know which kind of spirits have arrived the very day on which he begins an undertaking; if the good spirits are more numerous than the bad ones, the day will be a lucky one, and the more so if the man's tutelary deity is amongst the good spirits. This belief naturally offers a wide field of intrigue to the Lamas, who alone are able to decide the actual movements of the spirits. Amongst the evil spirits particular attention is to be paid to the abode of four demons, who, in astrological maps of the sky, are typified by the following figures: a black dog; a monster with a human body and the tail of a dragon, meaning a Mahōraga, in Tibetan Tophye chenpo; a man on horseback; and, finally, the fabulous bird Garuda. Their images are always encircled by a double square frame; the inner one is divided into twelve compartments, in each of which the name of a cyclic animal is written; the outer frame contains Dhāranīs supposed to be able and willing to hinder obnoxious attempts of the evil spirits. To each of these demons also a season is assigned; the black dog rules the spring, the Mahōraga the summer, the man on horseback the autumn, the bird Garuda the winter.

The linear arrangement of such a table is here given: the squares show the position of the respective four demons, the surrounding numbers the succession of the names of the twelve cyclic animals; the outer space is that containing the Dhāranīs.

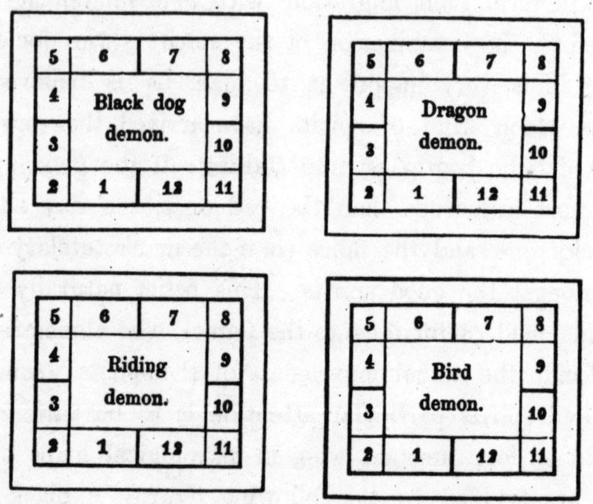

3. *Figures and oracles for the character of a day.*

A day which, according to its number in the series of the days of a year, should be lucky, may for the individual man become fatal by circumstances originating from the time of his birth and other important epochs in his life. But there are days which are lucky under all circumstances, whilst others are invariably unfavourable. The stability as well as the variable character of the thirty days of each month is illustrated by tables divided into thirty principle compartments; the compartments show the symbolical figures of the single days, and below each is written a mystical sentence which reveals its character. Such a table allows one to predict whether the chances of an undertaking are increased by the character of the day, or whether man needs the assistance of a Lama, to tell him from which spirit or from what direction danger threatens, as also to indicate the means of averting it. The answer is considered to be derived from most complicated computations; the cyclic animals and the elements of the present year, the abode of the tutelary deity, the birth-meba, and many other things must be taken into consideration. Only the most expert astrologers are believed to have the necessary knowledge, and consequently the remuneration demanded for their assistance and cooperation is high; so that none but the great and wealthy possess the means of getting indicated the reasons which render one day lucky, another unlucky. Chibu Lama said that such tables were generally consulted only by Rājas, and that copies of the book in which this kind of calculation is detailed are very rare in every Buddhist country; no copy had to be was in Síkkim.

The table which will be here described also forms part of the great roll which was bought by Hermann during his travels in 1855, who even obtained some explanations about the general meaning of the sentences. When I continued the analysis, first by getting transcribed the sentences which in the original are written with small characters, which could be done but very imperfectly, as by the frequent use of the roll about one-half of the squares had become quite illegible by friction, I found, also here, so many words used not introduced into Tibetan literature as known hitherto, that all that could be deciphered with sufficient accuracy was some few words; these I add in brackets to the verbal native information.

I now give the *description* of the table. In the upper left-hand corner (in space No. I.) Manjusrī[1] is represented sitting upon a throne; in the opposite corner (in No. II.) is the sword of wisdom, an emblem of his superior knowledge. Each of these two figures occupies the longitudinal space of two squares and the breadth of one. The rest of the plate is filled up by the following thirty figures and their corresponding sentences.

I.	1	2	3	4	5	6	II.
7	8	9	10	11	12	13	14
15	16	17	18	19	20	21	22
23	29	25	26	27	28	29	30

Although the arrangement is very plain, the delineation, combined with the numbers, will facilitate the representation to the reader of the position of the symbols.

1. A bird; good.
2. An elephant; middling.
3. The bird Garuda; good.
4. A wheel, the Buddhist symbol typifying the preaching of the Buddhas, as also the circle of existences, and the supreme power of the fabulous fabulous kings Chakravartin.[2] Good.
5. A bird; bad. (Words below: nine, bird, danger, evil spirit, tiger; *d*gu, bya, *g*nod, 'dre, *s*tag.)
6. A box within a frame; middling.

[1] See p. 65. [2] See p. 127.

7. Pot to keep water for worship. Good. (Thirteen, mouse, ox, two; *b*chu-*g*sum, byi, *g*lang, *g*zhis.)
8. The nine Mebas distributed in a circle similar to the centre of the tortoise described in one of the subsequent Nos.; middling.
9. A leopard; good.
10. A lion; good.
11. The three holy beings, Buddha, Dharma, Sangha,[1] typified by three gems set in a golden case. Good. (Seventeen, armour, shield, good, staff, bird, ape, two, from, perpetual; *b*chu-*b*dun, go, khrab, *b*jang, ber, bya, *s*prel, *g*zhis, nas, *r*tag.
12. A deer; not very good.
13. Nine human skulls; bad.
14. An instrument for rattling at worship; good.
15. Two peacocks; middling.
16. A horse; good.
17. Another bird; middling.
18. A serpent; middling. (Three, dorje, a young sheep, bird, serpent, two, from, perpetual; *g*sum, *r*dorje, lu-gu, bya, *s*brul, *g*nyis, nas, *r*tag.)
19. The tree of blue colour of turquoise; good.
20. A sleeping sick man leaning back in a chair; bad. (Two, hare, sleeping, refreshment, motiv, man, from, perpetual; *g*nyis, yos, nyal-du, sim, *r*gya, mi, nas, *r*tag.)
21. A three-headed man; bad. (The twenty-ninth, head, three, hog, hare, perpetual; nyer-*d*gu-pa, *m*go, *g*sum, phyag, yos, *r*tag.)

[1] See p. 184.

22. The Svastica, a Buddhist symbol most frequently met with in images; good.
23. A temple in the Lhássa style; good.
24. A Yak; good.
25. A Dorje; good.
26. A dragon; good. (The fourth, of the Bon, sheep, two, from, perpetual; *b*zhi-pa, bon-kyi, lug, *g*nyis, nas, *r*tag.)
27. Another bird; bad. (The ninteenth, bird, mouse, ox, two, from, perpetual; *b*chu-*d*gu-pa, bya, byi, *g*lang, *g*nyis, nas, *r*tag.)
28. A headless man; the worst. (Twenty-three, man, dead-body, eight, of the belly, bird, ape, from, the upper, perpetual; nyer-*g*sum, mi, ro, *b*rgyad, grod-gyi, bya, *s*prel, nas, yas, *r*tag.)
29. The Dorje; good. (Twenty-seven, ape, perpetual; nyer-*b*dun, *s*prel, *r*tag.)
30. The tortoise-shell; good. (Thirty, lotus-flower, leaf, eight, dog, thunder, two, the first, perpetual; sum-*b*chu, padma, 'dab, *b*rgyad, gyi, 'brug, *g*nyis, yas, *r*tag.)

II.

TABLES FOR DIRECTION IN IMPORTANT UNDERTAKINGS.

1. *The square tortoise.*

The essential figure of such tables is a tortoise, the feet of which are often drawn as hands (*see* Plates XIV., XV., XVI.); its shell is divided into numerous compartments, in each of which an allegorical figure is traced symbolizing some part or direction of the universe. The tortoise is considered by the Tibetan Buddhists to support the universe; and it is in allusion to this belief that it is generally drawn surrounded by water, signifying the ocean which washes the shores of the different continents. The legend having reference hereto, and which Pallas[1] also found to be spread amongst the Mongolian tribes, is this: As often as the universe, after its destruction, has to be re-moulded, the chaos, a fluid and incoherent mass, is somewhat dried by the winds, and the liquid ingredients separated from the solid. At the time of the creation of the present world, Manjusrī caused a tortoise of enormous size to emanate from him and to float in this chaos. Then considering, as god of wisdom, that the continents to be formed needed a solid basis, he rose up into the atmosphere and discharged a golden arrow, which struck the tortoise in its right side causing it to turn over and sink down through the chaotic mass, dropping blood from its wound, leaving behind its excrements, and vomiting fire, thus increasing the elementary parts dissolved in the waters; and when the consolidation took place, it furnished the basis of the universe, which now rests upon the flat under side of its shell.

This surface is quite distinctly characterised, in all representations I have before me, as the under shell, *not* as the back of the tortoise. The head is turned upwards to show the face, and what makes it more evident still,

[1] Compare Pallas, "Mongol. Völkerschaften," Vol. II., p. 21. The fullest account of it was told by the Lamas to stand in the Tibetan book Shecha rabsal "history of science."

the human hands connected with the tortoise, have distinctly a position of the thumb which shows the lower part to the observer. For astrological purposes this lower part of the tortoise-shell is drawn either square or circular, which necessarily also causes a very different arrangement of its component parts. The shell here described is a square one. The accompanying sketch shows the distribution

24			17			18
	5	6	13	7	8	
	4				9	
23	16		In this circle Mebas are inscribed.		14	19
	3				10	
	2	1	15	12	11	
22			21			20

of the compartments; the numbers I have inserted have reference to the figures, which will be subsequently explained.

In the centre is traced a circle with eight Mebas in this order:

4	9	2
3		7
8	1	6

; the central square is here empty, but in other diagrams of the tortoise it contains a numeral. A square frame surrounding the circle is the next division, and contains compartments with the twelve cyclic animals (their position is indicated in the sketch by the numerals from 1 to 12); it also contains the symbolical signs of the four principal corners of the universe: No. 13, fire (flames) = north; No. 14, iron (two angles meaning the Phurbu) = east; No. 15, water (waves) = south; No. 16, tree (leaves) = west. The rest of the shell is divided into eight principal divisions

(No. 17 to 24 of the sketch), which are distinguished by a frame of double lines; each is subdivided again into nine compartments. In the central part of every one of these groups we find a mystical sign, one of the "eight symbolical forms," in Tibetan Parkha chakja chad, meaning one of the eight regions of the universe, of which there are ten in all.[1] For astrological purposes mystical names are given to them, and generally they are symbolized by the following signs (see also Plate XIV., XV.):

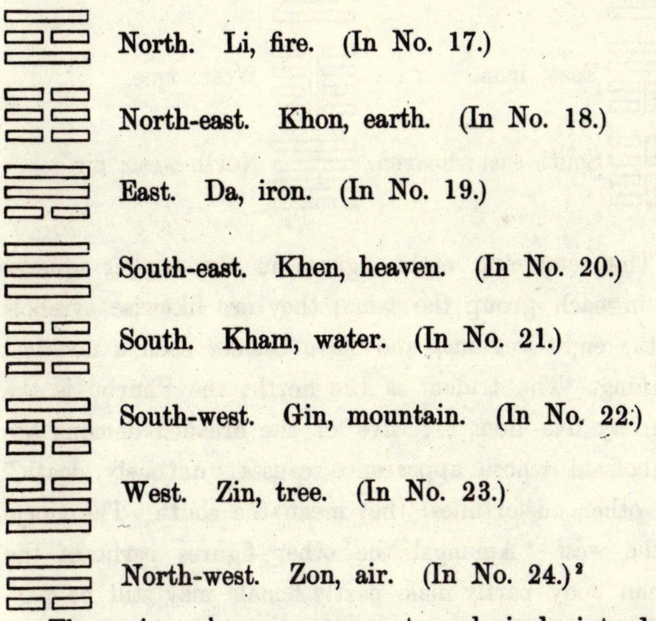

These signs, however, are not exclusively introduced in this form: other types may be occasionally considered

[1] See p. 126, 259.

[2] Pallas, "Mongol. Völkerschaften," Vol. II., p. 229, has likewise inserted the allegorical names for the eight corners of the universe: his names are the same as above, but the region they typify differs. I shall have occasion in the next pages to prove, byt he place which they in a occuppy compass, that in their explanation he is wrong.

to be more useful, or more damaging to the influence of evil spirits; and famous astrologers do not unfrequently invent quite new ones; a specimen of such a deviation is that printed on Plate XVI. where the signs are these:

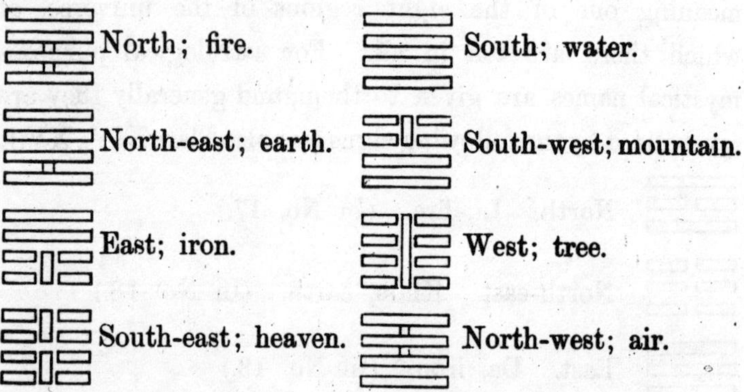

The remaining eight figures in the smaller squares are in each group the same; they are likewise symbols of the eight regions, and have besides each a mystical meaning. The trident is the north; the Phurbu is the east; by five dots, :·:, five of the dreaded demons are symbolized whose appearance causes "untimely death," and other misfortunes; they mean the south. The Dorje is the west. Amongst the other figures parts of the human body partly male partly female may still be particularly mentioned. Their relative position varies, and each different combination shows the region desired for a specific purpose, such as whither to direct the prayers and the Phurbu in order to ward off successfully the demons; what direction a bridegroom or a warrior must take on leaving the house, &c.

DIVINATION FORMULÆ.

TAKEN FROM FIGURE-TABLES FROM LHÁSSA.

1. To calculate the direction favourable to an undertaking.

1.

དབུས་ན་གནམ་ལྷུགས་རི་བོ་དང༌། ། མེ་རྒྱ་ས་ཤིང་རླུང་ལ་ཞཁོར། །

2.

ཕོ་ལོ་བོན་བསྐོར་གནམ་གྱི་སྐོར། ། མོ་ལོ་ནམས་ཀྱི་ཆོས་བསྐོར་ཐ། །

2. For learning beforehand the issue of an illness.

1.

ཐང་ཤིང་དབུགས་སྨོན་པ་ཆགས་པ་དང་ཕྱི་མ་ཆགས་སོ། །

2.

གཡུ་ཤིང་སྨོན་མ་ཆགས་པ་དང་ཕྱི་མ་ཆགས་སོ། །

3.

དཔག་བསམ་ཤིང་དུ་སྨོན་ཆགས་པ་ཕྱི་མ་ཆགས་སོ། །

4.

....སྨོན་པ་དཔལ་ཁྱིམ་ར་ཕྱི་མ་སྒྱུར་ཕྱི་མ། །

5.

སྨོན་པ་ཤི་མིག་ཕྱི་མ་གསོད་སྐྱེག། །

In order to discover the region required, various circumstances have to be taken into consideration; of the numerous books in which they are detailed the greatest variety of rules . is contained in the books Yangsal Domi (already quoted p. 280), Chungpa kundus tsis, and Thangshin-gi tsis. The astrologers are very reserved in communicating these laws; this would make their art too popular and would deprive it of the character of sublime mysticism and science, with which they now array it. All I can say is this: A quantity of numerals corresponding to the number of years of the questioner is inscribed successively in the nine compartments of a circle in the order in which the symbolical names of the quarters of the world are enumerated in the following verses:—

"The centre, the heaven, the iron, the mountain and
"The fire, the water, the earth, the tree, the air, turning."

Air (North-west)	Fire (North)	Earth (North-east)
Tree (West)	Centre	Iron (East)
Mountain (South-west)	Water (South)	Heaven (South-east)

The centre means the nadir, the tenth of the regions of the universe which the Tibetans acknowledge (the ninth region, the zenith, is omitted). From the number which takes the place of the nadir, the succession of the others depends; which number has to occupy the centre I do not know, I have been only informed that attention must be paid to the sex, as the central number is one with males, another with females.

[1] The Tibetan text is printed sub No. I., 1, in Plate XVIII.

When the central number has become known, the other numerals are grouped so that the next higher is written in the compartment heaven, the next higher in the compartment iron, and so on as detailed in the verses. If the number 9 is reached, it is not 10 which follows but the series is continued again with 1, 2, &c., till the quantity of the numerals inscribed is identical with the number of years of the questioner. The highly mystical character of the rules concerning the distribution of the Mebas seems to be well illustrated by those respecting the influence of the sex upon the calculation; they are brought in the form of verses, and run thus:

"The year of man must be counted by the sign of
the heaven, turning like Bon,
"The year of women like the doctrine (chos)."[1]

For facilitating the correct inscription of the numerals in the succession required, such representations of the tortoise have not only in their own centre a circle with nine compartments and the numerals inscribed in due order, but beneath the tortoise an appendix of eight other circles is added, which show the due succession of the numerals in case any one of the nine numerals should fall into the central position. Also our large roll contains, in Tibetan characters, the following eight combinations bordered by circles:

[1] For the Tibetan text see Plate XVIII., No. I. Bon the dictionaries explain by an adherent to the Bon religion, about which see p. 74. The book *bs*Tan-*r*tsis-'dod-*s*byin-*g*ter-bum-zhes-bya-va-*g*zhugs, "Accomplishment of the desire for instruction in astrology, vessel of the hidden treasure," which Hermann obtained in Síkkim, has, added, on leaf 25, in a linear arrangement, several Lugs, or "methods" of computation.

1	6	8	3	8	1	8	4	6	6	2	4
9	2	4	2	4	6	7	9	2	5	7	9
5	7	3	7	9	5	3	5	1	1	3	8

2	7	9	9	5	7	5	1	3	7	3	5
1	3	5	8	1	3	4	6	8	6	8	1
6	8	4	4	6	2	9	2	7	2	4	9

2. *The circular tortoise.*

The shell of the tortoise drawn as a circle is particularly used for calculating from the combination of the planets with the constellations at the time of one's birth, from the birth Meba, and other moments, which deity an individual man has to address as tutelary god in every year of the sixty years circle. Its surface shows:

Head of the Tortoise.

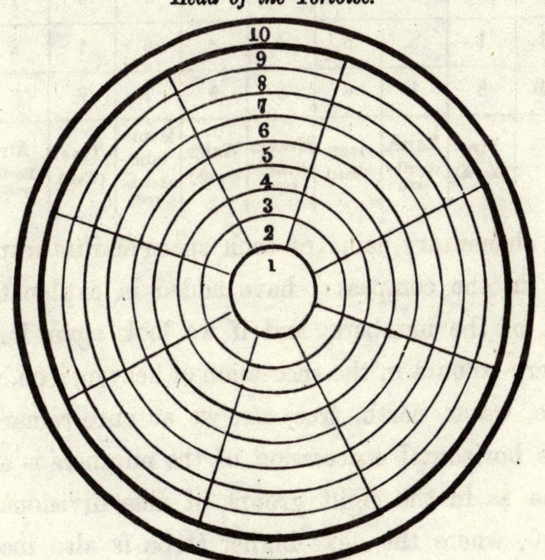

Tail of the Tortoise.

1st. Compartment. A central circular space containing the nine Mebas, identical with the central part of the square tortoise-shell described p. 305.

2nd. to 9th. Compartments. These consist of eight concentric divisions subdivided by eight radii into eight parts each; the resulting 64 spaces contain inscribed the numbers I here give in their cyclic succession; and I begin where I have placed the numbers in the preceding diagram of concentric circles, going through the circle from left to right.

2d.	1	3	8	7	2	9	4	5
3d.	2	4	9	8	3	1	5	6
4th.	3	5	1	9	4	2	6	7
5th.	4	6	2	1	5	3	7	8
6th.	5	7	3	2	6	4	8	9
7th.	6	8	4	3	7	5	9	1
8th.	7	9	5	4	8	6	1	2
9th.	8	1	6	5	9	7	2	3
	Fire (North)	Earth (North-east)	Iron (East)	Heaven (South-east)	Water (South)	Moun-tain. (South-west)	Tree (West)	Air (North-west)

The elementary name of each space and its respective position in the compass I have added in explanation at the foot of the numbers; and if we look again for these elementary colours in the succession of heaven, iron, mountain, fire, water, earth, tree, air, we at once remark that then the horizontal successsion of the numbers is exactly the same as in the eight groups of nine divisions each, page 310, where the next higher Meba is also inscribed in the succession of heaven, iron, &c.

10th. Compartment. This last circle is divided into

64 spaces; in 60 the names of the cyclic animals (byi, *g*lang, &c.) are written; the four remaining symbolical figures of the four principal points of the compass occupy a position as on our geographical maps; fire, or the north, being next to the head of the tortoise; Phurbu, or east, to the right; water, or south, at the tail; leaves, or west, to the left.

III.

TABLES OF DESTINY IN CASES OF SICKNESS.

1. *The human figures.*

Sixteen human figures are drawn in two rows; in cases of sickness seeds or small pebbles are cast upon them to foretell the development and final result. The succession of these human figures and their appendices are:—

Upper line.	Lower line.
1. A woman with a hook.	9. A woman with an axe.
2. A woman with a spoon.	10. A Lama holding a vessel.
3. A man with a firebrand.	11. A Lama with his left hand supporting a book.
4. A Lama with a water vessel on his back.	12. A woman holding a vessel.
5. A woman falling down from sickness.	13. A woman with hands raised in prayer.
6. A man with empty hands.	14. A woman with a water vessel on her back.
7. A Lama wearing a yellow trimmed hat.	15. A woman with food for cattle in her hand.
8. A woman holding a dagger.	16. A Lama with a sacred stick.

2. *Allegorical figures and dice.*

A rectangular table 6 inches long, and 4 inches broad, divided into 24 parts.

1	2	3	4	5	6
7	8	9	10	11	12
13	14	15	16	17	18
19	20	21	22	23	24

The squares 1, 2, 3, 4 are filled up by representations of the twelve cyclic animals, in groups so arranged that one animal is ridden by three others. They are considered here as introductory figures and have their particular importance when a marriage is contracted, but not in reference to sickness; they shall be explained in the subsequent section, IV. Squares 5 to 16 are the spaces which contain the objects and sentences consulted in illness; they are: 5. Two coniferous trees. 6. Buildings during inundation. 7. Two coniferous trees. 8. One tree. 9. Two sacred buildings. 10. Two eyes. The sentences in 10 to 16 are written in running-hand with abbreviations, so that a literal transliteration was not possible for square 12. These sentences[1] follow in the succession my diagram gives:—

11. The flourishing (green) tree of life will be broken now or later.—No. 1.
12. [The golden tree will now be broken].—This, however, stands under the image of the buildings in inundation, in which no allusion to a tree could be discovered.
13. The tree of the blue colour of turquoise will be broken now or later.—No. 2.

[1] Number 12, of which the exact translation could not be given, is marked by brackets. In the other sentences the numerals after "No." have reference to the Tibetan text in Plate XVIII., II.

14. The tree *d*Pag-*b*sam-shing[1] will be broken now or later.—No. 3.

15. The celebrated houses and enclosures will be destroyed now or later.—No. 4.

16. Now or later the eyes of death shall meet you.—No. 5.[2]

The spaces 19 to 24 represent the six surfaces of a die. The dots upon dice used for soothsaying purposes show here. the following arrangment, one half of the dots being white, the other black.

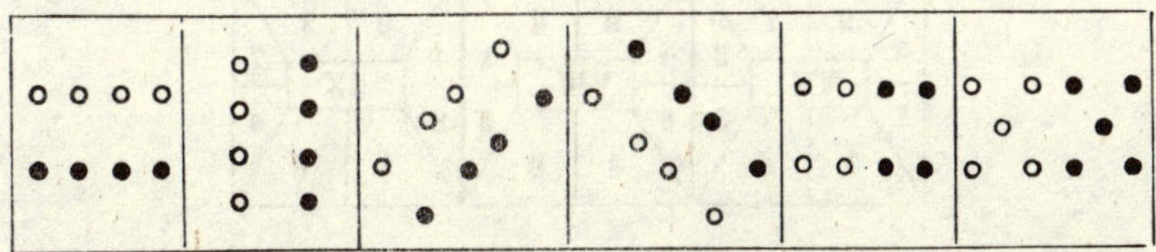

The dice are either cubes, like the European ones, or rectangular parallepidedons, sometimes comparatively very long. The latter, in consequence of their form, have two sides blank.

IV.

TABLES FOR MARRIAGE.

1. *Table with numerals.*

One diagram of this kind shows a table of nine squares, each divided again into nine spaces; the central is a rectangle, in which is inscribed a short sentence; the eight surrounding

[1] It is a fabulous tree which accomplishes every wish. Schmidt, "Tíbet. Lexicon."

[2] A great number of similar oracles have been compiled in the book Jed-tho yangi zamatog "handbook of oracles."

spaces contain each the number of a Meba. The arrangement of the numerals is as given in the accompanying figure.

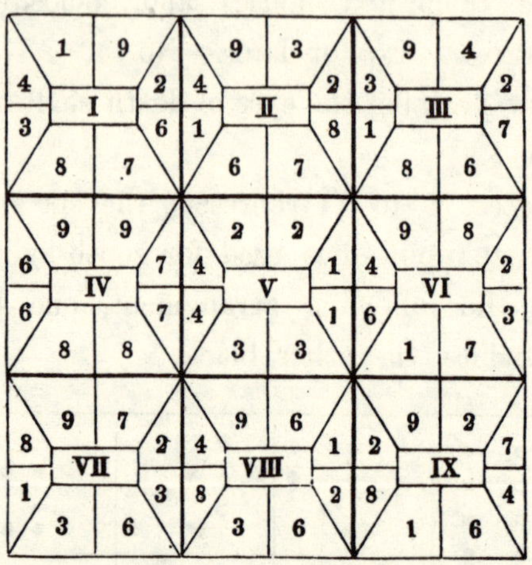

The sentences in the rectangles were explained to Hermann to run thus:[1]

I. Medicine of the sky, true.
II. Medicine of the sky, middle.
III. Medicine of the sky, partly true.
IV. Imaginarily true according to man's knowledge.
V. Of middle fortune, mediocre (the Lama said: Imaginarily true, but doubtful).
VI. Imaginarily true, and bad by imagination.
VII. Utterly bad.
VIII. Likely to be bad.
IX. A little better than the regular bad ones.

This table is consulted by the parents of the young people to be married, who throw a sacred seed upon it;

[1] The inscriptions had been so much injured that I could only verify the fifth.

the inscription of the square upon which the seed rests, is taken as the general character of the answer as to the felicity of the ensuing marriage, but the answer allows a variety of interpretations, according to the birth Meba of the young people, and to the Meba of the square, if the seed happens to rest upon a numeral and not upon the inscription. Also the elements under which they were born, are taken into consideration. In this respect it is universally admitted that the circumstance, that the elements under which the young people were born are not the same would entail discord and strife, if the element which is superior in power were not neutralized by ceremonies which, of course, can only be performed with efficacy by the Lamas. The relations of the elements are detailed in the following sentences; their Tibetan text is given in Plate XIX., II.

"The mother of wood is water, the son of wood fire;
"The enemy of wood is iron, the friend of wood earth;
"The mother of water is iron, the son of water wood;
"The enemy of water is earth, the friend of water fire;
"The mother of iron is earth, the son of iron water;
"The enemy of iron is fire, the friend of iron water;
"The mother of earth is fire, the son of earth iron;
"The enemy of earth is wood, the friend of earth iron."

These notions[1] are evidently founded upon considerations on the conditions of growth and decay of the existing objects; for wood, or the plants, grow in

[1] Comp. Pallas, l. c., p. 236.

the earth and are fed by water; wood furnishes the material for fire, but wood, or trees, are felled by iron. Iron (shovels) are indispensable for irrigation-canals, to furnish the plants (wood) with the necessary water, of which, however, they are deprived to a certain extent by the earth, into which a part sinks and is lost.[1] Fire again renders possible the use of water for cooking, and thus increases its importance for man.

2. *Table with cyclic animals.*

All the tribes of Central Asia[2] suppose that the different natures of the elements which constitute the cycle of twelve years, cause mutual affection or aversity; the rules, however, which the Tibetans have established on this head, are very arbitrary; they believe, *e. g.* that the bird would pick the horse, &c. They speak of six varieties of relative feelings, viz.: very great affection; mediocre affection; indifference; disinclination; great hatred; deadly hatred. Deadly hatred is incurable, and under such auspices young people should, properly, not be permitted to marry; but if the parties are wealthy and liberal, the hatred may be prevented from breaking out. All other relations of the animals can be modified—the influence of the unfavourable weakened or totally counteracted, that of the favourable strengthened and increased.

Diagrams in the divisions of which such groups of animals are formed, are very frequent; their arrangement

[1] The general dryness of the climate in Tibet makes cultivation much more dependent upon irrigation than in nearly any inhabited part of the globe.

[2] Comp. Pallas, l. c., pp. 236, 263.

To face p. 318.

DIVINATION FORMULÆ.

TAKEN FROM FIGURE-TABLES FROM GNÁRI KHÓRSUM.

1. For the interpretation of oracles.

The oracles to which they refer are given on Plate XX.

1. ས་ཁར་གནམ་ལོ་རྒྱལ་པོ་ནས་རྩིས། །

2. ཤིང་གིས་···ནས་རྩིས་ལྕགས་སྟག་ནས། །

3. ཆུ་སྟག་ནས་རྩིས། །

4. ས་སྟག་ནས་རྩིས། །

5. ལྕགས་སྟག་གཡོས་ནས་རྩིས། །

6. མེ་གཡོས་ནས་རྩིས། །

7. ཤིང་གཡོས་ནས་རྩིས། །

8. ཆུ་གཡོས་ནས་རྩིས། །

9. ཡར་ཀྱིས་གསུམ་ནས་རྩིས། །

10. མེ་སྟག་ནས་རྩིས། །

11. ཆུ་སྦྲེལ་ནས་རྩིས། །

12. ཡར་ཀྱིས་ལྔ་ནས་རྩིས། །

13. མར་ཀྱིས་ལྔ་ནས་རྩིས། །

14. གནམ་ལོ་ནས་རྩིས། །

2. Rythmical sentences concerning the influence of the elements, for good or bad, upon a proposed marriage.

1. ཤིང་མ་ཆུ་ལ་ཤིང་མེ། །

2. ཤིང་དགྲ་ལྕགས་ལ་ཤིང་གྲོགས་ས། །

3. ཆུ་མ་ལྕགས་ལ་ཆུ་བུ་ཤིང་། །

4. ཆུ་དགྲ་ས་ལ་ཆུ་གྲོགས་མེ། །

5. ལྕགས་མ་ས་ལ་ལྕགས་བུ་ཆུ། །

6. ལྕགས་དགྲ་མེ་ལ་ལྕགས་གྲོགས་ཆུ། །

7. ས་མ་མེ་ལ་ས་བུ་ལྕགས། །

8. ས་དགྲ་ཤིང་ལ་ས་གྲོགས་ལྕགས། །

is either that the head of two animals are delineated within one division, or that their names are inscribed instead: occasionally also an animal is ridden by a monster in human shape with the heads of one or even more of the cyclic animals. Whether the hatred or disinclination will become fatal to the couple, is determined by the casting of dice.

Tables of this sort had been appended to the astrological roll from Lhassa (see p. 293).

The one which shows the combinations of animals between which feelings of averseness very probably exist, has 36 compartments; the twelve squares of the first two lines have the heads of the animals drawn turned away from each other; the remainder contain their names; the entire series is this:—

Tiger Ape	Hare Bird	Dragon Dog	Serpent Sheep.	Horse Mouse.	Sheep Ox
Hare Bird	Tiger Ape	Serpent Hog	Dragon Dog.	Sheep Ox	Horse Mouse
Dragon Dog	Ox Sheep	Horse Mouse	Hare Bird	Ape Tiger	Serpent Hog
Serpent Hog	Mouse Horse	Ox Sheep	Tiger Ape	Bird Hare	Dragon Dog
Horse Mouse	Hog Serpent	Ape Tiger	Ox Sheep	Dog Dragon	Hare Bird
Sheep Ox	Dog Dragon	Bird Hare	Mouse Horse	Hog Serpent	Tiger Ape

Another combination shows the animals which *may* but do not necessarily prove unfavourable; it comprises four divisions, and in each is seen an animal ridden by a monster with the heads of three animals. In the first division the hog is ridden by the bird, serpent and dog; in the second the ape by the mouse, sheep, and tiger; in the third the tiger by the horse, ox and ape; in the fourth the serpent by the dragon, the hog and hare. These figures are the same as those which occupy the four first spaces of the table which is described on p. 313, as used for consultation in cases of sickness.

V.

A SOOTHSAYING TABLE WITH NUMEROUS FIGURES AND SENTENCES.

It was but after great hesitation on the part of the Lamas that Adolphe and Robert obtained this table at Mángnang, in Gnári Khórsum; they were repeatedly assured that no other copy could be procured, except after much delay, direct from Lhássa. As my brothers did not succeed in obtaining information from the Lamas of Mángnang concerning its application, I addressed myself to Mr. Schiefner, in order to obtain details about analogous objects; but though he inquired with his usual kindness about such materials, I remained limited to the translation of the inscriptions, and, for the interpretation of the figures, to the analogy of the forms with those on other tables.

The original is 21 inches long, and 18 inches broad; its principal part is divided into 78 rectangles which contain either a figure, or a sentence, or both combined; some, however, are empty. Along its sides two vertical stripes are left to receive explanatory directions for the use of the table; of these, however, one is empty. In order to facilitate the explanation, I give as usual the outlines of the compartments; where a number is omitted, the space is empty.

B			A				B
	1	2	3	4	5	6	1
	7	8	9	10	11	12	2
	13	14	15	16	17	18	3
	19	20	21	22	23	24	4
	25	26	27	28	29	30	5
	31	32	33	34	35	36	6
	37	38	39	40	41	42	7
	43	44	45	46	47	48	8
	49	50	51	52	53	54	9
		56	57	58	59	60	10
	61	62	63	64	65	66	11
		68	69	70	71	72	12
			75	76	77	78	13
							14

In the translation here given the sentences, in order to the distinguishing of them from the figures, are placed between marks of quotation.

A. *The central table with its figures and sentences.*

The numbers at the commencement of the line have reference to those in A of the preceding diagram; the numbers at the end of the sentences refer to Plate XX., where the respective sentences are printed in Tibetan characters.

1. "The celestial chair, is it empty or not?" (No. 1.)
2. A lion.
3. "The twisted snare, shall it slip through (under the object) or not?"[1] (No. 2.) A twisted rope.
4. The skin of a man.
5. The walls of a religious establishment.
6. "Shall every track be lost of the residence of the king of eloquence or not?"[2] (No. 3.) A Lama.
7. "The peacock beneath the throne of lions,[3] shall it be victorious or not." (No. 4.)
8. The peacock riding a lion: this is a symbol of the throne of lions.
9. "The residence of turquoise colour, shall it be destroyed or not?" (No. 5.) The figure is meant for an altar with a cone of sacrifice (Zhalzai)[4] upon it."
10. A string of beads, symbolizing human skulls.
11. The vessel Namgyal bumpa,[5] with flowers put into the neck.
12. "The golden Dorje, shall it open itself like a

[1] The snare, in Tibetan Zhagpa, is a symbol of power, see pp. 213, 216. It occurs again sub Nos. 18, 21, 48. The words in parentheses are paraphases of the Tibetan texts.

[2] Manjusrī is meant, the god of eloquence and wisdom (see p. 65).

[3] See p. 211. [4] See p. 228. [5] See p. 247.

Plate XX.

QUERIES AND ANSWERS.

TAKEN FROM A SOOTHSAYING-TABLE FROM GNÁRI KHÓRSUM.

1.

ལྷ་ཁྲི་སྟེང་གདན་ས་སྟོང་སོ་སམ་བེ་སྟོང། །

2.

ཞགས་ཆེང་སྤུལ་ཞོག་ཏུ་ཤོར་རམ་མ་ཤོར། །

3.

ས་པ་དག་རྒྱལ་པོ་སྤྲུགས་པའི་གདན་ས་སྟོང་སོ་སམ་མི་སྟོང། །

4.

སེང་ཁྲི་སྟེང་ནས་རྒྱ་བྲ་རྒྱལ་མ་རྒྱལ། །

5.

གཡུའི་གདན་ཞིག་སོ་སམ་མ་ཞིག། །

6.

གསེར་གྱིས་རྡོ་རྗེ་གནམ་ཏུ་འབར་སོ་སམ་མ་འབར། །

7.

མུ་སྟེགས་ངན་རག་འབྱུང་སོ་སམ་མ་འབྱུང། །

8.

ཐུགས་ལྡན་སྟན་སྐྱོལ་སོ་སམ་མ་སྐྱོལ། །

9.

ནམ་མཁའ་བྱང་བྱ་འདྲེ་ལ་ཐལ་ཚོད་སོ་སམ་མ་ཚོད། །

10.

སློན་པོའི་གདན་ས་སྟོང་སམ་མི་སྟོང། །

11.

སྤྲུལ་གྱི་བར་ཀ་ཕྲུག་སོ་སམ་མ་ཕྲུག། །

12.

བོན་པོའི་ཐབ་ར་སྟོང་སོ་སམ་མ་སྟོང། །

13.

···གྱི་ཡིད་རྣ་རབ་མི་དང་བྲལ་སོ་སམ་མི་བྲལ། །

14.

ཟ་འོག་ལྷམ་ཆུང་ཆུའི་ཁྱེར་རམ་མ་ཁྱེར། །

15.

ལྷ་བྲལ་རྩིས་ས་སྟོང་སོ་སམ་མ་སྟོང། །

16.

བོས་གྱི་མང་གཡུ་ལོ་ལག་ནས་ཤོར་སོ་སམ་མ་ཤོར། །

17.

མི་བྲང་ཁར་སྤྲི་ཞིག་སེ་སམ་མ་ཞིག། །

18.

སྲིད་པའི་ཆུ་མིག་སྐམ་སོ་སམ་མ་སྐམ། །

19.

མ་ཕྲིམ་··རོག་ལ་ཤོར་མ་ཤོར། །

20.

སྤྲུལ་གྱི་མེ་ལོང་དོ་ལ་ནོམ་སོ་སམ་མ་ནོམ། །

21.

ཀ་སྟོང་གྱི་སྟེར་ཟུར་ལྷུག་སོ་སམ་མ་ལྷུག། །

22.

རབ་ཞིང་གི་གྱིལ་ཏུ་ལྷ་··དཀར་པོ་གཙུགས་སོ་སམ་མི་གཙུགས། །

flower (appear) in the sky?" (No. 6.) A Dorje, the symbol of power.[1]

13. "The bad speech of the unbelievers,[2] will it come forth or not?" (No. 7.)
14. An unbeliever.
15. "The mat, shall it be made to melt (be destroyed) by fire or not?" (No. 8.) A figure similar to a chess-board.
16. The Phurbu, the symbol of power over the evil spirits. (See p. 257.)
17. A circle for divination.
18. Twisted ropes, meaning the snare. (Comp. Fig. 3.)
19. "The celestial .... and the twisted .... shall they be cut or not?"[3] (No. 9.)
20. The figures of "Byang-bu" and "Thal;" the former is a stalk with green leaves, the latter a parallelogram fastened to a stick.
21. The snare (comp. Fig. 3.). No meaning found for the respective sentence.
22. An arrow with ribands.
23. Two astrological instruments.
24. The trident, the symbol of power over the evil spirits. (See p. 215.)
25. "The magistrate's residence shall it become empty or not." (No. 10.)
26. A bridge, of which three arches are seen.

[1] See p. 215.

[2] In Sanskrit Tīrthika; see p. 25.

[3] The two Tibetan words which I could not translate, are byang-bu, and thal. Byang-bu the Dictionaries explain by "a title, an address;" for thal they give "dust, ashes," for thal-mo they have "palm of the hand."

27. "The magic wand, shall it break or not?" (No. 11.) Two staffs, one standing upright, the other with its upper end bent.
28. The walls of a religious building. (Comp. Fig. 5.)
29. A Lama.
30. A Lama.
31. "The enclosure of the fire-place of the followers of the Bon religion, shall it be empty or not?" (No. 12.)
32. A priest of the Bon religion, holding a sword and a shield.
33. "The excellent horse[1] and the man, shall they go away in opposite directions or not?" (No. 13.) A man on horseback.
34. A sword.
35. A bow in a case, and a quiver with four arrows.
36: An arrow without ribands.
37. "The shoes, shall they be carried away by the water or not?" (No. 14.)
38. Two shoes standing on the slopes of a hill.
39. "The divine astrology, shall it become known or not?" (No. 15.) Two astrologers in religious garments.
40. A bow and a arrow.
41. Two fishes swimming in water.
42. A bird sitting upon a flower.
43. Water. (Comp. Fig. 49.)

[1] The Lungta, or airy horse is to be understood here, and its faculty of keeping off the dangers which might arise from the disharmony of the cyclic animals, the elements and the planets. See Plate XI., and p. 253.

44. "The garment and the umbrella with the handle of turquoise, shall it fall down (to the earth) or not?" (No. 16.) The handle of a turquoise.
45. "The lodgings, shall they be destroyed by the servant, or not?" (No. 17.) Walls.
46. A Lama wearing the magic mirror.
47. A snare hanging down from a rope. (Comp. Fig. 3.)
48. Several snares hanging down from a rope.
49. "The spring of the universe, shall it dry up or not?" (No. 18.) It must refer to Fig. 43.
50. "The paternal house, shall it come into the possession of the enemies, or not?" (No. 19.) Walls.
51. "The magic mirror, shall it appear or not?" (No. 20.) The mirror supported by a flower.
52. Three Lamas.
53. A full-blown flower.
54. Five arrows and a bow.
56. "The pillars (of the Buddhist faith) and the thousand offerings, shall they be sprěad far and wide, or not?" (No. 21.) Three vessels for offerings upon a table.
57. Three Lamas, the first clad in red and green; his two companions are left uncoloured.
58. A Lama with the magic mirror.
59. A Lama clad in red, leaving the house.
60. Its upper part is filled with the point of the arrows and bow (comp. Fig. 54.); to its lower and reaches the flower from the square underneath.
61. "The white genius of the excellent land, shall he submit himself or not?" (No. 22.)

62. A sentence, but no meaning was found.
63. A conch, with which the Lamas are summoned to prayers.
64. The magic mirror.
65. A leaf.
66. An open flower, its upper part is formed by the magic mirror.
68. A hog.
69. A pillar (supporting a monastery, or Buddhism in general).
70. An altar with an offering vessel, and a flame burning under it.
71. Walls.
72. A house.
75. The black celestial dog.[1]
76. A yak.
77. A tiger.
78. A hare.

B. *Directions for finding out the due answer.*

The numerals at the commencement are those in B of the diagram on p. 321, and those at the end of the line refer to the Tibetan texts in Plate XIX, 1.

1. "Begin to count the terrestrial fortress from the celestial king." (Manjusrī.) (No. 1.)
2. [The quantity of letters which could be read was not sufficient to guess the meaning]. (No. 2.)
3. "Count the water from the tiger." (No. 3.)
4. "Count the earth from the tiger." (No. 4.)

[1] See p. 299.

5. "Count the iron from the tiger and the hare." (No. 5.)
6. "Count the fire from the hare." (No. 6.)
7 "Count the wood from the hare." (No. 7.)
8. "Count the water from the hare." (No. 8.)
9. "Count the preceding (hare) from these three (elements)." (No. 9.)
10. "Count the fire from the tiger." (No. 10.)
11. "Count the water from the ape." (No. 11.)
12. "Count the preceding (ape and tiger) from the five (elements)." (No. 12.)
13. "Count the subsequent from the five." (No. 13.)
14. "Count from the year of the heaven." (No. 14.)

Having arrived at the conclusion of the descriptive part of this volume, I may be allowed to add still a few remarks, though of a general bearing, in allusion to the contributions which the inquiries into Buddhism have afforded for the explanation of monumental remains in Europe, particularly in Norway, as well as for the interpretation of ancient mythological terminology. Prof. Holmboe of Stockholm, when comparing the tumuli and long walls extant in many parts of Norway with the Topes in India and Afghanistan and the Chortens and Manis of Tíbet, found so many surprising analogies, that he at length declared that, in his opinion, it is highly probable, "the teachers of Buddhism advanced as far as Scandinavia, after having passed through the vast provinces of Russia."[1] And, what may be more unexpected still, even in Mexico Buddhism was discovered to have had followers as late as the 13th century, a circumstance made evident from the details and descriptions contained in a Chinese author of the end of the fifteenth century of our era concerning "the far distant land into which pious men and heavy storms had transferred the sacred doctrine."[2]

[1] For details see Holmboe, "Traces de Buddhisme en Norvège," p. 69. Even the name of the god Odin, or Wodan, the highest god in German mythology, Holmboe says, may be referred to Buddhist terms and to the Sanskrit word *Budh* and its derivations *Buddha, Bodhin, Bodhān, Bodhant*. The change of *b* into *v* has taken place already in Sanskrit, and the dropping of the *v* in the ancient language of Norway is said to be very frequent in words in which it is followed by *o* or *u*.—A brief summary, with critical remarks, of Holmboe's book is given by Rajendralal Mitra in Journ. As. Soc. Beng., Vol. XXVII., p. 46.

[2] See Neumann, as quoted by Lassen, "Indische Alterthumskunde," Vol. IV., p. 749.—In the United States of America, too, artificial mounds have been found bearing such a curious analogy with the tumuli in Norway, that it has been suggested by American antiquarians, that a people coming from Norway discovered America already about the year 1000 of our era. Rafn, as quoted by Holmboe, p. 23.

APPENDIX

A.

LITERATURE

AN ALPHABETICAL LIST OF THE WORKS AND MEMOIRS CONNECTED WITH BUDDHISM, ITS DOGMAS, HISTORY, AND GEOGRAPHICAL DISTRIBUTION.

TITLES OF THE PERIODICALS AND COLLECTIVE PUBLICATIONS CONSULTED.—ALPHABETICAL LIST OF THE AUTHORS.

THE following register gives the full title of all notable publications on Buddhism, including memoirs contained in periodicals, as well as separate works. The literature of the various languages of Europe is so vast that I dare not hope that this list is sufficiently detailed and complete. But I may be allowed at least to add, as an apology for my compilation, that I was not aided by a previous enumeration of this kind.

For official assistance I am particularly indebted to the director of the Royal and State Library at Munich, Professor Halm.

An arrangement of the literature in reference to the *principal objects* is easily found in the "Index," where the respective publications are added to the other details.

TITLES OF THE PERIODICALS AND OTHER PUBLICATIONS EXAMINED.

(The words in brackets are the abbreviations I use.)

ABHANDLUNGEN der königlichen Akademie der Wissenschaften zu Berlin. Up to 1860. (Abh. d. Berl. Akad.)

ARBEITEN der russischen Mission in Peking. Deutsche Uebersetzung von Abel und Mecklenburg. Berlin, 1858. Vols. I., II. (Arb. d. russ. Mission.)

ARCHIV für die wissenschaftliche Kunde von Russland, von Erman. Vols. I. to XX. (Erman's Archiv.)

ASIATIC RESEARCHES, or Transactions of the Society instituted in Bengal. Calcutta. Vols. I. to XX. The octavo edition is distinguished by 8°. (As. Res.)

BULLETIN scientifique publié par l'Académie des Sciences de St. Pétersbourg. Vols. I. to X. (Bull. sc. St. Pétersb. Acad.)

BULLETIN de la classe historico-philologique de l'Académie Impériale des Sciences de St. Pétersbourg. Vols. I. to XIV. (Bull. hist.-phil. St. Pétersb.)

BULLETIN de l'Académie Impériale des Sciences de St. Pétersbourg. Vols. I. to V. (Bull. St. Pétersb. Acad.)

CHINESE REPOSITORY. Canton. Vol. III. (Chin. Rep.)

DENKSCHRIFTEN der k. k. Akademie der Wissenschaften in Wien. (Denkschr. d. Wien. Akad.)

GLEANINGS IN SCIENCE. Calcutta. Vols. I. to III. (Glean. in sc.)

JOURNAL Asiatique, ou Recueil de Mémoires, d'Extraits et de Notices relatifs à l'histoire, à la philosophie, aux sciences, à la litterature et aux langues des peuples orientaux. Vols. I. to V. (Journ. As.)

JOURNAL of the American Oriental Society. New-York. (Journ. Amer. Or. Soc.)

JOURNAL of the Asiatic Society of Bengal. Vols. I. to XXX. (Journ. As. Soc. Beng.)

JOURNAL of the Bombay branch of the Royal Asiatic Society. Vols. I. to V. (Journ. Bomb. R. As. Soc.)

JOURNAL of the Ceylon branch of the Royal Asiatic Society. Colombo, 1845, 1848, 1850, 1853. (Journ. Ceylon. R. As. Soc.)

JOURNAL of the Indian Archipelago and Eastern Asia. Singapore. New series. Vols. I. to III. (Journ. Ind. Arch.)

JOURNAL (also Transactions) of the Royal Asiatic Society of Great Britain and Ireland. Vols. I. to XIX. (Journ. R. As. Soc.)

JOURNAL des Savants. Paris. From 1820-1856. (Journ. des Sav.)

JOURNAL of the Shanghai Literary Society. (Journ. Shanghai Lit. Soc.).

MADRAS JOURNAL of Literature and Science. Madras. New Series. Vols. I. to VII. (Madras Journ.)

MÉMOIRES de l'Institut Impérial de France, Académie des Inscriptions. (Mém. de l'Inst. de Françe.)

MÉMOIRES présentés à l'Académie Impériale des Sciences de St. Pétersbourg par divers savants. Vols. I. to VI. (Mém. des sav. étrang. St. Pétersb.)

MÉMOIRES de l'Académie Impériale des Sciences de St. Pétersbourg. Série I. to VII. (Mém. de l'Acad. St. Pétersb.)

NOUVEAU JOURNAL ASIATIQUE ou Recueil de Mémoires, d'Extraits et de Notices relatifs à l'histoire, à la philosophie aux langues, et à la littérature des peuples orientaux. Paris. 1826-1861. (Nouv. Journ. As.)

TRANSACTIONS of the Literary Society of Bombay. Vols. I. to III. (Trans. Lit. Soc. Bombay.)

ZEITSCHRIFT der deutschen Morgenländischen Gesellschaft. Vols. I. to XI. (Ztschr. d. d. Morg. Ges.)

ZEITSCHRIFT für die Kunde des Morgenlandes. Vols. I. to V. (Ztschr. f. d. K. d. Morg.)

ALPHABETICAL LIST OF THE AUTHORS.

ACKERMANN, B. The history and doctrine of Buddhism. 1829.

ANDERSON, W. An attempt to identify some of the places mentioned in the Itinerary of Hiuan Thsang. Journ. As. Soc. Beng., Vol. XVI., p. 1183.

See also for other publications on this subject: Cunningham, Müller.

Critic. diss.: Cunningham, Journ. As. Soc. Beng., Vol. XVII., Part. I., p. 476; Part. II., p. 13.

BAILEY, E. C. Note on some sculptures found in the district of Peshawur. Journ. As. Soc. Beng., Vol. XXI., p. 606.

See also on this subject a paper by Jaquet.

BARTHÉLEMY ST. HILAIRE: Sur les travaux de M. Eugène Burnouf. Journ. des Sav., 1852, pp. 473, 561.

—— Du Buddhisme. Paris, 1855.

Barthélemy St. Hilaire: Le Bouddha et sa religion. Paris, 1860. For critical dissertations by this author see: Burnouf, Foucaux, St. Julien.

Bazin, M. Recherches sur l'origine, l'histoire et la constitution des ordres religieux dans l'empire chinois. Nouv. Journ. As., V. Série, Vol. VIII. (1856).

Benfey, Th. Bemerkung zu einer Mittheilung des Megasthenes in Bezug auf Indische Geschichte. Zschr. f. d. K. d. Morg., Vol. V., p. 218.

—— Einige Bemerkungen über die Götternamen auf den indoscythischen Münzen. Ztschr. d. d. Morg. Gés., Vol. VIII., p. 450.

Bennet, C. Life of Gaudama, a translation from the Burmese book entitled Ma-la-len-ga-ra Wottoo. Journ. Amer. Or. Soc., Vol. III., pp. 1-165.

Bergmann: Nomadische Streifereien unter den Kalmücken in den Jahren 1802 u. 1803. 4 Vols. 1805. (Compare also Morris.)

Bigandet, Legend of the Burmese Budha, called Gaudama. Journ. Ind. Arch., Vol. VI., pp. 278, 499; Vol. VII., p. 159; Vol. VII., pp. 349, 373; Vol. IX., pp. 139, 325, 483.

Biot. For critical dissertations by this author see Burnouf.

Bird, J.: Historical Researches on the Origin and Principles of the Buddha and Jaina Religions. Journ. Bombay R. As. Soc., Vol. II., p. 71.

Bochinger, J. J.: La vie contemplative, ascetique, et monastique chez les Indous et chez les peuples Bouddhistes. Strasbourg, 1831.

Boehtlingk: Rapport sur un mémoir intitulé: "Eine tibetische Lebensbeschreibung Sākjamuni's, des Begründers des Buddhathums," im Auszuge mitgetheilt von A. Schiefner. Bull. hist.-phil. St. Petersb. Vol. V., p. 93.

BOHLEN, P. v.: De Buddhaismi Origine et Aetate conscripsit Petrus a Bohlen. Regimont. Pruss., 1827.

—— Das alte Indien, mit besonderer Rücksicht auf Egypten dargestellt. 2 Vols. Königsberg, 1830.

BROCKHAUS, H.: Soma Deva, Gründung der Stadt Pātaliputra und Geschichte des Upakosa. Leipzig, 1835.

See also on this subject a paper by Francklin.

BUCHANAN, FR.: On the religion and literature of the Burmas As. Res., 8°. Vol. VI., p. 136.

BURNES, A.: Account of the Jain temples at Mount Ábu in Guzerát. Journ. As. Soc. Beng., Vol. II., p. 161.

—— Travels into Bokhara; being an account of a journey from India to Caboul, Tartary and Persia. 2 Vols. 1834.

See also Ephinstone.

BURNEY, H. ST.: Translation of an Inscription in the Burmese language, discovered at Buddha Gaya, in 1833. As. Res., Vol. XX., p. 161.

See also about this town a paper by Kittoe.

Critic. diss.: Lassen, Chr.: Zeitschr. f. d. K. d. Morg., Vol. I., p. 108.

—— Discovery of Buddhist Images with Deva-nāgari Inscriptions at Tagoung, the ancient Capital of the Burmese Empire. Journ. As. Soc. Beng., Vol. V., p. 157.

Critic. diss.: Lassen, Chr.: Zeitschr. f. d. K. d. Morg., Vol. I., p. 228.

BURNOUF, E. (et Ch. Lassen): Essai sur le Pāli, ou la Langue sacrée de la presqu'île au-dela du Gange, avec six planches lithographiées. Paris, 1826.

BURNOUF, E. (et Ch. Lassen): Observations grammaticales sur quelques passages de l'Essai de MM. Burnouf et Lassen. Paris, 1827.

—— Introduction à l'Histoire du Buddhism Indien. Paris, 1844.

Critical diss.: Roer, E.: Journ. As. Soc. Beng., Vol. XIV., Part II., p. 783; Biot: Journ. des Sav., 1845, pp. 233, 257, and 337.

—— Le Lotus de la Bonne Loi, traduit du Sanskrit, accompagné d'un commentaire et de vingt et un mémoires relatifs au Buddhisme. Paris, 1852.

Critical diss.: Barthélemy St. Hilaire: nine articles in Journ. des Sav. 1854 and 1855 (in connexion with Foucaux's Rgya Tcher Rol pa). A. Weber, "Indische Studien," Vol. III., p. 135.

For *critical diss.* by this author see Rémusat, Upham.

BURT, F. S.: More Dānams from the Sanchi Tope near Bhilsa, taken in impression. Journ. As. Soc. Beng., Vol. VII., p. 562.

See also about this tope: Cunningham, Prinsep.

—— A description, with drawings, of the ancient stone pillar at Allahabad, called Bhim ten's Gadā or Club, with accompanying copies of four inscriptions engraved in different characters upon its surface. Journ. &c. Vol. III., p. 105.

See also for other papers on this pillar: Hodgson, Mill, Prinsep, Troyer, Turnour.

CALLAWAY, JOHN: *Yakkun Nattannawa*; A Cingalese Poem descriptive of the Ceylon System of Demonology, to which is added: The Practices of a Capua or Devil Priest, as described by a Buddhist: and *Kolan Nattannawa*, a Cingalese Poem, descriptive of the characters assumed by natives of Ceylon in a Masquerade. London, 1829.

Campbell, A.: Journal of a trip to Síkkim. Journ. As. Soc. Beng., Vol. XVIII., p. 482.

—— Diary of a Journey through Síkkim to the frontiers of Thibet. Journ. As. Soc. Beng., Vol. XXI., pp. 407, 477, 563.

Carey, W.: An account of the funeral ceremonies of a Burman Priest. As. Res., Vol. XII., p. 186.

Carte, W. E.: Notice of Amulets in use by the Trans-Himalayan Boodhists, with remarks by Csoma de Körös. Journ. As. Soc. Beng., Vol. IX., Part. II., p. 904.

Catalogue des Manuscrits and Xylographies Orientaux de la Bibliothèque Impériale Publique de St. Pétersbourg. 1852.

Chapmann, I. I.: Some additional remarks upon the ancient city of Anurājapura or Anurādhapura and the Hill Temple at Mehentēlē in the island of Ceylon. Journ. R. As. Soc., Vol. XIII., p. 164.

Chitty, S. C.: The sixth Chapter of the Tiruvathavur Purana. Journ. Ceylon R. As. Soc. 1845. No. I., Part. I., p. 63.

Colebrooke, H. T.: Observations on the sect of Jains. As. Res., Vol. IX., p. 287.

Congreve, H.: A brief account of the ancient Buddhist Sculptures at Masulipatam. Madras Journ., Vol. VI., May 1861, p. 44.

Court, A.: Further information on the Topes of Manikyāla, being the translation of on extract of a manuscript memoir on ancient Taxila. Journ. As. Soc. Beng., Vol. III., p. 556.

—— Note on the brown liquid contained in the cylinders from Manikyāla. Journ. As. Soc. Beng., Vol. III., p. 567.

See also for other papers on this tope: Cunningham, Prinsep.

Crawfurd, J.: On the ruins of Boro Budor in Java. Trans. Lit. Soc. Bomb., Vol. II., p. 154.

—— History of the Indian Archipelago. Edinburgh, 1820. Vols. I., II., III.

Csoma de Körös: Translation of a Tibetan fragment, with remarks by H. H. Wilson. Journ. As. Soc. Beng., Vol. I., p. 269.

—— Geographical notice of Tibet. Journ. &c., Vol. I., p. 121.

—— Note on the origin of the Kāla-Chakra and Adi-Buddha Systems. Journ. &c., Vol. II., p. 57.

—— Translation of a Tibetan passport. Journ. &c., Vol. II., p. 201.

—— Origin of the Shākya race, translated from the La, or the 26th volume of the *m*Do class in the Kah-gyur, commencing at the 161st leaf. Journ. &c., Vol. II., p. 385.

—— Extracts from Tibetan works. Journ. &c., Vol. III., p. 57.

—— Analysis of a Tibetan Medical Work. Journ. &c., Vol. IV., p. 1.

—— Notices on the different systems of Buddhism extracted from the Tibetan authorities. Journ. &c., Vol. VII., Part. I., p. 142.
Critical diss.: Zeitschr. f. d. K. d. Morg., Vol. IV.

—— Enumeration of Historical and Grammatical works to be met with in Tibet. Journ. &c., Vol. VII., p, 147.
Critical diss.: Zeitschr. f. d. K. d. Morg., Vol. IV.

—— Remarks on the "Notice of amulets in use by the Trans-Himálayan Boodhists by W. E. Carte." Journ. &c., Vol. IX., Part. II., p. 905.

Csoma de Körös: Interpretation of the Tibetan inscription on a Bhotian banner, taken in Assam. Journ. &c., Vol. V., p. 264.

—— Translation of a Tibetan sloka found on a white piece of China scarf. Journ. &c., Vol. V., p. 384.

—— Analysis of the Tibetan work entitled the Kah-gyur. As. Res., Vol. XX., pp. 41, 393.

—— Abstract of the contents of the *B*stan-*h*gyur. As. Res., Vol. XX., p. 553.

—— Notices on the life of Shākya. As. Res., Vol. XX., p. 285.

—— A Grammar of the Tibetan language, in English. Calcutta, 1834.

—— Essay towards a Dictionary, Tibetan and English. Calcutta, 1834.

—— A brief notice of the Subhāshita Ratna Nidhi of Saskya Pandita. Journ. As. Soc. Beng., Vol. XXIV., p. 141; Vol.XXV., p. 257.

Cunningham, A.: Correction of a mistake regarding some of the Roman coins found in the Tope of Manikyāla opened by M. Court. Journ. &c., Vol. III., p. 635.

See also for other papers on this tope: Court, Prinsep.

—— An account of the Discovery of the Ruins of the Buddhist City of Samkassa. Journ. R. As. Soc., Vol. VII., p. 241.

—— Opening of the Topes, or Buddhist Monuments, of Central India. Journ. R. As. Soc., Vol. XIII., p. 108.

—— The Bhilsa Topes, or Buddhist monuments, of Central India. London, 1854.

—— Ladák, physical, statistical, and historical; with notices of the surrounding countries. London, 1854.

Cunningham, A.: Verification of the Itinerary of Hivan Thsang through Afghanistan and India, through the first half of the 7th. century. Journ. &c., Vol. XVII., Part. II., p. 13.

—— Verification of the Itinerary of Hivan Thsang through Ariana and India, with reference to Major Anderson's hypothesis of its modern compilation. Journ. &c., Vol. XVII., Part I., p. 476.

See also the paper of Müller.

—— Satraps, with Greek inscriptions. Journ. &c., Vol. XXIII., p. 679.

—— An Essay on the Arian order of Architecture as established in the Temples of Kashmir. Journ. &c., Vol. XVII., Part II., p. 274.

Davis: China and the Chinese. German edition by Drugulin. Stuttgart, 1852.

Deshauterayes: Recherches sur la Religion de Fo, professée par les Bonzes Ho-chang de la Chine. Journ. As. 1825, pp. 150, 228, 311; 1826, pp. 40, 74, 179, 219.

Eckstein, Baron d': Théologie et Philosophie booddhiques, comparées à celles des Védantins. (In the article, entitled: "Narasinha Oupanichat"). Nouv. Journ. As. 3e série, Vol. II. (1836), p. 470.

A *critical review* is noticed under Julien.

Edkins, E.: Translation of a Shastra Buddhist. Journ. Shanghai Lit. Soc., 1858. No. 1. (*See* also Wilson).

—— Notes of a Correspondence with Sir John Bowring on Buddhist literature in China, by Prof. Wilson. With Notice of Chinese Buddhist works translated from the Sanskrit. Journ. R. As. Soc., Vol. XVI., p. 316.

Elphinstone, M.: An account of the kingdom of Caboul, and its dependencies in Persia, Tartary, and India. 1819.

See also Burnes.

ERSKINE, W.: Account of the cave temple of Elephanta. Trans. Lit. Soc. Bomb. Vol. I., p. 198.

—— Note to F. Dangerfield's "Account of the caves near Bang called the Panch Pandoo." Trans. &c., Vol. II., p. 194.

—— Observations on the remains of the Buddhists in India. Trans. &c., Vol. III., p. 494.

FA HIAN: The Pilgrimage of; from the French edition of the Foe koue ki of MM. Rémusat, Klaproth, and Landresse. With additional notes and illustrations. (Anonymous. Cunningham quotes Laidley as the author.) Calcutta, 1848. 8°.

For an other paper on the Itinerary of Fa Hian see Kittoe.

FERGUSSON, J.: On the Rock-cut temples of India. Journ. R. As. Soc., Vol. VIII., p. 30. Also Published in 8°, with an Atlas in Roy. Fol., London, 1845.

FINLAYSON: The Mission to Siam and Hué, the capital of Cochin China, in the years 1821-22. With a memoir by the author, by Sir Th. St. Raffles. 1826.

FORBES, J.: Notes on the Buddhas, from Ceylonese authorities: with an attempt to fix the dates of the appearance of the last four. Journ. As. Soc. Beng., Vol. V., p. 321.

Critical diss.: Lassen, Chr.: Ztschr. f. d. K. d. Morg., Vol. I., p. 235.

FOUCAUX, PHIL. ED.: Spécimen du Gya-Tcher-Rol-Pa. Partie du Chapitre VII., contenant la naissance de Çakya-Muni. Texte Tibétain, traduit en français et accompagné de notes. Paris, 1841.

FOUCAUX, PHIL. ED.: Rgya Tcher Rol pa, ou Developpement des jeux, contenant l'histoire du Bouddha Çakyamuni, traduit sur la version Tibétaine du Bkah Hgyour, et revu sur l'original sanscrit (Lalitavistāra). 2 Vols. Paris, 1847.

Critical diss.: Schiefner. Bull. hist.-phil. St. Pétersb. Vol. VII., pp. 118, 225, 261, 501.—Barthélemy St. Hilaire; nine articles in connexion with Burnouf's "Le Lotus de la Bonne Loi." Journ. des Sav. 1854. 1855.

For other papers on this historical book, see: Lenz, Rajendralal Mitra.

—— Parabole de l'enfant égaré, formant le Chaptre IV. du *Lotus de la Bonne Loi.* Paris, 1854.

—— Grammaire de la Langue Tibétaine. Paris 1858.

—— Le Trésor des belles Paroles: choix de sentences, composées en tibétain par le Lama Saskya Pandita, suivies d'une élégie tirée du Kanjur, traduites pour la première fois en français. Paris, 1858.

FRANCKLIN, W.: Researches on the Tenets and Doctrines of the Jeynes and Boodhists; conjectured to be Brahmanes of ancient India. London, 1827.

—— Inquiry concerning the site of ancient Palibothra, conjectured to lie within the limits of the modern district of Bhaugulpoor. Parts. I-IV. London, 1815-22.

For another paper on this town see Brockhaus.

FRIEDERICH: Over Inscriptien van Java en Sumatra, voor het eerst ontcjferd. Batavia, 1857.

GABET, see *Huc.*

GEORGI, A. A.; Alphabetum Tibetanum. Missionum apostolicorum commodo editum. Romæ, 1762.

Gerard, A.: Koonawur, edided by G. Lloyd. London, 1841.

Gogerly, D. J.: On Buddhism. Journ. Ceylon R. As. Soc., 1845. No. I., Part I., p. 7; 1848, p. 111; and 1853, p. 1.

Grindlay, R. M.: An account of some sculptures in the Cave Temples of Ellora. Trans. R. As. Soc., Vol. II., p. 326.

See also on these temples the papers of Sykes, Tod.

de Guignes, J.: Recherches historiques sur la religion Indienne, et sur les livres fondamentaux de cette religion, qui ont été traduits de l'Indien en Chinois. Acad. R. d. Inscript., Vol. XI. Paris, 1780.

—— Histoire générale des Huns, des Turcs, des Mongols, et des autres Tartares occidentaux &c., avant et depuis Jésus Christ jusqu'à présent. 4 Vols. 1756-58.

Gurius, O.: Das Gelübde der Buddhisten, und die Ceremonien ihrer Ablegung bei den Chinesen. Arb. d. russ. Miss., Vol. II., p. 315.

Gützlaff, C.: Remarks on the present state of Buddhism in China. Journ. R. As. Soc., Vol. XVI., p. 73.

Halbertsma, J. H.: Het Budhism en zyn stichter. Deventer, 1843.

Hammer-Purgstall: Ueber einen halb buddhistischen, halb moslimischen Talisman. Denkschr. d. Wien. Akad., Vol. I., 1850.

Harington, J, H.: Introductory remarks to Capt. Mahony's paper on Ceylon, and the doctrines of Buddha. As. Res. 8°. Vol. VIII., p. 529.

HARDY, R. Spence: Eastern Monachism: an Account of the origin, laws, &c., of the order of Mendicants founded by Gōtama Buddha. London, 1850.

—— A Manual of Buddhism, translated from Singhalese Manuscripts. London, 1853.

Critical diss.: A. Weber, "Indische Studien." Vol. III., pp. 117-35.

HAY, W. C.: Report on the Valley of Spiti. Journ. As. Soc. Beng., Vol. XIX., p. 429.

HILARION: Die Beziehungen China's zu Tibet. Arb. d. russ. Miss. Vol. I., p. 313.

HODGSON, B. H.: Notices on the Languages, Literature, and Religion of the Bauddhas of Nepaul and Bhot. As. Res., Vol. XVI., p. 409.

—— Sketch of Buddhism, derived from the Bauddha scriptures of Nepaul. Journ. R. As. Soc., Vol. II., p. 222.

—— Quotations from original Sanskrit authorities in proof and illustration of his Sketch of Buddhism. Journ. As. Soc. Beng., Vol. V., pp. 28, 71.

Critical diss.: Lassen: Zeitschr. f. d. K. d. Morg., Vol. I., p. 234.

—— European Speculations on Buddhism. Journ. &c., Vol. III., p. 382.

—— Further remarks on M. Rémusat's Review of Buddhism. Journ. &c., Vol. III., p. 425.

—— Notice on some ancient inscriptions in the characters of the Allahabad column. Journ. &c., Vol. III., p. 481.

For other papers on this column see also: Burt, Mill, Prinsep, Turnour.

HODGSON, B. H.: Note on an inscription from Sarnath. Journ. &c., Vol. IV., p. 196.

See also on this inscription the paper of Śykes.

—— Notice on Adi Buddha and of the seven mortal Buddhas. *Printed under the title*: Classification of Néwars, in Journ. &c., Vol. III., p. 215.

—— Remarks on an Inscription in the Ranja and Tibetan (U'chhen) characters, taken from a Temple on the confines of the Valley of Nepaul. Journ. &c., Vol. IV., p. 196.

—— Account of a visit to the Ruins of Simroun, once the Capital of the Mithila Province. Journ. &c., Vol. IV., p. 121.

—— Note on the Primary language of the Buddhist writings. Journ. &c., Vol. VI., p. 682.

Crictical diss.: Lassen: Zeitschr. f. d. K. d. Morg. Vol. III., p. 159.

—— (*Of the same subject treats an*) Extract of Proceedings of the R. As. Soc. January, 1836.

—— A Disputation respecting Caste by a Buddhist, in the form of a series of Propositions supposed to be put by a Saiva and refuted by the Disputant. Journ. R. As. Soc., Vol. III.

—— On the extreme resemblance that prevails between many of the Symbols of Buddhism and Saivism. Quarterly Oriental Magazine, 1827. Nos. 14, 16.

All these papers are reprinted in:

—— Illustrations of the Literature and Religion of the Buddhists. Serampore, 1841.

—— The Pravrajia, Vrata or Initiatory Rites of the Buddhists to the Paja Kand. Illustrations, p. 212.

—— Notice on Buddhist symbols. Journ. R. As. Soc., Vol. XVIII., p. 393.

HOFMANN: Buddha Pantheon von Nippon. With an Atlas of 63 Plates. Vol. V. of "v. Siebold, Archiv zur Beschreibung von Japan." Leyden.

HOLMBOE, C. A.: Trace de Buddhisme en Norvége avant l'introduction du Christianisme. Paris, 1857.

A brief summary is given by Rajendralal Mitra in the Journ. As. Soc. Beng., Vol. XXVII., p. 46.

HOOKER, J. D.: Himalayan Journals. 2 Vols. London, 1854.

HUC et GABET: Souvenirs d'un voyage dans la Tartarie, le Tíbet et la Chine pendant les années 1844, 1845, 1846. Vols. I. and II. 1853.

—— Notice sur la Prière bouddhique: Om mani padme hum. Nouv. Journ. As. 4e Série. Vol. IX., p. 462.

—— Les quarante-deux points d'enseignement proférés par Bouddha, traduit du Mongole. Nouv. etc., Vol. XI., p. 535.

See on this Sūtra also the paper of Schiefner.

—— Le Christianisme en Chine, en Tartarie and en Thibet. Vols. I.-IV. (Also translated into English.)

HÜLLMANN, C. D.: Historisch-kritische Abhandlung über die Lamaische Religion. Berlin, 1795.

HUMBOLDT, W. v.: Ueber die Kawi Sprache auf der Insel Java, nebst einer Einleitung über die Verschiedenheit des menschlichen Sprachbaues und ihren Einfluss auf die geistige Entwickelung des Menschengeschlechts. Berlin, 1836.

IDELER: Ueber die Zeitrechnung der Chinesen. (Read in the Berl. Ac. 1837; printed with addenda 1839.)

IMPEY, E.: Description of a colossal Jain figure nearly 80 feet high, discovered on a spur of the Satpurah Range. Journ. As. Soc. Beng., Vol. XVIII., Part II., p. 918.

Jacob, L. G., and Westergaard, N. L.: Copy of the Asoka Inscription at Girnar. Journ. Bomb. R. As. Soc., April 1843, p. 257.

Japan, nach den besten vorhandenen Quellen geschildert von einem Vereine Gelehrter. 1860.

Jaquet, E.: Notice sur les découvertes archéologiques faites par Honigberger pendant son séjour dans l'Afghanistan. Nouv. Journ. As. 1836, p. 234; 1837, p. 401.

Compare in reference to Peshaur the paper of Bailey.

Joinville: On the Religion and Manners of the People of Ceylon. As Res 8°. Vol. VII, p. 397.

Jones, J., Taylor: Some account of the Thrai Phun. Journ. Ind. Arch. 1851., Vol. V., p. 538.

Julien, Stan.: Mémoires sur les Contrées Occidentales, traduits du Sanskrit en Chinois, en l'an 648, par Hiouen Thsang, et du Chinois en Français. Paris, 1858. Vols. I. and II.

Critical diss.: Baron d'Eckstein. Nouv. Journ. As., 5e Série, Vol. X., p. 475 et seq. Barthélemy St. Hilaire: eight articles in Journ. des Sav. 1855 and 1856. For further critical dissertations see: Anderson, Cunningham, M. Müller.

—— Listes diverses des noms des dix-huit écoles schismatiques qui sont sorties du Bouddhisme. Nouv. Journ. As., Vol. XIV. (1859.), p. 327.

—— Renseignements bibliographiques sur les relations des Voyages dans l'Inde et les descriptions du Si-yu, qui ont été composées en Chinois entre le 5e et le 18e siècle de notre ère. Nouv. Journ. As. 4e Série, Vol. X. (1847.), p. 265.

JULIEN, STAN.: Concordance Sinico-Sanskrite d'un nombre considérable de titres d'ouvrages bouddhiques, recueillie dans un catalogue chinois de l'an 1306, et publiée, après le déchiffrement et la restitution des mots indiens. Nouv. Journ. As. 4e Série, Vol. XIV., pp. 351-446.

—— Histoire de la vie de Hiouen Thsang et de ses voyages dans l'Inde entre les années 629 and 645 de notre ère. Paris, 1853.

Critical diss.: Schiefner: A: Mélanges Asiatiques. Vol. II.

KISHEN KANT BOSE: Some account of the country of Bhutan. As. Res., Vol. XV., p. 128.

KITTOE, M.: Note on an Image of Buddha found at Sherghatti. Journ. As. Soc. Beng., Vol. XVI., Part I., p. 78.

—— Note on the sculptures of Bōdh Gya. Journ. &c., Vol. XVI., Part. I., p. 334.

Compare also on Buddha Gaya the paper of Burney.

—— Notes on Places in the Province of Behar, supposed to be those described by Chi-Fa-Hian, the Chinese Buddhist priest who made a pilgrimage to India, at the close of the 4th. century. Journ. &c., Vol. XVI., p. 953.

KLAPROTH, J.: Reise in den Kaukasus und nach Georgien. Vol. I. and II. 1812.

—— Beleuchtung und Widerlegung der Forschungen über die Geschichte der Völker Mittelasiens von I. J. Schmidt. 1824.

Critical diss.: Sylvestre de Sacy. Journ. des Sav., 1825.

KLAPROTH, J.: Description du Tubet, traduite du chinois en russe par le Père Hyacinthe, et du russe en français par M***; revue sur l'original chinois et accompagnée de notes. Nouv. Journ. As., Vol. IV., pp. 81, 241.; Vol. VI., pp. 161, 321.

Fragmens Bouddhiques. (Extrait du Nouv. Journ. As., Mars 1831.) Paris, 1831.

—— Table Chronologique des plus célèbres patriarches et des événements remarquables de la Religion Bouddhique, redigée en 1678, traduite du Mongol et commentée. Nouv. Journ. As., Vol. VII. (1831), p. 161.

—— Explication et Origine de la formule bouddhique Om mani padme hoûm. Nouv. Journ. As., Vol. VII., p. 185.

For his edition of Timkowsky see this name.

KNOX: The ceremonial of the ordination of a Burmese priest. Journ. R. As. Soc., Vol. III.

KÖPPEN, C. F.: Die Religion des Buddha und ihre Entstehung. Vols. I. and II. Berlin, 1857, 1859. (Vol. II. is also entitled: Die lamaische Hierarchie und Kirche.)

Critical diss.: Zeitschr. f. d. K. d. Morg. Vol. XVIII. (1859), p. 513. Göttinger Gelehrte Anzeigen, 1858, p. 401.

KÖRÖSI, see *Csoma de Körös.*

KOWALEWSKY: Mongolian Crestomathy (written in Russian). Kasan, 1836. Vols. I-III.

—— Extrait d'une lettre addressée a M. Jacquet (que les livres bouddhiques sont quelquefois échangés à Kiakhta entre des fourrures russes). Nouv. Journ. As. 3e Série, Vol. VII. (1839), p. 181.

LASSEN, CHR.: Zur Geschichte der griechischen und indoscytischen Könige in Baktrien, Kabul und Indien, durch Entzifferung der altkabulischen Legenden auf ihren Münzen. Bonn, 1834. Also in Journ. As. Soc. Beng., Vol. IX., pp. 251, 339, 449, 627, 733.

—— Ueber eine alte indische Inschrift der kgl. Satrapen von Surāhstra, worin Chandragupta und sein Enkel Asoka erwähnt werden. Zeitschr. f. d. K. d. Morg., Vol. IV., p. 146.

—— Eine auf einer Kupfertafel in Sattāra gefundene Inschrift Varavarma's aus dem J. 1104. Zeitschr. f. d. K. d. Morg. Vol. VII., p. 294.

—— Indische Alterthumskunde. Vols. I. to IV.

Critical dissertations by this author are noticed under: Burney, Burnouf, Csoma de Körös, Forbes, Turnour.

LATTER, T.: Remarks on a Boodhist Coin. Journ. As. Soc. Beng., Vol. XIII., Part. II., p. 571.

—— On the Buddhist Emblems of Architecture. Journ. &c., Vol. XIV., Part. II., p. 623.

LENZ, R.: Analyse du Lalita-Vistara-Pourana, l'un des principaux ouvrages sacrés des Bouddhistes de l'Asie centrale, contenant la vie de leur prophète et ĕcrit en sanscrit. Bull. sc. Pétersb. Acad., Vol. I., pp. 49, 57, 71, 75, 87, 92, 97.

Compare about this historical book: Foucaux, Rajendralal Mitra.

LEPSIUS, R.: Ueber chinesische und tibetische Lautverhältnisse und über die Umschrift jener Sprachen. Berlin, 1861. (From the Abh. d. Berl. Acad., 1862.)

LOGAN, J. R.: The West Himalaic or Tibetan tribes of Assam, Burma, and Pegu. Journ. Ind. Archip. New Series, Vol. II., pp. 68, 230.

LOW, J. ST.: General Observations on the contending claims to antiquity of Brahmans and Buddhists. Journ. As. Soc. Beng., Vol. XVIII., Part. I., p. 89.

—— On the Buddha and the Phrabāt. Journ. R. As. Soc., Vol. III. (1835).

—— Gleanings in Buddhism, or translations of passages from a Siamese version of a Pali work termed in Siamese "Phrâ Pat'hom:" with passing observations on Buddhism and Brahmanism. Journ. As. Soc. Beng., Vol. XVII., Part. II., p. 72.

McGOVAN, D. J.: An Inscription from a Tablet in a Buddhist Monastery at Ningpo, in China. Journ. As. Soc. Beng., Vol. XIII., Part. I., p. 113.

MAKENZIE, C.: Account of the Jains, collected from a priest of this sect. As. Res., Vol. IX., p. 244.

MARCO POLO: The Travels of Marco Polo in the thirteenth century, by *W. Marsden.* London, 1818.

—— A recent paper of *Thomas*, "Zu Marco Polo, aus einem Cod. ital. Monacensis," read in the Bavarian Academy of science, March 4, 1862, contains many a geographical detail concerning the places visited by this audacious traveller.

MALCOLM, SIR JOHN: Inscriptions from the Boodh Caves, near Joonur. Communicated in a letter to Sir John Malcolm. Journ. R. As. Soc., Vol. IV. (1837), p. 287.

MARSHALL, W. H.: Four Years in Burmah. 1860.

MASON, FR.: Mulamuli, or the Buddhist Genesis of Eastern India from the Shan, through the Talaing and Burman. Journ. Amer. Or. Soc., Vol. IV., p. 103-19.

MASSON, CHR.: A memoir on the buildings called Topes. London, 1841. (Reprinted with further remarks on coins in Wilson's Ariana Antiqua.)

—— Narrative of various journeys in Balochistan, Afghanistan, the Panjab and Kalāt, during a residence ín those contries. Vols. I-IV., 1844.

MILL, W. H.: Restoration of the Inscription No. 2 on the Allahabad Column. Journ. As. Soc. Beng., Vol. III., pp. 257, 339.

See also for other papers on this column: Burt, Hodgson, Prinsep, Troyer, Turnour.

—— Restoration and translation of the Inscription on the Bhitāri Lāt, with critical and historical remarks. Journ. As. Soc. Beng., Vol. VI., p. 1.

MOORCROFT, W., and TREBECK, G.: Travels in the Himalayan; Travels in Hindustan and the Panjab; in Ladakh and Kashmir; in Peshawar, Kabul, Kimduz and Bokhara. Edited by H. H. Wilson. London, 1841. Vols. I. and II.

—— A Journey to Lake Mansorovara in Undes, a province of Little Tibet. As. Res., Vol. XII., p. 375.

MOORE, G.: The lost tribes and the Saxons of the East and of the West, with new views of Buddhism, and translations of Rock-Records in India. London, 1861.

MORIS: Exposé des principaux dogmes Tibétains-Mongols. Extrait de l'ouvrage de D. Bergmann. Journ. As. 1823, p. 193.

MÜLLER, MAX: The languages of the seat of war in the East. With a survey of the three Families of Language, Semitic, Arian, and Turanian. With an Appendix on the Missionary alphabet, and an Ethnographical Map, drawn by A. Petermann. London, 1855.

—— Letter to Chevalier Bunsen, on the Classification of the Turanian Languages. Journ. As. 1823. p. 193.

—— Buddhism and Buddhist Pilgrims. A review of Mr. Stanisl. Julien's "Voyages des Pélerins Bouddhistes." Reprinted from the "Times" of April 17th. and 20th., together with a letter on the original meaning of Nirvāna. London, 1857.

For other papers on Buddhist pilgrims see: Anderson, Cunningham, Fa Hian, Schiefner.

NEUMANN, C. F.: Coup d'œil historique sur les peuples et la littérature de l'Orient. Nouv. Journ. As.; 2e série, Vol. XIV. (1834.)

—— Mexico im fünften Jahrhundert nach Christus. Nach chinesischen Quellen. Ausland, 1845.

—— The Chatechism of the Shamans, or the Laws of the Priesthood of Buddha. Translated from the Chinese. London, 1831.

NÈVE, FEL.; De l'état présent des études sur le Bouddhisme et de leur application. (Extrait de la Révue de la Flandre, Vol. I.) Gand, 1846.

——. Le Bouddhism, son fondateur et ses écritures. Paris, 1854.

NIL (Archbishop of Yaroslaw): Buddhism in Sibiria. (Written in Russian.) St. Petersb. 1858.

NORRIS, E.: On the Kapur-di Rock inscription. Journ. R. As. Soc., Vol. VIII., p. 301.

OVERBECK: Jets over Boeddhoe en zyne Leer. Verh. d. Batav. Genoot., Vol. XI., p. 293.

PALLAS, P. S.: Reise durch verschiedene Provinzen des Russischen Reiches. 3 Theile. St. Petersburg, 1773-1801.

—— Sammlungen historischer Nachrichten über die Mongolischen Völkerschaften. 2 Theile. St. Petersburg, 1776, 1801.

PALLADJI, O.: Das Leben Buddhas. Arb. d. russ. Mission, Vol. II., p. 197.

—— Historische Skizze des alten Buddhismus. Erman's Arch. Vol. XV. (1856), p. 206. Also contained in: Arb. d. russ. Miss., Vol. II., p. 467.

—— Lebensbeschreibung des Buddha's Schakjamuni. Erman's Arch., Vol. XV. (1856), p. 1.

PAUTHIER: Faits relatifs au culte Bouddhique, d'après les sources Chinoises (in the article entitled "Examen méthodique des faits qui concernent le Thien-tchu"). Nouv. Journ. As.; 3e série, Vol. VIII. (1839).

PAVIE, T.: Étude sur le Sy-yeou-Schin-tsuen, roman bouddhique chinois. Nouv. Journ. As.; 5e serie, Vol. IX. p. 357, and Vol. X., p. 308.

PEMBERTON, R. B.: Report on Bhután. Calcutta, 1839.

PERRY, ERSKINE: Account of the great Hindu Monarch, Asoka, chiefly from Lassen's "Indische Alterthumskunde." Journ. Bombay R. As. Soc., Vol. III., Part. II., p. 149.

PICKERING, CH.: The Buddhist Caves. United States exploring expedition. Philad., 1848., Vol. IX., p. 349.

PITSCHURINSKI, HYACYNTH: Description of Tibet in its actual state. (Written in Russian.) St. Petersb. 1828.

POSTANS, W.: An account of the Jain temple at Badrasir; and ruins of Badranagirs in the province of Cutch. Journ. As. Soc. Beng., Vol. VII., Part. I., p. 431.

PRINSEP, J.: Interpretation of the most ancient of the inscriptions of the pillar called the Lāt of Feroz Shāh, near Delhi, and of the Allahabad, Radhia, and Mattiah pillar, or Lāt, inscriptions which agree therewith. Journ. As. Soc. Beng., Vol. VI., p. 566.

In reference to these pillars see also: Burt, Hodgson, Mill, Troyer, Turnour.

—— Note on the Facsimiles of the various Inscriptions on the ancient column at Allahabad, retaken by Edw. Smith. Journ. &c., Vol. III., p. 114.; Vol. VI., p. 963.

—— Note on the Facsimiles of Inscriptions from Sanchi near Bhilsa, and on the drawings of the Buddhist monument presented by Captain W. Murray. Journ. &c., Vol. VI., p. 451.

—— On the Edicts of Piyadasi, or Asoka, the Buddhist monarch of India. Journ. &c., Vol. VII., Part. I., p. 219.

—— Discovery of the name of Antiochus the Great, in two of the edicts of Asoka, king of India. Journ. &c., Vol. VII., p. 156.

—— Note on Inscriptions at Udayagiri, and Khandgiri, in Cuttak, in the Lāt characters. Journ. &c., Vol. VI., p. 1072.

PRINSEP, J.: On the coins and relics discovered by Chev. Ventura in the tope of Manikyāla. Journ. As. Soc. Beng., Vol. III., pp. 313, 436.

See also on this Tope the paper of Cunningham.

—— Note on the Coins discovered by M. Court. Journ. &c., Vol. III., p. 562.

For additions and corrections see: Cunningham.

—— Essays on Indian Antiquities, historic, numismatic, and palæographic of the late, to which are added his "Useful Tables," illustrative of Indian History, Chronology, modern Coinages, Weights, Measures, &c. Edited, with notes and additional matter, by Ed. Thomas. Vols. I. and II. London, 1858.

RAJENDRALAL MITRA, BABU: Buddhism and Odinism, their similitude; illustrated by Extracts from Professor Holmboe's Memoir on the "Traces de Buddhisme en Norvége." Journ. As. Soc. Beng., Vol. XXVII., p. 46.

—— The Lalita-Vistara, or Memoirs of the life and doctrines of Sakya Sinha. Vol. V. of the *Bibliotheca Indica*, by Roer.

See also the translation of Foućaux, and Lenz.

RÉMUSAT, ABEL: Note sur quelques épithétes descriptives de Bouddha. Journ. des Sav., 1819, p. 625.

—— Sur la succession des 33 premiers patriarches de la religion de Bouddha. Journ. des Sav., 1821, p. 4.

—— Aperçu d'un Mémoire sur l'origine de la Hiérarchie Lamaique. Journ. As., Vol. IV., 1824, p. 257.

—— Mélanges Asiatiques, ou Choix de morceaux de critique, et de mémoires relatifs aux religions, aux sciences, à l'histoire, et à la géographie des nations orientales. Vols. I. and II. Paris, 1825.

RÉMUSAT, ABEL: Nouveaux Mélanges Asiatiques, on Recueil de morceaux, &c., Vol. I. and II. 1829.

—— Essai sur la cosmographie et la cosmogonie des bouddhistes d'après les auteurs chinois. In the "Mélanges Asiatiques."

—— La Triade Bouddhique (in the article entitled "Observations sur trois Mémoires de De Guignes insérés dans le tome XL. de la Collection de l'Académie des Inscriptions et Belles-Lettres, et relatifs à la religion samanéenne). Nouv. Journ. As., 2e série, Vol. VII. (1831), pp. 265, 269, 301.

—— Observations sur l'histoire des Mongols orientaux, de Ssanang-Ssetsen. Paris, 1832.

—— Mémoires sur un voyage dans l'Asie Centrale, dans le pays des Afghans, et des Beloutches, et dans l'Inde, exécuté à la fin du IVe Siècle de notre ère par plusieurs Samanéens de Chine. Mém. de l'Inst. royal de France, Acad. d. inscr. 1838, p. 343.

—— Foe koue ki, ou Relations des Royaumes Bouddhiques: Voyages dans la Tartarie par Fa Hian. Paris, 1836.

Critical diss.: Neumann: Zeitschr. f. d. K. d. Morg., Vol. III., p. 105; and two articles by E. Burnouf in Journ. des Sav., 1837, pp. 160, 358; and H. H. Wilson, in Journ. R. As. Soc., Vol. V. (1839), p. 108.

For remarks on these voyages see Kittoe; an English translation of Rémusat's work is noticed under Fa Hian.

—— Mélanges posthumes d'histoire et de littérature orientales. Paris, 1843.

RENOU et LATRY: Relation d'un Voyage au Tibet par l'Abbé Krick. Paris, 1854.

Ritter, C.: Die Stupas, oder die architektonischen Denkmale an der indo-baktrischen Königsstrasse, und die Colosse von Bamian. Berlin, 1838.

See also the Narrative of Burnes.

—— Die Entstehung der lamaischen Hierarchie und der weltl. Suprematie der Chinesen über das Volk der Tübeter. "Erdkunde," Vol. III., pp. 274-87.

Salisbury, E.: Memoir on the history of Buddhism. Journ. Amer. Orient. Soc., Vol. I., pp. 79-136.

Salt, H.: Account of the caves in Salsette. Trans. Lit. Soc. Bombay, Vol. I., p. 41.

Schiefner, A.: Tibetische Studien. Einleitung und erster Artikel. Bull. hist.-phil. St. Pétersb. Vol. VIII., pp. 212, 259, 292, 303.

—— Beiträge zur Tibetischen Lautlehre. Bull. &c., Vol. VIII., pp. 267, 337.

—— Ueber den sogenannten Artikel. Bull. &c., Vol. VIII., p. 341.

—— Ueber die Verschlechterungsperioden der Menschheit, nach buddhistischer Anschauungsweise. Bull. &c., Vol. IX., p. 1.

—— Bericht über die in Peking für die Akademie angekauften tibetischen Werke. Bull. &c., Vol. IX., pp. 10, 17.

—— Das buddhistische Sutra der zweiundvierzig Sätze. Bull. &c., Vol. IX., p. 65.

—— Ueber das Werk; Histoire de la vie de Hiouen Thsang, &c. Bull. &c., Vol. XI., p. 97.

—— Ueber eine eigenthümliche Art tibetischer Composita. Bull. &c., Vol. XV., p. 7.

SCHIEFNER, A.: Ergänzungen und Berichtigungen zu Schmidt's Ausgabe des Dsanglun. St. Petersb., 1852.

—— Eine tibetische Lebensbeschreibung Sākyamuni's. Mém. des sav. étrang. St. Petersb. Vol. VI., p. 231.

—— Buddhistische Triglotte, d. h. Sanskrit-Tibetisch-Mongolisches Wörterverzeichniss. St. Petersb., 1859.

—— Sur le grand nombre des Buddhists. Bull. St. Petersb. Acad., Vol. V., No. 5.

SCHILLING DE CANNSTADT, Baron: Bibliothèque bouddhique, ou Index du Gandjour de Nartang. Bull. hist.-phil. St. Pétersb., Vol. IV., p. 321.

—— Mahāyānasūtra, d. i. das ehrwürdige, mit Namen "Das unermessliche Lebensalter und die unermessliche Erkenntniss." Ed. by the Imp. Academy. St. Petersb., 1845.

SCHLAGINTWEIT, H., A., and R. DE: Results of a scientific Mission to India and High Asia. The *Atlas* contains various representations of Buddhist temples, monasteries and objects of Buddhist worship.

—— EMIL: Ueber das Mahāyānasūtra Digpa thamchad shagpar terchoi. Bull. der bayer. Akad., 1863, p. 81. (Also contained in Chapter XI. of this volume.)

SCHLEGEL, FR., Professor: Mode of expressing numerals in the Sanskrit and Tibetan language. Journ. As. Soc. Beng., Vol. III., p. 1.

SCHOEBEL, C.: Le Bouddha et le Bouddhisme. Paris, 1857.

SCHMARDA, L. K.: Reise um die Erde in den Jahren 1853-1857. Braunschweig, 1861. (Vol. I. in reference to Buddhism in Ceylon.)

SCHMIDT, I. J.: Forschungen im Gebiete der älteren religiösen, politischen und literarischen Bildungsgeschichte der Völker Mittel-Asiens, vorzüglich der Mongolen und Tibeter. St. Pétersb., 1824.

—— Würdigung und Abfertigung der Klaproth'schen "Beleuchtung der Forschungen &c." Leipzig, 1826.

—— Ueber die Verwandtschaft der gnostisch theosophischen Lehren mit den Religionssystemen des Orients, vorzüglich des Buddhaismus. Leipzig, 1828.

—— Geschichte der Ostmongolen und ihres Fürstenhauses, verfasst von Ssanang Ssetsen Chungtai dschi der Ordus; übersetzt von .... St. Petersb., 1829.

For critical diss. see: Klaproth, Rémusat.

—— Die Thaten Bogda Gessers Khan's, des Vertilgers der Wurzel der zehn Uebel in den zehn Gegenden. Eine ostasiatische Heldensage, aus dem Mongolischen übersetzt. St. Petersb., 1839.

—— Ueber das Mahāyāna und das Prajnā Parāmita der Bauddhen. Bull. scient. St. Petersb. Acad., Vol. I., p. 145, and Mém. de l'Acad. de St. Petersb., Vol. IV., p. 124.

—— Ueber die Begründung des Tibetischen Sprachstudiums in Russland und die Herausgabe der dazu nöthigen Hülfswerke. Bull. sc. &c., Vol. I., p. 28.

—— Ueber Lamaismus und die Bedeutung dieses Namens. Bull. sc. &c., Vol. I., p. 11.

—— Ueber einige Eigenthümlichkeiten der Tibetischen Sprache und Schrift. Bull. sc. &c., Vol. III., p. 225.

Schmidt, I. J.: Ueber den Ursprung der Tibetischen Schrift. Mém. de l'Acad St. Pétersb., Vol. I., p. 41.

—— Ueber einige Grundlehren des Buddhismus. Mém. &c., Vol. I., p. 93.

—— Ueber die sogenannte dritte Welt der Buddhaisten. Mém. &c., Vol. II., p. 1.

—— Ueber die tausend Buddhas einer Weltperiode der Einwohnung, oder gleichmässigen Dauer. Mém. &c., Vol. II., p. 41.

—— Grammatik der Tibetischen Sprache. 1839.

—— Tibetisch-deutsches Wörterbuch nebst deutschem Wortregister. 1841.

—— Dsanglun, der Weise und der Thor; aus dem Tibetischen übersetzt und mit dem Originaltexte herausgegeben. 1843.

For Addenda and corrections see Schiefner.

—— Der ILdex des Kanjur. St. Petersb., 1845.

—— and Boehtlingk, O.: Verzeichniss der tibetischen Handschriften und Holzdrucke im Asiatischen Museum der K. Akademie der Wissenschaften. Bull. hist.-phil. St. Petersb., Vol. IV., Nos. 6, 7, 8.

Schönberg, E. von: Blick auf die buddhistischen Felsentempel Indiens. Zeitschr. d. deutsch. Morg. Ges., Vol. VII. (1853), pp. 101-3.

Schott, W.: Ueber den Doppelsinn des Wortes Schamane, und über den tungusischen Schamanencultus am Hofe der Mandshu Kaiser. Abh. Berl. Acad. 1842.

SCHOTT, W.: Ueber den Buddhaismus in Hoch-Asien und in China. Abh. Berl. Acad. 1844.

SELKIRK: Recollections of Ceylon, after a residence of nearly thirteen years; with an account of the church Missionary Society's operations. 1844.

SIEBOLD, PH. FR. v.: Nippon, Archiv zur Beschreibung von Japan und dessen Neben- und Schutzländer &c. 5 Vols. Leyden, 1837.

SIRR: China and the Chinese, their religion, character, customs, and manufactures, &c. 2 Vols. 1849.

SMITH, J.: Specimen of a Burmese drama. Journ. As. Soc. Beng., Vol. VIII., p. 535.

SPIEGEL, FR.: Kammavakya, Liber de officiis sacerdotum Buddhicorum. Palice et Latine primus edidit, atque adnotationes adjecit. 1841.

—— Anecdota Palica. Nach den Handschriften der kgl. Bibliothek in Copenhagen im Grundtexte herausgegeben, übersetzt und erklärt. Leipzig, 1845.

STEVENSON: Analysis of the Ganesa Purāna, with special reference to the history of Buddhism. Journ. R. As. Soc., Vol. VIII. (1846), p. 319.

—— On the intermixture of Buddhism with Brahmanism in the religion of the Hindus of the Dekhan. Journ. R. As. Soc., Vol. VII. (1843), pp. 1-8.

—— An account of the Buddho-Vaishnavas, or Vitthal-Bhaktas of the Dakhan. Journ. R. As. Soc., Vol. VII. (1843), p. 64.

Strachey, H. Captain: Narrative of a Journey to Cho Lagan and Cho Mapan. Journ. As. Soc. Beng., Vol. XVII., Part. II., pp. 98, 128, 327.

Stuhr: Die Religionssysteme der heidnischen Völker des Orients. Berlin, 1836.

Sykes, H. W.: On a Catalogue of Chinese Buddhistical Works. Journ. R. As. Soc., Vol. IX. (1848), p. 199.

—— An Account of the Caves of Ellora. Trans. Lit. Soc. Bombay, Vol. III., p. 265.

See also on these caves: Grindley, Tod.

—— On the Miniature Chaityas and Inscriptions of the Buddhist religious dogma, found in the ruins of the Temple of Sárnáth, near Benares. Journ. R. As. Soc., Vol. XVI., p. 37.

See also on the fundamental dogma of the Buddhist faith: Hodgson's paper on Sarnath.

—— Specimens of Buddhist inscriptions, with symbols, from the West of India. Journ. As. Soc. Beng., Vol. VI., Part. II., p. 1038.

Sylvestre de Sacy: A critic is noticed under Klaproth.

Taylor, Cooke: Ancient and modern India. Revised and continued to tke present time by Mackenna. 1857.

Tennent, Sir, Emerson: Christianity in Ceylon, its Introduction and Progress under the Portuguese, the Dutch, the British, and American Mission; with an historical Sketch of the Bramanical and Buddhist Superstitions. London, 1850.

TENNENT, SIR, EMERSON: Ceylon, an account of the island, physical, historical, and topographical; with notices of its natural history, antiquities, and productions. London, 1859.

THOMAS, E.: Note on the present state of the excavations of Sārnāth. Journ. As. Soc. Beng., Vol. XXIII., p. 469. (For further notices see Vol. XXV., p. 395.)

—— For his edition of J. Prinsep's *Useful Tables* see Prinsep.

THOMSON, T. D.: Western Himálaya and Tíbet. London, 1852.

TIMKOWSKI: Travels of the Russian mission through Mongolia China, and residence in Peking in years 1820-21. With corrections and notes by Klaproth. 2 Vols. London, 1827.

TOD, J.: Remarks on certain sculptures in the Cave Temples of Ellora. Trans. R. As. Soc., Vol. II., p. 328.

See also about these caves: Grindley, Sykes.

TORRENS, L.: Travels in Ladâk, Tartary and Kashmir. London, 1862.

TROYER, A.: Announcement of the work: Histoire du Bouddha Sakya-Mouni, par Ph. Ed. Foucaux. Nouv. Journ. As. 4e série, Vol. XIV., pp. 252-4.

—— Remarks upon the second inscription of the Allahabad pillar. Journ. As. Soc. Beng., Vol. III., p. 118.

In reference to these pillars see also: Burt, Hodgson, Mill, Prinsep, Turnour.

TURNER, S.: An account of an embassy to the Court of the Teshoo Lama in Tibet; containing a narrative of a journey through Bootan, and part of Tibet. London, 1800.

TURNOUR, G.: Account of the Tooth relic of Ceylon, supposed to be alluded to in the opening passage of the Ferog lāt inscription. Journ. As. Soc. Beng., Vol. VI., p. 963.

—— Further Notes on the Inscriptions on the columns at Dehli, Allahabad, Betiah, &c. Journ. &c., Vol. VI., p. 1049.

See also in reference to these columns: Burt, Hodgson, Mill, Prinsep, Troyer.

—— Examination of the Pāli Buddhistical Annals. Journ. As. Soc. Beng., Vol. VI., pp. 501 and 713; and Vol. VII., Part. II., pp. 686, 789, 919, 991.

Critical diss.: Zeitschr. f. d. K. d. Morg., Vol. III., p. 157, and Vol. IV.

—— The first Twenty Chapters of the Mahāwanso: and a prefatory essay on Pāli Buddhistical literature, originally published as an introduction to the above-mentioned portion of the Mahawanso and to the epitome of the history of Ceylon, and the historical inscriptions, printed in the Ceylon Almanac of 1833 and 1834. Ceylon, 1836.

—— The Mahāwanso in Roman characters, with the translation subjoined, and an Introductory Essay on Pāli Buddhistical Literature.

—— Examination of some points of Buddhist Chronology. Journ. As. Soc. Beng., Vol. V., p. 521.

Critical diss.: Lassen, Chr.: Zeitschr. f. d. K. d. Morg., Vol. I., pp. 235-9.

UPHAM, E.: The history and doctrine of Buddhism, popularly illustrated; with notices of the Kappoism, or Demon worship, and of the Bali, or planetary incantations of Ceylon. London, 1829.

UPHAM, E.: The Mahavānsi, the Rājāratnācari, and the Rājāvali, forming the sacred and historical books of Ceylon; also a collection of tracts illustrative of the doctrines and literature of Buddhism. Translated from the Singhalese. London, 1833.
Critical diss.: Burnouf, Journ. des Sav., 1833, 1834.

VIGNE, G. T.: Travels in Kashmír, Ladak, Iskardo, &c. 2 Vols. London, 1842.

WASSILJEW, W.: Notices sur les ouvrages relatifs au Buddhism qui se trouvent dans la bibliothèque de l'Université de Kasan. Bull. hist.-phil. St. Pétersb., Vol. XI., p. 337.

—— Notices sur les ouvrages en langues de l'Asie orientale qui se trouvent dans la bibliothèque de St. Pétersbourg. Bull. &c. Vol. XIII.. Nos. 14 *et seq.*

—— Der Buddhismus, seine Dogmen, Geschichte und Literatur. Deutsche Uebersetzung. St. Petersb., 1860.
Notice is given of this work by A. Schiefner, in Bull. hist.-phil. St. Pétersb., Vol. XIII.

WEBER, A.: Die neueren Forschungen über das alte Indien. Printed in the "Histor. Taschenbuch von F. Raumer." 3rd. series, Vol. VI., 1854, pp. 103-43.

—— Ueber das Çatrunjaya Māhātmyan. Ein Beitrag zur Geschichte der Jaina. Leipzig, 1858.

—— Indische Skizzen. Berlin, 1857.

—— Die neuesten Forschungen auf dem Gebiete des Buddhismus. Separatabdruck aus den "Indischen Studien." Vol. III., p. 1. Berlin, 1853.

WESTERGAARD, N. L.: A brief account of the minor Bauddha caves of Beira and Bajah, in the environs of Karli. Journ. Bombay Branch R. As. Soc., Vol. I. (Aug. 1844), p. 438.

—— Ueber den ältesten Zeitraum der indischen Geschichte mit Rücksicht auf die Literatur. — Ueber Buddha's Todesjahr und einige andere Zeitpunkte in der älteren Geschichte Indiens. Translated from the Denish by Stenzler. Breslau, 1862

WILFORD, T.: An Essay on the sacred Isles in the West, with other essays connected with. As. Res., Vol. VIII., p. 245.

For other memoirs by this author see As. Res., Vols. II., III., IV., V., VI., X.

WILSON, H. H.: Ariana antiqua. A descriptive account of the antiquities and coins of Afghanistan: with a memoir on the buildings called Topes, by E. Masson. London, 1841. 4°.

—— Buddhist Emblems. Journ. R. As. Soc., Vol. VI., p. 451.

—— Analysis of the Kah-gyur. Journ. As. Soc. Beng., Vol. I., p. 375.

—— Buddhist Inscription of King Priyadarsi. Journ. &c., Vol. XVI., p. 357.

—— On the Rock inscription of Kapur di Giri, Dhauli and Ginar. Journ. R. As. Soc., Vol. XII., p. 153.

—— On Buddha and Buddhism. Journ. &c., Vol. XIII., p. 229.

—— Note on the Literature of Thibet. Glean. in Science. Vol. III. p. 243.

—— Notes of a Correspondence with Sir John Bowring on Buddhist Literature in China. With notices of Chinese Buddhist Works translated from the Sanskrit. By E. Edkins. Journ. R. As. Soc., Vol. XVI., p. 316.

WILSON, H. H.: Notices sur trois ouvrages bouddhiques reçus du Nepal par ..... Nouv. Journ. As., 1831, p. 97.

WILSON, J.: Memoir on the Cave Temples and Monasteries and other ancient Buddhist, Brahmanical, and Jaina remains of Western India. Journ. Bombay R. As. Soc., Vol. III., Part. II., p. 36, and Vol. IV., p. 340.

YULE: A narrative of the Mission sent by the Governor General of India to the Court of Ava in 1855, with notices of the Country, Government and People. With numerous Illustrations. London, 1858.

B.

GLOSSARY OF TIBETAN TERMS,

THEIR SPELLING AND TRANSLITERATION.

WITH QUOTATIONS OF THE EXPLANATION CONTAINED IN THIS VOLUME.

ALPHABETICALLY ARRANGED.

In order to facilitate the printing, the spelling in native characters has been excluded from the text, and I present here a general synopsis in which every term met with in the preceding parts can easily be found.

The first column gives the pronunciation; the second the Tibetan spelling; the third the transliteration; in the fourth the page is added in which details about the respective term are contained.

The Tibetan terms may be monosyllabic or they may consist of several words, but the Tibetan language also shows frequent examples of compositions; several words which of themselves have a distinct meaning, and are as such in general use, often occur combined and forming one term.

Many words show a considerable difference between the pronunciation and the spelling. In most cases the difference is based upon grammatical rules; in others we have to explain it by supposing the influence of dialects, in consequence of which many words have become invested with a form different from that which they have in the classical stationary language of the sacred Buddhist literature. I have already had occasion to allude to this introduction of numerous new forms into the modern popular Tibetan, when analysing the historical document obtained at Hímis (see p. 183).

The alphabet I use for the transliteration in the third column is given in full detail p. XI-XIV. The consonants not pronounced are printed in Italics; the Tibetan inter-syllabic points are rendered, as is usually done, by small horizontal lines.

Phonetic Transcription.	Tibetan Characters.	Transliteration.	Page.
Argai choga.	ཨརྒྷའི་ཆོ་ག	Arga'i-chho-ga.	179
Atisha.	ཨ་ཏི་ཤ	A-ti-sha.	69, 136
Badang.	བ་དང	Ba-dang.	191
Bagtsis.	བག་རྩིས	Bag-*r*tsis.	274
Bardo.	བར་དོ	Bar-do.	109
Bardo phrang-grol gyi sol deb jig grol gyi pavo zhechava.	བར་དོ་འཕྲང་སྒྲོལ་གྱི་གསོལ་འདེབས་འཇིགས་སྒྲོལ་གྱི་དཔའ་བོ་ཞེས་བྱ་བ	Bar-do-'phrang-*s*grol-gyi-*g*sol-'deb*s*-'jig*s*-*s*grol-gyi-*d*pa'-vo-zhes-bya-va.	110
Bechon.	བེ་ཅོན	Be-chon.	215
Bihar gyalpo.	བི་ཧར་རྒྱལ་པོ	Bi-har-*r*gyal-po.	177
Bon.	བོན	Bon.	74
Brakhug.	འབྲས་ཁུག	'Bra*s*-khug.	240
Brikungpa.	འབྲི་ཁུང་པ	'Bri-khung-pa.	74
Bromston.	འབྲོམ་སྟོན	'Brom-ston.	69, 73
Brug.	འབྲུག	'Brug.	255, 276
Brúgpa.	འབྲུག་པ	'Brug-pa.	74
Brul.	སྦྲུལ	*s*Brul.	276
Budzad.	དབུ་མཛད	*d*Bu-*m*dzad.	155
Bumapa.	དབུ་མ་པ	*d*Bu-ma-pa.	32
Bumpa.	བུམ་པ	Bum-pa.	239
Cha.	ཇ	Ja.	169

Phonetic Transcription.	Tibetan Characters.	Transliteration.	Page.
Chag.	ལྕགས	*l*Chag*s*.	281
Chagpa thogmed.	ཕྱགས་པ་ཐོགས་མེད	Phyag*s*-pa-thog*s*-med.	32
Chagtong khorlo.	ཕྱག་སྟོང་འཁོར་ལོ	Phyag-*s*tong-'khor-lo.	89
Chagye chin.	ཕྱག་གཡས་སྦྱིན	Phyag-*g*ya*s*-*s*byin.	208
Chakdor.	ཕྱག་རྡོར	Phyag-*r*dor.	114
Chakna dorje.	ཕྱག་ན་རྡོ་རྗེ	Phyag-na-*r*do-rje.	
Chag zhipa.	ཕྱག་བཞི་པ	Phyag-*b*zhi-pa.	89
Chakhan.	ཕྱ་མཁན	Phya-*m*khan.	156
Chakja.	ཕྱག་རྒྱ	Phyag-*r*gya.	56, 208
Chakna padma karpo.	ཕྱག་ན་པདྨ་དཀར་པོ	Phyag-na-padma-*d*kar-po.	89
Champai chos nga.	བྱམས་པའི་ཆོས་ལྔ	Byam*s*-pa'i-chhos-*l*nga.	32
Chamzhug.	བྱམས་བཞུགས	Byam*s*-*b*zhug*s*.	211
Chandren.	སྤྱན་འདྲེན	*s*Pyan-'dren.	260
Changpo.	འཆང་པོ	'Chhang-po.	256
Chantong.	སྤྱན་སྟོང	*s*Pyan-*s*tong.	90
Chebu damchan.	སྐྱེས་བུ་དམ་ཅན	*s*Kye*s*-bu-dam-chan.	158
Chenresi vanchug.	སྤྱན་རས་གཟིགས་དབང་ཕྱུག	*s*Pyan-ras-*g*zhig*s*-*d*vang-phyug.	88
Chi.	ཁྱི	Khyi.	276
Chinsreg.	སྦྱིན་སྲེག	*s*Byin-sreg.	249
Chod.	གཅོད	*g*Chod.	163
Chodpa.	མཆོད་པ	*m*Chhod-pa.	260

Phonetic Transcription.	Tibetan Characters.	Transliteration.	Page.
Chodpan.	ཅོད་པན	Chod-pan.	209
Chogi dangpoi sangye.	མཆོག་གི་དང་པོའི་སངས་རྒྱས	*m*Chhog-gi-dang-po'i-sang*s*-*r*gyas.	50
Choichi gyalpo.	ཆོས་ཀྱི་རྒྱལ་པོ	Chhos-kyi-*r*gyal-po.	185
Choichi gyalpoi shed dul.	ཆོས་ཀྱི་རྒྱལ་པོའི་ཤེད་འདུལ	Chhos-kyi-*r*gyal-po'i-shed-'dul.	110
Choichong.	ཆོས་སྐྱོང	Chhos-*s*kyong.	156
Choigyal.	ཆོས་རྒྱལ	Chhos-*r*gyal.	93, 185
Chorten.	མཆོད་རྟེན	*m*Chhod-*r*ten.	192 & *seq.*
Chorva.	འབྱོར་བ	'Byor-ba.	240
Chos ku.	ཆོས་སྐུ	Chhos-*s*ku.	38
Chu.	ཆུ	Chhu.	281
Chugchig zhal.	བཅུ་གཅིག་ཞལ	*b*Chu-gchig-zhal.	89
Chungpa kundus tsis.	འབྱུང་པ་ཀུན་འདུས་རྩིས	'Byung-pa-kun-'dus-*r*tsis.	309
Chusrang.	ཆུ་སྲང	Chhu-srang.	289
Da.	ཌ	Da	307
Da.	དགྲ	*d*Gra	109, 258
Dabchad.	འདབ་བརྒྱད	'Dab-*br*gyad.	248
Dachan.	སྒྲ་གཅན	*s*Gra-*g*chan.	115
Dalha gyalpo.	དགྲ་ལྷ་རྒྱལ་པོ	*d*Gra-lha-*r*gyal-po.	157
Damchan dorje legpa.	དམ་ཅན་རྡོ་རྗེ་ལེགས་པ	Dam-chan-*r*do-rje-leg*s*-pa.	158
Dampai de.	དམ་པའི་སྡེ	Dam-pa'i-*s*de.	39

Phonetic Transcription.	Tibetan Characters.	Transliteration.	Page.
Darnai janba.	དར་སྣ་ལྔའི་བརྒྱན་པ	Dar-*s*na-*l*nga'i-*br*gyan-pa.	261
Darzab.	དར་ཟབ	Dar-zab.	178
Dashol.	ཟླ་བཤོལ	Zla-*b*shol.	288
Dava.	ཟླ་བ	Zla-ba.	289
Dava dagpa.	ཟླ་བ་གྲགས་པ	Zla-ba-grag*s*-pa.	41
Dechad.	སྡེ་བརྒྱད	*s*De-*br*gyad.	109
Dechog.	བདེ་མཆོག	*b*De-*m*chhog.	108
Dechogi gyut.	བདེ་མཆོག་གི་རྒྱུད	*b*De-*m*chhog-gi-*r*gyud.	109
Dejung.	བདེ་འབྱུང	*b*De-'byung.	47
Devachan.	བདེ་བ་ཅན	*b*De-ba-chan.	101
Dezhin shegpa.	དེ་བཞིན་གཤེགས་པ	De-*b*zhin-*g*sheg*s*-pa.	4, 126
Digpa thamchad shagpar terchoi.	སྡིག་པ་ཐམས་ཅད་བཤགས་པར་གཏེར་ཆོས	*s*Dig-pa-tham*s*-chad-*b*shag*s*-par-*g*ter-chhos.	123
Digshag ser chi pugri.	སྡིག་བཤགས་གསེར་གྱིས་སྤུ་གྲི	*s*Dig-*b*shag*s*-*g*ser-gyis-*s*pu-gri.	124
Digug.	གྲི་གུག	Gri-gug.	264
Do.	མདོ	*m*Do.	78
Dodne vangpo.	གདོད་ནས་དབང་པོ	*g*Dod-nas-*d*bang-po.	263
Doljang.	སྒྲོལ་ལྗང	*s*Grol-*l*jang.	66
Dolkar.	སྒྲོལ་དཀར	*s*Grol*d*-kar.	66
Dolma.	སྒྲོལ་མ	*s*Grol-ma.	66
Dolzin.	གྲོལ་ཟིན	Grol-zin.	42
Dom.	སྡོམ	*s*Dom.	106, 162

Phonetic Transcription.	Tibetan Characters.	Transliteration.	Page.
Donchen chonga.	གདོན་ཆེན་བཅོ་ལྔ	*g*Don-chhen-*b*cho-*l*nga.	267
Dondampai denpa.	དོན་དམ་པའི་བདེན་པ	Don-dam-pa'i-*b*den-pa.	35
Dorje.	རྡོ་རྗེ	*r*Do-rje.	215
Dorjechang.	རྡོ་རྗེ་འཆང	*r*Do-rje-'chhang.	50 *& seq.*
Dorjedan.	རྡོ་རྗེ་གདན	*r*Do-rje-*g*dan.	178
Dorjedzin.	རྡོ་རྗེ་འཛིན	*r*Do-rje-zin.	50 *& seq.*
Dorje kyilkrung.	རྡོ་རྗེ་དཀྱིལ་དཀྲུང	*r*Do-rje-*d*kyil-*d*krung.	210
Dorjesempa.	རྡོ་རྗེ་སེམས་དཔའ	*r*Do-rje-sem*s*-*d*pa'.	50 *& seq.*
Dote.	མདོ་སྡེ	*m*Do-*s*de.	68
Dragpo chinsreg.	དྲག་པོ་སྦྱིན་སྲེག	Drag-po-*s*byin-sreg.	110, 252
Dragshed.	དྲག་གཤེད	Drag-*g*shed.	111
Drilbu.	དྲིལ་བུ	Dril-bu.	53
Drimed shelphreng.	དྲི་མེད་ཤེལ་ཕྲེང	Dri-med-shel-phreng.	114
Dubjed.	སྒྲུབ་བྱེད	*s*Grub-byed.	247
Dudo.	དུད་འགྲོ	Dud-'gro.	92
Dudpo.	བདུད་པོ	*b*Dud-po.	110
Dug.	གདུགས	*g*Dug*s*.	191
Dug karchan.	གདུགས་དཀར་ཅན	*g*Dug*s*-*d*kar-chan.	257
Dulva.	འདུལ་བ	'Dul-ba.	78
Dulva-zhi.	འདུལ་བ་བཞི	'Dul-va-*b*zhi.	125
Dungtsi.	གདུང་རྩི	*g*Dung-*r*tsi.	264

Phonetic Transcription.	Tibetan Characters.	Transliteration.	Page.
Dus kyi khorlo.	དུས་ཀྱི་འཁོར་ལོ	Dus-kyi-'khor-lo.	47 *& seq.*
Dusmayinpar chi.	དུས་མ་ཡིན་པར་འཆི	Dus-ma-yin-par-'chhi.	109
Dutsi.	བདུད་རྩི	*b*Dud-*r*tsi.	114
Dzadpa chugnyi.	མཛད་པ་བཅུ་གཉིས	*m*Dzad-pa-*b*chu-gnyi*s*.	86
Dzambhala.	ཛམ་བྷ་ལ	Dzam-bha-la.	263
Gabtsis.	གབ་རྩིས	Gab-*r*tsis.	274, 294
Galdanpa.	དགའ་ལྡན་པ	*d*Ga'-ldan-pa.	73
Gang zar.	འགང་གཟར	'Gang-*g*zar.	250
Gaũ.	གཨུ	Gau.	174
Gavo.	དགའ་བོ	*d*Ga'-bo.	39
Gebkoi.	དགེ་བསྐོས	*d*Ge-b*s*kos.	155
Geg.	བགེགས	*b*Geg*s*.	109, 258
Geldanpa.	དགེ་ལྡན་པ	*d*Ge-ldan-pa.	73
Gelong.	དགེ་སློང	*d*Ge-*s*long.	162
Gelukpa.	དགེ་ལུགས་པ	*d*Ge-lug*s*-pa.	73
Genyen.	དགེ་བསྙེན	*d*Ge-*bs*nyen.	149, 162
Genyen darma.	དགེ་སྙེན་དར་མ	*d*Ge-*s*nyen-dar-ma.	98
Getsul.	དགེ་ཚུལ	*d*Ge-ts'hul.	162
Gin.	གིན	Gin.	307
Gonpa.	དགོན་པ	*d*Gon-pa.	179
Gonpo.	མགོན་པོ	*m*Gon-po.	261
Gonyan serpo.	མགོ་བརྙན་སེར་པོ	*m*Go-*br*nyan-ser-po.	234
Grubchen tsul-khrim gyatso.	གྲུབ་ཆེན་ཚུལ་ཁྲིམས་རྒྱ་མཚོ	Grub-chhen-ts'hul-khrim*s*-*r*gya-*m*ts'ho.	97

Phonetic Transcription.	Tibetan Characters.	Transliteration.	Page.
Grubtsis.	གྲུབ་རྩིས	Grub-*r*tsis.	274
Gungdun.	དགུང་བདུན	*d*Gung-*b*dun.	289
Gyalcheṅzhi.	རྒྱལ་ཆེན་བཞི	*r*Gyal-chhen-*b*zhi.	109
Gyalpo chenpo namthoras chi kang shag.	རྒྱལ་པོ་ཆེན་པོ་རྣམ་ཐོས་སྲས་ཀྱི་བསྐང་བཤགས	*r*Gyal-po-chhen-po-*r*nam-thos-sras-kyi-*bs*kang-*b*shag*s*.	264
Gyaltsan.	རྒྱལ་མཚན	*r*Gyal-*m*ts'han.	264
Gyelrap salvai melong.	རྒྱལ་རབས་གསལ་བའི་མེ་ལོང	*r*Gyal-rab*s*-*g*sal-ba'i-me-long.	71
Gyelva rinpoche.	རྒྱལ་བ་རིན་པོ་ཆེ	*r*Gyal-ba-rin-po-chhe.	153
Gyut.	རྒྱུད	*r*Gyud.	48, 56, 78
Gyut zhi.	རྒྱུད་བཞི	*r*Gyud-*b*zhi.	265
Hala hala.	ཧ་ལ་ཧ་ལ	Ha-la-ha-lā.	115
Hēruka.	ཧེ་རུ་ཀ	He-ru-ka.	108
Ja.	བྱ	Bya.	276
Jabyol.	རྒྱབ་ཡོལ	*r*Gab-yol.	212
Jamjang.	འཇམ་དབྱངས	'Jam-*d*byang*s*.	65
Jampaijang lhai thama shesrab od.	འཇམ་པའི་དབྱངས་ལྷའི་ཐ་མ་ཤེས་རབ་འོད	'Jam-pai-*d*byang*s*-lha'i-tha-ma-shes-rab-'od.	97
Jang.	བྱང	Byang.	259
Jed-tho yangi zamatog.	བརྗེད་ཐོ་གཡང་གི་ཟ་མ་ཏོག	*br*Jed-tho-yang-gi-za-ma-tog.	315
Je Tsonkhapa.	རྗེ་ཙོང་ཁ་པ	*r*Je-tsong-kha-pa.	97
Ji.	བྱི	Byi.	276
Jigten Gonpo.	འཇིག་རྟེན་མགོན་པོ	'Jig-*r*ten-*m*gon-po.	90

Phonetic Transcription.	Tibetan Characters.	Transliteration.	Page.
Jolsong.	བྱོལ་སོང	Byol-song.	92
Jungpo.	འབྱུང་པོ	'Byung-po.	109
Ka.	བཀའ	*b*Ka'.	73
Kadampa.	བཀའ་གདམས་པ	*b*Ka'-*g*dam*s*-pa.	73
Kalba.	སྐལ་བ	*s*Kal-ba.	93
Kanjur.	བཀའ་འགྱུར	*b*Ka'-'gyur.	78 *& seq.*
Kantsai.	བསྐང་རྫས	*bs*Kang-*r*dzas.	260
Kapāla.	ཀ་པཱ་ལ	Ka-pa-la.	216
Kargyutpa.	བཀའ་རྒྱུད་པ	*b*Ka'-rgyud-pa.	73
Karmapa.	ཀརྨ་པ	Karma-pa.	74
Kartsis.	དཀར་རྩིས or སྐར་རྩིས	*d*Kar-*r*tsis or *s*Kar-*r*tsis.	156, 274
Kartsi-pa.	སྐར་རྩིས་པ	*s*Kar-*r*tsis-pa.	156
Khado.	མཁའ་འགྲོ	*m*Kha'-'gro.	248
Kham.	ཁམ	Kham.	307
Khangtsig.	ཁང་བརྩིགས	Kang-*br*tsig*s*.	264
Khanpo.	མཁན་པོ	*m*Khan-po.	155
Kharsil.	འཁར་བསིལ	'Khar-*b*sil.	214
Khatak.	ཁ་བཏགས	Kha-*b*tag*s*.	190
Khen.	ཁེན	Khen.	307
Khetup chakdor gyatso.	མཁས་གྲུབ་ཕྱག་རྡོར་རྒྱ་མཚོ	*m*Khas-grub-phyag-*r*dor-*r*gya-*m*ts'ho.	97
Khetup sangye.	མཁས་གྲུབ་སངས་རྒྱས	*m*Khas-grub-sang*s*-*r*gyas.	97
Khiral.	ཁི་རལ	Khi-ral.	76

Phonetic Transcription.	Tibetan Characters.	Transliteration.	Page.
Khon.	ཁོན	Khon.	307
Khorlo.	འཁོར་ལོ	'Khor-lo.	53
Khorloi phanyon.	འཁོར་ལོའི་ཕན་ཡོན	'Khor-lo'i-phan-yon.	232
Khorten.	འཁོར་བརྟེན	'Khor-*b*rtěn.	229
Khrim.	ཁྲིམས	Khrim*s*.	159
Khyung.	འཁྱུང	'Khyung.	255
Kontseg.	དཀོན་བརྩེགས	*d*Kon-*b*rtseg*s*.	78
Kundzob chi denpa.	ཀུན་རྫོབ་ཀྱི་བདེན་པ	Kun-*r*dzob-gyi-*b*denpa.	35
Ku nga gyalpo.	སྐུ་ལྔ་རྒྱལ་པོ	*s*Ku-*l*nga-*r*gyal-po.	157
Ku nga gyalpoi kang shag.	སྐུ་ལྔ་རྒྱལ་པོའི་བསྐང་བཤགས	*s*Ku-*l*nga-*r*gyal-po'i-*bs*kang-*b*shag*s*.	157
Kuntag.	ཀུན་བརྟགས	Kun-*br*tags.	34
Labri.	བླ་བྲི	*b*La-bri.	191
Labtse.	ལབ་ཙེ	Lab-tse.	199
Lagoi.	བླ་གོས	*b*La-gos.	172
Lai bumpa.	ལས་བུམ་པ	Las-bum-pa.	248
Lama.	བླ་མ	*b*La-ma.	156
Lamrim.	ལམ་རིམ	Lam-rim.	77, 104
Lang.	གླང	*g*Lang.	276
Langdar.	གླང་དར	*g*Lang-dar.	68
Langpo.	གླང་པོ	*g*Lang-po.	54
Lantsa.	ལན་ཚ or ལཉྩ	Lan-ts'ha.	80
Las.	ལས	Las.	93
Leutho.	ལེའུ་ཐོ	Le'u-tho.	274

Phonetic Transcription.	Tibetan Characters.	Transliteration.	Page.
Lha.	ལྷ	Lha.	91, 108
Lhachen.	ལྷ་ཆེན	Lha-chhen.	234
Lhagpa.	ལྷག་པ	Lhag-pa.	289
Lhakhang.	ལྷ་ཁང	Lha-khang.	188
Lhamayin.	ལྷ་མ་ཡིན	Lha-ma-yin.	92, 109
Lhamo.	ལྷ་མོ	Lha-mo.	112, 119
Lhatug.	ལྷ་ཕྲུག	Lha-phrug.	234
Lho.	ལྷོ	Lho.	258
Lhonub.	ལྷོ་ནུབ	Lho nub.	258
Lhungzed.	ལྷུང་བཟེད	Lhung-*b*zed.	210
Lhunpo.	ལྷུན་པོ	Lhun-po.	92
Li.	ལི	Li.	307
Lo.	ལོ	Lo.	276
Longchod dzog-pai ku.	ལོངས་སྤྱོད་རྫོགས་པའི་སྐུ	Long*s*-*s*pyod-*r*dzog*s* pa'i-*s*ku.	38
Lonpo.	བློན་པོ	*b*Lon-po.	53
Lotho.	ལོ་ཐོ	Lo-tho.	274
Lotsava.	ལོ་ཙཱབ	Lo-tsava.	76
Lug.	ལུག	Lug.	276
Lug.	ལུགས	Lug*s*.	246, 310
Lugrub.	ཀླུ་སྒྲུབ	*k*Lu-*s*grub.	30, 136
Lugzar.	བླུག་གཟར	*b*Lug-*g*zar.	250
Lungta.	རླུང་རྟ	*r*Lung-*r*ta.	253
Luvang gyalpo.	ཀླུ་དབང་རྒྱལ་པོ	*k*Lu-*d*bang-*r*gyal-po.	157
Maglon.	དམག་བློན	*d*Mag-*b*lon.	54

Phonetic Transcription.	Tibetan Characters.	Transliteration.	Page.
Mani.	མཎི	Mani.	196, 229
Mani choskhor.	མཎི་ཆོས་འཁོར	Mani-chhos-'khor.	230
Mani kambum.	མཎི་བཀའ་འབུམ	Mani-*b*ka-'kum.	84
Manii rilbu grub thab.	མཎིའི་རིལ་བུ་གྲུབ་ཐབས	Mani'i-ril-bu-grub-thab*s*.	266
Manla.	སྨན་བླ	*s*Man-*b*la.	266
Me.	མེ	Me.	281
Meba gu.	སྨེ་བ་དགུ	*s*Me-ba-*d*gu.	297
Melha.	མེ་ལྷ	Me-lha.	207, 251
Melong.	མེ་ལོང	Me-long.	239
Mi.	མི	Mi.	92
Migmar.	མིག་དམར	Mig-*d*mar.	289
Monlam.	སྨོན་ལམ	*s*Mon-lam.	119
Muliding.	མུ་ལི་དིང	Mu-li-ding.	113
Myalba.	དམྱལ་བ	*d*Myal-ba.	92
Myangan las daspa.	མྱ་ངན་ལས་འདས་པ	Mya-ngan-las-'das-pa.	98
Myangdas.	མྱང་འདས	Myang-'das.	78, 98
Nagpo chenpo.	ནག་པོ་ཆེན་པོ	Nag-po-chhen-po.	261
Naktsis.	ནག་རྩིས	Nag-*r*tsis.	274
Naljor chodpa.	རྣལ་འབྱོར་སྤྱོད་པ	*r*Nal-'byor-*s*pyod-pa.	32
Naljor ngonsum.	རྣལ་འབྱོར་མངོན་སུམ	*r*Nal-'byor-*m*ngon-sum.	44
Nam chu vangdan.	རྣམ་བཅུ་དབང་ལྡན	*r*Nam-*b*chu-*d*vang-*l*dan.	121

Phonetic Transcription.	Tibetan Characters.	Transliteration.	Page.
Namgyal bumpa.	རྣམ་རྒྱལ་བུམ་པ	*r*Nam-*r*gyal-bum-pa.	247
Namtog.	རྣམ་རྟོག	*r*Nam-*r*tog.	44
Namthosras.	རྣམ་ཐོས་སྲས	*r*Nam-thos-sras.	264
Nathongzha.	སྣ་མཐོང་ཞ	*s*Na-*m*thong-zha.	171
Netan.	གནས་བརྟན	*g*Nas-*b*rtan.	97
Netan chudrugi todpa.	གནས་བརྟན་བཅུ་ དྲུག་གི་ བསྟོད་པ	*g*Nas - *b*rtan - *b*chu-drug-gi-*bs*tod-pa.	97
Ngagi lhamo.	ངག་གི་ལྷ་མོ	Ngag-gi-lha-mo.	65
Ngagpa.	སྔགས་པ	*s*Ngag*s*-pa.	156
Ngagvang lob-zang gyamtso.	ངག་དབང་བློ་བཟང་རྒྱ་མཚོ	Ngag - *d* bang - *b*lo-bzang-*r*gya-mts'ho.	154
Ngoizhi.	དངོས་གཞི	*d*Ngos-*g*zhi.	241
Ngontog.	མངོན་རྟོགས	*m*Ngon-*r*tog*s*.	260
Ngovó chig.	ངོ་བོ་གཅིག	Ngo-bo-*g*chig.	42
Ngovonyid med-par mrava.	ངོ་བོ་ཉིད་མེད་པར་སྨྲ་བ	Ngo - bo - nyid - med-par-*s*mra-ba.	43
Norbu.	ནོར་བུ	Nor-bu.	53
Nubjang.	ནུབ་བྱང	Nub-byang.	259
Nyangdas Nyangan las daspa.		*see under* Myangdas, Myangan las daspa.	
Nyigmapa.	རྙིག་མ་པ	*r*Nyig-ma-pa.	72
Nyima.	ཉི་མ	Nyi-ma.	289
Nyingpo.	སྙིང་པོ	*s*Nying-po.	39
Nyompa.	སྙོམས་པ	*s*Nyom*s*-pa.	54
Nyungne.	སྙུང་གནས	*s*Nyung-*g*nas.	95, 240

Phonetic Transcription.	Tibetan Characters.	Transliteration.	Page.
Nyungpar nepai choga.	སྙུང་པར་གནས་པའི་ཆོ་ག	*s*Nyung - par - *g*nas-pa'i-chho-ga.	240
Odpagmed.	འོད་དཔག་མེད	'Od-*d*pag-med.	52 *& seq.*
Odpagmed kyi zhing kod.	འོད་དཔག་མེད་ཀྱི་ཞིང་བཀོད	'Od - *d*pag - med - kyi-zhing-*b*kod.	101
Ombu.	འོམ་བུ	'Om-bu-	228, 249
Padma jungne.	པདྨ་འབྱུང་གནས	Padma-'bgung-*g*gnas.	67
Pag.	ལྤགས	*l*Pag*s*.	233
Paldan lhamoi kang shag.	དཔལ་ལྡན་ལྷ་མོའི་བསྐང་བཤགས	*d*Pal - *l*dan - lha-mo'i-*bs*kang-*b*shag*s*.	112
Panchen Rinpoche.	པཎ་ཆེན་ར་ནི་པོ་ཆེ	Pan - chhen - rin - po-chhe.	153
Parkha chakja chad.	སྤར་ཁ་ཕྱག་རྒྱ་བརྒྱད	*s*Par - kha - phyag-*r*gya-*br*gyad.	307
Pasang.	པ་སངས	Pa-sang*s*.	289
Penpa.	སྤེན་པ	*s*Pen-pa.	289
Phag.	ཕག	Phag.	276
Phagpa chenresi.	འཕགས་པ་སྤྱན་རས་གཟིགས	'Phags-pa-*s*pyan-ras-*g*zhig*s*.	89
Phagpai denpa zhi.	འཕགས་པའི་བདེན་པ་བཞི	'Phag*s*-pa'i-*b*den-pa-*b*zhi.	16
Phalchen.	ཕལ་ཆེན	Phal-chhen.	78
Phan.	འཕན	'Phan.	190
Pharchin.	ཕར་ཕྱིན	Phar-phyin.	33
Phurbu.	ཕུར་བུ	Phur-bu.	215, 257
Phurbui davo.	ཕུར་བུས་གདབ་པོ	Phur-bus-*g*dab-bo.	257

Phonetic Transcription.	Tibetan Characters.	Transliteration.	Page.
Phurkha.	ཕུར་ཁ	Phur-kha.	259
Prel.	སྤྲེལ	*s*Prel.	276
Progzhu.	སྤྲོག་ཞུ	Prog-zhu.	209
Prulku choichong chenpoi kang shag.	སྤྲུལ་སྐུ་ཆོས་སྐྱོང་ཆེན་པོའི་བསྐང་བཤགས	*s*Prul - *s*ku - chhos-*s*kyong-chhen-po'i-*bs*kang-*b*shag*s*.	157
Prulku thongva dondan.	སྤྲུལ་སྐུ་མཐོང་བ་དོན་ལྡན	*s*Prul - *s*ku - *m*thong-ba-don-*l*dan.	97
Prulpai ku.	སྤྲུལ་པའི་སྐུ	*s*Prul-pa'i-*s*ku.	38
Rabne zhugpa.	རབ་གནས་བཞུགས་པ	Rab-*g*nas-*b*zhug*s*-pa.	206
Rabsal.	རབ་གསལ	Rab-*g*sal.	96
Ralgri.	རལ་གྲི	Ral-gri.	264
Ralpachen.	རལ་པ་ཅན	Ral-pa-chan.	76
Rangi nying gar thalmo charva.	རང་གི་སྙིང་གར་ཐལ་མོ་སྦྱར་བ	Rang-gi-*s*nying-gar-thal-mo-*s*byar-ba.	208
Rikhrodpa.	རི་ཁྲོད་པ	Ri-khrod-pa.	163
Rimate.	རི་མ་ཏེ	Ri-ma-te	113
Rinchen na dun.	རིན་ཆེན་སྣ་བདུན	Rin-chhen-*s*na-*b*dun.	53
Ritha.	རི་ཐ	Ri-tha.	274
Ruibal chenpoi dokjed.	རུས་སྦལ་ཆེན་པོའི་བཟློག་བྱེད	Rus-*s*bal-chhen-po'i-*b*zlog-byed.	297
Sa.	ས	Sa.	281
Sa chupa.	ས་བཅུ་པ	Sa-*b*chu-pa.	126
Sadag gyalpo.	ས་བདག་རྒྱལ་པོ	Sa-*b*dag-*r*gyal-po.	271
Sagpar.	སག་པར	Sag-par.	204
Sakyapa.	ས་སྐྱ་པ	Sa-*s*kya-pa..	73

Phonetic Transcription.	Tibetan Characters.	Transliteration.	Page.
Samtan	བསམ་གཏན	*b*Sam-*g*tan.	54
Sangbai dagpo.	གསང་བའི་བདག་པོ	*g*Sang-ba'i-*b*dag-po.	50
Sangye chi ku sung thug chi ten.	སངས་རྒྱས་ཀྱི་སྐུ་གསུང་ ཐུགས་ཀྱི་རྟེན	Sang*s*-*r*gyas-kyi-*s*ku-*g*sung - thug*s* - kyi-*r*ten.	179
Satsa (*Comp. Tsatsa.*)	ས་ཚྪ, འ ཚ	Sa-chchha.	194, 206
Sa tsoma.	ས་འཚོ་མ	Sa-'ts'ho-ma.	5
Semtsamo.	སེམས་ཙམ་མོ	Sem*s*-tsam-mo.	39
Senge chad ti.	སེངྒེ་བརྒྱད་ཁྲི	Seng - ge - *br*gyad-khri.	211
Sengei nyal tab.	སེང་གེའི་ཉལ་སྟབས	Seng-ge'i-nyal-*s*tabs.	241
Senge Nampar Gyalva.	སེང་གེ་རྣམ་པར་རྒྱལ་བ	Seng - ge -*r*nam - par-*r*gyal-ba.	185
Sengti.	སེང་ཁྲི	Seng-khri.	211
Shagpa.	བཤགས་པ	*b*Shag*s*-pa.	260
Shakya Thub-pa.	ཤཱཀྱ་ཐུབ་པ	Shakya-thub-pa.	4
Shar.	ཤར	Shar.	258
Sharlho.	ཤར་ལྷོ	Shar-lho.	258
Shecha rabsal.	ཤེས་བྱ་རབ་གསལ	Shes-bya-rab-*ǵ*sal.	305
Sherchin.	ཤེར་ཕྱིན	Sher-phyin.	33, 78
Shesrab ralgri.	ཤེས་རབ་རལ་གྲི	Shes-rab-ral-gri.	66
Shesrab chan.	ཤེས་རབ་སྤྱན	Shes-rab-*s*pyan.	210
Shid.	ཤིད	Shid.	269
Shing.	ཤིང	Shing.	281
Shinje.	གཤིན་རྗེ	*g*Shin-*r*je.	93

Phonetic Transcription.	Tibetan Characters.	Transliteration.	Page.
Shintsis.	གཤིན་རྩིས	*g*Shin-*r*tsis.	274
Sobyong.	གསོ་སྦྱོང	*g*So-*s*byong.	95
Sregpa.	སྲེག་པ	Sreg-pa.	249
Srongtsangampo.	སྲོང་བཙན་སྒམ་པོ	Srong-*b*tsan-*s*gam-po.	65
Sringan.	སྲི་ངན	Sri-ngan.	109
Ta.	རྟ	*r*Ta.	276
Tachog.	རྟ་མཆོག	*r*Ta-*m*chhog.	53
Tag.	སྟག	*s*Tag.	255, 276
Ta gom.	ལྟ་གོམ	*l*Ta-gom.	240
Tamdin.	རྟ་མགྲིན	*r*Ta-mgrin.	258
Tamdin gyalpoi sri nanpa.	རྟ་མགྲིན་རྒྱལ་པོའི་སྲི་མནན་པ	*r*Ta - mgrin - *r*gyal-po'i-sri-*m*nan-pa.	110
Tanbin shi.	བསྟན་པའི་ཤིས	*bs*Tan-pa'i-shi*s*.	232
Tanjur.	བསྟན་འགྱུར	*bs*Tan-'gyur.	78 *& seq.*
Tashi khatak.	བཀྲ་ཤིས་ཁ་བཏགས	*b*Kra-shi*s*-kha-*b*tag*s*.	190
Tashi tsig jod.	བཀྲ་ཤིས་ཚིག་བརྗོད	*b*Kra - shis - ts'hig-*br*jod.	178
Tenbrel.	རྟེན་འབྲེལ	*r*Ten-'brel.	43
Tenbrel chugnyi.	རྟེན་འབྲེལ་བཅུ་གཉིས	*r*Ten - 'brel - *b*chu-*g*nyis.	23
Tenkab.	སྟེང་བཀབ	*s*Teng-*b*kab.	211
Tensumni.	རྟེན་གསུམ་ནི	*r*Ten-*g*sum-ni.	137
Thabdang shes-rab.	ཐབས་དང་ཤེས་རབ	Thab*s* - dang - shes-rab.	208
Thabkhung.	ཐབ་ཁུང	Thab-khung.	249

Phonetic Transcription.	Tibetan Characters.	Transliteration.	Page.
Thabshes.	ཐབས་ཤེས	Thab*s*-shes.	208
Thal gyurva.	ཐལ་འགྱུར་བ	Thal-'gyur-ba.	41
Thangshin gi tsis.	ཐང་ཤིང་གི་རྩིས	Thang-shing-gi-*r*tsis.	309
Thegpa chenpoi do.	ཐེག་པ་ཆེན་པོའི་མདོ	Theg-pa-chhen-po'i-*m*do.	125
Thegpasum.	ཐེག་པ་གསུམ	Theg-pa-*g*sum.	104
Thengpa.	ཕྲེང་པ	Phreng-pa.	174
Thisrong de tsan.	ཁྲི་སྲོང་ལྡེ་བཙན	Khri-*s*rong-*l*de-*b*tsan.	67
Thonglam.	མཐོང་ལམ	*m*Thong-lam.	54
Thonka.	མཐོངས་ཀ	*m*Thong*s*-ka.	204
Thor.	ཐོར	Thor.	240
Thothori Nyan tsan.	ཐོ་ཐོ་རི་གཉན་བཙན	Tho-tho-ri-*g*nyan-*b*tsan.	63
Thugdam kantsai.	ཐུགས་དམ་བསྐང་རྫས	Thug*s*-dam-*bs*kang-*r*dza*s*.	260
Thugje chenpo chugchig zhal.	ཐུགས་རྗེ་ཆེན་པོ་བཅུ་གཅིག་ཞལ	Thug*s*-*r*je-chhen-po-*b*chu-gchig-zhal.	89
Thumi Sambhota.	ཐུ་མི་སམ་བྷོ་ཊ	Thu-mi sam-bho-ta.	65
Togpa nyid.	རྟོགས་པ་གཉིས	*r*Tog*s*-pa-*g*nyi*s*.	42
Tokchoi gyalpo.	ཐ་འོག་ཆོས་རྒྱལ་པོ	Tha-'og-chhos-*r*gyal-po.	157
Tongpanyid.	སྟོངས་པ་ཉིད	*s*Tong*s*-pa-nyid.	33
Tophye chenpo.	ལྟོ་འཕྱེ་ཆེན་པོ	*l*To-'phye-chhen-po.	271
Tsang.	རྩང	*r*Tsang.	39
Tsangpa.	ཚངས་པ	Ts'hang*s*-pa.	114

Phonetic Transcription.	Tibetan Characters.	Transliteration.	Page.
Tsatsa *(Comp. Satsa.)*	ཚ་ཚ	Chha-chha	194, 206
Tsavanas.	རྩ་བ་ནས	*r*Tsa-va-nas.	95
Tsei.	ཚེས	Ts'hes.	289
Tsemo.	རྩེ་མོ	*r*Tse-mo.	54
Tsepagmed.	ཚེ་དཔག་མེད	Ts'he-*d*pag-med.	129
Tserab las-tsis.	ཚེ་རབས་ལས་རྩིས	Ts'he-rab*s*-las-*r*tsis.	274
Tsesum.	རྩེ་གསུམ	*r*Tse-*g*sum.	215
Tsikhan.	རྩིས་མཁན	*r*Tsi*s*-*m*khan.	156
Tsonkhapa.	ཙོང་ཁ་པ	Tsong-kha-pa.	69
Tsovo.	གཙོ་བོ	*g*Tso-vo.	51
Tsugtor.	གཙུག་ཏོར	*g*Tsug-tor.	209
Tsulkhrim kyi phungpo.	ཚུལ་ཁྲིམས་ཀྱི་ཕུང་པོ	Ts'hul-khrim*s*-kyi-phung-po.	43
Tsunpo.	བཙུན་པོ	*b*Tsun-po.	53
Tuisol.	བཀྲུས་གསོལ	*b*Krus-*g*sol.	95, 239
Tungshakchi sangye songa.	ལྟུང་བཤགས་ཀྱི་སངས་རྒྱས་སོ་ལྔ	*l*Tung-*b*shag*s*-kyi-sang*s*-*r*gyas-so-*l*nga.	96
Urgyen.	ཨུ་རྒྱན	Ur-gyan.	67
Urgyenpa.	ཨུ་རྒྱན་པ	Ur-gyan-pa.	73
Utpala.	ཨུད་པ་ལ	Ut-pa-la.	66
Vajrapani.	བཛྲ་པཎི	Vajra-pani.	114
Vangi chinsreg.	དབང་སྦྱིན་སྲེག	*d*Vang-*s*byin-sreg.	252
Vuchan.	དབུ་ཅན	*d*Vu-chan.	80
Vumed.	དབུ་མེད	*d*Vu-med.	80

Phonetic Transcription.	Tibetan Characters.	Transliteration.	Page.
Yab yum chudpa.	ཡབ་ཡུམ་འཁྱུད་པ	Yub-yum-'khyud-pa.	112
Yangchob.	གཡང་སྐྱོབས	*g*Yang-*s*kyob*s*.	263
Yangdag den.	ཡང་དག་བདེན	Yang-dag-*b*den.	39
Yangsal domi.	གཡང་གསལ་སྒྲོན་མེ	*g*Yang-*g*sal-*s*gron-me.	281
Yangug.	གཡང་འགུགས	*g*Yang-'gug*s*.	263
Yiḍag.	ཡི་དྭགས	Yi-dags.	92
Yiḍam.	ཡི་དམ	Yi-dam.	245
Yong grub.	ཡོངས་གྲུབ	Yong*s* grub.	34
Yos.	ཡོས	Yos.	276
Zamatog.	ཟ་མ་ཏོག	Za-ma-tog.	64
Zanad.	གཟའ་ནད	*g*Za'-nad.	267
Zastang.	ཟས་གཙང	Zas-*g*tsang.	4
Zhagpa.	ཞགས་པ	Zhag*s*-pa.	213, 216
Zhalthang.	ཞལ་ཐང	Zhal-thang.	190
Zhalzai.	ཞལ་ཟས	Zhal-zas.	228
Zhanvang.	གཞན་དབང	*g*Zhan-*d*bang.	34
Zhine lhagthong.	ཞི་གནས་ལྷག་མཐོང	Zhi-*g*na*s*-lhag-*m*thong.	54
Zhiva.	ཞི་བ	Zhi-ba.	108
Zhivai chinsreg.	ཞི་བའི་སྦྱིན་སྲེག	Zi-ba'i-*s*byin-sreg.	250
Zhiva tso.	ཞི་བ་མཚོ	Zhi-ba-*m*ts'ho.	67
Zin.	ཟིན	Zin.	307
Zodmanas zhiva.	གཟོད་མ་ནས་ཞི་བ	*g*Zod-ma-nas-zhi-ba.	33

Phonetic Transcription.	Tibetan Characters.	Transliteration.	Page.
Zodpa.	བཟོད་པ	*b*Zod-pa.	54
Zon.	ཟོན	Zon.	307
Zundui.	གཟུངས་བསྡུས	*g*Zung*s*-*bs*dus.	96
Zung.	གཟུངས	*g*Zung*s*.	55
Zung zhug.	གཟུངས་བཞུགས	*g*Zung*s*-*b*zhug*s*.	206

C.

ADDITIONS TO CHAPTER XI,

pp. 122—42.

In reference to the Address to the Buddhas of Confession Prof. Ph. Ed. Foucaux of Paris had the kindness to communicate to me some details taken from a copy contained in the Imperial library. The Paris document, which had not yet been published, enables me to supply the hiatus at the end of Part I. of my original, which was here considerably injured: it also shows that the separation into two parts is an arbitrary alteration, for the concluding sentence of Part I. should be carried on to the phrase beginning Part II.; at the same time the concluding sentence of Part I. differs in my original from the Paris document.

Beginning with page 7, line 3 of the native print in Plate V., the Paris document runs as follows:—

"When they care but for actual pleasures; when bad actions shall be accumulated; when there shall be no more gratuities; when there shall be enemies, war, and illness, and famine be spread; when many shall be heaped up in the interior of those hells, *m*Nar-med, where are the human beings who have performed bad actions; —might then they meet this *s*Dig-*b*shags-*g*ter-chhos. The prayer of the teacher *k*Lu-*s*grub, will be spread; the creatures of this period of distress and misery shall read it, and on account of telling it with loud voice, all sins shall be taken away. This hidden doctrine, a protector of creatures (delivered) by the divine, the best *k*Lu-*s*grub, which had been concealed under the treasures, like the rock-lion in the grove of reeds,[1] will be spread as a blessing."

This passage tells us also that Lugrub, or Nāgārjuna (see p. 29), is viewed as the author of this prayer.

The copy which I had occasion to translate also varies in the title. At its head it has written the words: "Repentance of all sins, doctrine of the hidden treasure;" in the text it is denominated "the golden razor which takes away the sins." The Paris document has this latter title also at the head of the treatise; it is styled *s*Dig-*b*shag*s*-*g*ser-gyi-*s*pu-gri-zhes-bya-va-*b*zhug*s*-so, "this is the golden razor of the confession of sins."

Another deviation still to be noticed is the omission of the concluding prayers and of the details in reference to the writer and the time it took him to copy it. Also the Dhāranīs differ; the Paris copy has the Sanskrit sentences "Om supratishthita vajrāya; subham astu sarva jagatam; sarva mangalam; yasas mahā."

I add in Roman characters the text translated above, and a list of the readings of the Parisian text which differ from mine; the pages and lines quoted are those of Plates Nos. V. to VIII.

[1] An allusion to Sākyamuni's retirement and austerities in the woods previous to his obtaining the Buddhaship.

Tibetan text in Roman characters; page 7, line 4 to 9.

Ts'he-phyi-ma-ma-drin-'di-ka-bsam-pa'i-das; dus-kyi-ma-lan-las-ngan-bsags-pa'i-lan; dus-mi-'gyur-te-mi-mi-rnams-'gyur-bas-lan; pha-rol-dmag-ts'hogs-nad-dang-mu-ge-dar-ba'i-dus; dmyal-mnar-med-du-skye-ba'i-sems-chan-las-ngan-chan-mang-po-yod-pa-de-rnams-kyi-nang-na-bsags-pa-chan-'ga'-yod-pas; sdig-bshags-gter-chhos-'di-dang-'phrad-par-shog-ches-slob-dpon-klu-sgrub-kyi-smon-lam-btab-pa-lags-so; 'di-bskal-pa-snyigs-ma'i-sems-chan-bsags-pa-chan-rnams-kyis-'di-klog-dang; kha-'don-byas-na-sdig-pa-thams-chad-byang-bar-gsungs-so; 'di-grong-chig-na-bzhugs-na-grong-khyer-de'i-sdig-pa-thams-chad-byang-bar-gsungs-so; gter-chhos-'di-'gro-ba'i-mgon-po-klu-sgrub-snying-pos-lhas-smig-mang-ts'hal-gyi-brag-seng-ge-'dra-pa'i-'og-tu-gter-du-sbas-nas-smon-lam-bstab-skad.

Readings differing from my original.

Page 2, line	1:	thams-chad-bshags-pa'i-mdo.
»	3	'khor-lo-bskor-du-gsol.
»	5	baidu'rya.
»	6	gzugs-lta-bu'i.
»	6	rnam-par-spras.
»	9	gser-gyi-gdugs-nam-mkha'-lta-bu'i.
»	10 to 11:	'jig-rten-gyi-khams-kun-tu.
» 3 »	1	bag-ts'ha-ba-mi.
»	3	gang-la-la-zhig-gis-yi-ger-bris-sam; 'chhang-zhing-klog-gam.
»	8	zhing-'od-bzang-po-na.
» 4 »	5 to 6:	chhos-kyi-dkor-la.
» 5 »	5	bzhon-pa-zhon-pa'i-sdig-pa-'dag-go.
»	6, 8, 10:	sdig-pa-'dag-go.
» 6 »	10	gser-gyi-spu-gri.
»	13	snags-byed-pa'i-dus.
»	3	ma-grol-grol.
»	12	'khor-mi-sred-do.
» 8 »	1	gchig-la-'dus; don-dam-par-sems.

INDEX

THE names of the authors quoted in the text have been excluded, as the various publications on Buddhism have been enumerated, in the alphabetical order of the editors, in the Appendix "Literature," pp. 331-69.

The Tibetan terms are given in native characters, and exact transliteration in the Appendix "Glossary," pp. 371-93. Terms of more frequent occurrence and greater importance have been referred to in this Index again.

THE END.

3 For the PLATES OF THE ATLAS such objects have been selected as illustrate the worship of the deities, the ornamental decoration of the interior of the temples, and the strong belief in the beneficial influence of magical sentences and figures upon the welfare of man; the number of Buddhas, kings, and deified sages is particularly great.

The explanations given in the text in reference to the drawings are quoted below the objects; here, therefore, I limit myself to the communication of such details as concern the execution of the plates and the reproduction of the materials used in the originals.

Method of drawing. The paintings were traced in Tíbet by means of patterns (see p. 204) upon paper, or canvass prepared with chalk, lime, and flour-paste. A variety of colours is most minutely applied, and these tints are not only used for increasing the plastic effect, but their colour is also directly combined with the sacred character of the object, as I have frequently had occasion to allude to. Here, in the Atlas, the reproduction of the outlines is particularly given; it was obtained by an immediate process, viz. by putting transparent paper upon the objects and by transferring their contours directly upon the stone, after having traced them with lithographic ink. As it was my special object to give fac-similes of native art, I have limited myself to a plain reproduction of figures and pictures, even where the representation might easily have been improved and corrected.

The materials which had to be reproduced were woven manufactures, different varieties of paper, wood, and stone. A transfer system of a rather novel nature, first employed by Hermann, who, for various objects, had used it already during the journey, allowed of giving, in many cases without any other addition, the predominant character at least of the material used; and so the plates also show the selection at present made for the Lamaic work in the Buddhist monasteries. This circumstance, though of an ethnographical as well as a religious character, may justify my entering here into some more details.

Woven Manufactures. The Plates Nos. 1, 3, 4, 7, 9, 11, 16, 17, 20 show various specimens of Tibetan industry. — Nos. 1 and 4 are coarse silks; in their natural colours. — No. 3 is a red cotton; the borders are covered with a colour partly rubbed off again from having been frequently rolled up. — Nos. 7 and 9 are specimens of coarse Tibetan woollen cloth; in No. 7 the distance of the longitudinal borders shows at the same time the total breadth of the piece of cloth; above and below the image two borders of stronger cloth are stitched on. — No. 11 is a peculiar precious stuff from China, richly interwoven with metallic thread; the cross we see upon the marginal parts is the symbol of peace (see p. 182). — No. 16 is a sacred symbol drawn upon cotton by a cane-pen; it formed a part of a long prayer-flag. One side of it was fastened to a pole, the opposite side shows pieces of stronger rags, separately attached. — No. 17 shows a flag of cotton with a broad stripe of deeper shading; when coloured, the central part of such flags, containing the sacred image, is covered by a particular stratum facilitating the application of colours. When complete, as hung up in the Temples (see p. 215), sticks supporting the borders are added, as in the present case. As plates showing flags without the sticks being added to their borders, I quote Nos. 3, 5, 10 and 11. — In No. 20 the blue cloth is a very coarse Tibetan woven stuff of Lepcha hemp.

Of Wood I have but one example, No. 13, where a light-coloured poplar wood is seen. The apricot and the poplar *(Populus euphrasica)* are the trees which follow the Lamaic priests up to their highest settlements where the climate allows of it; the latter tree not unfrequently attains considerable dimensions.

The Stones here represented are: the granite of Bhután in No. 6, which, however, is only found within very narrow limits in the Eastern Himálaya; the micaschist of Síkkim in No. 12, and the jurassic slate of Central Tíbet in No. 14. Gneiss is also used in the Eastern Himálaya.

Paper is manufactured in great variety in the different provinces of the Himálaya and Tíbet; in general these papers are very tough when dry, but they are too liable to destruction when exposed to moisture, from want of the necessary glutinous substances. – Nos. 2 and 9 show a paper which is rather smooth and pretty well made; such kinds of paper are frequently found. – No. 8 is a paper covered with a reddish stratum of colour considerably rubbed off again. – Nos. 15 and 19 are papers from the central part of Tíbet of a very uniform texture, but nevertheless of a very unbleached colour. – No. 18 is particularly characteristic of the paper manufactory in the Himálaya. It is made of vegetable fibres without having previously undergone the process of wear and tear by man. The material used for this paper is the inner bark of the *Daphne cannabina* (Lour.), a shrub from 4 to 5 feet high. This paper is of a rough surface, but unusually strong and tough.

(They face in the book the pages stated.)

(The pages have reference to the explanations in the Text)

Group I. Representations of Deities.

1. The thirty-five Buddhas of Confession, in Tibetan Tungshakchi sangye songa, with various mythological persons. See p. 96.
2. Vajrasattva, in Tibetan Dorjesempa, the God above all. See p. 53.
3. The Dhyâni Buddha Amitâbha, in Tibetan Odpagmed. See p. 53

   The four-armed figure is Padmapâni (see Plates 4 & 12), the other to his right is Guru Dragpo, a protector against evil spirits.
4. Padmapâni, in Tibetan Chenresi, the particular Protector of Tíbet. See p. 88.

   The figures in a standing position are Hêrukas (see p. 108), the sitting figure is Amitâbha (see p. 53).
5. Maitreya, in Tibetan Jampa, the Buddha to come. See pp. 209, 210.

   The figures in an upright attitude are the goddesses Dolma (see p. 66); the figures above the head are the Manlas, or Buddhas of medicine (see p. 266), & two ancient priests; the figures beneath the throne are men reputed for sanctity.
6. Manjusrî, in Tibetan Jamjang, the God of wisdom. See p. 65.
7. The goddess Doljang, the deified Consort of King Srongtsan Gampo (A.D. 617–98). See p. 66.
8. Dzambhala, or Dodnevangpo, the God of wealth, with his assistants. See p. 263.
9. Bihar Gyalpo, the Patron of monasteries and temples. See p. 177.
10. Choichong Gyalpo, the God of astrology and protector of man against evil spirits. See p. 157.
11. Dzambhala, or Dodnevangpo, the God of wealth. See p. 263.

    The two Buddhas are Dîpankara (see p. 131), and a Buddha of medicine (see p. 266).
12. Padmapâni, in Tibetan Chenresi, the particular Protector of Tíbet. See p. 88.
13. Padma Sambhava, a deified Indian sage of the eighth century A. D. See p. 67.

Group II. Sentences & Figures for averting the dangers arising from Evil Spirits.

14. The six-syllabic prayer "Om mani padme hum". See p. 120.
    In the central circle is added the syllable "Hri", a mystical imploration of Padmapâni. See p. 266. – The sentence in smaller characters means: "The diamond benediction (= supernatural faculty) is begged for what is engraved."
15. The six-syllabic prayer "Om mani padme hum".
    The combination of the letters so as to form an anagram, is called Namchu vangdan, "the ten entirely powerful". See p. 121.
16. The magical figure Dabchad, "octagon", containing in each compartment the name of a Dâkinî, in Tibetan Khado. See p. 248.
17. Mystical sentences with the figure of the Airy Horse. See p. 253.
18. The magical figure Phurbu with the face of Tamdin and charms directed against evil spirits. See p. 257.
19. A Soothsaying Table with numerous figures & sentences. See p. 320–327.
20. Table to indicate lucky and unlucky periods, as well as the chances of undertakings. See pp. 293–320.

Plate 13. Renderings of Figures on Amulets: [illegible]

14. The syllable [illegible] "Om mani padme hum". See p. 240.
In the central circle is the syllable "Hri", a mystical representation of Padmapani. See p. 206. The [illegible] characters [illegible]
[illegible]

15. The [illegible]. See p. [illegible]
The combination of the letters [illegible] form an [illegible]
[illegible]. See p. [illegible]

16. The magical figure [illegible] containing in each [illegible]
name of a [illegible]. See p. 245.

17. Mystical sentence with the figure of the [illegible]. See p. [illegible]

18. [illegible] figure [illegible]
against evil spirits. See p. [illegible]

19. A [illegible] table with [illegible] figures [illegible]. See p. 226-227.

20. Table to indicate lucky and unlucky [illegible] as well as the [illegible] of
undertakings. See pp. 226-230.

PLATES

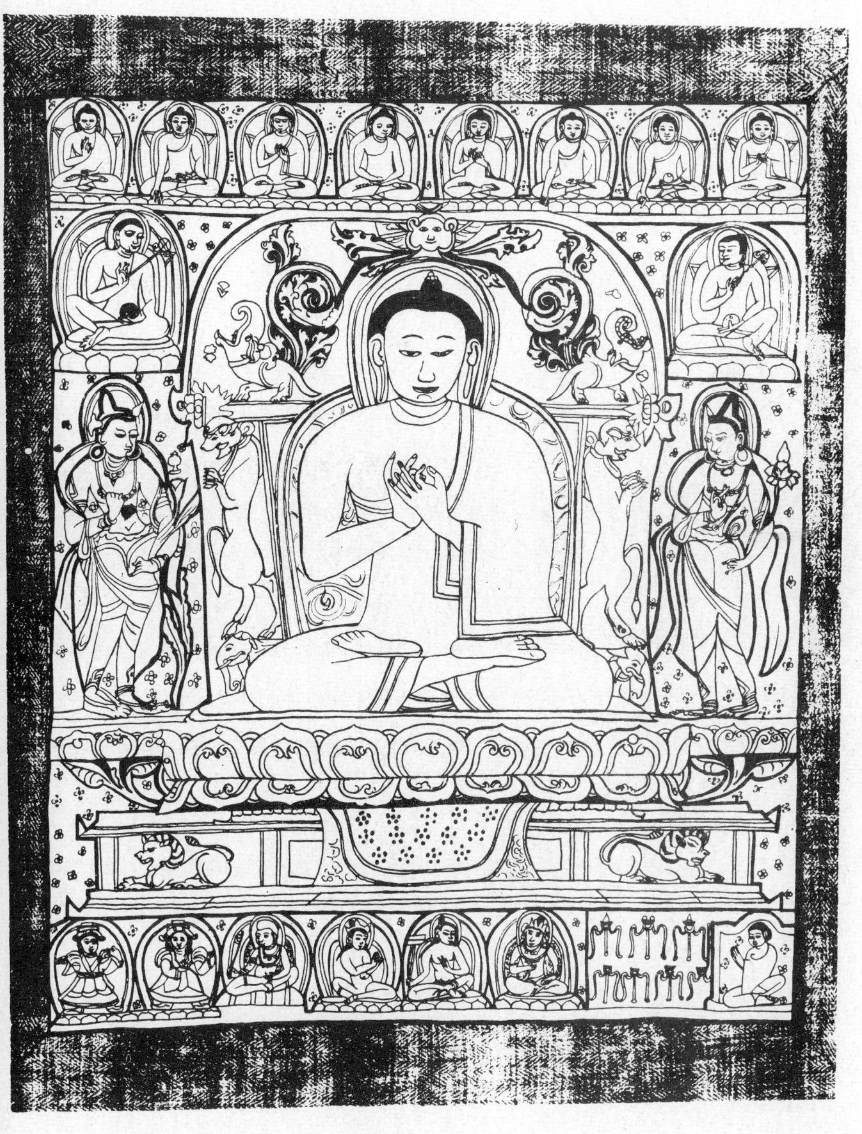

བཀོས་བཀྲ་ཤིས་རྡོ་རྗེ་ཞུས་པའོ།།

༄། །ཨོཾ་མ་ཎི་པདྨེ་ཧཱུྃ། ཨོཾ་མ་ཎི་པདྨེ་ཧཱུྃ། ཨོཾ་མ་ཎི་པདྨེ་ཧཱུྃ། ཨོཾ་མ་ཎི་པདྨེ་ཧཱུྃ། །
ཨོཾ་མ་ཎི་པདྨེ་ཧཱུྃ། ཨོཾ་མ་ཎི་པདྨེ་ཧཱུྃ། ཨོཾ་མ་ཎི་པདྨེ་ཧཱུྃ། ཨོཾ་མ་ཎི་པདྨེ་ཧཱུྃ། ཨོཾ་མ་ཎི་པདྨེ་ཧཱུྃ། །
ཨོཾ་མ་ཎི་པདྨེ་ཧཱུྃ། ཨོཾ་མ་ཎི་པདྨེ་ཧཱུྃ། ཨོཾ་མ་ཎི་པདྨེ་ཧཱུྃ། ཨོཾ་མ་ཎི་པདྨེ་ཧཱུྃ། ཨོཾ་མ་ཎི་པདྨེ་ཧཱུྃ།
ཨོཾ་མ་ཎི་པདྨེ་ཧཱུྃ། ཨོཾ་མ་ཎི་པདྨེ་ཧཱུྃ། ཨོཾ་མ་ཎི་པདྨེ་ཧཱུྃ། ཨོཾ་མ་ཎི་པདྨེ་ཧཱུྃ། ཨོཾ་མ་ཎི་པདྨེ་ཧཱུྃ། །
ཨོཾ་མ་ཎི་པདྨེ་ཧཱུྃ། ཨོཾ་མ་ཎི་པདྨེ་ཧཱུྃ། ཨོཾ་མ་ཎི་པདྨེ་ཧཱུྃ། ཨོཾ་མ་ཎི་པདྨེ་ཧཱུྃ། ཨོཾ་མ་ཎི་པདྨེ་ཧཱུྃ། །

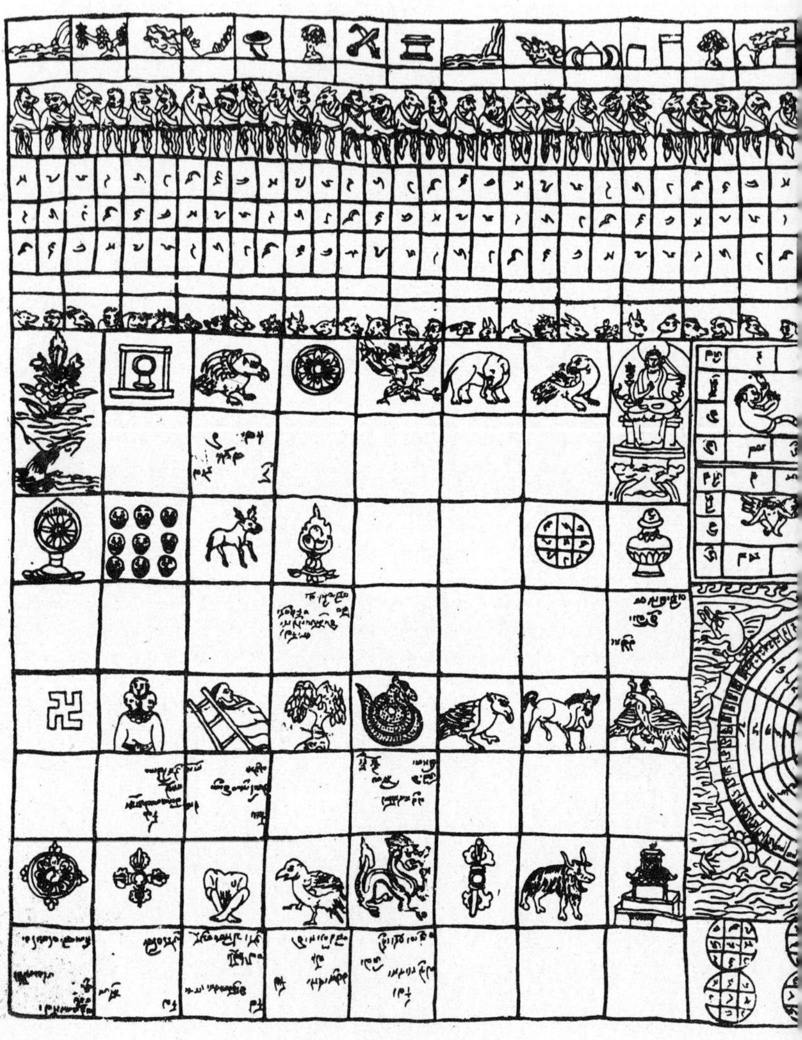

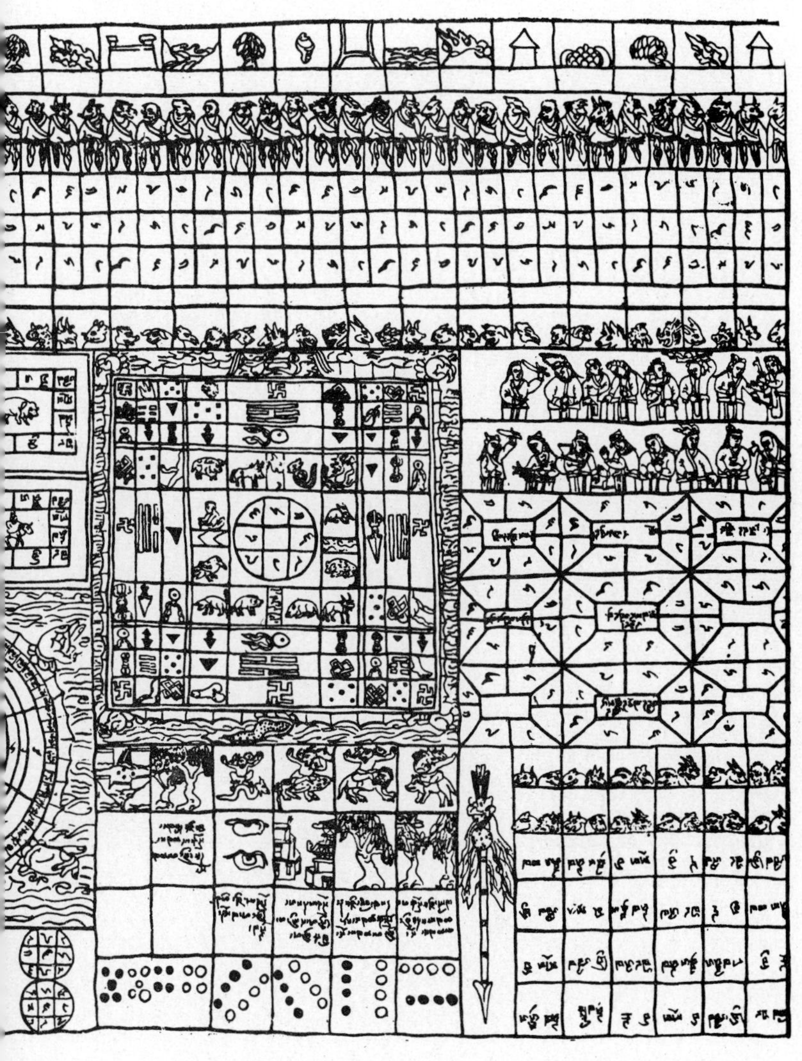

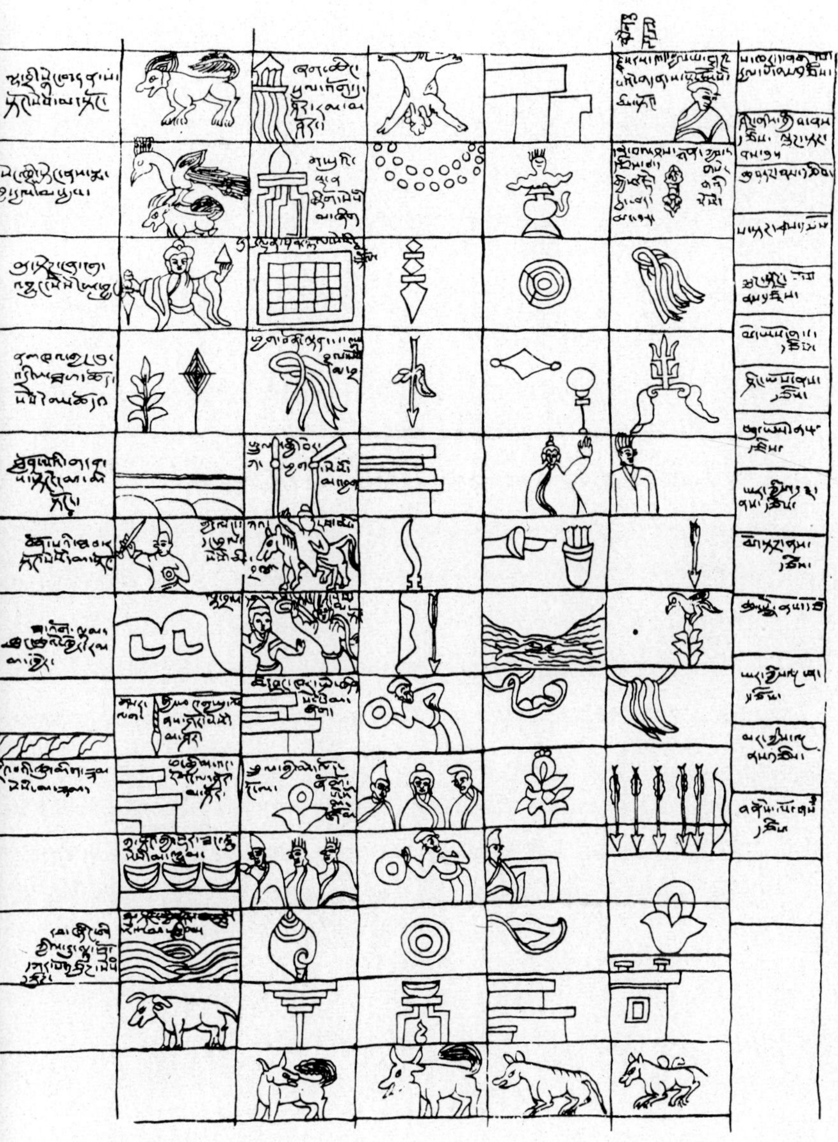

Some of the Titles on

BUDDHISM

from

BOOK FAITH INDIA

- A Buddhist Bible ______ *Dwight Goddard*
- Pilgrims Quotations from the Buddhist Scriptures ______ *Keshar Lal*
- The Message of Buddha ______ *A.S. Wadia*
- Buddhism: Its Essence & Development ______ *E.Conze*
- Oracles and Demons of Tibet

  The Cult and Iconography of the Tibetan Protective Dieties ______ *Rene De Nebesky-Wojkowitz*
- The LIfe of Milarepa ______ *Translated by L. P. Lhalungpa*
- Shambhala ______ *Nicholas Roerich*
- The Doctrine of the Buddha ______ *George Grimm*
- Buddhist Parables ______ *Translated by E.W. Burlingame*
- Tibetan Religious Dances ______ *R. De N. - Wojkowitz*
- The Buddhist Conception of Spirit ______ *B.C. Law*
- Buddhist Rules for the Laity ______ *Compiled by D.J. Subasinha*

For Catalog and more Information Mail or Fax to:

PILGRIMS BOOK HOUSE

Mail Order, P.O.Box 3872, Kathmandu, Nepal

Fax: 977-1-424943

e-mail: pilgrims@wlink.com.np

website : www.pilgrimsbooks.com